The Redesign of the Global Financial Architecture

More than ten years on from the most intense phase of the global financial crisis, and the collective international response in the G20 summit in London, a 'new normal' has emerged with systems in place to mitigate against further banking crises. This updated new edition analyzes this post-crisis international and national regulatory framework and asks whether the current paradigm is fit for purpose as new dangers gestate and develop.

This new edition includes a discussion of the impact of the aggressively deregulatory and anti-globalist policies of the Trump administration and its pursuit of an 'America First' policy and explores its implications for the regulatory landscape constructed and tended by previous leaders. The author addresses new and future systemic risks, many outside the regulated banking sector, which have grown in importance since 2015. He develops possible future scenarios for the international regulatory architecture, both negative and positive, asking, 'Are we better prepared for future banking crises?' New risks, including the COVID-19 pandemic and economic crash, are testing the global system; and the G20, without US leadership, may be failing in this latest most severe crisis of our lifetimes. This book provides a unique narrative explanation drawn from leading actors of key events and policy changes as they unfolded immediately post-crisis. The author builds upon the first edition to capture key developments that have occurred during the past five years, while raising key questions and vulnerabilities and looking at future risks and challenges that may emerge.

This text will be of great interest to students, teachers and researchers of financial frameworks, globalisation and political economy.

Stuart P. M. Mackintosh is Executive Director of the Group of Thirty, an international financial think tank. He is past President of the National Association of Business Economics, the largest and most influential organisation of professional economists in the USA. Dr Mackintosh speaks widely before diverse audiences, from central banks, to investor events, to general audiences. He continues to write widely, with recent work appearing in *Reuters*, *EuropeNow* magazine, the *Journal of Business Economics*, the *Journal of World Economics* and *Financial World* magazine.

Rethinking Globalizations

Edited by Barry K. Gills
University of Helsinki, Finland

Kevin Gray
University of Sussex, UK

This series is designed to break new ground in the literature on globalization and its academic and popular understanding. Rather than perpetuating or simply reacting to the economic understanding of globalization, this series seeks to capture the term and broaden its meaning to encompass a wide range of issues and disciplines and convey a sense of alternative possibilities for the future.

BRICS and MICs: Implications for Global Agrarian Transformation
Edited by Ben Cousins, Saturnino M. Borras Jr., Sergio Sauer and Jingzhong Ye

Migration, Civil Society and Global Governance
Edited by Carl-Ulrik Schierup, Branka Likic-Brboric, Raúl Delgado Wise and Gülay Toksöz

Authoritarian Neoliberalism
Philosophies, Practices, Contestations
Edited by Ian Bruff and Cemal Burak Tansel

The Redesign of the Global Financial Architecture
State Authority, New Risks and Dynamics
Stuart P. M. Mackintosh

Challenging Inequality in South Africa
Transitional Compasses
Edited by Michelle Williams and Vishwas Satgar

Between Class and Discourse: Left Intellectuals in Defence of Capitalism
Boris Kagarlitsky

Questioning the Utopian Springs of Market Economy
Damien Cahill, Martijn Konings and Adam David Morton

For more information about this series, please visit: www.routledge.com/Rethinking-Globalizations/book-series/RG

The Redesign of the Global Financial Architecture

State Authority, New Risks and Dynamics

Second edition

Stuart P. M. Mackintosh

Routledge
Taylor & Francis Group
LONDON AND NEW YORK

Second edition published 2021
by Routledge
2 Park Square, Milton Park, Abingdon, Oxon OX14 4RN

and by Routledge
605 Third Avenue, New York, NY 10017

First issued in paperback 2022

Routledge is an imprint of the Taylor & Francis Group, an informa business

First edition published in 2015

Publisher's Note
The publisher has gone to great lengths to ensure the quality of this reprint but points out that some imperfections in the original copies may be apparent.

British Library Cataloguing-in-Publication Data
A catalogue record for this book is available from the British Library

Library of Congress Cataloging-in-Publication Data
Names: Mackintosh, Stuart P. M., author.
Title: The redesign of the global financial architecture : state authority, new risks and dynamics / Stuart P. M. Mackintosh.
Description: Second edition. | Abingdon, Oxon ; New York, NY : Routledge, [2021] | Series: Rethinking globalizations | Includes bibliographical references and index.
Identifiers: LCCN 2020019724 (print) | LCCN 2020019725 (ebook) | ISBN 9780367857479 (hardback) | ISBN 9781003014799 (ebook)
Subjects: LCSH: International finance. | Financial crises
Classification: LCC HG3881 .M2715 2021 (print) | LCC HG3881 (ebook) | DDC 332/.042—dc23
LC record available at https://lccn.loc.gov/2020019724
LC ebook record available at https://lccn.loc.gov/2020019725

ISBN 13: 978-0-367-56278-6 (pbk)
ISBN 13: 978-0-367-85747-9 (hbk)
ISBN 13: 978-1-003-01479-9 (ebk)

DOI: 10.4324/9781003014799

Typeset in Times New Roman
by Apex CoVantage, LLC

In memory of Una, Bernard and John, without whose example and support this would not have been possible.

Contents

Illustrations

Figures

Boxes

Tables

Acknowledgement

I would like to thank all those who have supported me during my research for this new edition. My particular thanks to Barry Gills for his continued support encouragement, support and intellectual guidance.

I cannot name, but must warmly acknowledge and thank, the scores of individuals who were so generous of their time and who allowed me to interview them regarding the 2007–2008 financial crisis and G20-led intergovernmental response since then. I feel honoured to have been given the time and counsel of presidential and prime ministerial advisers, finance ministers, G20 sherpas, central bank governors and deputy governors, treasury and ministry of finance officials, numerous IMF executive directors, academics and former senior policy makers. Without their frank insights and personal narratives of the events that they experienced, often first-hand, this research would not have been possible. Any errors in the book are mine. The lion's share of the illumination that the book contains on global summitry, policy making and processes comes from those leaders, experts and actors who graciously permitted me to interview them.

I must thank my wife, Jean, for her constant encouragement. I would also thank my mentors, Jean-Claude Trichet and Sir David Walker, for their ongoing support. I must also thank my good friend Diane Stamm for her careful eye as to style and presentation, and my hardworking researcher John Harkness, who worked with me on the new edition. Finally, I must thank Emily Ross and Hannah Rich, both superb editors, who shepherded the book from its raw form to completion.

Stuart P. M. Mackintosh
Washington, DC, April 2020

Abbreviations

AI	artificial intelligence
AIIB	Asian Infrastructure Investment Bank
BCBS	Basel Committee on Banking Supervision
BIS	Bank for International Settlements
CO_2	carbon dioxide
COP21	21st Conference of Parties
DSPs	dispute settlement procedures
EU	European Union
FASB	Financial Accounting Standards Board
FDIC	Federal Deposit Insurance Corporation
FOREX	foreign exchange
FSB	Financial Stability Board
FSF	Financial Stability Forum
GAAP	Generally Accepted Accounting Principles
GDP	gross domestic product
GSIFIs	Global Systemically Important Financial Institutions
G20	European Union plus Argentina, Australia, Brazil, Canada, China, Germany, France, India, Indonesia, Italy, Japan, Mexico, the Russian Federation, Saudi Arabia, South Africa, South Korea, Turkey, the United Kingdom and the United States
IASB	International Accounting Standards Board
ICCP	International Climate Change Partnership
IFRS	International Financial Reporting Standards
IMF	International Monetary Fund
IOSCO	International Organization of Securities Commissions
IT	information technology
LIBOR	London Interbank Offered Rate
MAP	Mutual Assessment Process
NGFS	Network for Greening the Financial System
OECD	Organisation for Economic Co-operation and Development
OTC	over-the-counter
SDR	special drawing rights
SIVs	structured investment vehicles

SPEs	special purpose entities
SSB	standard-setting body
TBTF	too big to fail
TCFD	Taskforce on Climate-related Financial Disclosure
TLAC	total loss-absorbing capacity
UN	United Nations
WTO	World Trade Organization

Introduction

In the years prior to the 2007–2008 economic and financial crisis leaders and their governments allowed and facilitated a progressive erosion and diffusion of state power to other actors, through a series of deliberate decisions and nondecisions (Bachrach and Baratz, 1963). Governmental acts or refusal to act were underpinned by ideological and economic beliefs, a worldview that championed unregulated markets ahead of state prerogatives (Akerlof and Shiller, 2009; Padoa-Schioppa, 2010; Stiglitz, 2010). There was a weakening of state power and a gradual retreat of the state's desire and authority to regulate a rapidly growing global financial system and bank and nonbank actors as a corollary to this deregulatory neoliberal paradigm (Strange, 1986, 1996).

As state power retreated there was a concomitant increase in the size, impact and influence of the liberalised financial sector, and within that of systemically important interconnected financial firms and banks, and the levels and magnitude of the compensation of their traders and investment bankers spiked upwards (FCIC, 2011, p. 62). Unregulated or underregulated the shadow banking sector grew simultaneously with a series of unregulated new complex derivatives markets (Tett, 2009), nonbank housing finance firms (McLean and Nocera, 2010) and products that increased leverage and magnified risk (Lewis, 1989, 2010).

This financial engineering brought the illusion of wealth but did little to support genuinely sustainable growth. As with booms in the past during the period of irrational exuberance, rising asset prices, rising house prices, low inflation and solid employment numbers (boosted by housing construction jobs) made consumers feel wealthier. The immediate short-term effects therefore appeared positive. Credit-fuelled personal consumption (mortgage re-fis, anyone?) sustained modest economic growth rates, despite real median wages being flat in much of the developed world, as the Chinese economy opened up and placed downward pressure on wages. Observers, market participants, policy makers and the many viewers of such reality TV gems as *Flip this House* and *Million Dollar Listing* felt the positive effects of leveraging equity in their principal assets – their houses. The negative downsides of leverage were, of course, overlooked (Mian and Sufi, 2014).

A deregulatory, laissez-faire, neoliberal Anglo-Saxon worldview and narrative championing economic markets over regulatory vigour underlay these developments. This was parroted by leaders, such as Bill Clinton, George W. Bush and

Gordon Brown, and major regulators such as the US Federal Reserve and the UK Financial Services Authority. Policy makers thought this deregulatory approach appeared to pay dividends, and so determined to *laissez les bons temps rouler*.

Markets were said to be self-correcting and would always return to stable equilibrium unaided. Excessive risk, speculation, manias and dangerous booms and busts were a thing of the past, or so many policy makers believed, blind to the lessons of economic history (Kindleberger and Aliber, 1978; Minsky, 2008). The 'great moderation' was said to be underway. According to this mind-set financial engineering made the markets safer, not riskier.

During this period of excess credit, liquidity and the worship of the deregulatory gods, the magnitude and frequency of boom and bust cycles grew (Allen and Gale, 2007) and the number and severity of banking crises rose to a level last seen in the pre-World War I era (King, 2011).

In theory financial risk was spread. In reality no one could gauge the risk or who held it. Few regulators lost any sleep over or thought to question this narrative or to consider the dangers they might engender. Those who did express concern, such as Raghuram Rajan, former International Monetary Fund chief economist, or the officials at the Bank for International Settlements (BIS), were not heeded (Rajan, 2005; BIS, 2008).

The dominant deregulatory, largely Western and Anglo-American narrative provided intellectual justification for the progressive erosion of conservative prudential supervision of major financial institutions and actors in major markets, including the US and the UK, in particular, as regulators became 'captured' by those firms they regulated, i.e. the major financial market actors. Neoclassical economic beliefs – in market equilibrium, in rational actors, and in the efficiency of liberalised markets – were championed, and behavioural economics languished, notwithstanding the latter's greater explanatory power regarding the business cycle and the nature of booms and busts.

Historical memory of the drivers of individuals and investors, of the commonalities in past boom and bust cycles, was forgotten. Too few (almost none) of the existing policy-making community had experienced severe crises. Instead they viewed events discretely, individually, not systemically as a whole and across entire markets. Regulators and central bankers had seen small numbers of individual bank failures. Certainly. Systemically linked, synchronised collapse or near collapse of hundreds and thousands of small banks and scores of regionally and globally significant firms in a very short period? Certainly not.

Just as in past booms 'this time' was thought to be 'different'. It was not (Galbraith, 1954; Rogoff and Reinhart, 2009). Ultimately the latest, largest, most interconnected, highly leveraged, opaque credit and US-real-estate-driven boom, fuelled by a great many market and regulatory failings, turned to bust. The mania turned to panic and near global economic collapse, as house prices collapsed, families' marginal propensity to consume collapsed, firms toppled, markets shook and economies contracted.

In 2007–2008 the global economy faced the worst economic crisis in 80 years. The autumn of 2008 saw the bankruptcy of Lehman Brothers, the

US government takeover of American International Group (AIG), the forced merger of Merrill Lynch with Bank of America and action to secure the remaining two American investment banks, Goldman Sachs Group Inc. and Morgan Stanley (Federal Reserve Bank of St. Louis, 2008). Scores of other large banks and financial firms closed their doors (FDIC, 2013). Elsewhere across the globe other giants of finance were already wards of the state, such as the RBS and HBOS.

By September 2008 the global financial system was under huge stress and the economic crisis in the US had accelerated. Credit remained tight or almost nonexistent. International trade flows had collapsed (OECD, 2009). Markets and investors were in a panic. Certain types of asset classes or 'socially worthless' instruments (Turner, 2009), composed of poorly underwritten subprime mortgages sold in the US and securitised, had collapsed in value or could not be sold at any price. The overnight repo market had frozen (Gorton, 2010, 2012). The US plunged into its most severe contraction in 80 years. Families saw a loss of a greater proportion of their net worth than occurred in the Great Depression, and jobs disappeared at the rate of 800,000 per month (Goolsbee, 2011). Many other nations, such as the UK, China, France and Spain, also faced economic contractions that would develop into full-blown recessions.

Policy makers confronted 'the limits of unrestricted globalization [and] . . . the intrinsic tension between global financial markets and sovereign states' (Subacchi, 2010, p. 258). Leaders were faced 'not only with the collapse of a financial system, but also with the collapse of a worldview' (Assenza, Sokolickova, and Martynau, 2011; Fergusson *et al.*, 2009). Laissez-faire neoliberalism confronted a legitimacy crisis (Chorev and Babb, 2009), and the spell of the 'mystical Anglo-Saxon model of liberalization and deregulation' was broken (El Erian, 2009). Market fundamentalism was dead (Stiglitz, 2008).

Leaders, shocked, were galvanised into action. Only governments and their central banks could act as the economic backstop, as lenders of last resort, *in extremis*, for private markets and firms. In taking action political leaders and their central bank governors would move rapidly away from the deregulatory laissez-faire neoliberal worldview. They would reassert state authority over markets. The retreat of the state would be reversed. Leaders and their elite central banking community would begin a rare paradigm shift in their overarching crisis-altered regulatory policy narrative and worldview (Constancio, 2010).

This book examines the internationally coordinated, state-led response to the 2007–2008 economic and financial crisis. It involves the examination of the construction of 'alternative narratives' which encompass a rejection of the laissez-faire neoliberal paradigm, with a particular emphasis on the role of international financial regulatory authority, its rules, and institutionalisation. The book addresses the manner in which acute and severe crisis episodes such as this one provoke and also reveal the underlying tension and contestation between 'market authority' and 'state authority' in relation to the regulation of the world economy and especially the financial system and firms, with the goal of ensuring maximisation of long-term systemic stability and crisis prevention. The construction of alternative crisis-driven narratives is in part a reaction to the previous ideological hegemonic domination of the laissez-faire 'neoliberal' beliefs as applied to deregulation (i.e. of self-regulation by markets and private sector actors in the financial sector). The book identifies and examines a paradigm shift underway in response to the crisis: a move from the dominance of market authority to the reassertion of state authority over financial markets and actors. It addresses this crisis as an instance of the greater set of historical cases of severe financial crises which transmute into economic crises and illuminates the way in which crisis narratives are constructed in response to such episodes and the policy outcomes of a paradigm shift when they occur.

The book examines the elite state-level crisis response, the institutional reforms most important to the construction of a 'new global financial architecture,' and the policy outcomes. Calls for a new architecture have occurred in the past; there were similar demands following the 1997-1998 global and East Asian financial crisis. A principal argument within the book is that the severity of the financial crisis in this case precipitated an important shift in the policy narrative, a paradigm shift, and a series of reforms and policies designed to collectively apply and internationally coordinate regulatory authority over global financial markets and private sector actors in a more robust manner.

The book assesses the resilience of the global architecture more than a decade after its construction, seeking to gauge whether the constructs built in response to events on 2008–2009 are still effective, resilient to undermining and additive in 2020.

At the diplomatic level of G20 summitry the book finds an erosion of the consensus, which becomes a break, with the election of nativist nationalist Donald Trump as America's president and his pursuit of his America First policy. Absent American hegemonic leadership the effectiveness of the G20 was seriously undermined. This is particularly evident in the disappointing failure of G20 leadership in the response to the COVID-19 pandemic and global economic disaster.

But the paradigmatic prognosis is not uniformly bleak. State authority (fiscal, monetary and institutional) was reasserted across the globe in response to the horrific COVID-19 crises. State power is in the ascendant once again as crises again clarify, create new possibilities and force action. Evidence shows that the technocratic central banking community instrumental in re-regulating global financial markets in 2008–2009 continues its work, identifying risks and building new additions to the global architecture. Neoliberalism remains in retreat and the state and its technocratic communities continue to shape policy and outcomes.

This book draws upon a series of high-level, qualitative interviews with many of the governmental, central bank, and supervisory principals present and active in key decision-making meetings and roles from 2008 onwards. Those actors and officials interviewed played central roles in the paradigm shift, crisis response, architectural redesign and, since then, the maintenance and strengthening of the re-regulatory paradigm. Chapter 1 addresses the importance of these sources and of their collective remembrances of and narratives constructed around the crisis response.

References

Akerlof, G.A. and Shiller, R.J. (2009) *Animal spirits: How human psychology drives the economy, and why it matters for global capitalism*. Princeton: Princeton University Press.

Allen, F. and Gale, D. (2007) *Understanding financial crises*. Oxford: Oxford University Press.

Assenza, G., Sokolickova, Z., and Martynau, A. (2011) 'The ideational background of the global economic crisis', *Humanicus*, Issue 6.

Bachrach, P. and Baratz, M.S. (1963) 'Decisions and nondecisions: An analytical framework', *American Political Science Review*, 57(3), pp. 632–642.

BIS (Bank for International Settlements). (2008) '78th annual report 2007–2008', 30 June [Online]. Available at: www.bis.org/publ/arpdf/ar2008e8.htm (accessed: 7 January 2012).

Chorev, N. and Babb, S. (2009) 'The crisis of neoliberalism and the future of international institutions: A comparison of the IMF and the WTO', *Theory and Society*, 38(5), pp. 459–484.

Constancio, V. (2010) 'The future of economic governance in Europe in a global perspective', *Speech delivered at the Centre Culturel Calouste Gulbenkian*, Paris, 7 December.

El-Erian, M. (2009) 'Market fatigue: The Anglo-Saxon model has taken a knock', *The Economist*, 1 October [Online]. Available at: www.economist.com/node/14530138 (accessed: 10 November 2009).

FCIC (Financial Crisis Inquiry Commission). (2011) [Online]. Available at: http://cybercemetery.unt.edu/archive/fcic/20110310172443/http://fcic.gov/ (accessed: 5 February 2015).

FDIC (Federal Deposit Insurance Corporation). (2013) 'Failed bank list' [Online]. Available at: www2.fdic.gov/hsob/hsobRpt.asp (accessed: 8 January 2013).

Federal Reserve Bank of St. Louis. (2008) 'The financial crisis: a timeline of events and policy actions' [Online]. Available at: http://timeline.stlouisfed.org/index.cfm?p=timeline (accessed: 4 February 2011).

Fergusson, N., Brady, B., Wells, R., Krugman, P., and Soros, G. (2009) 'The crisis and how to deal with it', *New York Review of Books*, 30 April.

Galbraith, J.K. (1954) *The great crash of 1929*. Boston: Houghton Mifflin Harcourt.

Goolsbee, A. (2011) Speech delivered to the National Association for Business Economics, Washington, DC, 8 March.

Gorton, G. (2010) *Slapped by the invisible hand: The panic of 2007*. Oxford: Oxford University Press.

———. (2012) *Misunderstanding financial crises: Why we don't see them coming*. Oxford: Oxford University Press.

Kindleberger, C.P. and Aliber, R. (1978) *Manias, panics and crashes: A history of financial crises*. Hoboken: John Wiley & Son.

King, M. (2011) 'Global imbalances: The perspective of the Bank of England', *Financial Stability Review. Banque de France*, February [Online]. Available at: www.bankofengland.co.uk/publications/speeches/2011/speech473.pdf (accessed: 8 March 2011).

Lewis, M. (2010) *The big short: Inside the doomsday machine*. New York: W.W. Norton & Company.

———. (1989) *Liar's poker: Rising through the wreckage on Wall Street*. New York: W.W. Norton & Company.

McLean, B. and Nocera, J. (2010) *All the devils are here: The hidden history of the financial crisis*. New York: Portfolio.

Mian, A. and Sufi, A. (2014) *House of debt: How they (and you) caused the Great Recession, and how we can prevent it from happening again.* Chicago. University of Chicago.

Minsky, H. (2008) *Stabilizing an unstable economy.* New York: McGraw Hill.

OECD (Organisation for Economic Co-operation and Development). (2009) 'Trade flows collapse in Q4 2008 but signs of falls easing in early 2009' [Online]. Available at: www.oecd.org/dataoecd/29/36/42668007.pdf (accessed: 2 March 2011).

Padoa-Schioppa, T. (2010) 'Markets and government before, during, and after the 2007–20XX crisis', *Per Jacobsen Lecture*, Basel, Switzerland, 27 June.

Rajan, R.G. (2005) 'Has financial development made the world riskier?', presented at Jackson Hole, August.

Rogoff, K. and Reinhart, C. (2009) *This time is different: Eight centuries of financial folly.* Princeton: Princeton University Press.

Stiglitz, J. (2008) 'Market fundamentalism is dead', *FORA*, 20 October [Online]. Available at: www.youtube.com/watch?v=x_2-Tv2GPs0 (accessed: 6 August 2011).

———. (2010) 'Needed: A new economic paradigm', *Financial Times*, 19 August [Online]. Available at: www.ft.com/intl/cms/s/0/d5108f90-abc2-11df-9f02-00144feabdc0.html#axzz1yGalnhcl (accessed: 19 June 2012).

Strange, S. (1986) *Casino capitalism.* Manchester: Manchester University Press.

———. (1996) *The retreat of the state: The diffusion of power in the world economy.* Cambridge: Cambridge University Press.

Subacchi, P. (2010) 'The role of the United States in the post-crisis economic order', in Niblett, R. (ed.) *America and a changed world: A question of leadership.* London: Wiley-Blackwell/Chatham House, pp. 258–274.

Tett, G. (2009) *Fool's gold: How the bold dream of a small tribe at J.P. Morgan was corrupted by Wall Street greed and unleashed a catastrophe.* New York: Free Press.

Turner, A. (2009) 'How to tame global finance', *Prospect Magazine*, 27 August.

1 Crises and paradigm shift[1]

In 1543 a little-known amateur astronomer published his *magnum opus*. *On the Revolutions of Heavenly Spheres* secured Nicolaus Copernicus's place in the history of science and constituted the beginning of what Thomas Kuhn (1962) described as a paradigm shift in scientific thought. Before Copernicus the sun and the planets were believed to revolve around the earth. But astronomers had increasingly been bothered by growing observational anomalies with the Aristotelian, geocentric view. Copernicus hypothesised that contrary to the dominant view, the earth revolved around the sun, as did the planets – a new, radical, heliocentric model. He was right. But Copernicus's theory did not result in a sudden or instantaneous shift in worldview. The shift took longer to become solid as the scientific consensus adjusted, and then, more slowly, it was accompanied by a more gradual process, a societal and cultural shift supporting the new model, with empirical observations, such as Galileo's discovery of the moons of Jupiter, underpinning its validity. These types of rare disjunctive shifts occur not only in the scientific realm but also in the economic and regulatory policy spheres, and this book addresses one: a narrative and international regulatory policy consensus shift that began in 2008 and which continues today.

Economic cycles: crises, response and relapse

Global and national economies and markets operate in cycles of growth that, when unrestrained, can turn into booms, which are eventually punctured by busts resulting in recessions of varying severity (Galbraith, 1954; Kindleberger and Aliber, 1978; Minsky, 2008). During the boom phase, few remember economic history, believing this time is different (Rogoff and Reinhart, 2009; Shiller, 2006), but it never is, and booms always eventually turn to bust. Global economic cycles operate on a longer frequency than national cycles, because it is rare that the credit expansions and contractions of national economies align to create a synchronous collapse of the global economy as a whole. Normally, a national recession or a banking calamity in one part of the world is balanced partially by growth and prosperity elsewhere.

The rhythm within these cycles is not only economic but also conceptual and ideological. 'Constructionists' are right: ideas do matter in the political and economic calculus of policy making. Economies are underpinned by and linked to ideological narratives, a prevailing policy consensus that places limits on policy actions and options and constitutes a dominant worldview or paradigm.

In some, but by no means all, financial crises, a paradigm shift (Kuhn, 1962) can be triggered and becomes part of the cycle and process, particularly in severe economic crises. For instance, economic failures and stagflation in the United Kingdom (UK) (a slow-motion bust) in the 1970s paved the way for the Thatcher victory in 1979 and a significant ideological and economic policy shift that affected the UK for decades thereafter (Blyth, 2002; Gamble, 1988).

On the international level, as with economic cycles, the ideological cycle is also of a longer frequency, measured in decades, not years. But when a sufficiently severe exogenous event or economic and financial crisis occurs, it can shake the prevailing worldview. More rarely still a shock may result in a paradigm shift in ideological and regulatory concepts held by leaders and policy makers. In such cases a rapid evolutionary burst of action and reform, a shift in the policy consensus and worldview, can occur.

In 1971 one economic and financial paradigm, embedded liberalism and the system of globally managed exchange rates (Ruggie, 1982), ended with US president Richard Nixon's closure of the gold window. The end of that era gradually gave birth to another, which over time came to be characterised in part by laissez-faire neoliberalism (Gamble, 2009, pp. 71–86), or market fundamentalism (Stiglitz, 2008), and later by the Washington Consensus (Wade, 2008; Williamson, 1993, 1994). This ideological worldview involved a championing of deregulated, unfettered global markets and firms. This shift moved economies and the financial system away from a rules-based system (Elson, 2011, pp. 208–209), to competing based on flexible exchange rates and fostering the success of their national economic models within increasingly globalised economies reliant on (it was assumed) efficient markets (Wade, 2008, p. 2). The series of policy decisions and nondecisions that flowed from this deregulatory narrative took shape in the late 1970s, gathered strength in the 1980s and thundered forward in the 1990s and early years of the 21st century.

During the decades before the 2007–2008 financial crisis governments allowed and facilitated the erosion and diffusion of state power to other actors – a weakening of state power coupled with a retreat of the state's willingness to supervise growing global markets and firms (Strange, 1986, 1996). Markets grew. Governmental acts or refusal to act were underpinned by the ideological and economic belief in unregulated markets rather than state regulatory power (Akerlof and Shiller, 2009; Padoa-Schioppa, 2010; Stiglitz, 2008). Firms grew and morphed from national retail banks into global behemoths with operations interconnected across the globe. The size, impact and influence of these firms rapidly grew, as did the complexity of markets and instruments (McLean and Nocera, 2010; Tett, 2009), the leverage seen (Turner, 2009, p. 19), the risks taken and levels of compensation paid to their employees (FCIC, 2011, p. 62; Johnson and Kwak, 2010).

There were voices raised against the dominant paradigm (Rajan, 2005; White, 2008). But they did not alter the worldview. The macro-level neoliberal narrative defended questionable economic truths and orthodoxies, blocked historical memory of previous crises, allowed regulatory laxity, overlooked the 'capture' of the regulators by the regulated, permitted dangerous market and firm-level risks to build up and resisted action to mitigate the worst effects until the crisis was all but upon us.

As in other previous ideological and economic cycles the existing worldview blotted out historical memory amongst leaders and technocrats. Deregulation and self-regulation (the latter now viewed as an oxymoron) was the norm. During this period the frequency of national boom and bust cycles grew (Allen and Gale, 2007), and the number and severity of national banking crises rose (King, 2011), but few paid attention. The Anglo-Saxon paradigm and narrative worshipped by political leaders and regulators precluded actors from seeing the 'black swan', or the extreme exogenous event or crisis, coming (Taleb, 2010); instead, a great moderation was supposed to be underway.

In this manner the worldview provided ideological justification for the boom of the 1990s and 2000s. It fostered the creation of markets, firms and instruments that would in 2007 rapidly transmit price declines in houses and condos in Nevada and Florida sold to poor, credit-challenged Americans to banks in the UK and Germany, and then around the globe. As the credit crunch and economic contagion spread the panic grew, and leaders faced the most significant economic and financial crisis since the Great Depression in 1929.

Confronted by a crisis of historic proportions old solutions were insufficient. A breakpoint occurs and as a result, 'the possibilities for major change are particularly great and scope of possibilities and outcomes is unusually wide' (Ikenberry, 1992, p. 318; see also Helleiner, 2009, p. 16). This time the US could not fashion the solution alone or solely with its G7[2] colleagues and allies, as it had in the past. The days when two men, Paul Volcker, chairman of the US Federal Reserve from 1979 to 1987, and Robin Leigh-Pemberton, governor of the Bank of England from 1983 to 1993, could do a deal on international bank regulation that was pressed upon the rest of the world were long gone (Goodhart, 2011; Kapstein, 1992).

In 2008 US hegemonic power was in decline, and rising powers, especially China, Brazil and India, demanded a voice and a role, and they had the reserves to back their demands. Emerging countries had to be included. Recognising this reality and making the switch to a larger leadership grouping at the topmost tier of international economic and financial diplomacy would be necessary to make any possible solutions truly global in impact and to ensure the legitimacy of the decisions taken in response to the crisis. As a result while the crisis response in 2007–2008 exhibits common elements with prior cycles, the constructs created as a result of the architectural impulse would be markedly different, indicative of the evolution of geopolitical power relations and balances since the last major shift in 1971.

The internationally coordinated collective response in 2008 and since is part of this history of cycles of booms and busts, crisis management and reform and gradual relapse. This especially severe crisis forced a financial regulatory paradigm shift in worldview amongst government leaders, states and their technocratic central banking community. There was a rapid evolution in the collective policy-making narrative, which underpinned new and refurbished international political, regulatory and architectural constructs. This was 'a new phase' (Wade, 2008, p. 3) – one which entailed the rejection of key aspects of the laissez-faire neoliberal worldview and its assumptions.

Using Kuhn and Hall to understand crisis response

Thomas Kuhn described the process of paradigm shift. A shift occurs when anomalies arise that can only be effectively described, answered and dealt with by new hitherto controversial explanations (theories) and an accompanying worldview. Only after a paradigm shift occurs does a series of different truths take their place at the centre of the new worldview constructed of new scientific facts and a new orthodoxy. Peter Hall applied the concept of paradigm shift to analyse intellectual and political forces centred on economic policy making in Britain and a dramatic shift from established Keynesian norms to neoliberal monetarist supply-side economics in the 1980s; this was the construction of a new policy paradigm. Hall posited three orders of change.

First-order changes are forms of normal policy making, 'a process that adjusts policy without challenging the overall terms of a given policy paradigm' (Hall, 1993, p. 279). This is 'paradigm maintenance' (Skogstad, 2008, p. 16) adjustments or small changes in focus and direction within an agreed narrative construction. Existing truths are not challenged and are not in dispute. Second-order changes are moderately more significant, where the instrument of a policy is adjusted but not the overarching policy. Both first- and second-order changes are characterised by incrementalism (Hall, 1993). Third-order changes reflect radical changes to the overarching terms of the discourse and indicate a paradigm shift or replacement is occurring. They involve the accumulation of anomalies, experimentation, failures and a reappraisal of existing truths. The process is likely to be contested. An intensification of debate about economic issues will occur. Issues of authority (i.e. power) are central. Third-order change, the paradigm shift described by Kuhn in the scientific world and Hall in the economic context, is a major reappraisal, an event at least an order of magnitude greater than first- and second-order changes. This book identifies a shift in narrative worldview to some extent amongst political leaders, but especially amongst the elite of the world's central banking community, who adjust their policy consensus and champion first-, second- and third-order changes that collectively constitute the beginning of a paradigm shift.

Paradigms tend to be championed by leaders, experts and transnational actors and are characterised by periods of stability followed by abrupt episodes of substantial change (Wilson, 2000), via a process of punctuated equilibrium. This is what we saw in the crisis response particularly in 2008–2009. For a policy paradigm shift to take place, policy-making actors must be challenged by model failures and growing anomalies (Weir and Skocpol, 1983). The paradigm or era can be said to end when its basic illusions are seen as false. The financial crisis created conditions for a paradigm replacement because the dominant laissez-faire neoliberal deregulatory model of financial architecture of the last three decades was compromised (Wade, 2008). This allowed the intellectual economic beliefs behind the prevailing paradigm to be increasingly challenged (El-Erian, 2009; Stiglitz, 2009, 2010), leading some to suggest the Anglo-American deregulatory laissez-faire, neoliberal, neoclassical economic paradigm had become exhausted (Palley, 2009). A strong challenge to the dominant worldview is then possible because the severe economic crisis creates a transformational opportunity, a paradigmatic moment (Assenza, Sokolickova, and Martynau, 2011; Fergusson *et al.*, 2009; Soros, 2008).

In essence, for a paradigm shift to occur, the consensus policy narrative in a community must make a jump, when confronted by increasing anomalies; there has to be the abandonment of the old and the taking up of a new theory, and related policy positions in response to recognised anomalies and failures in the past worldview. This is what began in 2008 and which is still underway in 2015.

Whether or not a paradigm shift is underway is a matter of dispute. Some observers, such as Eric Helleiner (2014), see the current crisis and response as simply a maintenance of the status quo. He is joined by Mark Blyth (2013), who views changes underway as only first and second order; in Blyth's formulation 1+ 2 does not equal 3, i.e. incrementalism alone does not signal a paradigm shift. Still others try to bridge the 'paradigm gap' by stretching Hall's definition and arguing that paradigms can indeed shift via progressive incremental steps alone (Moschella and Tsingou, 2013).

This book rejects the proposition that the 2008–2009 crisis resulted in little or no change in community narratives and policy outcomes, and finds that, when the response and reform waves are viewed as a whole and within the broader cultural context, with sufficient temporal distance from events, the crisis response was not just an exercise in incrementalism, but something much more significant. There was in fact a break, a jump, a third-order shift, which is then supported by smaller, less substantial, first- and second-order changes: a crisis-induced narrative shift. The replacement narrative moves away from market authority and towards a broad-based reassertion of state authority, and it signals a rejection of aspects of laissez-faire neoliberalism, as it was applied to the regulation of global financial markets and firms.

At this point, 11 years on from the apogee of the crisis, the shift is largely confined to a macroprudential policy consensus and to regulatory policies that are controlled and directed by the central banking community. Critics are right that the shift does not encompass a rejection of the neoliberal market economy model as a whole; it is presently a narrower, technical paradigm shift. But, because of the power and authority of the central bank community promulgating and defending the narrative, architecture and agreed policies, what is underway has strength and permanence, and effect upon national and international financial markets' importance for the markets, firms and the operation of real economy. What has taken place is a narrative and technocratic shift with macroeconomic implications. That was a goal of the architects who designed the new global structures – to apply technical policy changes, collectively and individually, that would, it was hoped, enhance the stability of the global financial system in the future.

The narrative and policy shift that underpinned collective policy actions after 2008 is recognised by leaders, participants and actors as a 'new consensus' based on agreed macroprudential policies and tools applied to the world's largest banks, and other actions designed re-regulate global financial markets. This is significant, because this collective realisation of a shift in the community consensus strengthens the position of those who hold the new worldview, and they henceforth view the policy-making process through a new lens, one that comports with the new worldview and one, which, once it is in place, is resistant to attack and dismemberment.

Why narratives matter

Narratives matter in political economy because they help clarify and provide a foundation for decision making and policy actions. Faced by sudden severe events the narratives adopted by a community help it address key questions that arise in response to crises: how we got there, what went wrong and what to do to stop it from happening again. These narratives reduce uncertainty and galvanise action. In analysing and dissecting the crisis response and policy process that began in 2008 and continues in 2020 the underlying narratives allow us a window into the crisis dynamics and formulation of the new policy consensus, which underpins and supports the policy paradigm shift that follows from it.

The book draws upon a series of 34 high-level, qualitative interviews with many of the governmental, central bank and supervisory principals present and active in key decision-making meetings and roles from 2008 onwards (from 11 G20 and five non-G20 states). These interviews involved the social production of knowledge; they provided a conversational window into events which is 'contextual, linguistic, narrative and pragmatic' (Kvale and Brinkmann, 2009, p. 18). In using such narrative material we are 'putting oneself in the place of the other' (Crotty, 1998, p. 76). Of course recalled narratives around events in the past are subjective and reflective of the individuals' own biases and perspectives. Nonetheless the sources can, according to the interactionist tradition, 'give an authentic insight into people's experiences' (Silverman, 2001, p. 87). The subjects interviewed had direct personal experience of the crisis management from 2007 to 2008, of the response since then, and were senior actors in the decision-making processes. Seniority is important, especially when analysing an opaque, elite, leader-driven diplomatic and technocratic policy-making process with relatively few key actors and players. The interviews provided a view of the policy consensus, political economy and diplomatic factors behind the evolution of the post-crisis international architectural and regulatory policy response, through the creation of the G20, and the creation of the Financial Stability Board (FSB).

Fundamentally it is these policy narratives, their strengths and weaknesses, the disputes seen and policy outcomes observed which enable us to understand what occurred in response to the crisis, and what continues to unfold today. The book finds that the extent to which a common narrative and a new policy consensus emerges is linked to the strength of the outcomes observed and the robustness (or not) of the paradigm shift that results. Policy change is about narratives, but it is also, in this case, about the negotiating processes in international diplomacy and G20 summitry, which exhibits its own dynamics and rhythm.

The 'two-level game' in normal times and crisis

Readers require models to understand the dynamics in international diplomacy and G20 summitry. This book applies Robert Putnam's two-level game to the G20 summit process (Putnam, 1988; Putnam and Bayne, 1984). Putnam used game theory to design a model in which international negotiations between states comprise simultaneous negotiations at the international level, between governments (level-one negotiations) and at the intranational level, or domestic internal negotiations, between actors (level-two negotiations). In the domestic negotiations the government weighs demands by actors and constructs coalitions. At the international level the government seeks to address demands without committing to anything that could prove unacceptable to major domestic interests. Agreements in summitry are composed of what Putnam calls 'win sets', which occur when the positions of the actors at both the international and national levels overlap and permit agreement. This two-level game analytical framework illuminates the G20 process.

The book identifies a difference between Putnam's construct in non-crisis periods, and when it is applied in a period of economic crisis, as in Figure 1.1. In non-crisis periods level-one negotiation positions of A and B may indeed have limited overlap. Each actor's position is distinct and can be in conflict. For example in non-crisis periods, US negotiators rarely see overlap with the level-one goals of their Chinese counterparts. In normal times domestic interests on both sides also drive them apart, creating little if any win sets. For example domestic US demands for market access by major US financial firms to Chinese markets fall on deaf ears in Beijing because this conflicts with the position of China's state-owned banks to restrict new entrants into the domestic market. Result: no level-one or level-two win-set space, and no progress. In crisis periods the nature of the two-level game is distinctly different.

In a period of global economic crisis the diplomatic negotiating calculus changes. The goals of level-one negotiators in country A and country B converge or overlap. Win sets open up as domestic interests either temporarily diminish in importance or can be overridden by level-one goals. Result: a consensus, and policy actions can be agreed and acted upon. Putnam suggests, and we see in the G20-FSB crisis-response that 'the greater the autonomy of central decision makers from their level two constituents the larger the win set' (Putnam, 1988, p. 449). The crisis provides evidence of this, with G20 leaders negotiating and agreeing to deals, fashioned by central bank and supervisory technocrats (who were independent and faced no electoral pressure). Those G20 leaders and, especially their senior central banking proxies, in phases one and two of the crisis, were able to take positions opposed by their own national level-two constituents (i.e. the world's largest banks). A senior participant in the G20 process captured the effect of crisis upon the two-level game, leaders understood the 'need for comprehensive action' and this view was 'widely shared'. There was a 'real changing of views', a consensus amongst level-one actors (Mackintosh, 2012, 24, pp. 3–4).[3] Figure 1.1 graphically represents the two-level game operating in non-crisis and crisis periods.

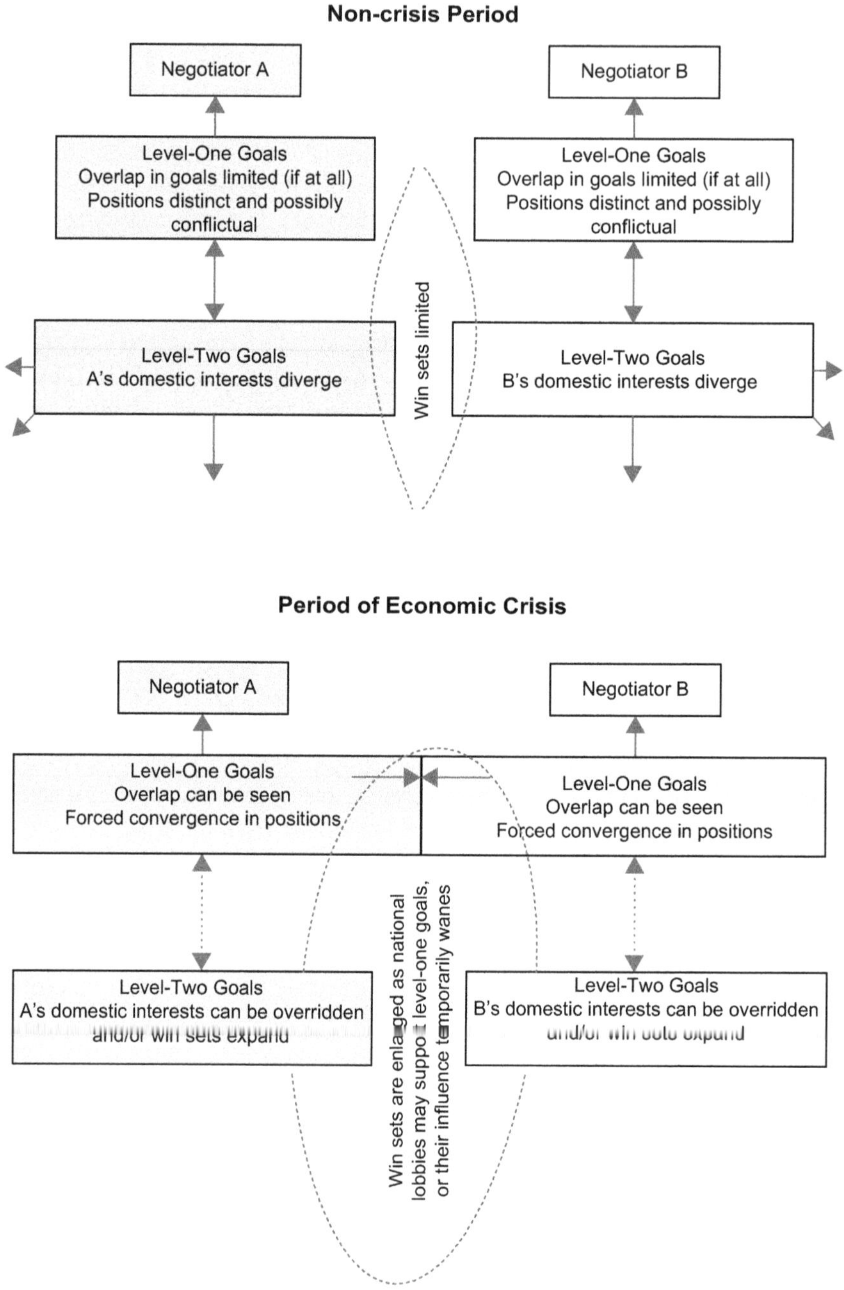

Figure 1.1 Two-level games in a non-crisis period and during a period of economic crisis

Putnam's two-level game also operates in complex or contentious financial reform areas. The book identifies instances where the G20 technical negotiators went back for legislative solutions to a problem agreed to at the macro-G20 level. In those cases leaders and technocrats had to engage in parliamentary and national negotiations with level-one domestic interests. As a result the complexity and difficulty of securing final ratification, and agreement amongst national actors, and thus implementation, increased. This is in line with Putnam's model.

As the financial and economic crisis eased in severity from 2010 onwards, especially in areas where the lead central banking community had weaker (or no) levers of policy control, the outcomes were notably less robust, because wins sets are once again limited, and level-one and level-two interests clash. With little or no consensus there is much less progress, and only first-order changes in policies. Putnam's model thus helps the reader understand the dynamics in G20 summitry and in the technical negotiations below them. But we must also be alert to the impact of the central banking community that dominated those technical negotiations below the G20, which was and remains pivotal to the policy reforms and paradigm shift observed.

The central banking epistemic community and paradigm shift

The book explores not only G20 summitry but also focuses on the narrative shift and technical-level architectural and policy outcomes that were agreed in principle by the G20 but which were designed and executed by a cohesive, elite, central banking community, led by North American and European figures. These individuals operated as the dominant epistemic community during the crisis response and reform processes. This same community continues to drive the building, maintenance and defence of the new re-regulatory worldview, and the reassertion of state authority over global financial markets and firms in 2020.

An epistemic community is a network of professionals with recognised expertise and policy competence and knowledge in a specific field. While all members of the community need not come from the same speciality, community members share in common a set of normative and principled beliefs, which underpin the interaction of the community; causal beliefs based on an analysis of the shared problems they confront, possible policy actions and desired outcomes; notions of validity – of intersubjective, internally defined criteria for judging knowledge in their area of expertise; and they will be engaged in a common policy enterprise addressing the identified common problems related to their area of expertise which they believe will result in improvements to the commonwealth (Haas, 1992, p. 3).

The G20 leaders relied on trusted central bankers and this small epistemic community. Leaders stood side by side with their central bankers in the immediate responses to the global economic crisis, rescuing the system with exceptional fiscal and monetary policy actions. Leaders often deferred to the community's technical knowledge and looked to the central bankers for solutions. After all the G20 politicians did not have the time or the ability to determine the detailed reform agenda. But they knew action was needed, and needed fast. And they were prepared to strongly back the central banking community's reform agenda. That agenda was girded and anchored in a crisis-altered new narrative and policy consensus within the central banking community. The narrative centred on the importance of enhanced institutionalised international regulatory coordination and cooperation, and a championing of macroprudential policy tools and mechanisms to ensure the future financial stability of the global economy.

The book will show that the success of a particular reform endeavour is related to the extent to which the central banking community recognises anomalies, its international and national policy-making strength in the policy space and the degree to which it has a common policy narrative and consensus. It is the combination of these three factors that influences the strength, the success or the failure of policy reforms in particular cases, and hence the degree of paradigm shift. It is useful at this point to view these interactions graphically, as is done in Figure 1.2. The axes are:

1 The build-up of recognised critical anomalies in the system (top X-axis)
2 The strength of the central banking epistemic community in policy making and implementation (bottom X-axis)
3 The strength of the policy consensus seen in the policy area (right-hand Y-axis)
4 The Kuhn/Hall paradigm shift and first-, second-, and third-order changes (left-hand Y-axis).

The sloping line running diagonally through the chart represents different policy outcomes.

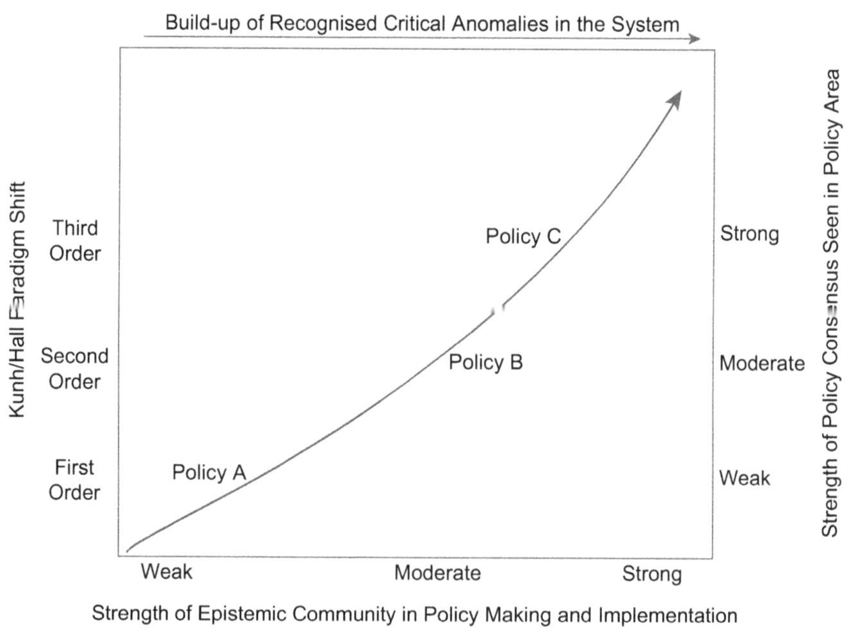

Figure 1.2 The epistemic community, policy consensus and paradigm shift

In Policy A: The number of collectively recognised anomalies is small. The central banking epistemic community is weak in the policy area. The resulting policy consensus is also weak and the results are first-order changes. The combination of these factors (too few anomalies, a weak or conflicted policy community and a weak consensus) together produces poor policy outcomes.

In Policy B: A greater number of anomalies are recognised. The central epistemic community is stronger in the policy arena. The policy consensus is more robust. The resulting policy outcome can therefore be stronger and of second-order magnitude.

In Policy C: Huge anomalies are present and are recognised by a majority of the central banking community and actors. The community is in control of policy and recognises the anomalies. A strong new policy consensus is agreed. The community has power and influence in the policy area. This results in a third-order paradigm shift.

What the figure underscores is that it is the combination of these factors that affects the policy outcomes and orders of change, or degrees of paradigm shift. This dynamic will be observed in particular in Chapter 6, on FSB policy outcomes.

Watching and dissecting the shift underway

To conclude this book addresses the crisis response in 2007–2008 by advanced and emerging-country leaders and their most trusted technocrats from central banks. It identifies a crisis-influenced change in the underlying policy narratives amongst both groups, but especially amongst the community composed of advanced and emerging country leaders. This worldview signalled a reassertion of state authority over financial markets and firms and a retreat of market authority and laissez-faire neoliberalism in the regulatory sphere.

The wave of crisis management actions and reforms began in 2008, gathered momentum in 2009 and 11 years later now continues at a slower pace in 2020, bedevilled by a US administration which has abandoned leadership and replaced it with hostility to the international community and architecture of cooperation and coordination.

G20 actors and the FSB have been since 2017 engaged in triage and defence of the processes that have worked and are still needed, despite the lack of global leadership from the US under President Trump. In pursuit of America First the US president has abandoned the international order created by his predecessors, and this has undermined the effectiveness of the G20. But it has not undermined central banking coordination to the same degree, as that technocratic grouping continued to operate, much less affected by America First. Figure 1.3 illustrates the reform response as a series of waves which rise together in response to the global financial crisis peak together and then decline to varying degrees depending on the extent of the narrative and policy cohesion seen in each community of actors area as the crisis impetus dissipates and normality returns.

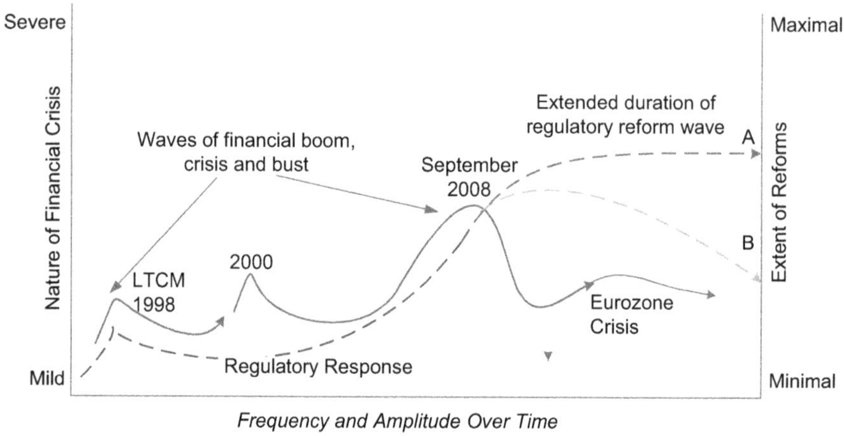

Figure 1.3 The regulatory reform waves

COVID-19 – the ultimate stress test of the global architecture

As this book went to press the G20 appeared to be failing its most important crisis stress test. It had failed to provide an effective mechanism for crisis management and reaction when confronted in the spring of 2020 with the COVID-19 pandemic. Without American leadership, the forum could not act, and G20 states descended into national inwardly looking partial solutions, to the most significant threat to economic stability since the 1929 Great Depression. The G20 was unable defend the system. Instead Mr Trump levied accusations at allies, competitors and key coordinators, such as the World Health Organization (WHO). Donald Trump was no Gordon Brown. Leadership was lacking and the G20 failed to help stabilise the globe.

State authority to the rescue

But the multifaceted extreme pandemic and economic fallout did nonetheless push leaders from across the political spectrum to vastly extend state authority, action and control. The pandemic forced actors towards similar solutions, opening national win sets and creating new (temporary) coalitions of necessity and urgency.

We saw that when all face possible death by suffocation, and the grim reaper is knocking, few politicians or voters hold to libertarian Randian shibboleths and fantasies. Only the state, its doctors, nurse, technocrats and central bankers acting together could save us and the global economy from disaster. So, while the G20 failed, crippled by Mr Trump, state authority was extended and asserted on a scale never witnessed (whether medical, fiscal, monetary or physical) in the modern era. Yet again crisis caused policy leaps from reality to another. Yet again a severe crisis made possible what was previously considered impossible.

The COVID-19 pandemic has clearly demonstrated the continuing essential stabilising role of state power, and central bank authority over markets and economies in crises. Confronted by the pandemic all leaders individually massively increased state action and intervention in their economies. The central bank community reacted by swiftly reactivating mechanisms used in 2008–9 in response to the COVID-19 pandemic. The mechanisms – quantitative easing, central bank swap lines, massive directed bond buying and lending – were hugely expanded to deal with the worst economic crisis in 100 years. Central bankers and supervisors also took regulatory actions to support and constrain markets. In summary the COVID-19 pandemic, and national responses, taught us all further lessons about leadership, crisis dynamics and the centrality of state authority when these terrible events strike.

We now turn our attention to the first G20 summit, which took place in Washington in November 2008. The financial and economic crisis was surging. Political leaders frantically sought a mechanism through which to respond. They began crisis management. But this would not just be the old G7 club taking charge. This time many more leaders were called to sit at the diplomatic table and join the crisis response, as the crisis was at the core and not at the periphery, and the former needed the help and the resources of the latter to address the global crisis. Leaders would seek to calm the panicked markets. Even at this very early stage leaders and central bankers also began to delineate the contours of the financial reform endeavour that they would engage upon collectively. State authority over markets was reasserted. The retreat of the state would halt and change direction. A new paradigm would start to become visible.

Notes

1 This chapter draws on work previously published by the author in 'Crises and paradigm shift', *The Political Quarterly*, 84(4), Winter 2014, pp. 406–412.
2 The Group of Seven is composed of leaders, finance ministers and central bank governors from the following countries: Canada, France, Germany, Italy, Japan, the UK and the US.
3 Author's note: interviews are referenced throughout the text as follows: author's name, year of the interview, number of the interview and page number or numbers of the transcript, as in Mackintosh (2012, 24, pp. 3–4).

References

Akerlof, G.A. and Shiller, R.J. (2009) *Animal spirits: How human psychology drives the economy, and why it matters for global capitalism*. Princeton: Princeton University Press.

Allen, F. and Gale, D. (2007) *Understanding financial crises*. Oxford: Oxford University Press.

Assenza, G., Sokolickova, Z., and Martynau, A. (2011) 'The ideational background of the global economic crisis', *Humanicus*, Issue 6.

Blyth, M. (2002) *Great transformations: Economic ideas and institutional change in the twentieth century*. Cambridge: Cambridge University Press.

———. (2013) 'Paradigms and paradox: The politics of economic ideas in two moments of crisis', *Governance: An International Journal of Policy, Administration, and Institutions*, 26(2), pp. 197–215.

Copernicus, N. (1543) *On the revolutions of heavenly spheres* (1995 edition). New York: Prometheus.

Crotty, M. (1998) *The foundations of social research: Meaning and perspective in the research process*. London: Sage.

El-Erian, M. (2009) 'Market fatigue: The Anglo-Saxon model has taken a knock', *The Economist*, 1 October [Online]. Available at: www.economist.com/node/14530138 (accessed: 10 November 2009).

Elson, A. (2011) *Governing global finance: The evolution and reform of the international financial architecture*. New York: Palgrave.

FCIC (Financial Crisis Inquiry Commission). (2011) 'Final report' [Online]. Available at: www.fcic.gov/report (accessed: 2 April 2011).

Fergusson, N., Brady, B., Wells, R., Krugman, P., and Soros, G. (2009) 'The crisis and how to deal with it', *New York Review of Books*, 30 April.

Galbraith, J.K. (1954) *The great crash of 1929*. Boston: Houghton Mifflin Harcourt.

Gamble, A. (1988) *The free economy and the strong state*. Durham: Duke University Press.

———. (2009) *The spectre at the feast: Capitalist crisis and the politics of recession*. New York: Palgrave Macmillan.

Goodhart, C. (2011) *The Basel Committee on Banking Supervision: A history of the early years, 1974–1997*. Cambridge: Cambridge University Press.

Haas, P.M. (1992) 'Introduction: Epistemic communities and international policy coordination', *International Organization*, 46(1), pp. 1–35.

Hall, P.A. (1993) 'Policy paradigms, social learning, and the state: The case of economic policymaking in Britain', *Comparative Politics*, 25(3), pp. 275–296.

Helleiner, E. (2009) 'Special forum: Crisis and the future of governance', *Global Governance*, 15, pp. 1–28.

———. (2014) *The status quo crisis: Global financial governance after the 2008 meltdown*. Oxford: Oxford University Press.

Ikenberry, J.G. (1992) 'A world economy restored – Expert consensus and the Anglo-American post-war settlement', *International Organization*, 46(1), pp. 289–321.

Johnson, S. and Kwak, J. (2010) *13 bankers: The Wall Street takeover and the next financial meltdown*. New York: Pantheon.

Kapstein, E. (1992) 'Between power and purpose: Central bankers and the politics of regulatory convergence', *International Organisation*, 46(1), pp. 265–287.

Kindleberger, C.P. and Aliber, R. (1978) *Manias, panics and crashes: A history of financial crises*. Hoboken: John Wiley & Son.

King, M. (2011) 'Global imbalances: The perspective of the Bank of England', *Financial Stability Review. Banque de France*, February [Online]. Available at: www.bankofengland.co.uk/publications/speeches/2011/speech473.pdf (accessed: 8 March 2011).

Kuhn, T. (1962) *The structure of scientific revolutions*. Chicago: University of Chicago Press.

Kvale, S. and Brinkmann, S. (2009) *InterViews: Learning the craft of qualitative research interviewing*. London: Sage.

Mackintosh, S. (2012) Interview, 24, p. 3. G20 Central Bank Governor, 2 July.

McLean, B. and Nocera, J. (2010) *All the devils are here: The hidden history of the financial crisis*. New York: Portfolio.

Minsky, H. (2008) *Stabilizing an unstable economy*. New York: McGraw Hill.

Moschella, M. and Tsingou, E. (eds.). (2013) *Great expectations slow transformations: Incremental change in post-crisis regulation*. Colchester: European Consortium for Political Research (ECPR).

Padoa-Schioppa, T. (2010) 'Markets and government before, during, and after the 2007–20XX Crisis', *Per Jacobsen Lecture*, Basel, Switzerland, 27 June.

Palley, T.I. (2009) 'America's exhausted paradigm: Macroeconomic causes of the financial crisis and Great Recession', *New America Foundation* [Online]. Available at: www.newamerica.net/files/Thomas_Palley_America%27s_Exhausted_Paradigm.pdf (accessed: 20 June 2012).

Putnam, R. (1988) 'Diplomacy and domestic politics: The logic of two-level games', *International Organization*, 42(3), pp. 427–460.

Putnam, R. and Bayne, N. (1984) *Hanging together: The seven-power summits*. London: Royal Institute for International Affairs.

Rajan, R.G. (2005) 'Has financial development made the world riskier?', presented at Jackson Hole, August [Online]. Available at: www.kansascityfed.org/publicat/sympos/2005/pdf/rajan2005.pdf (accessed: 12 December 2010).

Rogoff, K. and Reinhart, C. (2009) *This time is different: Eight centuries of financial folly.* Princeton: Princeton University Press.

Ruggie, J.G. (1982) 'International regimes, transactions, and change: Embedded liberalism in the post-war economic order', *International Organization*, 36(2), pp. 379–415.

Shiller, R.J. (2006) *Irrational exuberance* (2nd edition). Princeton: Princeton University Press.

Silverman, D. (2001) *Interpreting qualitative data*. London: Sage.

Skogstad, G. (2008) *Internationalization and Canadian agriculture: Policy and governing paradigms*. Toronto: Toronto University Press.

Soros, G. (2008) *The new paradigm for financial markets: The credit crash of 2008 and what it means*. New York: Public Affairs.

Stiglitz, J. (2008) 'Market fundamentalism is dead', *FORA*, 20 October [Online]. Available at: www.youtube.com/watch?v=x_2-Tv2GPs0 (accessed: 6 August 2011).

———. (2009) *Freefall: Free markets and the sinking of the global economy*. New York: W.W. Norton & Company.

———. (2010) 'Needed: A new economic paradigm', *Financial Times*, 19 August [Online]. Available at: www.ft.com/intl/cms/s/0/d5108f90-abc2-11df-9f02-00144feabdc0.html#axzz1yGalnhcl (accessed: 19 June 2012).

Strange, S. (1986) *Casino capitalism*. Manchester: Manchester University Press.

———. (1996) *The retreat of the state: The diffusion of power in the world economy*. Cambridge: Cambridge University Press.

Taleb, N. (2010) *The black swan: The impact of the highly improbable*. New York: Random House.

Tett, G. (2009) *Fool's gold: How the bold dream of a small tribe at J.P. Morgan was corrupted by Wall Street greed and unleashed a catastrophe*. New York: Free Press.

Turner, A. (2009) *The Turner review: A regulatory response to the global banking crisis*. London: Financial Services Authority.

Wade, R. (2008) 'Financial regime change', *New Left Review*, 53 (September–October), pp. 5–21.

Weir, M. and Skocpol, T. (1983) 'State structures and social Keynesianism: Responses to the Great Depression in Sweden and the United States', *International Journal of Comparative Sociology*, 24.

White, W. (2008) 'International governance and management of financial crises', *Speech delivered at the Bank of France*, Paris, 10 June [Online]. Available at: www.bis.org/speeches/sp080708.htm (accessed: 31 January 2013).

Williamson, J. (1993) 'Democracy and the "Washington consensus"', *World Development*, 21(8), pp. 1329–1366.

———. (1994) *The political economy of policy reform*. Washington, DC: Peterson Institute for International Economics.

Wilson, C.A. (2000) 'Policy regimes and policy change', *Journal of Public Policy*, 20(3), pp. 247–274.

2 The creation of the G20 leaders' forum

> 'The formation of the G20 group of world leaders is likely to be the most lasting institutional consequence of the global financial meltdown of 2008'.
>
> (The Economist, 2009)

> 'The G20 has evolved into the closest thing to a board of directors for the world economy'.
>
> (Davis and Poletta, 2010)

> 'No longer the CEO of Free World Inc., the United States is now the largest minority shareholder in New World Order LLC'.
>
> (Jones, 2011)

G20 summitry and crisis management

The first summit of the reformulated Group of Twenty (G20) focused on emergency global crisis management efforts. National leaders seized upon the G20 forum and elevated its status from a finance ministers' forum to provide a hastily arranged venue for leaders to debate and address a still unfolding financial crisis emanating out of the US. During this crisis management phase, much of the corrective and economic stimulus activity was nation-state focused; it was bilateral and ad hoc. Broad-based international solutions were only partly formed or in the initial design stages. Participants at the summit realised the scope of the crisis they confronted, and there was 'a sense of collective denouement' (Mackintosh, 2012, 20, p. 3); this was, recalled another participant, 'a real meeting, and real changing of views' (Mackintosh, 2012, 24, p. 4).

Many of the officials present during this period used similar descriptions. They talked of recognising the chasm ahead, of having no alternative. Government leaders faced a real and present danger. It was at the summit, one participant recalled: 'palpably clear this was a global crisis' notwithstanding the American origins (Mackintosh, 2012, 12, p. 2). Another one principal recalled:

> We did not know what tomorrow would be made of. We were on the brink really of a big cliff. So clearly there was a necessity to act . . . all the leaders

> were conscious that in fact they were looked at by public opinion . . . there had been excesses in the financial industry and there was a clear need for more regulation.
>
> (Mackintosh, 2012, 17, p. 6)

This is the pressure of crises, the fellowship of the lifeboat. Leaders knew they had to be seen to act and to deliver a modicum of calm, to begin to take charge as the 'board of directors' of the global economy in Washington, and they arguably succeeded in doing so. Importantly this crisis management reaction was coupled to an immediate recognition that the response should be a process – i.e. the start of reform, not a single event. As a result this first G20 leaders' summit would have objectives and deliverables of a breadth and complexity not seen in previous summit-based crisis management by weaker forums, such as the G7.

A reluctant host

The American called to act at the first G20 'firefighting summit' (Mackintosh, 2012, 24, p. 3) was an unlikely reluctant facilitator for what would prove to be the beginning of a paradigm shift. President George W. Bush was a lame-duck Republican, a neoliberal with an antiregulatory stance, confronted by stark economic reality. His Treasury secretary, Hank Paulson, a former chairman and CEO of the Goldman Sachs investment bank, also understood what was at stake in 2008; Paulson had been physically sick when the US Congress voted down the first Troubled Asset Relief Program (TARP) bailout on 27 September 27 2008. So when Bush and Paulson received increasingly strident calls to take collective international action from French President Nicolas Sarkozy, German Chancellor Angela Merkel, UK Prime Minister Gordon Brown, and others, they were receptive, although modest in their aims. As one adviser stressed, the president understood the need for 'comprehensive action to stabilize' the financial system, a view that was widely shared by those present (Mackintosh, 2012, 24, p. 3). It is unlikely that Bush anticipated the creation of the G20 could be 'the most lasting institutional consequence of the global financial meltdown of 2008' (*The Economist*, 2009). In fact the summit went further than simple stabilisation and began a reassertion of state power and authority over financial markets and major firms the world over, signalling a re-regulatory shift the likes of which had not been seen for decades.

The move to address the crisis through an emergency summit in 2008 was not carefully thought out. In a crisis decisions need to be made quickly. Many leaders urged action, proposing different configurations. President Sarkozy, Chancellor Merkel, and Prime Minister Brown all called for some type of emergency summit (Rieffel, 2008). Sarkozy floated the idea of an emergency summit of heads of state using a 'G8 plus five' structure, and Merkel leaned towards the old G7–G8 format.

President Bush and Paulson worried that a summit meeting could degenerate into a platform for grandstanding. Bush suspected that the participants would attack the existing global economic and financial system, which he did not see as broken. And he and Paulson struggled over the issue of who would attend and what the goals would be. They decided to avoid that problem by elevating the G20 finance ministers' forum into a leaders' summit, because they knew the grouping and believed a conversion was the simplest route. This was a pragmatic solution. Finance ministry officials in the forum could rapidly act as 'sherpas' for the new G20, smoothing planning and coordination. In addition there would be fewer complaints from emerging countries that their inclusion was an afterthought, as might happen with the Sarkozy proposal. Bush was joined by Brown, who agreed that using the G20 format involved the least complexity and avoided the need to create an entirely new body and the diplomatic difficulties that would ensue. In the end Merkel also came on board and backed the Brown-Bush jump to the G20. The hastily convened summit brought round the table almost all the major global economic powers including the leadership of key emerging economies (CSIS, 2009, p. 21). The G20's creation sent the message that the prior institutionalised format (G7 or G8, in particular) was inadequate to the task (Cooper, 2010). It was a recognition that the US as a weakened hegemonic power and its allies could no longer drive the process alone or just with its allies (Beeson and Bell, 2009).

Emerging-country leaders supported calling a G20 leaders' summit. They were eager to become full members of a new forum, rather than ad hoc additions to an existing smaller grouping. The rhetoric was sweeping. Brazilian Finance Minister Guido Mantega stated that they were 'creating a new international economic order . . . a new international economic architecture that has the G20 at the top of the pyramid, providing guidance and support to international financial institutions' (IMF, 2009, p. 2). With hindsight Minister Mantega would be proved largely correct.

The G20 proposal to include emerging-economy leaders from Brazil, China, India and Russia, as well as other influential players such as Saudi Arabia, South Africa and Turkey, was a reflection of the severity and global nature of the crisis, and of the need to bring the leaders of both creditor and surplus states to the table as equals. This time, the creditors were emerging-economy players and the debtors were in the G7, a role reversal from prior financial and banking crises that historically erupted more frequently in emerging economies (Rogoff and Reinhart, 2009, p. 160). Expressed most simply it signalled that 'we ought to have new institutions that reflect the world we live in' (Traub, 2009, p. 1). It was a rebalancing to reflect new geopolitical and global macroeconomic realities.

Boosting the role of key emerging economies had been a long-standing US Treasury goal, and the crisis afforded an opportunity to hasten that change. To the watching world of nervous voters and panicking investors a summit of the G20 would also show it was 'no longer business as usual' (*Financial Times*, 2008) and could help rebuild economic, market and investor confidence. But the change would still leave the core members calling the policy shots. In the heat of the crisis this did not matter, for all were confronted with the same reality and this pushed leaders together, focused minds, removed extraneous issues and pernicious influences and forced participants towards action. Only later did legitimacy concerns arise.

This enlarged group of leaders around the table knew they had delivered a modicum of calm to begin to take charge of the global economy. In Washington they began a process that succeeded in doing so.

Summitry as a process

The 'Summit on Financial Markets and the World Economy' took place in Washington, DC, on 14–15 November 2008 (G20, 2008a). President Bush had relatively limited goals for the meeting. He saw it, as did his Canadian counterpart, Prime Minister Stephen Harper, as the start of a process (Kirton and Guebert, 2009, p. 7). It was to be the start of reform, not the end. Nonetheless the first summit, convened under duress by a reluctant lame-duck US president, resulted in objectives and deliverables of a breadth and complexity not seen in previous summit-based crisis management by weaker forums. There was a focus on emergency global and national actions. In architectural terms the design outline was to be sketched out; the more detailed floor plans and elevations for the new re-regulatory constructions were incomplete, but the elements of a new paradigm could begin to be discerned. Leaders, galvanised, seized upon an elevated G20 forum to be the coordinator and decision-making centre for international economic diplomacy and their crisis response. Through it, they would begin to fashion the new policy paradigm, alter the regulatory architecture and reassert national state power over, and supervision and regulation of, financial markets and firms. From Washington onwards leaders moved to a partial rejection of the prevailing laissez-faire neoliberal or market fundamentalist (Stiglitz, 2008) worldview, which championed unrestrained and unregulated financial markets operating with as few barriers as possible. They began to lean away from the Anglo-American or 'Anglosphere' ideological stance (Gamble, 2009). In its place there was an embrace of the re-regulation of global financial markets, firms and instruments, with key input from the Western central banking community (see Chapters 5 and 6). The governments acting through the G20 from Washington and in subsequent summits began the start of a paradigm shift (Kuhn, 1962) in the approach of the leaders, and especially of the technocratic central banking community, towards regulation and oversight of global financial markets and firms. This paradigm shift in the policy consensus was not instantaneous. It did not have an equal effect across all points in time and all policy areas. It was 'lumpy, jerky, and uneven in important respects' (Biesterker, in Payne, 2005, p. 75). As with other paradigm shifts – scientific (Kuhn, 1962), atmospheric (Haas, 1992a), nuclear (Mitchell *et al.*, 2007), economic (Hall, 1993; Blyth, 2002), economic development (Gore, 2000) or agricultural (Skogstad, 2008) – the shift occurred over a longer period of time and would be spasmodic and fluctuating in different policy areas.

Such shifts have various elements. Anomalies build up and can be institutionalised until challenged by crises (Weir and Skocpol, 1983; Wilson, 2000). The current worldview cannot explain the failures and loses utility. A new worldview and policy consensus take shape and begin to be championed by more actors. A tipping point occurs – for the purposes of this research, the peak of the economic crises occurs in September 2008 – and over a period of time, months and years, the new worldview is clarified, solidified and made real on the ground, step by step.

Washington was the beginning of a fundamental shift, and the creation of the G20 and the structural redesign and policy actions the leaders agreed from 2008 suggest that: 'The G20 has led to a new paradigm in multilateral cooperation' (G20, 2012). The fraught and fluid environment allowed the rejection of previous regulatory truths. A new consensus (political and technical) took shape within which the G20 acted, summits took place, and policy goals were formulated. The scope and breadth of reforms that commenced in 2008 support the view that a shift began, and over time it amounted to a third-order change in the international regulatory architecture (Hall, 1993), even as some individual policy changes viewed in isolation from one another might be first or second order in nature.

The creation of the G20 leaders' forum and the developing policy consensus and regulatory agenda that the meetings produced, from Washington onwards, were evidence of a reassertion of collective state authority over markets and suggest that the retreat of the state (Strange, 1986, 1996), so long underway, had stopped and reversed direction. States, acting together, buttressed the world's economy and global financial markets with public funds, providing bailouts and guarantees that amounted to 27 per cent of the developed world's gross domestic product (GDP)(Trichet, 2010). G20 leaders, in return for the public's largesse, began to take back control over markets and institute much more aggressive coordinated supervision and re-regulation as the quid pro quo. This dramatic reassertion of state authority over global financial markets was, and in 2015 still is, led by the leaders of the established powers, principally from Europe and North America, aided by emerging powers in the forum.

All understood the depth of the economic chasm before them in September 2008. Using Putnam's two-level game (1988) applied to the financial crisis (see Figure 1.1) events in 2008 forced level-one negotiators together. There was an increase in the degree of level-one policy agreement and overlap amongst state actors. Normal level-two processes that act against accord, i.e. divergent national interests, were temporarily overridden by the severity of the events and by the pressure for action based on the common leader-backed and technocrat-driven policy viewpoint. G20 summitry results strengthened the position of the US, which was then and today still is operating as the gradually declining hegemonic power (Layne, 1993, 2006). By taking the initiative to set up the new structure and rules America shored up its position and those of its key allies and drew the emerging powers further into the new architecture and into the reformed forums and institutions, which were designed largely by technocrats from Europe and North America based on their norms and, albeit altered, rules. In this manner, from Washington onwards, the G20 summit process enveloped the rising powers within the reformed architecture. The summits helped postpone, or alternatively institutionalised, an otherwise more potentially disruptive direct clash between the declining power – the US – and the central rising power – China – as well as others – such as Brazil and India (Jacques, 2009; Rhoter, 2010; Subramanian,

2011). Having emerging-country leaderships reinvested in the altered structure's success, politically and financially, may have the effect of extending rather than diluting US influence as the declining power.

Crisis management – the G20 emerges

In meeting together in haste as a crisis management exercise to tackle the global financial and economic crisis, leaders and states began to make the paradigm shift. The first G20 summit marked the return of the state or the swinging of the pendulum (Gills, 2008) away from laissez-faire neoliberalism. Leaders signalled the start of an evolution of their policy worldview on the desirability of comprehensive global and national supervision and regulation of financial markets and major financial firms. Individual national governments, unable to deliver a return to economic stability alone, decided to act collectively and globally in order to regain control and restore a degree of market confidence and economic stability. Leaders sketched the outline of a new approach towards application of state power to regulate markets and firms more comprehensively and in a much more coordinated fashion than previously witnessed. Leaders representing 85 per cent of global GDP, from developed and emerging economies, worked to identify a way out of the crisis.

At the Washington G20 summit governments began to reassert a significant degree of state power and authority over financial markets. They signalled the intention to commence a redesign of the global regulatory architecture. States, in moving to re-regulate finance with the backing of the G20, demonstrated that the erosion of state power, informal and formal, had been overstated. The crisis and the G20 response to it in November 2008 underscore that 'the state is irreplaceable as a risk manager of last resort and as a regulator of irretrievable imperfect markets' (Constancio, 2010, p. 3).

A new paradigm and policy consensus began to take shape. G20 governments moved to regain control over underregulated and deregulated financial markets. A rebalancing of formal hard state power exercised individually and collectively over financial markets and firms commenced. But the severity of the crisis in phase one meant that much of the focus had to be on a series of immediate steps to be taken to stimulate the economy, essentially neo-Keynesian policy actions, in a drive to halt the slide and rebuild confidence. More detailed reform plans would follow later.

The Washington summit's results

US policy makers were correct in suspecting the summit would be used to mount an assault on free market orthodoxies. Brown and Sarkozy took direct aim and began sketching their own outlines of the future. Brown styled the meeting a 'Bretton Woods II' conference, an opportunity to reform global financial institutions (Kirkup and Waterfield, 2008; Parker, Barber, and Dombey, 2008). Sarkozy, joined by Merkel, called for a 'new constitution' for world financial markets and for the construction of a new regulatory architecture (Kennedy and McKee, 2008), and wanted financial regulation to be centre stage (Benoit, 2008). Europe's leadership hoped for a major breakthrough at the summit, while the White House was less ambitious, with Bush operating as a reluctant chair, albeit one who was willing to act.

There had been concern the Washington summit could result in broad policy statements and calls for reform but no action; simply a G20 version of a G7 post-summit communiqué; nice language but no real action. But the crisis pushed the G20 leaders and their technocrats together and forward into a multiyear refashioning of the structure of financial regulation, one that would extend the power of the state, expressed collectively via the G20, and recast the structure of new and existing forums, institutions and regulatory bodies in a significant and long-lasting manner.

The arguments before the first summit illuminated the tension between those (predominantly Europeans) whose narrative understanding of the crisis recognised a series of major market failures. They demanded a strong reassertion of state power, commitments to stimulus, a shift towards a re-regulation of markets and an abandonment of laissez-faire, neoliberal self-regulatory tropes. The host president was reluctant to agree. Ultimately the pressure forced the two groups together; on balance, the re-regulators won and the redesign began.

The crisis forced Putnam's level-one negotiators (the leaders and their sherpas) together, and in doing so created win sets more favourable to those calling for state supervisory and regulatory action. During this crisis management stage there was no real evidence of level-two impacts on the hasty deliberations. Banking lobbies and external interest groups were not part of the process. Market events were moving too quickly. It was left to the leaders and officials to fashion an agreement. This would prove to be largely the case in the reform phase in 2009, as well.

Broad political direction now, detailed plans later

The first G20 leaders' summit and the crisis management phase saw the securing of a series of commitments that were preparatory in nature, but nonetheless more concrete than expected. According to one participant leaders and their sherpas were galvanised by a 'sense of crisis and responsibility' (Mackintosh, 2011, 5, p. 8). Another former official characterised it as a 'fire-fighting summit' (Mackintosh, 2012, 24, p. 3). All leaders understood they could not return home to an unfolding economic crisis with nothing to show for it. To have done so would have risked worsening market panic and accelerating the collapse of investor confidence (Kirton and Guebert, 2009, p. 15).

During the negotiations sherpas rejected a last-minute effort by the French to substitute their own five-point text and held onto the more detailed, more specific, less incendiary US language. The US sought to blunt criticism of the market economy model, and this was backed by an Indian intervention in favour of more balanced language. Overall US negotiators were successful in retaining control of the drafting process, and they perceived the outcome as 'far more measured than the rhetorical build-up' (Mackintosh, 2011, 5, p. 10).

The declaration was nonetheless a relatively robust reassertion of state prerogatives and of the essential nature of nation-state fiscal and regulatory intervention in times of economic crisis. It appeared to be an assertion of an emerging new re-regulatory paradigm, a common narrative, which was at odds with market fundamentalism, the old norms of self-regulation and deregulation. The Washington summit started a paradigm shift and a financial reform and architectural redesign process that still shapes global markets five years later. There is little doubt the leaders understood the broad parameters of what needed to be done in Washington: first, send a message that world governments were acting together via a collective and bilateral stimulus to halt the slide into another great recession (Stevens, 2008); and second, signal that an era of re-regulation would begin via a series of specific actions and reforms.

By focusing on specific goals this first G20 summit avoided the pitfalls of past summits, which descended into acrimonious ideological disputes (Reynolds, 2009) or meaningless platitudes. Specifying timelines and tasking other institutions with deliverables was also a key development. Deadlines concentrate minds and provide impetus for process-based progress towards known goals.

In the communiqué leaders stressed the goal of restoring economic stability via joint and several stimulus actions, and of planning for post-crisis reforms, the details of which would be determined later. They underscored their belief in 'market principles, open trade and investment regimes' (G20, 2008a, p. 1), a fillip to the US, and then turned to the need for economic stimulus and a re-regulation of markets. Addressing the macroeconomy summit leaders agreed to 'take whatever further actions are necessary' to stabilise the financial system, supporting that recovery with monetary and fiscal measures to provide markets with liquidity (G20, 2008a, p. 2). More economic stimulus, tax and interest rate cuts (Elliot, 2008), together with central bank liquidity, would be provided by each country where needed. The leaders of Britain and Canada moved to increase the existing stimulus, for instance, as did others, following on from passage of the US$700 billion US TARP a few weeks earlier (Federal Reserve Bank of St. Louis, 2008), and China's announcement of a US$586 billion stimulus package just before the summit (Lander, 2008). President-elect Barack Obama, once in office, initiated a further stimulus of US$887 billion in February 2009 (ARRA, 2009).

As part of the move to boost economic stability and stimulus leaders committed to provide more resources to the IMF, after strong pressure from then-IMF Managing Director Dominique Strauss-Kahn. The World Bank and other multilateral development banks (MDBs) would also see a resource boost.

Turning to financial reform and regulation the leaders agreed on five broad parameters and 47 specific steps, which current and former central banking sources present during the debate and drafting say drew upon earlier analyses by the Financial Stability Forum (FSF) (FSF, 2008). But the declaration was tougher, the language stronger, and it specified goals and deadlines that were absent from the earlier, weaker, FSF discussion paper. The crisis acted as a galvanising external force, and the G20 reacted by empowering the technical and central banking community, which seized the initiative and enhanced their own position, and they set the policy agenda.

The outlines of the reforms (and the new narrative they represented) agreed to in Washington and championed by the US and its European allies were a significant innovation but were also a fundamentally Western project. As one participant observed, 'what you got was you got all the emerging markets to sign up to our whole financial regulatory agenda. Pretty damn good deal' (Mackintosh, 2012, 12, p. 11). In Washington the leaders agreed to measures designed to strengthen transparency and accountability, enhance sound regulation, promote integrity in financial markets, reinforce international cooperation and reform international financial institutions (G20, 2008a, p. 5).

Leaders allowed their technocratic epistemic central banking community, which had crafted large parts of the declaration itself, to take over much of the formulation of the detailed work streams to be considered by the political leaders at the next summit. Just as Peter Haas describes, we saw a deferral to the expert epistemic communities (Haas, 1992a). By passing key preparatory work down to national technical agencies and bodies the leaders increased the likelihood of progress. Leaders recognised they could not make these detailed judgements; instead, experts would do so with their strong backing.

Two decisions embedded within the Washington Declaration under the rubric of 'reforming the international financial institutions' were significant for the future shape of the global architecture: 1 the decision to enlarge the FSF to include emerging countries; and 2 the commitment to reform the IMF, to boost emerging market representation and IMF resources.

Both these reforms underscored that the old system run only by the few to the exclusion of the many was at an end and that, henceforth, the process of international financial regulatory redesign would involve input from more states and governments. Emerging-economy leaders would now sit around the table. Their representation and voice in the FSF and IMF would be enhanced, gradually rebalancing power in the IMF.

Behind the proposed enlargement the state actors pivotal to reform were US and European leaders, essentially the old core players acting within the G20, who sought to ensure that regulatory reform and oversight would be outside the control of the IMF. The IMF had urged the G20 to entrust it with regulatory remit and early warning, as well as with its usual balance-of-payment responsibilities, but this was rejected at the outset. Instead the G20 decided the leadership of the reform process would be led by the G20 and overseen by an enlarged FSF. Both bodies were (and even now in 2015 still are) dominated by European and North American voices. The end result refashioned and reinforced the Western powers' influence within the new architecture which they themselves were largely responsible for building. In this manner the universal, treaty-based IMF was strengthened monetarily and in its governance, but it was simultaneously downgraded structurally within the new architecture with the agreement of the leading and emerging powers, suggesting that the renewed legitimacy of a reformed IMF only goes so far.

As the G20 process developed from November 2008 onwards an enlarged FSF (refashioned as the bigger, stronger institutionally more credible FSB) would coordinate, manage and play the central role in the regulatory reform process. This process included but was not controlled by the IMF. Mario Draghi, then-chairman of the FSF, seized the initiative to the benefit of core states and their central banking and supervisory community, in particular. The central bankers understood, one principal recalls, that 'you couldn't institutionalise the FSF without broadening its membership to parallel the G20 membership' (Mackintosh, 2012, 24, p. 5). In fact a relatively small number of national regulators, a central banking 'SWAT team', retained great influence within the enlarged FSF-led process of financial reform during its first years of work from 2009 to 2012, reflective of their countries' and markets' importance and power (Mackintosh, 2012, 24, p. 9).

The Washington declaration, by its broad nature and considerable detailed specificity – 47 deliverables and timelines – and by its delegation of authority and tasks, eclipsed G7 documents of the past. It is striking because of its depth of content. By international standards the G20 had started off with a hyperactive plan for supervisory and regulatory action that would be detailed and enumerated still further in subsequent summits (Cooper, 2010, p. 745).

The crisis-fighting exercise in 2008 worked if measured by polls, market and leadership reactions. National leaders benefited domestically from their time on the world stage. Externally the summit played well. President Bush got a modest uptick of 2 per cent in his approval rating (Rasmussen, 2008). Prime Minister Brown saw his approval rating jump 11 percentage points after the summit, from 31 to 42 per cent (UKPollingReport, 2008), but the boost was fleeting. Each leader stressed slightly different versions of what was achieved. Bush administration officials underscored the pro-stimulus and pro-growth message and saw in it an 'affirmation of free market principles' (G20, 2008b) and a defence of the status quo. Prime Minister Brown lauded the 'route map to the global economic recovery and the stimulus' (Elliot, 2008), also choosing to stress stimulus rather than regulation as the main takeaway. In contrast German and French leaders underscored the perceived victory against markets and the commitments to ensure that 'all markets, products and participants are regulated or subject to oversight' (G20, 2008b).

The Sarkozy and Merkel position mirrors most closely the tone before, and the detailed content of, the declaration and the regulatory reform agenda actually agreed (Benoit, 2008; Kennedy and McKee, 2008). Whole sectors of global financial markets hitherto unregulated faced regulation or oversight. 'Self-regulation' was criticised, and closer supervision of financial markets and actors would begin. But the narrative shift was still limited. It did not encompass a rejection of neoliberal economics, only of laissez-faire neoliberal approaches to markets and regulation.

Overall the summit's conclusions and the breadth of the regulatory reform project made clear that the G20 leadership believed the process was not a cosmetic exercise or simply first-order changes. Indeed the process London started began a substantial re-regulation of key global financial markets and firms, backed by political capital pooled by the G20. The summit results were a concrete manifestation of the beginning of a reassertion of collective state authority, which was indicative of the changing policy consensus and paradigm regarding the desirability of internationally coordinated re-regulation of financial actors and markets. The reforms were directed by the central banking community, and the extent to which they controlled the process affected the 'strictness' and level of policy convergence and harmonisation (Holzinger and Knill, 2005, p. 777).

The Washington G20 Summit achieved more than many expected. *The Economist* opined that the summit had 'permanently changed the machinery of international economic cooperation', adding 'rich countries will no longer set the agenda on their own' (*The Economist*, 2008). Some, such as former IMF Chief Economist Simon Johnson, disagreed, saying this was 'plain vanilla stuff they could have agreed upon without holding a meeting,' i.e. it was objectively unnecessary and national in substance – but not actually very radical (Lander, 2008). Viewed with hindsight the critics were unduly pessimistic.

Why Washington mattered

During 2008 and the crisis management phase and the birth of the G20 as a leaders' forum the firefighting and decisions taken in Washington were crucial in a number of concrete respects and they signaled a 'convergence of political, national priorities, followed by collective action' (Mackintosh, 2012, 21, p. 8). The G20 became almost overnight 'the premier forum for global economic governance' (Cooper, 2010, p. 741). Washington started the process of arresting the crisis and helped restore a degree of calm. Through the G20 summitry begun in Washington 'collective leadership and institutions emerged in unforeseen ways as governments intervened in a myriad of rescue efforts' (Subacchi and Cooper, 2010, p. 607). Leaders also debated the policy narrative through which to view the failures and solutions to the crisis.

In Washington leaders began the paradigm shift in approach to the re-regulation of global financial markets, firms and instruments. Leaders from France, Germany, China and even Britain had demanded and got a reappraisal of laissez-faire neoliberal norms and approaches to financial market regulation (Lander, 2008; MacGregor, 2010). Europeans and others who sought a reapplication of the power of the state in large part won the argument, despite protestations from the US, and they began fashioning elements of a new policy paradigm. The G20 defended globalisation in general terms and sought to restore calm, led by leaders from the old core while including emerging-country leaders. But the G20 leaders did much more than this – they began an ideological shift from which followed a series of major reforms over the following months and years.

After this qualified victory in Washington in 2008 for the re-regulatory forces and their evolving new policy consensus the debate and the G20 financial reform agenda would focus on the extent, speed and depth of global re-regulation and financial markets reform, not whether such action should be taken at all.

This policy consensus, this commitment to re-regulation, was signposted in the plan presented in Washington, where the heat of the crisis helped create win space for a new consensus. National leaders and their technocrats were literally living through the nightmare of 2008 together. As a result the need for lasting regulatory reforms, the solidifying concrete basis for a new policy paradigm, based around agreement on less leverage, more capital, more oversight of markets and firms, and vigilance on systemic risks appeared clear to almost all the key leaders and their trusted technocrats.

G20 leaders understood that their countries faced terrible, interlinked crises, and the solutions they reached went beyond the expected and further than in previous, lesser, financial crisis response episodes from the 1990s. This time they formulated plans for a more ambitious reform of the global financial architecture. The severity of the crisis was a crucible for action. It forced clarity upon leaders and removed extraneous influences. In Putnam's terms the crisis created level-one win sets while level-two concerns were muted (Putnam, 1988). When everyone is in danger voices of narrow-minded national self-interest carry less weight or converge and overlap. Phase one of the evolution of the G20 and the reform process it started would ultimately result in meaningful substantive changes in financial markets and the supervision of those markets. As John Kirton and Jenilee Guebert observed the leaders fashioned 'an ongoing summit-guided, multilevel process . . . promising to produce a permanent G20 summit institution at the centre of global financial economic governance' (2009, p. 4).

In addition the creation of the G20 signalled an explicit recognition by North American and European leaders that the number of seats around the table would increase permanently, with key emerging-country states becoming part of the process. America would lead, but henceforth she would need to bring many other states with her while engaging in summitry. As Bruce Jones observed, 'No longer the CEO of Free World Inc., the United States is now the largest minority shareholder in New World Order LLC' (Jones, 2011). Those states supported the new re-regulatory consensus and paradigm. In return for a seat at the table emerging countries committed their political and actual capital via bilateral stimulus and commitments to IMF reform and recapitalisation in Washington. In phase one, however, emerging countries would not lead the G20 crisis management response. The G20 was led by US and European actors who sketched out the outline of a stimulus and reform agenda. The agenda would be pursued by a strengthened FSF and a reinvigorated IMF, with the former going on to dominate the international coordination and implementation of post-crisis global financial reform and redesign.

The G20 in 2008 made what would prove to be a pivotal decision – they turned to their central banking and supervisory regulators, a group that constitutes a distinct expert epistemic community (see Chapters 5 and 6), to design the structural plans and the detailed reform agenda that would be built and that would constitute the new global financial architecture. The key recommendation in phase one was the enlargement of the FSF, which Mario Draghi, an Italian central banker, economist, and chair of the FSF, who went on to succeed Jean-Claude Trichet as president of the European Central Bank, championed and the G20 leaders then endorsed, according to those present. Much of the G20 summits' future detailed policy prescriptions and agenda would go on to be based on work done by the self-same Financial Stability Forum (soon to become the FSB), also chaired by Draghi.

Through this gambit a central banking community which was deeply culpable in the run-up to the crisis and in the mishandling of the global economy pre-crisis, succeeded in grasping the opportunity to determine the plan of the new regulatory shift and structure and presented it to the leaders. From that point onwards a small coterie of principally North American and European central bankers would go on to dominate the policy-making process to an extent that remains striking even today. So Washington mattered a great deal. Decisions taken then telegraphed how the reform process in later years would be led and would proceed.

G20 summitry in Washington was a considerable success and proved to be the foundation upon which subsequent summits in the second concrete reform phase would build. Remarkably George W. Bush was, in hindsight, the creator of a forum and a process that would go on to dominate global economic and financial diplomacy in the years after 2008. As *The Economist* opined at the time, 'The formation of the G20 group of world leaders is likely to be the most lasting institutional consequence of the global financial meltdown of 2008' (*The Economist*, 2009). Few would argue with that assessment. As we will see, in the years since its creation, 'The G20 has evolved into the closest thing to a board of directors for the world economy' (Davis and Poletta, 2010). Its progeny, the Financial Stability Board, and its other reform measures, from adoption of a raft of macroprudential controls over bank activities to the re-energising of the International Monetary Fund, would all form part of the new, reformed, global financial architecture that would be the mechanism through which state power and authority would once again be asserted over financial markets and firms.

Box 2.1 The structure and membership of the G20

Membership: Membership of the G20 is composed of the following countries: Argentina, Australia, Brazil, Canada, China, France, Germany, India, Indonesia, Italy, Japan, Mexico, Russia, Saudi Arabia, South Africa, Korea, Turkey, the United Kingdom, and the United States. The European Union (EU) is represented by the rotating European Council presidency, and the president of the European Commission. Other institutional participants are the managing director of the IMF, the president of the World Bank, and the chair of the International Monetary and Financial Committee and Development Assistance Committees.

A small number of other countries' leaders have a seat at the table each year, either because of their institutional position or simply because of the influence of the individuals and governments in question. Invited guests change slightly each year. In 2020 under the Saudi Arabia G20 presidency these guests will include Egypt, Jordan, Senegal, Singapore, Spain (a permanent guest), Switzerland, United Arab Emirates and Vietnam.

G20 membership is not set in stone; its make-up fluctuates at the margins.

The summit presidency: The country that chairs a summit acts as president of the G20. It sets the agenda and writes the draft declaration, action plans and communiqués. The country in the chair has significant influence on the outcome because, according to participants, other members tend, within limits, to defer to the chairing state's leadership. After the first summit the declaration agreed at each summit contains consistent themes, i.e. follow-on work from previously agreed policy actions, some omissions and additions made by each chairing country as that leader and his or her ministers strive to create a successful summit that addresses matters of particular concern to the chair, both domestic and international.

Decision making: At a summit and at the ministerial pre-meetings during the year all decisions are taken based on consensus. This is a strength and a weakness. In times of crisis events push level-one negotiators together and decisions are brisk, win spaces open up amongst the leadership and the creation of a policy consensus is easier. This occurred in 2008 and 2009. Once a crisis passes a consensus is harder to secure. The quality of the declaratory and decision-making output of the G20 can also decline in non-crisis periods, because the compromises required to switch the last 'no' to a grudging 'yes' dilute the results.

The European voice: European leaders retain a loud voice in the G20. Eight of the 26 principals around the table are European leaders. It would be an oversimplification to suggest that this means, in a consensus-based forum, that Europeans dominate. But the evidence suggests that the Europeans, especially when in accord with the US and Canada, do largely determine the content of declarations. In total as many as 27 nations with a direct or indirect presence are included as a result of EU representation (Payne, 2010).

Therefore there remains a North America-EU de facto co-dominance within the G20. European leaders have leverage over and above their numerical advantage because of their economic and financial importance. Moreover EU leaders can and do pursue their individual pre-summit goals bilaterally, and they also adopt joint EU positions prior to summits, increasing their collective impact in this manner, as well. In general European leaders are very well versed in international interstate diplomacy – they practise it constantly in the EU – and this may give them an advantage in the G20 forum.

The emerging-country voice: Key emerging countries – Brazil, China, India, Mexico and Russia – are included in the G20. Others were included for geopolitical and economic reasons, such as Indonesia (the world's largest Muslim nation), Saudi Arabia (for oil revenues and sovereign wealth fund cash) and South Africa (as the dominant sub-Saharan economy). The Republic of Korea and Turkey are also included. The G20 inclusion of major emerging powers of global and regional significance is a lasting innovation and one which cannot be reversed; once a state is admitted within the core 20, they cannot easily be ejected.

Anomalies arise and the regional balance fluctuates. Saudi Arabia has in 2020 added more North African and Persian Gulf leaders to the grouping, for instance. Africa remains underrepresented. Yet Singapore, a country of only six million inhabitants has almost permanent participation.

Other participants: G20 leaders' meetings include finance ministers, deputy finance ministers, central bank governors and 'sherpas', who act as the drafters, coordinators and protectors of each country's respective positions.

Legal personality, resources and frequency of summits: The G20 was conceived as an informal grouping, not an institution. It has no legal personality, resources or institutional solidity besides that conferred on it by the seriousness with which the leaders treat its gatherings and policy outcomes. It is not a treaty-based organisation. The G20 has no founding document, there are no specified government signatories, it has no formal power, it creates no obligations and it has no resources of its own. It is simply a forum for periodic meetings staffed by national officials of the country chairing the next summit, assisted by the IMF and World Bank. The 2011 Cannes summit affirmed this approach; during this summit, leaders rejected calls to create a separate secretariat distinct from the national leadership of the summits. This lack of legal personality, resources and solidity should not be construed as meaning the forum lacks authority, when and if it acts, or directs other technocrats to act on the forum's behalf. To the contrary especially in the crisis management and the subsequent reform phases, the G20 was dominant. And, even as states began to argue, and diverged as the crisis eased, the G20 still remained the key venue and process through which leaders chose to act, in a directive manner, on their agreed financial reform agenda.

The G20's effectiveness year-to-year rests in part on the power of the presidency and the chairing country and its leadership. The more powerful (i.e. politically and economically dominant) countries can achieve more than the smaller, less influential countries (such as Canada or even Korea). The G20's effectiveness also depends on the ability of the host country leadership to harness the collective will of the leaders present and to foster a policy consensus regarding the particular issues the G20 seeks to address at any one point in time. This, in turn, is affected by what phase the G20 is in at the time. Consensus is always easier to create during a crisis; it is difficult to create and sustain when the crisis abates. As a result dissension amongst participants can be seen.

G20 summitry is controlled by the national actors themselves (in reality, certain powerful governments), and they therefore maintain the buy-in of leading states. This structure also results in the effectiveness of summits varying somewhat due to a country's ability to staff the summit process, the political weight of the country in question, and the urgency of the global economic matters set before the leaders. For some states, such as Mexico and Korea, hosting is a large task – one that, according to finance ministry and central bank officials, stretches institutional capacity and resources.

G20 leaders at Cannes in December 2011 cemented the summit process into a troika of leadership to include the immediate past country chair, the current country chair, and the next summit chairman, similar to the long-standing EU Council process prior to the appointment of a permanent council president. In doing so leaders aim to improve continuity and allow smooth institutional handovers from one summit to the next. This approach shows the continued European influence in the G20 form and construction.

Preparatory meetings: The first G20 summit and subsequent ones are buttressed by ongoing multilateral and bilateral exchanges and multilevel ministerial discussions that assist in preparing the agenda, declarations and action plans. To help prepare these summits and press the agenda forward G20 finance ministers, G20 sherpas, and central bank governors continue to meet several times a year, including on the fringes of the spring and annual meetings of the World Bank and the IMF. Progress on declaration drafting is monitored by the finance ministries, and the work feeds into the leadership summits. Working groups are established to formalise this process and monitor deliverables. By the time of a leaders' summit, according to a US G20 sherpa, the content of the declaration or communiqué should be 'pretty much pre-cooked' (O'Toole, 2009), with most policy differences ideally greatly minimised.

References

ARRA (American Recovery and Reinvestment Act). (2009) Available at: www.recovery.gov/Pages/default.aspx (accessed: 29 February 2012).

Beeson, M. and Bell, S. (2009) 'The G20 and international economic governance: Hegemony, collectivism, or both?', *Global Governance*, 15, pp. 67–87.

Benoit, B. (2008) 'Merkel seeks to keep regulation centre stage', *Financial Times*, 24 September [Online]. Available at: www.ft.com/cms/s/0/260529cc-a0cc-11dd-b0bd-00144feabdc0.html#axzz1DsCvzP16 (accessed: 13 February 2011).

Blyth, M. (2002) *Great transformations: Economic ideas and institutional change in the twentieth century*. Cambridge: Cambridge University Press.

Constancio, V. (2010) 'The future of economic governance in Europe in a global perspective', *Speech delivered at the Centre Culturel Calouste Gulbenkian*, Paris, 7 December.

Cooper, A.F. (2010) 'The G20 as an improvised crisis committee and or a contested "steering committee"', *International Affairs*, 86(3), pp. 741–757.

CSIS (Center for Strategic and International Studies). (2009) 'CSIS Sherpa Summit 2009: Pittsburgh and the future of the international leadership through the G-8/G-20/G-?', 17 September [Online]. Available at: http://csis.org/files/attachments/090917_scholl_sherpa.pdf (accessed: 2 March 2011).

Davis, B. and Poletta, D. (2010) 'U.S. gets rebuffed at divided summit', *Wall Street Journal*, 13 November [Online]. Available at: http://online.wsj.com/article/SB10001424052748704865704575610761647291510.html (accessed: 25 November 2010).

The Economist. (2008) 'Not a bad weekend's work', 16 November [Online]. Available at: www.economist.com/node/12623258 (accessed: 21 August 2013).

———. (2009) 'A modern guide to G-ology', 13 November [Online]. Available at: www.economist.com/node/14742524 (accessed: 12 February 2015).

Elliot, G. (2008) 'Brown claims G20 success as world leaders agree tax and interest rate cuts', *Sunday Times*, 16 November [Online]. Available at: http://business.timesonline.co.uk/tol/business/economics/article5163072.ece (accessed: 13 February 2011).

Federal Reserve Bank of St. Louis (2008) 'The financial crisis a timeline of events and policy actions' [Online]. Available at: http://timeline.stlouisfed.org/index.cfm?p=timeline (accessed: 4 February 2011).

Financial Times. (2008) 'The G20 summit', November 14.

FSF (Financial Stability Forum). (2008) 'Report of the Financial Stability Forum on enhancing market and institutional resilience' [Online]. Available at: www.financialstabilityboard.org/publications/r_0804.pdf (accessed: 2 December 2011).

G20 (Group of Twenty). (2008a) 'Declaration: Summit on financial markets and the world economy', Washington, DC, 14 November.

———. (2008b) 'Washington action plan', 14 November [Online]. Available at: www.pittsburghsummit.gov/resources/125137.htm (accessed: 8 February 2011).

———. (2012) 'Los Cabos Declaration' [Online]. Available at: www.g20.utoronto.ca/summits/2012loscabos.html (accessed: 20 June 2012).

Gamble, A. (2009) *The spectre at the feast: Capitalist crisis and the politics of recession*. New York: Palgrave Macmillan.

Gills, B. (2008) 'The swinging of the pendulum: The global crisis and beyond', *Share the World's Resources*, 18 November [Online]. Available at: www.stwr.org/global-financial-crisis/the-swinging-of-the-pendulum-the-global-crisis-and-beyond.html (accessed: 10 June 2012).

Gore, C. (2000) 'The rise and fall of the Washington consensus as a paradigm for developing countries', *World Development*, 28(5), pp. 789–804.

Haas, P.M. (1992a) 'Introduction: Epistemic communities and international policy coordination', *International Organization*, 46(1), pp. 1–35.

Hall, P.A. (1993) 'Policy paradigms, social learning, and the state: The case of economic policymaking in Britain', *Comparative Politics*, 25(3), pp. 275–296.

Holzinger, K. and Knill, C. (2005) 'Causes and conditions of cross-national policy convergence', *Journal of European Public Policy*, 12(5), pp. 775–796.

IMF (International Monetary Fund). (2009) 'Statement by Guido Mantega, Minister of Finance, Brazil', 4 October [Online]. Available at: www.imf.org/External/AM/2009/imfc/statement/eng/bra.pdf (accessed: 14 March 2011).

Jacques, M. (2009) *When China rules the world*. New York: Penguin.

Jones, B. (2011) 'Largest minority shareholder on global order LLC: The changing balance of influence and U.S. strategy', *Brookings Institution, Policy Paper 25* [Online]. Available at: www.brookings.edu/~/media/research/files/papers/2011/3/global%20order%20jones/03_global_order_jones.pdf (accessed: 10 June 2012).

Kennedy, S. and McKee, M. (2008) 'G-20 pits Bush versus Sarkozy-Merkel regulation push', *Bloomberg* [Online]. Available at: www.bloomberg.com/apps/news?pid=newsarchive&sid=aCUyoDMpC36A (accessed: 3 November 2014).

Kirkup, J. and Waterfield, B. (2008) 'Gordon Brown's Bretton Woods summit call risks spat with Nicholas Sarkozy', *Daily Telegraph*, 15 October [Online]. Available at: www.telegraph.co.uk/news/worldnews/europe/france/3205033/Gordon-Browns-Bretton-Woods-summit-call-risks-spat-with-Nicholas-Sarkozy.html (accessed: 3 February 2011).

Kirton, J. and Guebert, J. (2009) 'A summit of substantial success: The performance of the G20 in Washington in 2008' [Online]. Available at: G20@utoronto.ca (accessed: 17 February 2011).

Kuhn, T. (1962) *The structure of scientific revolutions*. Chicago: University of Chicago Press.

Lander, M. (2008) 'World leaders vow joint push to aid economy', *New York Times*, 16 November, p. A1.

Layne, C. (1993) 'The unipolar illusion: Why new great powers will arise', *International Security*, 17(4), pp. 5–51.

———. (2006) 'The unipolar illusion revisited: The coming end of the United States' unipolar moment', *International Security*, 31(2), pp. 7–41.

MacGregor, R. (2010) *The secret world of China's communist rulers*. New York: Harper.

Mackintosh, S. (2011) Interview 5. Former G20 Sherpa, 7 November.

———. (2012) Interview 12. G20 Finance Ministry Official, 27 January.

———. (2012) Interview 17. G20 Presidential Advisor, 3 March.

———. (2012) Interview 20. National IMF Official, 13 March.

———. (2012) Interview 21. National IMF Official, 23 March.

———. (2012) Interview 24. G20 Central Bank Governor, 2 July.

Mitchell, N.J., Herron, K.G., Jenkins-Smith, H.C., and Whitten, G.D. (2007) 'Elite beliefs, epistemic communities and the Atlantic divide: Scientists' nuclear policy preferences in the United States and European Union', *Journal of Politics*, 37(4), pp. 753–764.

O'Toole, J. (2009) 'Sherpas blazing diplomatic trail to the city', *Pittsburgh Post-Gazzette*, 30 August [Online]. Available at: www.post-gazette.com/pg/09242/994269-482.stm (accessed: 2 March 2011).

Parker, G., Barber, T., and Dombey, D. (2008) 'Leaders back call for "Bretton Woods II" summit', *Financial Times* [Online]. Available at: www.ft.com/cms/s/0/539f1834-9b19-11dd-a653-000077b07658.html (accessed: 3 February 2011).

Payne, A. (2005) *The global politics of unequal development*. New York: Palgrave.

———. (2010) 'The perspective of the marginal majority of the world's states', *International Affairs*, 86(3), pp. 729–740.

Press Briefing by Senior Administration Officials on the Summit on Financial Markets and the World Economy. (2008) 'The White House. Transcript of the postsummit press briefing', 15 November.

Putnam, R. (1988) 'Diplomacy and domestic politics: The logic of two-level games', *International Organization*, 42(3), pp. 427–460.

Rasmussen Reports. (2008) 'President Bush approval ratings' [Online]. Available at: www.rasmussenreports.com/public_content/politics/political_updates/president_bush_job_approval (accessed: 11 March 2011).

Reynolds, D. (2009) 'Summitry and inter-cultural communication', *International Affairs*, 85(1), pp. 115–127.

Rhoter, L. (2010) *Brazil on the rise*. New York: Palgrave MacMillan.

Rieffel, L. (2008) 'The G-20 summit: What's it all about? Opinion editorial', *Brookings Institution* [Online]. Available at: www.brookings.edu/opinions/2008/1027_governance_rieffel.aspx (accessed: 4 February 2011).

Rogoff, K. and Reinhart, C. (2009) *This time is different: Eight centuries of financial folly*. Princeton: Princeton University Press.

Skogstad, G. (2008) *Internationalization and Canadian agriculture*. Toronto: University of Toronto Press.

Stevens, G. (2008) 'Interesting times', *Speech delivered at the Australian Business Economists Annual Dinner*, Sydney, December 9 [Online]. Available at: www.rba.gov.au/publications/bulletin/2008/dec/pdf/bu-1208-2.pdf (accessed: 15 July 2013).

Stiglitz, J. (2008) 'Market fundamentalism is dead', *FORA*, 20 October [Online]. Available at: www.youtube.com/watch?v=x_2-Tv2GPs0 (accessed: 6 August 2011).

Strange, S. (1986) *Casino capitalism*. Manchester: Manchester University Press.

———. (1996) *The retreat of the state: The diffusion of power in the world economy*. Cambridge: Cambridge University Press.

Subacchi, P. and Cooper, A.F. (2010) 'Global economic governance in transition', *International Affairs*, 86(3), pp. 607–741.

Subramanian, A. (2011) 'Eclipse: Living in the shadow of China's economic dominance', Peterson Institute for International Economics, Washington, DC.

Traub, J. (2009) 'Shaking up the boardroom at World Government Inc.', *New York Times*, 4 January, p. 4.

Trichet, J.C. (2010) Speech at the *World Policy Conference*, Marrakech, 16 October [Online]. Available at: www.ecb.int/press/key/date/2010/html/sp101016.en.html (accessed: 4 June 2012).

UKPollingReport. (2008) 'YouGov Poll', 14 November [Online]. Available at: http://ukpollingreport.co.uk/leaders/brown (accessed: 11 March 2011).

Weir, M. and Skocpol, T. (1983) 'State structures and social Keynesianism: Responses to the Great Depression in Sweden and the United States', *International Journal of Comparative Sociology*, 24.

Wilson, C.A. (2000) 'Policy regimes and policy change', *Journal of Public Policy*, 20(3), pp. 247–274.

3 The 2009 G20 summits

The apogee of reformist zeal

Introduction

The 2009 G20 summits occurred during the period of maximum G20-directed reformist zeal, underpinned by a clear policy consensus and policy narrative, and the political capital of the G20 leaders. The summits marked a reassertion of state power by the core and emerging-country G20 leaders over financial markets and firms. This phase in crisis response and reform unfolded during the leadership of the UK and the US in summits that occurred in London and Pittsburgh, Pennsylvania, in 2009. With the immediate financial crisis morphing into a real economic threat and with global economic output slumping a series of major stimulus moves were announced. States needed to seize the initiative from the panicking markets. As one participant recalled:

> We were striving after something called confidence. It is a terrible difficult thing. It's rather like an elephant. To describe the thing is difficult, but you know [it] when you see it.
>
> (Mackintosh, 2011, 8, pp. 8–9)

In this second phase of G20 activism and crisis response leaders and technocrats would try and restore confidence. Joint and several fiscal stimulus and financial rescue measures saw states working in tandem via the G20 forum at this juncture. Crucially this period also resulted in the identification and enumeration of many key institutional and regulatory reforms by the G20 leaders, prompted by the assertive central banking technocratic epistemic community, which would be central to the post-crisis financial architecture.

During this time the G20 began the architectural redesign and reform with vigour. Leaders agreed on, and direct international and national regulatory actors and agencies began to negotiate, the details of the financial reform agenda. The G20 was confirmed as leading the international economic policy-making process. The Financial Stability Board (FSB) was created. The reform, major recapitalisation, and a rebalancing of voice and voting power between the North and South and the East and West within the International Monetary Fund (IMF) was commenced.

The collective urgency for action was clear, and G20 leaders seized the regulatory reform initiative. It is widely recognised that this period of the G20's evolution constituted the apogee of the forum's effectiveness. Big solutions were needed. British Prime Minister Gordon Brown, US President Barack Obama and others, closely advised by key central banking and regulatory figures, set forth an ambitious agenda. During this phase a broad G20 policy consensus on action can be identified even as differences are seen (over stimulus and exit strategies, for instance). Overall the G20 in 2009 and in this reformist phase adopted a wide-ranging agenda and ambitious work programme goals. The narrative and its policy products resulted in state power beginning to be reasserted over markets across many policy areas.

Financial reforms and the redesign begin in earnest

In two G20 summits in 2009, during phase two of the evolution of the G20, the extreme severity of the immediate financial crisis morphed into a new economic challenge as the global economic outlook deteriorated and many industrialised economies entered severe recessions (IMF, 2009). What had been seen as a US subprime problem rapidly became everybody's economic problem. The G20 moved to commit to further major economic stimulus even as disagreements over the scope and form of stimulus began to emerge. At the same time the G20 actors turned their focus to the causes of the crisis and fleshed out ambitious institutional and financial reform proposals. The G20 action plans unveiled in this period built upon the broad parameters sketched out in Washington as actors began to lay the foundations for a new regulatory architecture.

In the spring of 2009 UK Prime Minister Brown was under great pressure: the future stability of the global economy and his own electoral and political future were on the line. Brown needed three things from the G20 in 2009. First, he needed a deal of such magnitude, in terms of monetary figures, that it would surprise the markets on the upside and slow or halt the downward economic spiral. Second, he needed to back up headline numbers with a sweeping agenda of financial and regulatory reform that would underscore there would be no going back to business as usual. Brown understood he needed to shift the narrative and policy consensus. And to get what he wanted, the prime minister locked G20 leaders in a room until the deal was done (Darling, 2011). Third, Brown needed the London summit to shore up his own domestic political position by demonstrating his global leadership role at a time of crisis.

During this second phase in the G20's rapid evolution reform and redesign were uppermost in policy makers' minds. The 2009 summits would be the apogee of reformist zeal amongst G20 leaders. In London Brown secured his first two objectives. His third, enhanced domestic political stature, would be fleeting and not enough to ensure victory at the 2010 UK general election.

The package deal agreed in London under Brown's direction was subsequently supported and strengthened by US President Obama at the Pittsburgh summit. The re-regulatory paradigm shift was beginning to be realised via scores of planned policy actions and reforms. State authority was back and deregulatory and self-regulatory approaches to financial markets were banished from the policy lexicon.

Much was achieved in phase two because, as with past national financial crises, the period immediately following a crisis permits a process of critical self-examination, a search for a narrative through which to understand the causes and lessons to be learnt, matched by a desire amongst the policy-making elite to repair identified gaps in the regulatory system and redesign the structures that they believe had failed.

Kuhn (1962) describes this process of paradigm shift. Existing truths fail to explain new or current phenomena properly or account for anomalies. Triggered by events and discoveries actors seek new narratives and different explanations and solutions to increasingly commonly recognised anomalies. Just such a process of critical self-reappraisal occurred and is reflected in official sector reports such as the *Turner Review* (Turner, 2009) and *Run on the Rock* (House of Commons, 2008) reports in the UK undertaken by key policy makers. It was also seen in various individual national reform financial proposals. Mervyn King, then-governor of the Bank of England and chairman of its Monetary Policy Committee, called for the consideration of 'utility banking' (King, 2010). Paul Volcker called for limits on banking practices and heavily influenced the Obama administration's response (G30, 2009), and in doing so changed the scope of banking activities in the US. Philipp Hildebrand, then-governor of the Swiss National Bank, increased the required capital of Swiss banks and reasserted the central bank's supervisory policy-making prerogative over massive firms that had threatened the Swiss economy (Hildebrand, 2010). Supervisors and central bankers went through a collective process of identifying failures and causes and prepared to seize back the levers of control from the market actors. Note that it is not the G20 political leaders themselves who engaged in this process of self-analysis, as much as the technical central banking community, who acted as their expert advisers. Leaders did not have time for deconstructing the various contributory elements of a multilevel crisis. What they sought was considered advice from trusted advisers. The central banking community provided that.

In 2009 there was critical space for self-examination and reform due to a temporary weakening of the normal influence of domestic lobbies, Putnam's potentially pernicious level-two interests and their power over the policy and governmental decision-making processes. Put simply as the economic crisis unfolded, many major global commercial banks were silent or temporary wards of the state (AIG, Citigroup, Lloyds and RBS, for instance). The widely felt effects of the crisis meant that domestic institutional and private sector opposition was quiescent, allowing governments, their central banking community leaders and regulators more room to manoeuvre and more policy options. The developing international policy consensus also helped supply the level-one win sets Putnam speaks of (Putnam, 1988). It is for this reason that President Obama's chief of staff observed that 'you never want a serious crisis go to waste' (Emanuel, 2008). What the Financial Stability Forum could not do pre-crisis the FSB could do post-crisis because of a new urgency and clarity of mission and purpose from the leadership of the G20 and the central banks. There was also a change in the power relationship between public versus private actors in favour of the state. And, during this pivotal early period of the G20 summitry, there was, as a principal noted, 'a real changing of views' (Mackintosh, 2012, 24, p. 4).

Clear deliverables in London: but first some big numbers

At the London summit in April 2009 Prime Minister Brown and the G20 leaders sought to restore a degree of calm and confidence to markets and to underscore their commitment to support growth and restore economic stability. To succeed in that goal big numbers were needed. Just how large was an area of some controversy prior to the meeting. The leaders also began the reform and redesign of the global architecture, building on the sketched outlines seen in Washington.

In the run-up to the meeting there was disagreement over what exactly constituted stimulus (Bradford, 2009). US, UK and Chinese ministers suggested only discretionary measures should count (tax cuts, investment and expenditure increases) (Darling, 2011, pp. 209–210). European officials disagreed and stressed automatic stabilisers should also be factored in, i.e. unemployment and social welfare provisions which acted to cushion the public from destitution. Combined discretionary and automatic stabilisers amounted to 2.6 per cent of global GDP, more than the IMF said was necessary at that time, which helped defuse the issue. Ultimately a compromise approach was agreed on and G20 leaders announced that collective fiscal and economic commitments, discretionary and automatic, amounted to US$5 trillion in 2009, 'the largest fiscal and monetary stimulus and the most comprehensive support programme for the financial sector in modern times' (G20, 2009a, p. 2), a huge amount but a figure still dwarfed by the expansionary and war-related expenditure during World War II.

G20 leaders also struck a deal to boost resources of the international financial institutions (IFIs). The final number announced was impressive: US$1.1 trillion in new resources for the IFIs. This included a new Special Drawing Right (SDR)[1] allocation of US$250 billion, US$500 billion under the New Arrangements to Borrow (NAB), US$100 billion of additional lending by the multilateral development banks, US$250 billion of support for trade finance and IMF gold sales for concessional lending (G20, 2009b, 2009c).

UK and US leadership successfully pressed for maximum 'shock and awe' from summit participants. US Treasury Secretary Tim Geithner responded to a proposed IMF NAB allocation of US$250 billion by announcing: 'Let's make it US$500 billion' which left his stunned officials wondering 'how the hell are we going raise US$500 billion?' (Mackintosh, 2012, 12, p. 22). Geithner insisted, and he won the argument. Geithner was acutely aware that leaders needed the maximum impact from the announcement, and the bigger the number the greater the impact on market sentiment. Tim Geithner, Larry Summers (chairman of President Obama's National Economic Council), and Gordon Brown understood that during a crisis, to restore calm, the size of the action must exceed that which is expected or assumed. Doing so can change the market dynamic and reaction from panic to calm or to positive in tone. It does not matter if all the funds are used in the end – only that the amount is massive and its use clearly articulated at the outset. It is, in contrast, notable that Europeans failed to learn this lesson during the Eurozone sovereign debt crisis, and instead in 2010–2011 (and since then) have repeatedly announced proposals that were seen as too small, too late or too incoherent for the desired market impact.

The G20 leaders followed the stimulus pledges with a series of detailed, highly specific financial reform proposals for the financial system post-crisis. Principal amongst these were agreements on the following.

The creation of the Financial Stability Board (FSB): G20 leaders agreed to create the FSB to replace the Financial Stability Forum (FSF). Representatives would be included from G20 countries, Spain and a small number of other key states and international actors. Political and technical leaders 'realized you couldn't institutionalise the FSF without broadening its membership to parallel the G20' (Mackintosh, 2012, 24, p. 5). The FSB would be the principal coordinating body for the raft of regulatory work specified in the two-part action plan agreed in London. The FSB would increase its staff from seven (as the FSF) to 30 plus by 2015. It would grow into the key forum for international regulatory diplomacy and financial coordination, backed by a broad G20 mandate for action. It would have a complex institutional structure and modus operandi much closer to that of a formal international institution than to its ad hoc predecessor, the FSF (see Chapter 5).

Financial reform: A series of highly specific deliverables were identified in the action plans unveiled in April 2009 in London and which continued to provide the focus for reform from that point forwards. Almost all the financial reform G20 workload would be overseen, and where necessary actually carried out, by the members of the FSB. The G20 tasked the FSB with coordination roles that included assessing vulnerabilities affecting the financial system, acting as principal coordinator of an information exchange forum and undertaking strategic reviews of the policy development work of the international standard-setting bodies to ensure they deliver on G20 goals (G20, 2009b).

In London the new FSB was placed at the very centre of the regulatory reform. The scores of tasks it was given responsibility for coordinating were contentious and difficult to achieve. Much of the work stream coordinated by the FSB was delegated to technical bodies and international agencies, such as the Basel Committee on Banking Supervision (BCBS), the International Association of Insurance Supervisors (IAIS) and the International Organization of Securities Commissions (IOSCO), but all were overseen by the FSB. These aggressive regulatory goals were backed by a series of precise timelines, targets and institutional responsibilities. The G20 leadership had taken the 47 steps agreed in Washington in 2008 and made them yet more concrete, more specific and actionable by particular international and national agencies led by the FSB.

Reform of the IMF: G30 leaders recommitted themselves to implementing the package of IMF quota and voice (i.e. governance and representation) reforms agreed in April 2008, followed by a major review of quotas by January 2011.

Leaders signalled that a reapportionment of voting and representation in the IMF would occur so that it more closely reflected the importance of emerging market powers. In a further nod to the new geopolitical reality leaders agreed 'that the heads and senior leadership of the international financial institutions should be appointed through an open, transparent, and merit-based selection process' (G20, 2009a, p. 9). So they would continue reforms at the IMF, but this would be subsidiary to their financial reform goals, and the IMF would be following G20 directions.

The reaction of participants and observers to the London declaration and reforms was supportive. Prime Minister Brown lauded the 'largest fiscal expansion ever seen' (Weisman and MacDonald, 2009) which when coupled with a reshaping of capitalism meant 'the old Washington consensus is over' (*BBC News*, 2009a). President Obama saw London as 'a turning point for global economic recovery', calling the collective action 'unprecedented' (*BBC News*, 2009b). President Sarkozy applauded regulatory reform. Chancellor Merkel called it a 'historic compromise' (BBC, 2009c). Key actors saw the summit outcome in dramatic and significant terms; the degree of policy consensus and the large total committed collective state resources and the specific quantified reform measures had an impact. Markets rose immediately after the end of the summit. London's FTSE 100 index closed up 4.3 per cent, Germany's DAX index gained 6.1 per cent and France's CAC 40 rose 5.4 per cent on the 'G20 factor' (*BBC News*, 2009d). For *The Economist*, the summit 'marked a turning point in investor and business confidence' (2009).

Colin Bradford and Johannes Linn suggested that 'in coming years, the London G-20 Summit will be seen as the most successful summit in history' (Bradford and Linn, 2010). Participants in the summit concurred calling London 'The most remarkable summit I have ever been to' (Mackintosh, 2011, 2, p. 3), and another echoing this stressing that 'it set in train the [reform] process'(Mackintosh, 2012, 22, p. 11).

If London was about aggressive action, big numbers and bold construction of the future architecture, Pittsburgh was about maintaining those gains and incremental but important steps.

The Pittsburgh summit – an affirmation of the G20 role

President Obama at the Pittsburgh summit continued to support stimulus expenditure and press for and support the technical work underway. Leaders signed a 'Framework for Strong, Sustainable and Balanced Growth', and the summit concentrated on technical work underway on new Basel capital and liquidity standards, FSB compensation standards, over-the-counter derivative clearing, accounting standards and cross-border resolution (G20, 2009d).

Pittsburgh's most notable institutional achievement, coming as the economic crisis appeared to moderate, was the decision to make the G20 the permanent forum for their international economic diplomacy and cooperation – a signal of the forum's consolidation and dominance (Cooper, 2010). This was perhaps the most 'profound development in global governance since the creation of the World Trade Organization' (Patrick, 2009). Obama confirmed that the G20 had permanently eclipsed the G7 and the G8 as the principal summit forum for global economic diplomacy (the latter ceased to operate in 2013). This change made concrete what Paola Subacchi had already noted, namely the centrality of the more inclusive G20 process and the shift away from weaker forums (Subacchi, 2009). There would be no backsliding or the exclusion of major emerging powers via the old, less legitimate groupings. Even though leaders outside the G20 still viewed its work with a jaundiced eye, since the forum was exclusive and self-appointed, the wider membership further solidified the G20's leadership position atop the global architecture.

The Pittsburgh summit's toughest and most controversial debates took place over global economic imbalances and pitted deficit-financed contracting economies (such as the US) against creditors with surpluses (such as China and Germany). This conflict was a variant of the perennial debtor/creditor-importer/exporter clash (such as the petrodollar disputes in the 1970s and the US-Japan conflict in the 1990s), and it would arise repeatedly, especially during phase three of the G20's evolution and its return to dissension amongst members. President Obama pressed surplus nations to increase domestic demand to boost global demand as US consumers retrenched (*Reuters News*, 2009; G20, 2009d, 2009e). Matters were further complicated because of differences over exit strategies and stimulus. Chancellor Merkel disagreed with President Obama, who continued major fiscal and monetary stimulus, as did the Chinese on an even larger scale.

As it would in later summits the divide over imbalances proved practically impossible to bridge. It was not part of the new policy consensus. Regulatory coordination and control were achievable and part of the new normal. Changing national economic models was not. As Dominique Strauss-Kahn, then-IMF managing director, said, there simply was no general agreement over 'what the long-term growth model will be' (Guha, 2009). Major powers in the G20 could not agree over whom to blame for the imbalances. Creditor nations criticised profligate debtors and their consumers. Debtors complained of currency manipulation and excess savings. In the end Obama struck a modest compromise: G20 leaders agreed to the creation of an IMF-monitored Mutual Assessment Process (MAP), which would monitor national economic, fiscal and monetary policies, which might contribute to imbalances, and report to the G20. But the lack of agreement over imbalances and what to do about them meant the IMF was given no new enforcement powers. The IMF could only name and shame. The developing dispute over imbalances, papered over in Pittsburgh, would be mild compared to that which would erupt more forcefully in phase three.

One other issue roiled the summit: European leaders, led by France and Germany, wanted action on bankers' bonuses and compensation levels. Indeed President Sarkozy threatened to walk out if no deal on bonuses was secured (Guebert and Shaw, 2009). He did not do so, but Sarkozy's threat did force the G20 to direct reluctant technocrats in the FSB to take up the issue, after the US team led by Treasury Secretary Geithner refused to address compensation at the summit. Chapter 4 will address the policy results in this area.

The apogee of the reform wave

By the end of phase two and of 2009 many of the main parts of the new regulatory structure were in place (such as the FSB) or were being built (a reformed IMF), and 'a rapidly developed, internationally coordinated reform agenda' took shape (Helleiner, 2010, p. 632). The G20 processes could not deliver on all aspects of reform in 12 months, and many reform agenda items remained to be addressed in the years ahead. But during phase two the main agenda items were set and tasks were distributed within the new superstructure overseen by the FSB. New coordination processes were implemented by the end of 2009 that did not exist less than 18 months earlier and which could deliver results, albeit ones limited by the degree of policy consensus amongst G20 leaders, and in particular amongst the central banking lead community (see Chapter 6). The agenda set in this period would form the bulk of the regulatory reform workload in the years ahead. With the benefit of hindsight phase two was the apogee of reformist zeal, the crest of the wave of the new financial and regulatory paradigm shift, amongst national political leaders and their regulatory surrogates.

In phase two the G20 diplomatic, economic stimulus and regulatory and technical reform waves rose together and peaked at the London summit (see Figure 3.1). Chapter 4 will show that after 2009, the economic policy wave dissipated, with disputes arising between Keynesians and 'austerions' (Krugman, 2012), only for the economic consensus to re-form in a smaller wave as leaders sought a Eurozone deal in 2012. The diplomatic G20-led wave would also weaken in phase three as the dissension inherent in normal non-crisis geopolitics and diplomacy returned. The election of Donald Trump as America's president in 2016 would further undermine the G20 effectiveness as his America First policy fractured the consensus in the forum, and America became oppositional and hostile rather than a key leader in the process. The diplomatic effectiveness of the G20 continued to deteriorate from 2017, as is seen in Figure 3.1. Confronted in 2020 by the COVID-19 pandemic and global economic disaster the G20 would prove unable to react in the same decisive manner it had in 2008 and 2009 under more internationalist collaborative farsighted US and UK leadership.

In contrast the technical regulatory policy wave, supported by the key central banking epistemic community and their principals in the FSB, was and remains the most resistant to erosion, because the wave was underpinned by a new cohesive policy consensus amongst the central banking community charged with leading the reform process.

Crucially when faced with the 2020 COVID-19 crisis, the central banking community, led by the US central bank, would act in a coordinated fashion to prop up the global economy as they sought to calm markets and keep trade flowing in the midst of disaster. Hence the technical FSB collaborative wave rises again in 2020, even as the G20 diplomatic wave continues to ebb, due to the absence of American leadership under President Trump. The G20 central banking response to COVID-19 is addressed in Chapter 8.

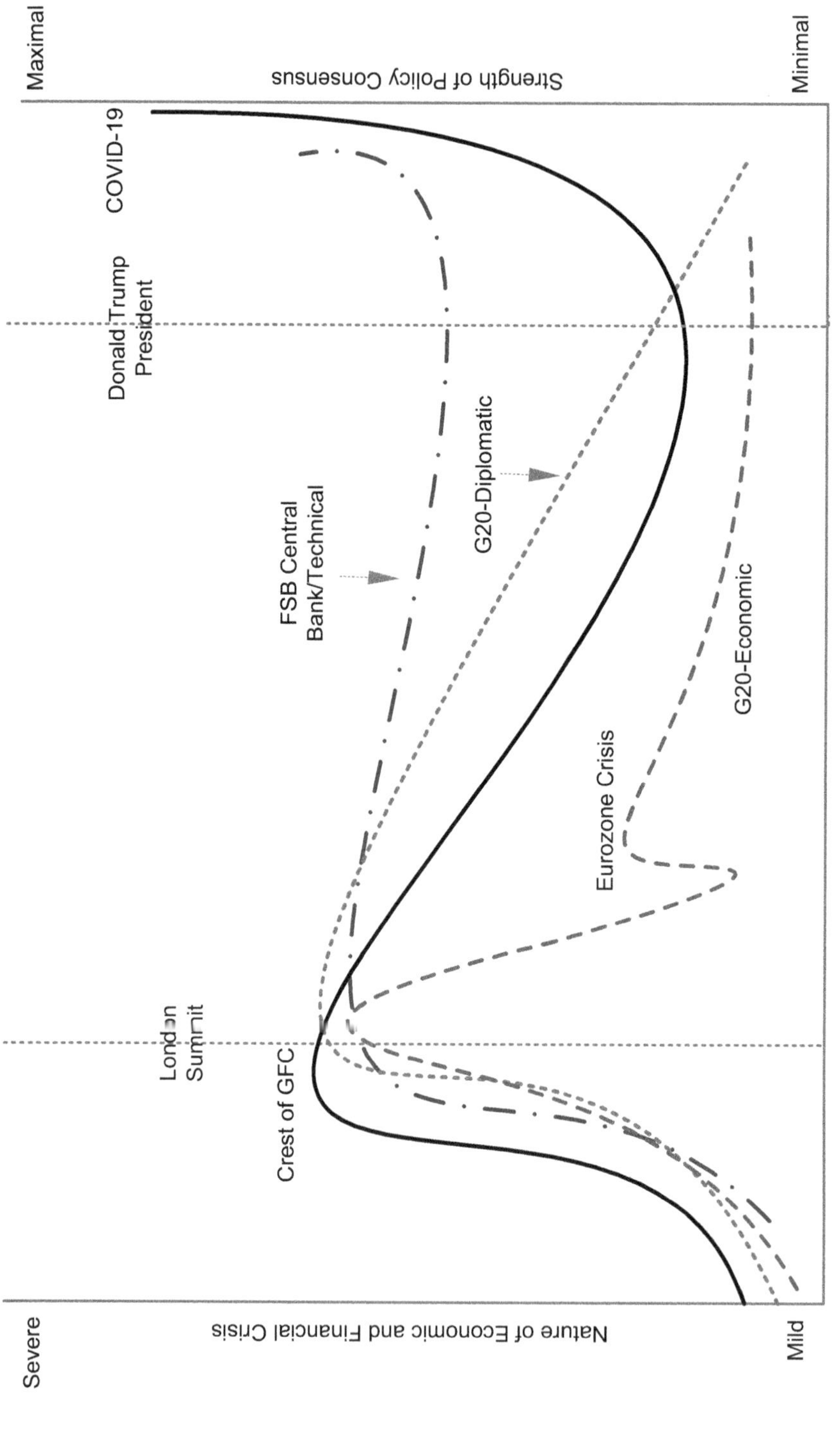

Figure 3.1 The diplomatic, economic and FSB technical reform waves

In 2009 we saw a new policy consensus that recognised the need for a state-power-driven, widespread re-regulatory agenda. The G20 backed this shift. It was a victory for the champions of a more aggressive global regulatory approach, advised by the central banking community, whose leaders were 'hawks', i.e. strongly supportive of the shift in worldview. The highly complex, multifaceted agenda and the aggressive timeline specified by the G20 in London was not their own creation. It was the 'wish list' of this same central banking community acting as the political leaders' advisers. They took goals, previously identified by the FSF, and which, absent the centripetal force of the crisis, would never have been achievable, and secured G20 backing for their rapid pursuit and implementation by national central banks, supervisors and standard-setting bodies.

This new worldview, policy narrative and consensus on action were strongest amongst the community of officials, regulators and technocrats who designed the details of the new coordination structure (i.e. the FSB) and advised on the broad work programme demanded by the G20. Those officials would lead the FSB, staff the new forum and chair the work streams emanating from phase two.

At the G20 level the decisions in this reformist period were largely driven by a relatively small group from North America and Europe, but the inclusion of the emerging-market countries whose leaders were supportive should not be discounted, because the new policy consensus shifted towards many of their statist/state corporatist viewpoints and preference for greater regulation and stronger regulatory systems.

The emerging countries' voice

The loud North American and European voices in 2008 and 2009, during the crisis management and concrete reform phases, partially obscured a significant change in the global architecture of economic diplomacy that became more visible from 2010 onwards: the permanent inclusion and enhanced role of major emerging powers within the G20, FSB and IMF. This inclusion was no trivial matter. Prior to 2008 none of these emerging state powers had regularly been included in discussions over global stimulus or the regulation of the global financial system and markets. Now that they were at the table, they could no longer be ignored. Others might be added in the future, but none can realistically be uninvited. In 2008–2009 there was relatively little evidence of emerging-market leaders having an impact, except at the margins, and indeed initially the emerging powers' voices were somewhat muted. But this is not surprising. Emerging-economy voices were drowned out by the existing powers who were leading and chairing the process, whose errors and omissions had led to the crisis and within whose markets the most needed to be done to re-regulate and restore a new balance between the state and markets.

Emerging-country leaders entered the room with varying degrees of familiarity with summitry, and some were at some disadvantage because of a lack of knowledge, technical capacity or political room to manoeuvre to engage effectively. A former finance ministry participant recalls a Chinese representative at an early summit reading out a position paper at the outset of the proceedings, and then reading exactly the same paper hours later at the conclusion of negotiations.

The relative silence from the new actors in 2008 and 2009 was also due to another key factor: the paradigm shift underway in 2009 moved the debate towards the stance already occupied by many of those leaders. China's leaders for example were supportive of greater financial macroprudential regulation and control of firms (they directly control all their major domestic banks). China also already had tougher capital and prudential standards at that time than existed in the West. Other emerging-country leaders, including Brazil, India and Russia, were critical of the US failures before the crisis and were supportive of the re-regulation of financial markets. In other words a lack of audible stridency by emerging countries in 2008 and 2009, in phases one and two of the crisis response, should not be read as a lack of support for the paradigm shift that commenced in 2008 which was increasingly visible in 2009.

The global financial architecture

The G20 at the centre

In 2009 the G20 backed a new global financial architecture to coordinate collective financial regulation of global markets and firms. Leaders agreed on a new structure that has proved resilient in the years since then, one which has been crucial to the pursuance of their common goals. In fashioning this architecture the leaders and their technocrats placed themselves (not unsurprisingly) in the lead and at the very centre of their new construction. While doing so they also agreed on reforms and refinancing of the IMF, but that organisation was not given a lead role. From 2009 on financial reform would be a G20 priority, and it would be led, coordinated and controlled by the central banking community and its dominant hawkish leaders from North America and Europe.

Figure 3.2 graphically displays the global financial architecture as built by the G20 states. It shows which forums and institutions are at the core of the structure, and which have grown in size and impact as regards supervision and regulation of financial markets.

At the top of the structure is the G20 (dark grey oval), providing political leadership, capital and collective state power reasserted to deliver financial regulatory reform in a way not seen prior to the crisis. The G20 was and is the key political forum in the new design. To a considerable extent the new architecture's effectiveness depends on the strength of the consensus in the forum and the ability of the G20 leaders to provide direction on the global macro policy and other major issues they confront. However, once the policy actions are delegated to the technical community, reforms can continue even when there is discord over outstanding controversial macro issues at the G20 level.

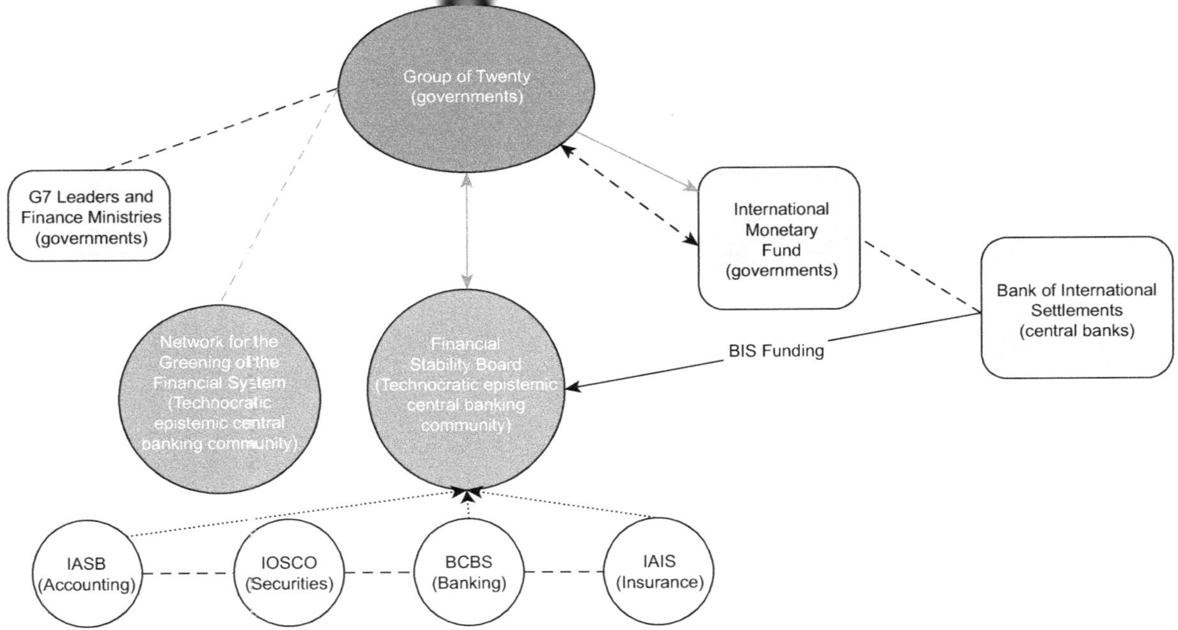

Figure 3.2 The global financial architecture

Sources: See Davies and Green, 2008, for a pre-crisis representation of the old architecture 'as was'.

Note: Dashed lines indicate information exchange and communication, with lines of communication between FSB and SSBs stronger than between SSBs themselves. Lines with arrows indicate directional authority and control. Double-faced arrows indicate two-way authority and coordination.

The newest addition to the landscape is the Network for Greening the Financial System, which modelled directly on the FSB, without at this stage being integrated with it.

Nation-state-level actors (such as the US Treasury), and substate agency actors, participate in certain levels of the international regulatory structure. For instance, the US Treasury participates in the G20 leaders and finance ministers meetings, while the SEC is a member of the FSB through IOSCO.

BCBS = Basel Committee on Banking Supervision; BIS = Bank for International Settlements; FSB = Financial Stability Board; IAIS = International Association of Insurance Supervisors; IASB = International Accounting Standards Board; IOSCO = International Organization of Securities Commissions; NGFS (Network for Greening the Financial System (NGFS)' SSB = standard-setting body.

The FSB role

The new structure includes the empowered FSB (large grey circle) playing the central coordinating role. The FSB was directed by the G20 and tasked by the G20 to oversee all major aspects of the financial reform process started in November 2008 and continuing through 2009 and beyond. It includes principals from all G20 members, central banks and finance ministries, as well as the leaders of standard-setting bodies. The FSB is a small forum, fighting above its weight because it reports directly to the G20 summits (not through finance ministries). Its strength lies in this tight linkage, coupled with the commitment of key FSB leaders to oversee the financial reform process. The board plays the key coordinating role at the centre of the structure.

Practically all leadership roles, the main working groups and standing committees during its formative period in 2008–2009, and through 2012, were occupied by leaders more critical of the past regulatory paradigm, such as Mark Carney (chairman of the FSB), Adair Turner (former principal supervisor in the UK) and Jaime Caruana (general manager of the BIS). These leaders were supportive of the change in worldview and shift they themselves directed and commenced. This initial FSB's leadership roster was not an accident and had implications for the robustness of key policies the community adopted. The FSB lacks a formal treaty basis, powers and responsibilities. But the power of the actors that lead it and their communication channel straight to the G20 leadership more than compensate for this formal weakness. It will be shown that the FSB's creators rapidly give it an internal structure more akin to an institution than to a mere talking shop.

Note, however, that the BIS plays an important parental and supporting role regarding the FSB, which it hosts and which it (from 2012) finances. This underscores the power of the central banking community in the new structure. It dominates the leadership of the FSB. The BIS – and by extension the community as a whole – provides the forum's financing. The BIS supports the FSB in a direct, tangible and ongoing manner, potentially ensuring its continued relevance and strength.

Enhanced and coordinated role for standard-setting bodies

The new architecture has significant changes below the level of the FSB, which coordinates the reform agenda and the related work of international standard-setting bodies (SSBs). SSB memberships are drawn from state regulatory agencies. Today they in large part carry out work delegated to them by the G20. Not only does the FSB monitor deliverables, but it also provides the forum within which the leadership of these bodies interact and collaborate. The FSB determines whether the SSBs are following the G20 summits' mandate. The FSB delivers a degree of coordination that was not previously evident. This is shown via the almost solid lines of communications between the FSB and SSBs, which remain independent, but are elevated and to a greater degree incorporated into the state-based system of technical cooperation and policy making.

The FSB is central to rapid progress in the deepening of the coordination amongst actors and amongst SSBs. The FSB technical-level work plays to the strengths of the core members and the outcomes are influenced by European and North American principals as leaders of the process, because it takes 'impressive expertise and stamina' to staff and operate multiple work streams (Cooper, 2010, p. 744). Larger emerging economies, such as China, can handle the demands, but others, such as South Africa, may strain their administrative capacity to contribute to the complex debates underway. This capacity will grow as G20 members engage regularly in these debates and discussions and become more familiar with them.

The SSBs until 2009 often worked alone and were at odds with the work of one another. There was no coordinating body of the strength and robustness of the FSB in which all participated (a joint forum did exist but it was weak and ineffective). Today the FSB draws the SSBs and their memberships inside the state-led reform drive. SSB leaders insist they are independent from the FSB. This is correct in formal terms, but in practice their agendas are being dictated by the G20, and the SSBs report to and are coordinating their work through the FSB. The new level of coordination seen amongst SSBs via the FSB process marks a valuable innovation. In forcing this structural reform, the G20 created direction and coordination amongst an obscure alphabet soup of organisations where little previously existed. This was a little-noted major achievement by the G20 and FSB leaderships as they sought a more cohesive, comprehensive, harmonised global regulatory structure.

The G7 is not central to the new global financial architecture. The group remains operative and does function and meet as another forum for the advanced world, but it is less important than in the past and has been eclipsed by the G20 (Subacchi, 2009). It is reasonable to assume that the G20 and FSB cannot swiftly be downgraded or pushed aside from its currently now dominant position. The G20-FSB nexus is now where the diplomatic and economic-regulatory power rests in 2020, even if Mr Trump's America First stymies G20 collective action.

The NGFS – a new institution to tackle climate change

In 2017 a new institution was added to the global architecture – the Network for Greening the Financial System (NGFS). The NGFS is modelled closely on the FSB (its internal structure is practically identical). It is designed to provide a forum in which member central banks can coordinate their approach to internalising climate change policies and climate change risk management within their mandates. Although only recently having been created (by Mark Carney, then-governor of the Bank of England), the NGFS signals a further major shift by key central banks on this key policy area. It is arguably a further instance of third-order paradigm shift by central banks and a majority of the community. Chapter 8 addresses the NGFS in detail.

The post-crisis position and role of the International Monetary Fund

The IMF in this new architecture was regenerated (its resources were almost quadrupled), but the institution was simultaneously diminished and is not in the lead on global financial reform. This is different from previous lesser crises; those tended to occur outside the core industrial nations and involved balance-of-payment issues in developing countries, and in those instances the IMF took a leading role. In 2008–2009 this was not the case; the IMF was in a weaker position structurally, even as it was rejuvenated with more resources thanks to the G20 governments.

A historical parallel and prior fight over crisis management roles is instructive. In the Asian and long-term credit management financial crises of the 1990s, a clash occurred between the chair of the Financial Stability Forum, Sir Andrew Crockett, (the FSF was itself an architectural response to those financial crises), and the deputy managing director of the IMF, Stan Fischer. Fischer asserted IMF supremacy in financial crisis response matters and sought to marginalise the smaller, new, much less powerful FSF. Fischer won and went on to run the crisis management responses as a result (Blustein, 2012, p. 9).

A similar clash occurred in 2008, but the outcome was very different. That year, Dominque Strauss-Kahn, managing director of the IMF, struggled with Mario Draghi, chairman of the FSB, over who would lead the financial crisis response and reform agenda. But unlike the 1990s, in 2008 Strauss-Kahn lost, and the central banking community took almost complete control over the financial reform agenda. The IMF got a lot more money but no real role in the financial reform space. The reforms were the prerogative of the FSB and its central bankers, backed by the G20 leaders. This is why, in the new architectural landscape, the IMF is simultaneously provided with new resources and downgraded in the global regulatory architectural redesign.

Finance ministers and central bankers worked feverishly together during the crisis. They understood and relied on one another. The former were willing to give the latter wide latitude in the design of regulatory reforms. In contrast, ministers and central bankers did not trust the IMF, and neither would allow the IMF a major role in the reform process. Marginal IMF policy adjustments were agreed. But the G20-backed FSB led on financial reform, despite its smaller size. G20 summits signaled a modified collective narrative adopted by the G20 on the utility of the IMF, an emergent adjusted policy consensus composed of:

1 An implicit agreement on a modified, improved, but simultaneously diminished, position of the IMF within the global architectural superstructure
2 An agreement on considerably increased IMF resources
3 An agreement on modest governance changes and adjustments in the relative power of emerging-market countries within the IMF itself to reflect global macroeconomic realities
4 An agreement on modest adjustments to the IMF's surveillance role.

This G20 policy consensus on the IMF's position and reforms did not change the nature of the institution in the short to medium term. The IMF reforms agreed in 2008–2009 and in later summits will result in relatively modest evolutionary governance and voice reforms that have aimed to draw emerging countries back into a stronger commitment to an IMF within which their role and voice would also be potentially more influential. Taken as a whole, the IMF reforms were incremental, first- and weak second-order reforms, emblematic of a slow and gradual rebalancing of power and influence away from the old core and towards the emerging countries within an existing structure and organisation. The IMF reforms went only so far.

The G20 memberships' collective recommitment to the IMF (especially emerging countries' recommitment) was noteworthy, particularly given how weak and irrelevant the IMF had become prior to the onset of the 2007–2008 crisis. The G20-led reform of the IMF made it once again a relevant, better-financed, marginally reformed organisation, tasked with assisting in the collective macroeconomic and financial response to the crisis. The G20 used the IMF to channel financing from states with excess surplus reserves to those states in crisis, swiftly but with conditions, to achieve identified common goals. The IMF's resource boost, internal reforms and policy changes depended on G20 summit deals amongst somewhat reluctant advanced economy leaders and more eager emerging-country leaders intent on seizing a greater degree of control over the IMF in return for their money.

But memories of past IMF failures in the 1990s lingered, and as a result the IMF was pushed to become to a degree subservient to the G20, to serve the G20 agenda and objectives. Today, compared with the other actors – the G20 and the FSB – the IMF has a 'limited role and visibility' (Beeson and Broome, 2008, p. 393). Why? Because the IMF performed poorly before the crisis and lacked legitimacy. In the end, as a senior national IMF figure stated: 'it comes down to a failure of the IMF, a failure to identify the crisis, and a failure to act' (Mackintosh, 2012, 19, p. 1). In 2020 the IMF is reinforced as the global lender of last resort to states facing balance-of-payment crises. The IMF once again has an important macroeconomic crisis-fighting role to play, but it is not in the lead on financial regulatory matters.

The agreed G20-led reforms mark a gradual evolution of the IMF away from one dominated by US and European officials, as the balance of state power shifts within the institution and emerging countries demand a larger role, albeit haltingly, and with many discordant voices. That being said, there was no paradigm shift inside the IMF, in its central neoliberal economic ideology, in its lending practices, or in its operation. Despite the organisation's past failures, there has been no rejection of existing 'truths', no revolution from within, and no adoption of a new approach to IMF macroeconomic oversight and management of the global economy. There is no evidence of a fundamental reappraisal of the IMF's mission, overall ideology or functioning. Remarkably, despite the IMF's pre-crisis mistakes, the number of anomalies was not enough to force a major shift in worldview amongst the staff or state shareholders. Instead, the internal policy consensus successfully resisted change. The community view within the IMF remains neoliberal, creditor-focused, firmly power-sensitive, member-driven, and internally ideologically resilient. This is the case even as the IMF adjusts its view of the merits and speed of austerity, and the merits of capital controls policies to halt capital flight, for example.

The IMF member states' refusal to take more radical reform steps shows their diverging national positions and the limits of the G20 policy consensus on the future role of the IMF. The IMF serves its creditor (finance ministry) members' interests first, and its lending and surveillance work reflects this reality, and neither will change with any rapidity. IMF shareholders control the rate of policy evolution, operating within an existing institutional structure and existing biases, and driven by national political and economic concerns. Unlike the G20 forum and the FSB, there was not a shift in worldview and approach within the IMF. It continues to operate within an existing (albeit slightly crisis altered and modified) worldview. The IMF is adjusting but not fundamentally altering its nature, ideology or consensus viewpoint.

In the post-crisis architectural structure, the IMF has been revived and it has much greater resources. Emerging countries have re-engaged with the organisation and the IMF is undergoing gradual, incremental institutional reforms. But it is not in the lead on financial reform. G20 leaders and central banking technocrats kept control within their grasp and rejected attempts by the IMF to play a bigger role in the financial reform space.

Ultimately, the G20 reforms might result in an IMF that more closely mirrors changes in the relative economic power and importance of developed and emerging countries. But it will take time for these reforms to alter the nature of the organisation and its culture, ideology, practices and policy stances. Taken together, the reforms amount to first- and, at most, second-order, changes (Hall, 1993).

The paradigm shift begins

In 2009 in London, as economic crisis loomed before G20 leaders and morphed from a financial panic into a global economic downturn, they grasped the need to act collectively, decisively, to provide stimulus and to chart a course ahead. Gordon Brown delivered. The summit gave 'high level direction' and it 'set in train the reform process', there was 'an alignment' (Mackintosh, 2012, 22, pp. 9–11). Even critics of the G20-FSB process recognise that 2009 saw G20 summitry at its best, as a reactive forum in which big directional decisions could be taken swiftly, when all were bound together by the fellowship of the lifeboat. London showed that 'the G20 is best when it is brokering rescue deals at the highest levels and thrashing out compromises on macroeconomic and financial reform issues' (Mackintosh, 2012, 19, p. 3).

Brown seized the initiative, the moment of maximal opportunity provided by the force of the crisis. He took advantage of and created win sets, delivering 'the most remarkable summit' (Mackintosh, 2011, 4, p. 3) that charted the way forward. In pursuing this Brown and the G20 leaders were advised by the central banking community, who laid out plans for the regulation of the global financial markets and the world's largest banks. Decisions in London in April 2009 formed the basis for a multiyear reassertion of state power, a return of state authority over markets and firms. Not only did the leaders agree on a broad and deep agenda, but they ensured that they 'had an institution in charge' i.e. the FSB (Mackintosh, 2012, 17, p. 8). It was then up to 'the technical experts, central bankers, the heads of supervision' to hammer out the details (Mackintosh, 2012, 22, p. 11). Decisions in London, which built on the Washington summit (as a process) began to extend 'the perimeter of regulation' (Mackintosh, 2012, 12, p. 15).

President Obama in Pittsburgh cemented these new constructs and the agreed goals, affirming the G20's leading role and the centrality of the FSB below it as reforms began to be pursued, most notably the Basel III Accord that had begun to be negotiated. The new and reformed structures created and the G20 technical agenda agreed on in this concrete reform phase constituted the beginning of a paradigm shift in the agreed consensus approach to the oversight and regulation of financial markets, to application of state power and authority and to the role of emerging markets in the diplomatic processes. The reforms signalled a new normal that would henceforth always include emerging as well as existing powers in economic and regulatory diplomacy and in the new and reformed institutions.

At the end of 2009, the G20-led process had achieved a great deal in a short time. Based on a shift in worldview, leaders agreed on an ambitious new architecture, centred on the FSB, and a state-power-driven re-regulatory reform agenda directed by their central banking technocrats. But certain political economy issues remained beyond the boundaries of the new policy consensus and paradigm. Thus, strains started to be seen over imbalances, as some leaders started to look forward from Pittsburgh perhaps 'a bit too positively' (Mackintosh, 2012, 33, p. 34), thinking the crisis was already behind them. That tensions began to be seen+ is no surprise.

Exits speeds from a crisis always differ. And the impasse over imbalances is a perennial area of discord and was and is outside the new consensus. A new international monetary system could not yet be fashioned. Indeed, numerous thorny perennial macroeconomic, political and ideological issues could not be solved, as the later history of the G20, as the crises dissipated, would demonstrate.

Does the observation that the paradigm has limits and boundaries mean we must downgrade the scale of the achievements of the G20 in 2009 to mere tinkering? Eric Helleiner's view is that the G20's failure to address imbalances, the maintenance of the leadership role of the US, the continuation of the dollar as reserve currency and other global macroeconomic factors suggest a status-quo crisis (Helleiner, 2014, pp. 55–91), i.e. one in which precious little changes. In my view this expects too much from the regulatory paradigm shift that had begun. In these areas of global macroeconomics paradigm conflict existed rather than consensus.

As Helleiner also notes, the international monetary system was not at the centre of the crisis in 2007–2008 (2014, p. 55). Despite fears the system would break, it did not. As such, it was not the focus of action – regulatory failures in the core were agreed to be at fault. Moreover, action by governments and central banks worked remarkably smoothly during the crisis, with the US and other leading central banks coordinating swaps, lines of credit, guarantees and much else. So while imbalances remain, the G20 and FSB community did not in 2009 try to address the international monetary system because it was not viewed as pivotal to a return to economic stability, and as we have also seen, this global macroeconomic subject remained outside the boundaries of the new narrative and policy consensus.

Helleiner underestimates what was begun and achieved in 2008 and in 2009. To be sure, the US and its allies played pivotal roles, and power dynamics were not disrupted; rather, they were augmented with emerging-country voices and input. But this was not business as usual with minor adjustments. This was the beginning of a change in worldview, visible to a degree in the G20 summits in 2009, and especially amongst the central banking community (as will become clear in Chapters 5 and 6). This was the start of a paradigm shift, one that is increasingly visible in 2015.

The response to the crisis and reforms laid out in 2009 are not simply incremental adjustments, as Manuela Moschella and Eleni Tsingou suggest (2013, p. 4). Rather, as Hall argued, a paradigm shift must be underpinned by indicators of high second- and third-order shifts. And third-order shifts are in fact seen. There was a jump in the technocrats' narrative policy consensus that underpinned the G20 summitry. The FSB's creation and its macroprudential policy output post-2009 are third-order changes. These shifts were accompanied by more modest first- and low second-order policy adjustments.

When all the institutional, policy and cultural shifts are viewed as a whole, they appear lasting and consequential. The policies were not an exercise in incrementalism. Moschella and Tsingou do get it partially right: paradigm shifts are, to a degree, the result of the cumulative effects of multiple, small changes in policy, but there still must be a precipitating event or crisis, *and* evidence of third-order shift (in narratives, institutions and ultimately, policies) for the changes to be durable and substantial, and for a paradigm shift to be judged as having occurred.

Looking at the events of 2009 with greater temporal distance, the decisions taken that year signalled a shift in the policy consensus; a reassertion of state authority in place of market authority, the creation of a new forum, the FSB, and the beginning of a multiyear, multifaceted policy process that is central to the new consensus.

The G20 and its FSB community technocrats backed the new consensus and designed in 2009 a structure and agenda that cannot be considered as flimsy or ephemeral or a 'G7-plus'. In its entire history, the G7 never produced this burst of post-crisis regulatory concrete activism of such robust design. The G20 reforms started in 2008 and given shape in 2009 collectively amounted to the beginning of a shift in worldview and policy consensus, and a major rebalancing of the state versus markets and regulator versus regulated, backed not only by the core members but also by emerging states. As will be seen, the process would not diminish or end in phase three.

The new global financial architecture with the G20 at the top and FSB at the centre (in Figure 3.2) constitutes a third-order change in international regulatory coordination and economic diplomacy. The G20 in 2009 laid the foundations for and began to construct the new policy consensus narrative during the crisis management and reform phases, including institutional alterations and building. But the G20 leadership could not identify the technical agenda and objectives (they would not know a macroprudential hammer from a microprudential screwdriver) or achieve them alone. So the politicians deferred to their central bankers, in the leadership of the FSB, whose expert membership is dominated by hawkish North American and European central bankers and supervisors operating as a distinct community.

It is this small elite group that led the drive to make the evolving policy consensus real via an aggressive agenda of policy reforms that they designed or would task others with designing. The crisis and concrete reform phases created a window of opportunity, enlarged win spaces, and permitted leaders and their technical surrogates to go much further than was possible in normal non-crisis circumstances. G20 leaders turned to their experts for the framework and solutions. Emboldened technocrats proposed a reform agenda that the G20 agreed on and which the central bankers could not previously have dreamt of securing.

In the third phase of the G20's development, from 2010 onwards, a diplomatic dialectic was balanced in part by a more robust technical reform process. In the diplomatic dialectic, the crisis created pressure for action, the G20 is created and leaders help restore some economic calm and stability through collective crisis management and reform actions. Once a degree of stability is evident, the pressure to maintain a G20 diplomatic consensus begins to wane and national prerogatives re-emerge as centrifugal forces acting against maintenance of diplomatic consensus or a further extension of the new policy consensus. Normality and dissention amongst G20 states is seen once more.

The crisis was the tipping point. The failures and anomalies were such that leaders, and especially the central bankers, began the paradigm shift. The crisis created enlarged win spaces and allowed leaders and their technocratic central banking elite, operating as the dominant financial regulatory epistemic community, to delineate and commence a multiyear series of reforms in 2009, based on a new narrative that championed the reassertion of state authority over markets via new macroprudential policies and tools. Summits after 2009 would be less productive, policy-wise. But this is not surprising, for not all summits can be as significant and dramatic as London, nor should we expect them to be. So the diplomatic crisis-induced cohesion weakened. The election of Donald Trump in the US and the end of American leadership within the G20 (and in many other international institutions) shook the foundations of the global financial architecture. American nationalist nativist populism would undermine the G20 summitry as Mr Trump abrogated leadership and replaced it with hostility to consensual international diplomacy and collaboration with allies.

The return to states' defence of parochial national objectives would be much less marked in the technical process, controlled by the central bankers and housed within the FSB structures and processes; in the FSB, in contrast, there was a continued collective movement forward, designed to construct the elements of the policy paradigm begun in Washington, drawn in detail in London and affirmed in Pittsburgh. The central banking community, backed by an increasingly disputative G20, continued to construct the new re-regulatory paradigm. The new normal would continue to take shape. This book finds that, as with previous shifts, after the disjunctive break caused by the crisis, sudden narrative and architectural and policy waves, subsequent evolution in global financial governance would occur more gradually (Helleiner, 2014, p. 165), and over a longer multiyear period.

Note

1 SDRs are how IMF contributions are calculated and held.

References

BBC News. (2009a) 'Gordon Brown's summit statement', 2 April [Online]. Available at: http://news.bbc.co.uk/2/hi/in_depth/business/2009/g20/7979746.stm (accessed: 2 March 2011).

———. (2009b) 'Obama hails historic summit', 2 April [Online]. Available at: http://news.bbc.co.uk/2/hi/in_depth/business/2009/g20/7980227.stm (accessed: 2 March 2011).

———. (2009c) 'Merkel on "historic compromise"', 2 April [Online]. Available at: http://news.bbc.co.uk/2/hi/in_depth/business/2009/g20/7980433.stm (accessed: 2 March 2011).

———. (2009d) 'Global markets rise on G20 deal', 2 April [Online]. Available at: http://news.bbc.co.uk/2/hi/business/7978948.stm (accessed: 9 February 2011).

Beeson, M. and Broome, A. (2008) 'Watching from the sidelines: The decline of the IMF's crisis management role', *Contemporary Politics*, 14, pp. 393–409.

Blustein, P. (2012) 'How global watchdogs missed a world of trouble', *CIGI Papers*, 5(7) [Online]. Available at: www.cigionline.org/publications/2012/7/how-global-watchdogs-missed-world-of-trouble (accessed: 1 May 2013).

Bradford, C.I. (2009) 'The G20 stimulus split: A false debate', *Brookings Institution*, Washington, DC, 1 April.

Bradford, C.I. and Linn, J.F. (2010) 'The April 2009 London G20 summit in retrospect', *Brookings Institution*, Washington, DC, 5 April [Online]. Available at: www.brookings.edu/research/opinions/2010/04/05-g20-summit-linn (accessed: 25 June 2010).

Cooper, A.F. (2010) 'The G20 as an improvised crisis committee and/or a contested "steering committee"', *International Affairs*, 86(3), pp. 741–757.

Darling, A. (2011) *Back from the brink: 1000 days at Number 11*. London: Atlantic Books.

Davies, H. and Green, D. (2008) *Global financial regulation: The essential guide*. New York: Polity.

The Economist. (2009) 'Market fatigue: The Anglo-Saxon model has taken a knock', 1 October [Online]. Available at: www.economist.com/node/14530138 (accessed: 25 October 2012).

Emanuel, R. (2008) Interview with the *Wall Street Journal*, November [Online]. Available at: www.youtube.com/watch?v=_mzcbXi1Tkk (accessed: March 2011).

G20 (Group of Twenty). (2009a) 'London Summit communiqué: Global plan for recovery and reform', 2 April [Online]. Available at: www.g20.utoronto.ca/2009/2009communique0402.html (accessed: 8 February 2011).

———. (2009b) 'Declaration on strengthening the financial system', 2 April [Online]. Available at: www.g20.utoronto.ca/2009/2009ifi.html (accessed: 8 February 2011).

———. (2009c) 'Declaration on delivering resources through the international financial institutions', 2 April [Online]. Available at: www.g20.utoronto.ca/2009/2009delivery.pdf (accessed: 11 February 2011).

———. (2009d) 'Leaders' statement: Pittsburgh Summit', 25 September [Online]. Available at: www.g20.utoronto.ca/2009/2009communique0925.html (accessed: 8 February 2011).

———. (2009e) 'Remarks by President Obama at G20 closing press conference', 25 September [Online]. Available at: www.whitehouse.gov/the_press_office/Remarks-by-the-President-at-G20-Closing-Press-Conference/ (accessed: 8 February 2011).

G30 (Group of Thirty). (2009) *Financial reform: A framework for financial stability*. Washington, DC: Group of Thirty.

Guebert, J. and Shaw, Z. (2009) 'Plans for the third G20 summit: Pittsburgh 2009', *G20 Information Center*, p. 5 [Online]. Available at: www.g20.utoronto.ca/g20plans/g20leaders090921.pdf (accessed: 16 March 2011).

Guha, K. (2009) 'IMF chief urges G20 focus on global imbalance', *Financial Times*, 18 September [Online]. Available at: www.ft.com/cms/s/0/3c4d3778-a479-11de-92d4-00144feabdc0.html#axzz1GlmTgluI (accessed: 16 March 2011).

Hall, P.A. (1993) 'Policy paradigms, social learning, and the state: The case of economic policymaking in Britain', *Comparative Politics*, 25(3), pp. 275–296.

———. (2014) *The status quo crisis: Global financial governance after the 2008 meltdown*. Oxford: Oxford University Press.

Hildebrand, P. (2010) 'Key factors for the Swiss economy – Financial market regulation in Switzerland', *Swiss Economic Forum*, 4 April.

House of Commons Treasury Select Committee. (2008) 'The run on the rock' [Online]. Available at: www.publications.parliament.uk/pa/cm200708/cmselect/cmtreasy/56/5602.htm (accessed: 14 August 2013).

IMF (International Monetary Fund). (2009) 'Global economic policies and prospects', *IMF Note*, 13 March.

King, M. (2010) 'Banking – From Bagehot to Basel, and back again', Second Bagehot Lecture, Buttonwood Gathering, New York, 25 October [Online]. Available at: www.bis.org/review/r101028a.pdf (accessed: 7 March 2011).

Krugman, P. (2012) 'Raygunomics', *The Conscience of a Liberal* blog, *New York Times*, 14 May [Online]. Available at: http://krugman.blogs.nytimes.com/?s=austerions (accessed: 30 July 2013).

Kuhn, T. (1962) *The structure of scientific revolutions*. Chicago: University of Chicago Press.

Mackintosh, S. (2011) Interview 2. Former Finance Ministry Official, 10 October.

———. (2011) Interview 4. National IMF Official, 1 November.

———. (2011) Interview 8. Former G20 Finance Minister, 8 December.

———. (2012) Interview 12. G20 Finance Ministry Official, 27 January.

———. (2012) Interview 17. G20 Presidential Advisor, 3 March.

———. (2012) Interview 19. National IMF Official, G20 Former Treasury Official, 12 March.

———. (2012) Interview 22. Former G20 Finance Minister, Central Bank Governor, 1 May.

———. (2012) Interview 24. G20 Central Bank Governor, 2 July.

———. (2012) Interview 33. Senior Finance Ministry Official and G20 Lead, follow-up meeting, 14 November 2012.

Moschella, M. and Tsingou, E. (eds.) (2013) *Great expectations slow transformations: Incremental change in post-crisis regulation*. Colchester: European Consortium for Political Research (ECPR).

Patrick, S.M. (2009) 'G20 present at the creation of a new economic order', *Council of Foreign Relations* [Online]. Available at: www.cfr.org/international-organizations/g20-present-creation-new-economic-order/p20296 (accessed: 14 March 2011).

Putnam, R. (1988) 'Diplomacy and domestic politics: The logic of two-level games', *International Organization*, 42(3), pp. 427–460.

Reuters News. (2009) 'Obama wants G20 to rethink global economy', 20 September [Online]. Available at: www.reuters.com/article/2009/09/20/us-g-idUSTRE58G34Z20090920 (accessed: 16 March 2011).

Subacchi, P. (2009) 'G-Force', *The World Today*, 65(8–9), pp. 32–33.

Turner, A. (2009) *The Turner review: A regulatory response to the global banking crisis*. London: Financial Services Authority.

Weisman, J. and MacDonald, A. (2009) 'Obama, Brown strike similar notes on economy', *Wall Street Journal*, 3 April [Online]. Available at: http://online.wsj.com/article/SB123871661163384723.html (accessed: 21 August 2013).

4 The emergence of dissension within the G20

When political and technocratic leaders entered the 2007–2008 economic and financial crisis, they did so with common concerns and a common desire to address perceived weaknesses and halt economic panic. They tackled the necessary firefighting and then turned to fashioning the needed reforms. A crisis spurs action and the reform impulse, but the window of opportunity for action is limited. As a crisis dissipates, in part because of the aggressive action in crisis management and the reform phases, the normal non-crisis dynamic of national diplomatic jockeying re-emerges, and centrifugal forces that fling actors apart on issues take over from the crisis-induced centripetal forces. This dialectic of crisis management, reform and finally relapse into diplomatic dissension was seen in G20 summitry from 2010 onwards. A G20 leaders' forum, created *in extremis* as a response, began to show its limits. G20 summits after 2010 all saw varying and generally increasing degrees of dissension and dispute that hampered the forum's utility to deliver on remaining desired goals, as the boundary of the crisis-induced common narrative was reached. The level of dissension and dispute increased again in 2017 after the election of Donald Trump as US president, and policy implications of his America First stance crystalised for all around the summit table.

At the Toronto summit (26–27 June 2010), this dissension dynamic began to play out. Canada's prime minister, Stephen Harper, could not bridge the gap between those still committed to stimulus (the US and France) and those turning towards erroneous stimulatory austerity (Skidelsky, 2018), or at least the exit from stimulus (Germany, the UK and China). While all entered the crisis together, countries exited at varying speeds, with differing views on the next (in particular) economic steps required. National models of economic development re-emerged as areas of natural disputation, disrupting the post-crisis G20 consensus.

The Seoul summit (11–12 November 2010) saw 'currency wars' erupting between the debt-laden, declining hegemon (the US) and creditor nations (Germany and China). The outer limits of the new policy consensus were tested and found. This is not surprising. During this phase in the G20's evolution, attempts were made to extend the policy consensus to perennial global macroeconomic matters, such as currency disputes and managing global imbalances. But these efforts resulted in practically no breakthroughs, as national narratives and political and economic goals clashed rather than converged. The G20 process was no longer, at the level of public posturing, if not in the technical financial policy realm, as productive.

The Cannes (3–4 November 2011) and Los Cabos (18–19 June 2012) summits ultimately reached consensus on how to address the Eurozone crisis, because the pressure of events created room for a renewed consensus, demonstrating again the clarifying and focusing effect that crises have on diplomatic summitry, at least in the short term. External pressures interrupted the growing discordance amongst leaders. The French and Mexican G20 presidencies were forced to grapple with the Eurozone troubles above all else, since the summits took place against a backdrop of increasingly frantic activity aimed at shoring up the Eurozone and the stability of the euro. This was a new, slightly smaller wave of the financial crisis, and the Eurozone crisis recreated some of the dynamics seen earlier in phase one of the G20's existence. That is to say, the crisis forced negotiators together, opened up win sets, temporarily muted domestic interests and allowed the fashioning of a US$461 billion International Monetary Fund (IMF) firewall for the Eurozone. The deal demonstrated that the G20's maximum utility is, in crisis circumstances, as a forum that places all the principals around one table and can get a deal done *in extremis*. Once this crisis was addressed, the return to dissension began again, spurred by increased geopolitical tensions between the US and Russia.

The Russian presidency and G20 summit (5–6 September 2013) produced mixed results. Russia, which had been largely disinterested in the G20 process prior to 2013, found common goals sabotaged in part by unexpected political events, centred on the leaking of confidential documents by the whistleblower Edward Snowden, which sparked antagonistic warmed-up Cold War responses from President Putin and President Obama. As a result, public comity was noticeably absent in St. Petersburg.

Ongoing tensions and a major new one, Russia's annexation of Crimea and the ensuing war in Eastern Ukraine, handicapped the 2014 G20 summitry process under the able technocratic leadership of Australia (15–16 November 2014). Matters became so disputatious that President Putin walked out of the summit before the final declaration, leading observers to suggest that the summitry was now 'G19 plus 1'. At the geopolitical level, the G20 process in 2014 simply could not bridge fundamental philosophical, ideological and territorial disputes between a current and former superpower, the former a slowly declining hegemon, and the latter an oil-dependent autocratic kleptocracy, being eclipsed by rising powers, most notably China. Nonetheless, despite stormy diplomatic waters, Brisbane still delivered, with bilateral breakthroughs (on climate change), and with progress on further financial regulatory reforms, demonstrating that the G20 diplomatic process remained useful.

The Turkish presidency and G20 summit (Antalya, 15 November 2015) took place in an atmosphere of tension as hundreds of thousands of refugees and migrants sought to cross from North Africa through Turkey into Western Europe, and horrific coordinated terrorist attacks in Paris heightened security concerns. On the economic front, China was slowing, the Greek crisis continued to fester and the US economy grew modestly, but faster than the rest of the advanced world. Despite this, some diplomatic progress was seen – on tax policy coordination and, more importantly, on the IMF quota adjustment, which was finally secured, and preparations for the Paris COP21 meeting occupied many minds. The Turkish presidency was not a complete bust.

Much was expected from the Chinese presidency and summit (Hangzhou, 4–5 September 2016), and they did deliver. Most important was a last-minute deal on the sidelines before the summit itself commenced in which the US and China agreed to ratify the Paris Climate Agreement. China built upon this breakthrough in the G20 by tasking the central banking community led by China and the Bank of England to begin a new workstream on green finance. Further work on tax havens was also agreed. Geopolitical events in 2016 also meant leaders were looking to what would happen in 2016 and beyond.

Political earthquakes occurred in the UK and US – a surprise vote for Brexit in the UK in June of 2016, and indications that Donald Trump was rising in the polls, signalling a close election in the US. Leaders worried about the rise of populism and the possible threat to the rules and structures that underpinned globalisation and trade. They were right to be alarmed.

Donald Trump and America First

The 6 November 2016 unexpected electoral victory of Donald Trump upset the consensus diplomatic and economic narratives in the G20 process. The dominant G20 narrative, which stands fundamentally upon a continued defence of the global architecture of free trade and the rules-based system (hitherto backed by the US *and* its allies), was challenged by the new US president. President Trump was a populist nativist nationalist who opposed the 'globalists' (Trump, 2017, 2018, 2019), i.e. the very cabal of experts and technocrats who ran the G20 process and its architecture of cooperation and coordination. Henceforth, it would be America first and everyone else second. For America to win, others would have to lose. Consensus and cooperation were for wimps. And, indeed, G20 summits since the election of President Trump have all been circumscribed by a need to manage a suddenly more confrontational US and ensure the G20 processes continue even as opposition from the most powerful country in the leaders' forum became the new normal.

In the German G20 presidency and summit (Hamburg, 7–8 July 2017), US participants clashed with their erstwhile allies on multiple issues related to trade, migration and security, while outside the summit, anti-US and anti-globalisation protestors fought with the police. Communiqué compromises were fashioned – of a sort – with the US administration showing a new hard line on globalisation, trade and climate change. Relations between President Trump and Chancellor Merkel were strained; Germany's long and close alliance with the US was called into question. All G20 allies took note and adjusted expectations and the resulting summit outcomes downward.

The Argentine presidency and summit (Buenos Aires, 30 November 2018) was swamped by dynamics Argentina had no control or influence over. The presidency took place as the US commenced a trade war with China. Additional geopolitical tensions occurred over the Saudi murder of journalist Jamal Khashoggi in Istanbul, and Russian aggression against Ukraine in the Black Sea complicated matters. In this environment, Argentina could not play referee between the giant American Eagle and the Chinese Dragon, or diplomatically deal with other tensions and issues. Technical progress continued, slowly, below the G20 level, but the Buenos Aires summit was a bust. The Japanese presidency proved little better.

The Japan presidency and summit (Osaka, 28–29 June 2019) took place as the US-China trade war continued to rage and a dispute between Japan and Korea worsened. The geopolitical backdrop was especially stormy in 2019, with ongoing disputes between Europe and the US (on trade and climate) and with Russia (on UK and US election meddling and attempted assassinations in the former) undermining the prospects for effective summitry. Once again, technical progress on certain issues, including taxation of multinational corporations and on Financial Stability Board (FSB) workstreams, showed the efficacy of the ongoing discussions below the level of principals.

Overall, this third phase of the G20's evolution has cast a harsher light on global summitry as a reactive process requiring consensus amongst leaders who, in non-crisis, normal times, do not exhibit concord, but who instead pursue national geopolitical and economic objectives. This period demonstrated the limitation of summitry. Summits generally do not deliver as much when normality returns, or when disputes are simply too large amongst the principals. At that point, negotiators diverge over goals, and domestic interests reassert themselves, and thus win sets shrink. The US turned away from leadership of the forum and process, and this significantly affected G20 comity, consensus and diplomatic progress. A sudden health and economic crisis would emerge in 2020 highlighting the G20's political atrophy.

COVID-19 and G20 impotence

In early 2020 with the Saudi Arabian presidency underway the growing weakness of the G20 process was rudely exposed. In late 2019 the COVID-19 virus jumped from wild animals to humans in Wuhan, China, setting off a global pandemic, of a scale not seen since the flu pandemic of 1918. Within weeks China was in lockdown and by February and March the virus was ravaging Italy, France, Spain, the UK and the US. The world economy ground to a sudden stop. Tens of millions of people lost their jobs. The world plunged into a recession and stock markets fell by over 30 per cent. The response of the G20? A damp squib, with leaders committing to beating the virus, but making no additional commitments collectively, instead referencing the size of individual fiscal and monetary actions underway. Unlike in 2008–2009 there was no collective additional commitment to action. With the US president hostile to the G20 process and blaming China for the virus, this was not a surprise even as it was a disappointment and a failure. There was no room or willingness for coordinated collective action. The G20 was created to confront global economic crises – and this was the health and economic crisis of our lifetimes – and the leaders' forum barely registered its relevance as nation states rushed to save their populations and economies, separately, without coordination.

State authority remains ascendant

As Chapter 8 will discuss, while the G20 was unable to act when confronted by COVID-19, due to an absence of leadership from the US, and leaders' uncoordinated responses, the crisis demonstrated some of the same dynamics as seen in the 2008–2009 crisis. State authority and the power of central banks to act in defence of economic stability were reconfirmed. For when crisis strikes the selfish, atomised, terrified, frozen private sector, it can do little or nothing to return stability and address the crisis. Only states and their agents have that ability. The COVID-19 pandemic underscored this reality. The crisis forced all leaders to assert power over markets, their economies and peoples. The US triggered wartime powers to compel firms to make ventilators. Spain nationalised all private hospitals to secure the needed beds. The pandemic could only be fought with state power applied through coordinated health systems, national fiscal policies and monetary policies. The colossal scale of the crises wrought by COVID-19 upon the globe meant leaders (in the US, UK, Germany and elsewhere) rejected economic orthodoxies to an extent and breadth not seen in 2008–2009. A possibly lasting shift was forced by the heat of the crisis towards the state and away from neoliberal economic norms, not just regulatory positions as we saw in 2008–2009. This shift was made possible in part because populist leaders, including Mr Trump in the US and Mr Johnson in the UK, could abandon past creeds when faced by the pandemic. These leaders, not bound by traditional conservative beliefs, backed by different electoral coalitions, could go further in their response than past leaders might have done. The COVID-19 governmental response is paradoxical – a failure of collectively applied state power via the G20, but a significant meaningful assertion of additional national state power vis-à-vis markets when the pandemic struck us all. It should be no surprise that there appear to be few libertarians left when collective state power and authority is required to save all our lives and livelihoods. Reality dawns. State power and action is demanded and required.

Globalist technocrats still working below the radar

The discord seen in the G20 during phase three was not reflected to the same degree amongst central bankers and technocrats in the FSB, who continued their work, less affected by political disputes above them, since the technical-level narrative and policy consensus remained largely intact. The paradigm shift in worldview and regulatory approach signalled in 2008 and drawn out in 2009 continued to be constructed and strengthened by the FSB and standard-setting bodies in 2010 and beyond. Progress on financial reform and on building the new architecture was not stymied by diplomatic discord at the summit table. Work on agency-level financial regulatory reforms remained underway in phase three, closely coordinated and overseen by the FSB leadership, conducted by other standard-setting bodies and national agencies. However, the reforms already underway in this period faced more sustained criticism, with efforts by opponents of reform to chip away at the new regulatory standards and their application in each jurisdiction. Bankers, suffering from exceedingly short memories, commenced a counterattack, seeking to weaken new regulatory rules, country by country. By 2020, the financial community had rebounded on the back of below-zero-percent real interest rates supplied by the central banking community of the world, and the banks turned towards undermining regulatory action. For instance, in the US, there were successful efforts by lobbyists to stop or scale back key aspects of the Dodd-Frank Act. Leading voices in finance began to object publicly to the re-regulation, with some declaring, 'The period of remorse needs to be over' (Moore, 2011). In addition, in this third phase a return to dissension meant that some of the key policy goals were affected by diverging national policy stances and national positions.

New voices, with differing degrees of impact

This third period in G20 summitry also included an important increase in the profile of, and leadership responsibilities for, emerging-market countries, with mixed results. Some presidencies were more successful (Turkey and China) than others (Argentina). This is no surprise as effectiveness is affected by the relative economic power of the presidency state and external economic and geopolitical factors outside their control. The power dynamics meant advanced economy leaders' views were still central to the forum's effectiveness as a venue. When leading powers choose to oppose and obstruct, the consensus-based forum cannot compel action. Realising this, emerging countries would call for institutional reforms at the technical level, but the subsequent adjustments outlined in Brisbane signalled only minor changes to the current summitry and FSB processes.

The following sections discuss the varying successes and the growing disputes seen during this phase in the G20's maturation. It includes discussion of the overwhelmingly negative impact of the Trump presidency on the G20 process and the forum's effectiveness.

Toronto: stimulus or austerity?

In Toronto (26–27 June 2010), G20 leaders disagreed over progress on financial regulation and on the amount of economic stimulus that was still needed. As a result, the message that emerged from the Toronto summit was muddled. Toronto's narrative contradicted the pro-regulation, pro-stimulus message that had come from Pittsburgh only a few months earlier. Certain G20 leaders, including those from Canada and Australia, neither of which had suffered a financial crisis due to the conservative prudential supervision of their banking and housing sectors, had begun to view the ongoing US-European regulatory drive within the

G20 with some hostility. Canadian Prime Minister Harper warned against 'excessive, arbitrary or punitive regulation' of the financial sector (Guebert, 2010), and he was joined in his criticism by French president Sarkozy.

Splits emerged between surplus and deficit countries and between creditors and debtors. By 2010, the economies of the Republic of Korea and Germany were experiencing accelerating economic growth; Germany faced the prospect of bailing out the Eurozone. Leaders of both countries disagreed with talk of sustained stimulus and urged those countries with high current account deficits to rebalance their economies and commence austerity moves. In addition, the UK leadership changed in May 2010, and the country was suddenly a stalwart supporter of austerity as opposed to stimulus. Participants in the Toronto summit recall what a difference this made to the balance of the debate between Keynesians and those calling for austerity. The US was more isolated, still backed by France on the need for stimulus, but opposed by German Chancellor Angela Merkel and a victorious British Prime Minister David Cameron, who revelled in championing austerity and lecturing G20 participants. Meanwhile, China was managing the inflationary effects of their massive 2009 domestic stimulus. Needing to cool its economy, it remained deaf to complaints from the US on currency levels, imbalances and surpluses.

As a result of all these factors, at the Toronto summit, national domestic regulatory and economic preoccupations and concerns created splits amongst states over the issues still on the negotiating table and shrank the level-one and level-two win sets. The Canadians tried to balance disparate and conflicting goals, and the declaration called for strong, sustainable, and balanced growth, relying also on 'growth friendly' fiscal consolidation, with a goal of halving deficits by 2013 (G20, 2010a, p. 2). The declaration was a slightly 'peculiar message' which 'overplayed it a little on consolidation', in the view of some (Mackintosh, 2012, 17, p. 11), evidence of the growing divergence between debtor and surplus states, and it was an exercise in the triumph of hope over actionable policy prescription.

Given the disagreements over exit strategies, austerity and rebalancing growth, any progress in Toronto was destined to be incremental. The Toronto summit moved the financial reform agenda gradually forward, but the other results were underwhelming. The summit highlighted national differences, not commonalities. Coordinating exit strategies – deciding on when stimulus should halt and austerity should start – was a disjointed, and by its nature, a state-by-state, matter. The difficult perennial nature of the remaining issues at hand, in particular, global imbalances and currency values, meant it was too much to expect continued breakthroughs. Progress was limited because we had got 'out of the lifeboat mentality of the crisis' (Mackintosh, 2012, 22, p. 16). Moreover, not every summit could announce major achievements, and a diminished sense of crisis and 'summit fatigue' was by now setting in (Dong-Hwi, 2010). If Toronto sent mixed messages on stimulus versus austerity and imbalances, the Seoul summit saw much louder disputes as the 'G2', i.e. China and the US, clashed head-on over imbalances.

Seoul and imbalances – the G20 has no solution

The Government of the Republic of Korea, the first emerging-country presidency of the G20 process, strove to succeed where the Canadians had failed. The Korean presidency had to referee a dispute between the declining hegemon (the US) and the rising power (China), made more complex because of electoral matters on the one hand and internal disputes within the leadership on the other. A single issue dominated the summit debates in Seoul: a dispute between key G20 members, and in particular the US and China, over the causes of and cures for global imbalances and currency mismatches. This clash created an impasse. US Treasury Secretary Timothy Geithner wanted targets for maximum permitted surpluses and deficits and for China to allow its currency to appreciate more rapidly. His proposals echoed previous international economic disputes, and historical comparisons continued to resonate when the two nation's ministers clashed.

The Seoul summit was not the first time a deficit-burdened US administration sought an accord aimed at managing imbalances, but this time it was China, not Japan, that was the culprit. In the 1980s, the Reagan administration proposed currency targets, with a similar goal. On that occasion, the US and Japan ultimately signed the Plaza Accord, which managed a devaluation of the dollar. But the deal failed to significantly alter the US trade deficit with Japan, which still persists today (Gilpin, 1987, p. 163). Geithner's attack on China was reflective of short-term political considerations, but it also echoed historic phenomena which remain unresolved. The 'currency war' that broke out at the Seoul summit reflected different national economic narratives.

China's leaders rejected the US imbalances narrative. Opposition to a cap on mercantilist growth strategies also came from other major export-oriented, surplus-country leaderships, including Germany and Brazil. They accused the US of its own currency manipulation and of embarking on a managed devaluation of the dollar, and they rejected calls for numerical targets for surplus and deficits. British Prime Minister Cameron joined in, chastising the US and opining that 'I am not one, and Germany is not one, who says growth and fiscal consolidation are contradictory' (Chen, Stolberg, and Sanger, 2010, p. 1).

The Korean presidency found it impossible to negotiate a compromise between fundamentally opposing positions. This meant that no substantive progress was possible. In the G20 context, a lack of a common narrative means no progress. It therefore led to a weak declaration. The Seoul Declaration committed G20 leaders to simply monitoring matters, via an FSB-IMF Mutual Assessment Process (G20, 2010b). In this manner, leaders kicked the imbalances can down the road. Only on development did Seoul open up a new area for G20 work, and they sought to highlight that as a success.

Summit disunity – but real progress in the regulatory sphere

Notwithstanding the rancour over exit strategies, imbalances, currency values and global macroeconomic disputes that mushroomed in the period encompassing the

Toronto and Seoul summits, regulatory reform measures continued. Of particular note were breakthroughs on bank regulation, capital and IMF reforms.

Financial reform: In Seoul in 2010, G20 leaders agreed on the Basel III Accord, which had been pushed forward by work done in Toronto and which was negotiated by the FSB and the Basel Committee on Banking Supervision in a few months, not years. As Chapter 6 will demonstrate, this single multifaceted deal, coordinated and driven by the FSB expert technocratic epistemic community, constituted evidence of a third-order paradigm shift in the regulation and supervision of global financial markets and of systemically important banks (Hall, 1993, p. 283).

G20 leaders at Seoul signed off on a deal fashioned by a central bank community led by hawks who agreed on a cohesive new macroprudential policy paradigm and narrative. G20 political leaders backed a deal over which they had essentially no input, since they were presented with a fully formed agreement in Seoul. This triumph of technocrats caused a backlash, as 'finance ministry deputies were really fed up, understandably' (Mackintosh, 2011, 7, p. 7). And this led them to conclude, going forward, that 'you cannot have something [the FSB] which is only a gathering of central bankers determining' parameters of such importance (Mackintosh, 2012, 17, p. 15). These complaints would lead to changes in the FSB in the future.

IMF reform: In 2010, leaders agreed to double quotas from 238.4 billion SDRs to 476.8 billion SDRs, equivalent to US$750 billion. The G20 was significantly recapitalising the IMF as agreed on at earlier summits. Leaders also agreed to voting reforms, and to an eventual shift of over 6 per cent of quota shares from overrepresented to underrepresented member countries, in particular moving the quotas to dynamic emerging economies and developing countries. The reforms and adjustments (when finally adopted in 2015) would result in China's quota and its voting power in the Executive Board doubling to over 6 per cent, approximately 40 per cent of the US quota level (of 16.5 per cent, in line with China's economic position globally). This would make China the third-largest member country in the IMF. In addition, three other major emerging economies – Brazil, India and Russia – would also be pushed into the top 10 shareholders in the IMF (IMF, 2011).

In this deal, the US got what it wanted – a rebalancing away from Europe and a recommitment of emerging states to the institution. The quota reforms were designed to draw rising powers into a recommitment to the IMF, which needed rejuvenation and renewed relevancy. The cash injections and reforms could eventually result in slow evolutionary change and could contain disputes within the existing institutional system. However, the failure to complete the changes promptly would force China to create a new institution to pursue its geopolitical goals – the Asian Infrastructure Investment Bank.

Seoul showed that even as disputes on outstanding irresolvable macroeconomic and fiscal matters were publicly aired and became much more marked, regulatory and reform processes continued successfully. This underscores that the paradigm shift observed – in worldview, policy reforms and prescriptions – was predominantly a supervisory and regulatory community-led shift. Effective policy response is limited to those areas over which these individuals collectively recognised critical anomalies, the strength of the central banking community charged with policy design and implementation and the degree to which a strong policy consensus existed as to action (see Figure 1.2). This broad theme and fundamental thrust of the book will be developed further in Chapters 5 and 6, on the FSB creation and its policy output.

The Seoul G20 Summit saw strident, nationally sparked arguments and disputes over the functioning of the international monetary non-system coupled to real progress, led by the FSB central banking epistemic community, towards the existing agreed regulatory reform goals. On global macroeconomic matters, however, consensus was a thing of the past. It had become every country for itself.

Former UK government minister Mark Malloch-Brown identified the emergence 'of a new pecking order' in which the US plays a more diminished role as China rises (Malloch-Brown, 2010). That rise, he added, would not be easy, and the G20 risks 'being reduced to the sum of its feuding parts as structural trade imbalances, currency wars and very different views of each other's relative economic prospects drive stakes into the enterprise' (Malloch-Brown, 2010). Larry Summers, then chairman of the US National Economic Council, took a slightly different view, noting that 'the world is more divided today than it was in London because nations not facing the prospect of a depression have that luxury' (Sanger, 2010). It was clear that the 'fellowship of the lifeboat' was gone, replaced by conflict (Vestergaard and Wade, 2010). Not everyone was giving up on the G20. Turkish economist and politician Kemal Dervis argued that the IMF-led monitoring of imbalances was major notwithstanding the lack of hard targets, maintaining that the process could yet succeed and that we should give it a chance to work (Dervis, 2010).

In 2010, the G20 reached the outer limits of the new policy consensus paradigm. This was partially balanced by continued technical success in actual regulatory policy making. National governments disagreed over exit speeds and over stimulus versus austerity. Leaders, especially but not only the US and China, playing to domestic interests and electoral and economic demands, clashed loudly over insoluble global macroeconomic differences and goals. These thorny issues are not new and they were not amenable to compromise and solution, because the G20 states' national narratives of causes and solutions clash and diverge.

Numerous actors and policy makers recognise the international monetary system was and is dysfunctional. As Tommaso Padoa-Schioppa noted, 'Those eager to envisage the post-crisis era in constructive terms need to promote the reconstruction of a fully fledged international monetary order' (Padoa-Schioppa, 2010a, p. 8). But periodic reform proposals have led nowhere (Palais Royale Initiative, 2011). The policy consensus and narrative does not extend that far. Neither level-one nor level-two win sets exist in this policy space. This is not the end of World War II; power is much more diffuse now (Cohen, 2008) and the US hegemon weaker, even if still first among equals.

In 2010, and since then, the policy consensus was confined to financial regulatory reform matters, where it was possible to discern the many fingerprints of the

Western central banking community on the G20 declarations and agenda, since it was progressively crafted and implemented in this period by those same individuals and their agencies. While public discord is the overriding acoustic note heard at both Toronto and Seoul, behind the scenes the regulators continued their work, agreeing to deals that could strengthen the system and potentially also the nature of the institutional politics in the IMF in favour of the rising emerging powers in the future. This public divergence on global macroeconomic issues would be interrupted by the crisis in the Eurozone in 2011 and 2012.

Cannes and Los Cabos: dealing with the Eurozone crisis

In 2011 and 2012, divergences amongst G20 leaders continued, but events in the Eurozone forced the actors to confront this latest manifestation of the financial crisis. Both summits focused almost exclusively on the Eurozone crisis, proving the ongoing utility of the G20 as *the* dominant global crisis management diplomatic forum.

Greece and the Eurozone

The French G20 presidency, despite an early desire to paint grand landscapes of the future global international monetary system, focused squarely on the crisis in Greece and the steps necessary to arrest the threat of a disorderly default in the Eurozone and possible contagion. But at this stage, the US and Europeans were unwilling to do a deal offered by emerging-country leaders.

Faced with the Greek and Eurozone crises, emerging countries offered to further increase SDR commitments at the IMF as a backstop. But other leaders baulked. US officials argued there was no need for more IMF resources – that the EU had the funds and could solve its own problems (Blackden, 2012). This was correct. It was an internal political and fiscal matter – whether Germany would pay to save the Eurozone; but it was more complex than that. The US resisted a further change in SDR quotas and votes that would have come with yet more emerging-market cash, and US officials knew they could not get further financing from Congress. Europeans did not wish to deal with more changes in the balance of power at the IMF, which would also diminish their votes and voice. The end result was that money was on the table from emerging countries but no deal on further finances for the IMF was reached at Cannes. A full deal would have to wait.

The G20 Cannes Declaration reflected the pressure of events in Greece, and there was a failure to advance on other fronts. On global macro issues, there were no major breakthroughs on the monitoring of imbalances, but there was some modest progress on the metrics of the monitoring process (G20, 2011). Language on commodities, capital flows and the international monetary system was included, but the tone was weak and unspecific, as were statements on a burgeoning list of issues from climate change, to the marine environment, to social cohesion, to the stone-dead global trade round. Sarkozy had reached for much at the outset and ended up with a declarative anodyne outcome which failed to live up to his hopes. It amounted to 'nice words, but no big deal' (Mackintosh, 2012, 33, p. 3). But, again, as in Seoul, the work of the central bankers was visible and additive to the new normal and new paradigm they were constructing, and under French leadership, the G20 did make progress on five architectural matters of future import.

First, leaders determined there would be no G20 secretariat. The G20 would continue to be informal and driven by the chairing country and national sherpas. Finance ministers saw this as a positive, because it retained the direct commitment by national leaders and ministers who would staff and act as negotiators on summit texts, deals and outcomes. National officials saw the rejection of formalisation as preserving the forum's flexibility and safeguarding its usefulness to political leaders while preserving state control over the process.

Second, leaders agreed there would be a troika of immediate past, current and future G20 presidents to enhance coordination and smooth transition from one country to another. This is a new and fitful construct, in that the current president and future presidency both tend to resist sharing information about their drafting and plans. This was designed to gradually improve continuity and assist those states less able to host the talks and the meetings that are needed around each summit. European fingerprints can be seen; this is practically the same format as has historically operated within the European Council.

Third, leaders agreed to the establishment of the FSB on an enduring organisational footing (G20, 2011). So, even as G20 leaders rejected greater formalisation and institutionalisation of their own ad hoc forum, they agreed on strengthening the technical coordinating body central to cement success on financial reform. This was a clear indication of the G20 leaders' support of the board. It also reflected the continuing impact of the central banking community.

Fourth, Cannes saw two institutional additions to the detailed structure of the financial reform architecture. Finance ministries, angry at being presented with the Basel III Accord as a fait accompli, secured limited representation on the Steering Committee of the FSB. And leaders backed the creation of a Bilateral Complaints Handling Process (FSB, 2012) to address claims of breach of agreed FSB compensation principles. Both were evidence of institution building by the G20 and central banking expert community, even as public disputes were seen in Cannes.

Fifth, Cannes marked the G20 leadership handover to non-core states. In Cannes, leaders agreed that, going forward, future summits would be led by Mexico in 2012, Russia in 2013, Australia in 2014 and Turkey in 2015. After 2015, leadership of the G20 would be chosen from rotating regional groups, starting with the Asian grouping comprising China, Indonesia, Japan and Korea (G20, 2011). Thus, Cannes signalled emerging countries would begin to take the lead in the G20. European and North American states would step back, providing an opportunity for emerging-market leadership and recognition of changing state power dynamics.

Cannes was a failure if evaluated on Sarkozy's ambitious goals, few of which he achieved. The summit also failed to secure a deal on the Eurozone, although it came close to doing so. However, leaders took a series of institutional decisions that solidified state control over G20 summitry, simultaneously strengthened the institutional foundation of the FSB and its dispute settlement procedures and laid out the future role of emerging markets. In the end, the Cannes outcome was mixed to positive.

Finally, a firewall

Mexico took over the presidency of the G20 in 2012 but confronted the same fundamental problem as the French: the need to halt the Eurozone market panic and restore some calm in markets to allow time for the solution of the troubles in the Eurozone. Ultimately, as a junior partner, the Mexican G20 presidency could do little but try and referee disputes amongst the principal G20 powers as they grappled with the Eurozone panic. Given that reality, 'they did a good job managing the cards they had been dealt' (Mackintosh, 2012, 33, p. 19).

In hurried negotiations that built upon an outlined deal formulated earlier at the April 2012 spring meeting of the IMF, the US argued that Europe must deal with its own crisis; they had the resources and they should act first (Blackden, 2012). At that point, the administration had no room domestically and could not provide more IMF funding; US negotiators had no negotiating space. US leaders wanted a deal, but they could not act because of opposition from level-two actors (i.e. Congress). Emerging-market leaders were again willing to fund a firewall, but Europeans opposed additional finance from emerging countries if the cost was quotas and voice reductions in the IMF. The US also opposed any further shrinkage of its voting power. Emerging countries, however, could not be excessively generous without changes in quotas and votes to assuage their own voters, who had no interest in bailing out the rich and foolish of the West.

Ultimately, a deal was forced by the urgency of events in Los Cabos. The threat of a default in Greece cascading into Spain and Italy focused minds. G20 leaders agreed on a massive US$461 billion package of additional bilateral funds. This was a success for both the G20 and IMF. Cash came from Europe (US$200 billion-plus) as exceptional bilateral financing and from emerging and other economies, especially Japan. It had the Europeans self-finance their bailout with the fig leaf of a potential IMF program for ailing economics, without any further reforms of IMF governance, thus dodging immediate fights over governance. On balance, in Los Cabos, the crisis made the G20 agree on a workable deal with a large additional resource boost.

Once again, this was not the only area of progress. Just as in Cannes, central bank technicians were busy in the FSB, building their structures and sending them to the G20 for their imprimatur. Two areas are worth brief comment. First, the FSB Charter was further clarified and the internal structure enhanced and detailed. Second, the FSB was put on a solid financial footing with five years of financing agreed to by the Bank for International Settlement (BIS), avoiding the need to return to the G20 states every time they required resources. These incremental but important first-order changes underscored how influential the FSB's central banking backers remained as the leaders, agenda setter, and direct financiers of the key coordinating forum and community within the global financial architecture.

St. Petersburg – Russian leadership and a mixed outcome

Russia's presidency of the G20 was overshadowed by a diplomatic dispute between the host and the US, demonstrating that if leading powers have fundamental disagreements over diplomatic goals, progress can be overshadowed or undermined. In the run-up to and during the summit President Putin and President Obama clashed over the fate of WikiLeaks whistleblower Edward Snowden, who was given temporary asylum by Putin, who rejected demands from Obama to hand Snowden over to face justice (i.e. a life sentence) in US gaol. The rhetoric warmed the hearts of cold warriors, with Obama accusing Putin of having a 'cold war mentality' (*The Moscow Times*, 2013). Perhaps so, but observers saw this development as a 'humiliating, wounding rebuff to the US' (*The Guardian*, 2013). Yet despite this very public dispute, some progress was made, albeit hidden by the headline news.

This was seen, in particular, in the summit discussions on aspects of climate change, on tackling tax havens and tax avoidance by multinational companies and the stress on the need for progress on a trade facilitation deal via the World Trade Organization (WTO) with leading emerging economies (G20, 2013). In this limited sense, Putin's G20 leadership was modestly successful, a reasonable outcome from a leader whose lack of engagement in previous G20 summits was often noted by other participants.

Of most significance from a financial and regulatory standpoint, the summit saw national leaders, facing fiscal and resource constraints, turn to taxation, with an emphasis on tax avoidance and anticorruption, and money laundering. Tax avoidance is damaging to larger advanced countries, which see their tax resources negatively affected by Apple, GE, Starbucks, and thousands of other firms that avoid taxation in their home countries through legal but ethically dubious methods, in connivance with tax havens like Ireland, Luxembourg and others. In this shift, the G20 committed to establishing global standards on tax data sharing as a first step.

Also in St. Petersburg, emerging and developing countries sought greater institutional clout within the FSB, demanding consultation on their roles, evidence of discontent at the technical community level, primarily from those who now understood that all were equal but some were more equal than others (Orwell, 1946). The G20 leaders agreed to report back on FSB procedural issues by Brisbane.

Thus, although the host and the US clashed vocally and publicly, the summit still allowed modest steps forward on a particularly difficult aspect of financial regulation. If the Russian presidency and St. Petersburg summit was publicly disputative, this would prove to be nothing compared to the discord between Russia and other G20 leaders at the Brisbane summit in 2014.

'G19 plus 1' in Brisbane

Australia's presidency was meant to be smoother, with some changes in emphasis, and more technocratic, i.e. a focus on deliverable goals, and a reduction in the number of areas coming under the G20 process. The brevity of the summit communiqué reflected this desire. But other foreign policy matters dominated much of the deliberations. In 2014, President Putin clashed with the West over a political and military crisis in Ukraine. Putin had invaded and annexed Crimea, a historically Russian region of Ukraine (King, 2013), leading to almost universal condemnation from G20 states. Throughout the year, the crisis deepened as Putin militarily backed an insurgency in Eastern Ukraine, and Russian-backed rebels allegedly shot down an Air Malaysia commercial airplane. In response, the US and Europe enacted tough economic and financial sanctions against Putin's closest domestic allies and closed off the Western financial system to Russia's largest banks, moves that, coupled to a rapid decline in global oil prices, sent Russia into recession late in 2014.

This rising diplomatic dispute between Russia and the West was clearly visible at the summit, with US, Japanese, Australian, UK, and Canadian leaders all excoriating Putin's actions in Ukraine (*The Telegraph*, 2014). German Chancellor Merkel, Putin's closest 'ally', sought to secure movement from Putin through a late-night, four-hour bilateral meeting, but it failed to deliver, and Merkel then moved towards other G20 leaders, increasing her own criticism of Putin. Ultimately, Putin could take no more attacks and left the summit before the issuance of the final declaration, leading some to conclude the summitry now really was 'G19 plus 1', since Russia's isolation was so stark. Although Russian actions in Crimea and Eastern Ukraine overshadowed other goals, they did not stop action in three other key areas.

Brisbane provided the opportunity for President Obama to close in on a bilateral climate change deal between the US and China. In the deal, both countries agreed to numerical reductions in CO_2 emissions by set dates (The White House, 2014). Although not stringent enough for critics, the deal showed the continued utility of the G20 summit process, it trumped Australian Prime Minister Abbott's efforts to keep climate change off the G20 agenda, and it boosted the prospects for multilateral International Climate Change Partnership (ICCP) talks in 2014 and 2015.

At the technical level of financial reform, shepherded by the FSB leadership, the G20 in Brisbane continued to support the reassertion of state power over market authority. The G20 summit backed FSB Chair Mark Carney as he sought to buttress the financial reform architecture via a proposed new standard for total loss-absorbing capacity (TLAC), which would require the largest banks in the world to issue large amounts of convertible debt that could be used to bail out, restructure or close failing big banks in the future. Total proposed capital required (Basel III and TLAC) was 20 per cent.

Tension between the states' dominant leaders in the FSB and emerging-country voices saw a compromise fashioned where both sides 'won' some concessions on further institutionalisation. Calls for an IMF-style 'constituency' representation in the FSB plenary were rejected. As a concession, the standard-setting bodies agreed to downgrade their voting members from two to one to increase the number of full members from the five emerging powers representatives in the plenary. Thus, the leading powers resisted the ossification of their flexible process, while acquiescing to adjustments in representation. Under Australian leadership, TLAC and the institutional adjustments show the lead community (advanced and emerging) still building on the new normal, in policies and institutionally, seven years into the process. This is what we should expect if the paradigm is becoming more durable over time – further first- and high second-order changes to the regulatory architecture.

In Brisbane the G20 delivered as a venue for important bilateral deal making. And we saw its utility as an ongoing process, despite considerable diplomatic disputes. So while unfolding events in Ukraine soured the tone at the top, the technocratic central banking community continued its work behind the scenes, shielded from the rancour over geopolitical developments above them.

Migrants and terrorism eclipse economic worries

Turkish leadership of the G20 (Antalya, 15–16 November 2015) was bedevilled with geopolitical and serious security developments. Huge numbers of migrants and refugees were floating across the Mediterranean, landing in Italy and Greece. In 2015, 1.3 million refugees sought asylum in the European Union (Pew, 2015), a much higher number than seen at the height of the 1992 events around the collapse of the Soviet Union and Warsaw Pact. A large number of those refugees sought to transit through Turkey. Most hoped to get to Western Europe, and to Germany, after German Chancellor Angela Merkel pledged an open-door policy to take most of those refugees, while her counterparts baulked (*The Atlantic*, 2015). Domestic politics in G20 countries was affected and major terrorist attacks heightened the fear of 'the other' amongst local populations. On 13 November 2015, three groups of Islamic State terrorists launched six attacks in Paris, targeting the Stadium of Paris; cafes and restaurants; and most horrifically, the concert in the Bataclan theatre. The attacks killed 130 people and wounded 413. Terrorism and the response dominated the summit two days later, and while G20 leaders adopted the usual prebaked communiqué and additional declaration on fighting terrorism, leaders focused understandably on sending a common message on the attacks.

Leaders in 2015 confronted different dynamics depending on where they sat. In America, the economy was outperforming other major G20 countries. This contrasted with a relative slowdown in China and continued weak lacklustre growth in the European Union. Leaders recognised as much, admitting 'economic growth is uneven and continues to fall short of our expectations, despite the positive outlook in some major economies' (G20, 2015, p. 1). Leaders continued to commit to achieving a 2 per cent growth target overall, but few expected it to happen. Once again little actual consensus on economic policy was seen.

At the multilateral level, 2015 also saw the US Congress finally legislate for the quota and voice adjustments agreed to in 2009. But this final progress came too late to assuage China, which had helped bail out the world economy in 2008–2009 only to have the US refuse to enact the IMF reforms. China could not wait and launched a competing institution in 2015, the Asian Infrastructure Investment Bank (see Box 4.1).

Box 4.1 Creating the AIIB: America's loss and China's gain

The six-and-a-half-year delay between the G20 agreeing to IMF voice and vote reforms and the US Congress reluctantly acquiescing in December 2015 forced China to look elsewhere during that period to exert its growing influence. It did so by announcing an institutional innovation: the creation of the Asian Infrastructure Investment Bank (AIIB) in October 2013.

Creation of the AIIB was a huge geopolitical victory for China. It had 22 founding state members and US$50 billion in funding committed at the outset. By 2020, that number had risen to 75 members and 26 further prospective members from across the globe. Callable capital stood at US$99 billion in 2019 (AIIB, 2019).

Practically all America's allies have joined as members. This was a major embarrassment and loss of prestige to the US (and for other international financial institutions). American congressional short-sightedness and unwillingness to pass the IMF reforms (changes that cost them nothing in terms of power or money), resulted in a dilution of America's influence and a strengthening of China's hand internationally. It was an entirely self-inflicted own goal.

The AIIB is based in Beijing and modelled on the World Bank (and led by many former World Bank staff). Unlike the IMF or World Bank, it does not have a resident Executive Board; this allows the president of the AIIB and his or her staff much greater room for daily decision making unencumbered by micromanagement by shareholders.

The creation of the AIIB demonstrates that other leading powers will not wait forever for America to lead and adhere to its agreements. When America fails to live up to its commitments, states will work around that failure. (See Chapter 7 on the creation of the Network for Greening the Financial System, for another example of this dynamic.)

Note: This text box draws on Mackintosh (2016).

As in past G20 processes and summitry, under the Turkish presidency a technocratic consensus was sustained below the level of G20 leaders. Additional progress was made on Base Erosion and Profit Shifting, a workstream designed by the Organisation for Economic Co-operation and Development to address the aggressive accountancy practices of major corporations that seek to pay as little tax as possible in the major jurisdictions in which they do almost all their business. Progress was seen with agreement of principles for implementation of TLAC (FSB, 2015). Work was also underway on parallel requirements for globally systemically important insurers by standard-setting bodies below the FSB.

Once again, G20 leaders, and in particular, central bankers and their colleagues in the regulatory superstructure below the G20 continued work, to a degree unaffected by the high-level concerns over security and geopolitics. These areas of modest progress show the interlinked multilevel G20 process delivering. As in the past, endorsement by the G20 provided downward pressure for continued engagement, and the technocratic consensus supported a workstream providing policy-specific actionable results for G20 signature in key areas.

China – a climate change deal as populist anger at elites rises

China sought to use the G20 presidency to cement its leadership role as the second-largest economy in the world and to underscore that geopolitical influence and power were shifting towards Asia, and towards China, in particular. The message: Any deal worth doing had to have China's imprimatur. Climate change was the clearest example of this new reality on display (BBC, 2016). President Barack Obama and President Xi Jinping used the eve of the summit to strike a bilateral deal on climate change that paved the way for a successful COP21 meeting in Paris and the ratification of the Paris Climate Agreement. President Obama heralded the deal: 'Where there is a will and there is a vision and where countries like China and the United States are prepared to show leadership and to lead by example, it is possible for us to create a world that is more secure, more prosperous and more free than the one that was left for us'. President Xi replied: 'Our response to climate change bears on the future of our people and the well-being of mankind' (*The Guardian*, 2016). This development, months in the making, was widely viewed as a major breakthrough – the G20 working as it should – a venue to strike the most difficult deals face-to-face when confronted with a crisis. But a hostile Republican-dominated Congress in the US, angry at being kept out of the process, vowed to revisit the matter.

China's leadership of the G20 occurred at an important political juncture, or tipping point. Its leadership coincided with the 23 June 2016 Brexit referendum result that shook the European establishment and global markets, signalling that populist, nationalist, anti-globalist, anti-technocrat anger was on the upswing. The summit itself took place as the Republican candidate for president, Donald J. Trump, closed the gap with his rival, Hillary Clinton. Populism appeared to be rising, and the elites present in Hangzhou were a main target.

In response, summit leaders took the opportunity to reaffirm their commitment to norms and rules of the global system, declaring a 'Hangzhou Consensus' on integration, openness and inclusiveness. Leaders made sure to 'reiterate our opposition to protectionism on trade and investment in all its forms' while also committing to strengthening policy coordination, to achieve growth targets and financial and regulatory goals (G20, 2016). The communiqué underscored the need to complete implementation of Basel III, TLAC standards, international tax coordination (i.e. Base Erosion and Profit Shifting) and other regulatory changes designed to strengthen the system against future risks. The central bank technocratic community was still at work in the FSB and in the standard-setting bodies. Hindsight is always 20/20. Reading the 2016 Hangzhou communiqué you can sense leaders' growing alarm at populism and its possible implications for coordination and cooperation in the years ahead. Those concerns would prove well founded only weeks later, with a US presidential election result that would go on to materially affect all subsequent G20 summits and test the robustness of the global architecture.

Trump and the end of Pax Americana

> 'What we see today is beginning to look like the world after the first world war about 100 years ago, in which none of the leading nations pulled together and we in the US rejected the idea of the League of Nations'.
>
> (Stavridis in the *Financial Times*, 2017b)

Donald J. Trump's election as president of the United States on 6 November 2016 fundamentally changed the policy-making, political, and diplomatic calculus globally, for all G20 leaders. A populist, nationalist, nativist, anti-globalisation, anti-elite president was elected by angry, left-behind, economically stressed voters who felt they were becoming strangers in their own land (Hoschild, 2016). President Trump's ideological views echoed past populist rhetoric, but they were shocking, nonetheless. We were witnessing the end of Pax Americana; the end of a generally benign US hegemony; the end of US support for a global system created by America and its allies after the Second World War. As Thomas Wright observes, 'Trump seeks nothing less than ending the US-led liberal order' (Wright, 2016). The election of Trump took international diplomacy dangerously back to the future, as James Stavridis warns. The implications for the efficacy of leaders' forum would be significant.

G20 leaders would spend the next four years grappling with a hegemon increasingly at odds with the global system which it had created. The G20 allies would find the US opposing norms, tenets, rules and systems that all previous presidents since the Second World War had supported. (Chapter 5 presents a detailed analysis of the broad impact of Trumpism on the global architecture.)

G20 summits from 2017 on have been characterised by US hostility and a rearguard action by other G20 leaders who sought to sustain the existing G20 process despite this disjunctive break from established norms by the US. As in the past, gradual progress would continue to be made at the technical FSB (and standard-setting body) level, but the G20's effectiveness as a forum would be hamstrung by an American president unwilling to engage, unwilling to compromise and unwilling to hear advice from other leaders.

G20 summitry since 2016 has been a diplomatic dance in which America's allies and competitors seek to grapple with the end of American institutional consensual collaborative leadership and its replacement with an oppositional, mercantilist, winner-takes-all approach to diplomacy. Deal making is not, for this president and White House, about seeking common ground. For the president to win, others must lose. If others appear to have done well, then *ipso facto* Mr Trump has done poorly. In this environment, G20 summitry became an exercise in damage containment, i.e. an attempt to minimise the damage the US administration could do to the forum and its processes.

The 2017 German presidency felt the first effects of Trumpian non-leadership. Tensions rose over trade, migration, security and climate change. This was seen in a US refusal to sign a statement that reaffirmed G20 opposition to 'all forms of protectionism' (*Financial Times*, 2017a). An angry US president indicated he thought Germany was winning on trade; German Chancellor Merkel responded, to no avail. The summitry in 2017 showed the rift between President Trump and Chancellor Merkel (Reuters, 2017). The German chancellor lamented, 'The times in which we could fully count on others are somewhat over, as I have experienced in the past few days. . . . We Europeans truly have to take our fate into our own hands' (NPR, 2019). On the US plan to exit from the Paris Climate Agreement, Merkel was similarly blunt: 'Unfortunately – and I deplore this – the United States of America left the climate agreement' (CBS, 2017). Germany was joined by almost all other major G20 leaders in deploring the US stance on the Paris Agreement. G20 leaders tried to get through the summit, and where possible, work around President Trump. An EU diplomat in the milieu responded acidly, 'The outcome is good. . . . We have a G20 communiqué not a G19 communiqué' (*Financial Times*, 2017b).

The 2018 Argentine presidency was affected by three significant external geopolitical factors and tensions over which it had no control. First, by 2018 the US was in the midst of a trade war with China, with tariff barriers rising on both sides, resulting in an increase in global policy and economic uncertainty. Second, the murder of Saudi journalist Jamal Khashoggi in the Saudi Consulate in Istanbul put the G20 under pressure to strongly rebuke one of its leaders. And third, Russian seizure of Ukrainian vessels in the Black Sea strained relations, with President Trump cancelling a bilateral meeting with President Putin as a result. The final Buenos Aires communiqué reflected the need for diplomatic flexibility, with carve outs and statements required by the US on climate change and trade rules. In the latter case, the G20 agreed to look at reforming the WTO, a nod to US complaints of unfairness, despite other G20 leaders disagreeing with this characterisation (G20, 2018).

During the Japanese presidency in 2019, G20 leaders sought to avoid and manage ongoing conflicts. The US-China trade dispute was still underway, with significant negative effects being seen (particularly in the export powers of Japan and Germany). The draft Osaka communiqué went so far as to completely drop a reference to climate change in deference to the US, but a reference to the Paris Agreement was reinserted before its signature (*The Guardian*, 2019). Overall, the Japanese had reason to be disappointed. They had done much to support the creation of the G20 and had supported the stimulus necessary to re-energise the global economy in 2008 and since. But ten years on, with the US president in a combative mood and the Japanese unable to control the agenda, they were unable to wrest success out of discord.

COVID-19 and the absence of American leadership

The 2019–2020 COVID-19 pandemic further illuminated the weakness of the G20 process in the Trump era. The health and economic crisis that unfolded rapidly in 2020 was not met by a coordinated response at the G20 level. To be sure massive stimulus fiscal and monetary actions were taken by individual nations. But the G20 proved unable to respond effectively collectively in this most severe interlinked global crisis in over a hundred years. No additional funds were made available for international organisations and interventions. Could US leadership have made a difference? Perhaps. It certainly would have made it a possibility rather than a dead end. China individually stepped in to assist other states, contrasting its willingness to lead with American unproductive accusations and national failures, by supporting the Italian government with massive shipments of masks and ventilators, even as China dealt with its own massive challenges. Confronting a global health and economic nightmare, the G20 forum did not deliver. But central bankers used the levers they had to a greater extent than in 2008–2009.

The pandemic prompted the central banking community, led by the US central bank, to take extraordinary measures, once again demonstrating the continuing strength of this key community and the important role of American leadership for the global financial system in which the US dollar is still the main medium of exchange. Chapter 8 analyses the COVID-19 response by the G20, states and central banks more fully.

Operating in an unfortunate Trumpian reality

In conclusion, the Trump presidency and US administration's shift in priorities on trade, economics, climate and other topics has adversely affected G20 summitry, causing increasing disputes rather than progress on (no longer) common problems. The summitry process could only seek to avoid and accommodate or agree to disagree. G20 consensus was a thing of the past. Summit discussions now resulted in carve-outs in place of US leadership and agreement with its allies.

Fortunately for supporters of the architecture and the re-regulatory consensus that formed after 2008, the central banking technocrats and their supporters in G20 governments were able to defend the progress made and continue gradual work as arguments raged at the summits. The FSB and their institutional allies continued to focus on Basel III implementation and monitoring. Further steps were taken on related financial stability: on too big to fail, on TLAC implementation, on central clearing of derivatives, on anti-money laundering and on the tax treatment of the earnings of multinational corporations. Beneath the G20, the FSB continued its coordinating and cooperative function. The strength it had built up prior to 2017 was not fundamentally undermined by the shock of the change in

US leadership. To be sure, changes in US leadership figures in central banking did have some effect. But the impacts were lessened by the independence of those actors and the strength of the narrative dominant community. Institutional innovation was still being seen, and FSB members' connections and commitments to the existing global financial architecture remained.

Watching a paradigm shift take place

The creation and evolution of the G20 since 2008 was marked by a narrative and paradigmatic shift in worldview in regulatory policy objectives, and more gradually, actual outcomes from 2008 and continuing more than a decade later. First, leaders fought over and began to construct a new worldview in 2008–2009 which rejected certain laissez-faire neoliberal truths and self-regulatory tropes. The new paradigm viewed self-regulation as an oxymoron. State authority would be reasserted over global markets. Leaders decided that, going forward, financial markets would be re-regulated and supervised more aggressively. A new era of international regulatory activism was ushered into existence.

The power of the G20 member states, long in retreat, was brought to bear to re-regulate global finance to an extent, scope and depth not seen since the 1970s and the end of the Bretton Woods system.

This worldview did not take shape instantaneously. It took time to create and make more solid and lasting through the building of new forums and through the reform of institutions and their resources. Making the shift real and lasting also required significant policy changes and reforms. To achieve this and to carry out detailed reforms, the G20 backed, relied on and empowered a particular epistemic community – the same central bankers who had failed to see the crisis coming in the first place. But the central bankers' culpability was not necessarily an impediment to action, because the community collectively grasped a new macroprudential worldview.

G20-sanctioned reforms were designed, enumerated and led by this chastened but re-empowered central banking community. They understood the dangers posed by too much market and not enough state power applied to the regulation of global financial markets. The community had a clear sense of the nature of the regulatory paradigm shift in worldview necessary to deliver financial stability. They began to build the new architecture headed by the FSB and commenced re-regulation swiftly in 2008–2009. As has been seen, even in the third phase, one marked by increasing dissension and disunity, the new paradigm was being built brick by brick by the central banking community that conceptualised it and supported its continuance and defence more than a decade later in 2020.

As with other crises responses in the past, there was a burst of construction followed by a process of gradual policy coordination and additions. These incremental steps were designed to strengthen the new forums and structures to make the new paradigm progressively more robust. The process of making the worldview actual on the ground was not yet complete in 2015.

In this third phase, public discord amongst G20 leaders became much more evident, as the effective actions taken in 2008 (the crisis management phase), and in

2009 (the concrete reform phase), were followed from 2010 onwards by a return to dissension amongst G20 states, as the fellowship of the lifeboat was replaced by normal defence of national objectives and economic models of development. Looked at individually, the G20 summits from 2010 onwards were much more publicly contentious overall, with disputes fluctuating from mild (in Toronto), to moderate (in Seoul), to severe (in Brisbane), to ongoing, chronic and related to America's retreat from leadership (in 2017 and since).

Crucially, this rise in diplomatic disputes, this period of increasing dissension amongst G20 leaders did not translate into a freezing of the policy process created by the ongoing summitry, and especially the technical reform process below the leaders' summits. This chapter has shown that despite the dissension, each summit saw a degree of meaningful progress, incremental first- and second-order reforms and additions to the architectural design agreed to in phases one and two. In this manner, the new normal continued to be constructed from 2010 through 2016 and was maintained and defended from 2017, despite a shift in the US stance vis-à-vis international cooperation and coordination. But America First signals 'that global governance in general has been marginalized, now that the US has abdicated its role as the custodian of the international order' (O'Neil, 2019).

Perspective matters

Critics, such as former IMF chief economist Simon Johnson and former World Bank chief economist and Nobel Laureate Joseph Stiglitz, maintain that what the G20 did in phases one, two or three did not amount to a meaningful paradigm shift – that the changes do not go far enough, that the same actors are in charge and that the adjustments are not radical enough. At best, the paradigm is said to be being constructed very slowly via incremental additions (Moschella and Tsingou, 2013). Whether one agrees with this position ultimately depends on the perspective and time frame through which events are viewed. Looked at from a greater distance, there appears to be a real shift in the policy consensus, and in the underlying re-regulatory narrative, a partial rejection of the laissez-faire neoliberal worldview as applied to regulation of financial markets and firms amongst leaders and the elite-level technocratic community.

The structures and actual policy outcomes that followed from the new narrative during the evolution of the G20 reflected this shift. The architectural and policy changes commenced in phases one and two were tested in phase three. But they have also been augmented and strengthened. Taken as a totality, the altered worldview and the reforms commenced are indicative of a paradigm shift in approach to international economic diplomacy and coordinated re-regulation, which is visible in ongoing processes and summitry. As a result, 'whether the task is developing ideas, reaching consensus on their desirability, or moving from ideas to implementation, the G20 which has working groups active in all these areas is where the action is' (Eichengreen, 2009). If the scope of the shift is still somewhat in doubt, that is because they are viewing events from the wrong perspective.

Previous international and national shifts are instructive. International and national economic paradigm shifts take a long time to become fully apparent. Just as the 'Bretton Woods system did not emerge from a single moment but rather from a much more extended historical process' (Subacchi and Cooper, 2010, p. 607), so a similar pattern is observed in this case. National paradigm shifts are similar in their pace of evolution.

The Thatcherite revolution 'did not spring upon the world fully formed and fully armed' (Payne, 2005, p. 74); it took years to be ideologically conceptualised (by thinkers such as Milton Friedman, Sir Keith Joseph and others), and it was then gradually realised via policy shifts. The winter of discontent, 1978–1979, in the UK created crisis conditions that set the stage for the election of Mrs Thatcher. She was swept to power and began contentious reforms. But the scale and long-term impact of her changes in Britain were not immediately apparent. Mrs Thatcher tackled some policy areas (the trade unions) and not others (the National Health Service). A new consensus did take shape. Looked at in totality over a longer period, it is now widely recognised that there was a Thatcherite revolution, a neoliberal paradigm shift in certain economic ideas and policies sparked in 1979 (Blyth, 2002; Gamble, 1998; Hall, 1993).

A partial answer to critics of the G20-led process is to suggest they look at the process and reforms underway with a different, longer and broader perspective. Then the paradigm shift can be seen to first emerge as a change in the ideological stance of G20 leaders and to a greater extent policy-making technocrats vis-à-vis the merits of regulating global markets and firms and the application of collective state power to that task. That narrative consensus is then applied to the difficult task of policy making. And this process continued even as public dissension mounted amongst G20 leaders from 2010 through 2016 and became especially marked and worrisome from 2017.

Policy makers rushed to react in Washington, London and Pittsburgh, creating a wave of reform, a shift in worldview and policy actions through 2009. In this third phase of the G20's evolution the process continues, although at a slower pace than in the first two phases. The full outlines of the reformed regulatory architecture are still being fashioned in 2015. The peak of the economic disaster is now far behind us. The amplitude of the regulatory reform wave remains and may not be fully appreciated at this point, for that is the nature of a large wave. The lone surfer cannot fully determine the size of the wave when riding it.

At present, we can reasonably assume the regulatory paradigm and policy shift will be sustained and continue beyond 2020. The G20 and more particularly its regulatory surrogates are maintaining vigilance and continuing to defend, and in some areas, construct, the architecture. The action is by no means as frenetic as in phases one and two, but the central banking creators of the new architecture have not abandoned it in phase three when faced with discord at the G20 level.

From 2010 onwards, there has been increasing public discord at the G20 summitry level. But paradigm maintenance is seen, nonetheless. In phase three, a majority of leaders are determined to maintain the G20's flexibility as an informal, state-led forum controlled by themselves and their finance ministries (i.e. not to institutionalise the summit process or extend its membership too far).

This informality in a non-crisis circumstance can be a weakness, for when no comity exists, action is stymied. But it is also true that crisis response forums do not work flat out all the time. That is not their intent. Rather, it may be sufficient that the central players continue to engage and cooperate within the structure and process. Having the structure operative for future crises is the lasting innovation, even if the G20 response to COVID-19 has been weak and disappointing, absent US leadership and commitment.

It is of course possible the policy paradigm and policy outcomes this produces could weaken beyond 2020, as could the reform wave in response to various factors, including G20 discord, national-political-economy-driven clashes, a global post pandemic recession and, potentially, poor implementation of agreed standards. Such an outcome cannot be dismissed. However, the indicators are that the policy shift and reform wave and redesign begun in 2009 are being sustained as a new equilibrium if we measure regulatory impact and other indicators, within certain boundaries.

In 2020 it is important to recognise the limits of the regulatory paradigm. All such shifts occur within particular science or policy universes and are subject to constraints based on the strength of the consensus narrative that compelled their adoption in the first place, and which then supports their maintenance once the shift occurs. It should not be expected, and the evidence does not show, a G20 paradigm shift that is constantly growing in size and volume; this is not an economic big bang and ever accelerating policy universe.

There are limits to the expansion of the G20- and FSB-led paradigm shift. The shift was a rejection of laissez-faire neoliberal truths and the adoption of a state-power-backed aggressive, re-regulatory approach and programme, not a complete abandonment of free market structures and national economic norms. According to Padoa-Schioppa, 'If the years before the crisis were years of over-reliance on markets and mistrust in government – or, more simply put, too much market and too little government – what we have seen in 2008 and 2009 has been a spectacular comeback of government' (Padoa-Schioppa, 2010b, p. 8). That comeback, that reassertion of collective state oversight and control, was and is real, but it has limits.

It did not extend to include perennial global macroeconomic issues such as trade and currency imbalances or national economic or currency policies. As this chapter has shown, there is no G20 policy consensus visible there, only discord, exacerbated by a US administration that has abrogated its leadership role. As has also been shown, a paradigm shift does not occur if there is a lack of consensus on anomalies, failures and solutions. Instead, disputes and the maintenance of the status quo occur. Such clashes are not necessarily a weakness of the G20-triggered shift itself but are instead the outer limits of it. Beyond that boundary, elements of 'paradigm wars' and paradigm conflict still exist.

This book suggests that what is notable in the case of the G20's creation, process and evolution is not how limited its policy effect has been, but how fast it moved in phases one and two and how many areas it affected and continues to affect. Bankers themselves (admittedly self-interestedly) complain of the huge effect of the multiple national and international regulatory processes started by the G20 and the FSB. But the bankers are correct that this is a significant, multifaceted and increasingly durable re-regulation process. The central banking community deliberately designed it to restrict risk taking and decrease the danger of another crisis; it is meant to make banking and risk taking more costly and less appealing, and more than a decade on, while there is some backsliding (see Chapter 5), it is not meant to be temporary. The results are positive so far. Bank leverage has been cut; return on equity has fallen to the high single digits, down from 20 per cent pre-crisis; and banks are exiting non-core businesses and have redesigned their business models to operate in the new normal. And the central banking and regulatory community retains the initiative; witness the aggressive pursuit of illegal actions by bankers taken in the 'fixing' of the LIBOR (*The Economist*, 2012) and FOREX. Regulatory fines against the world's largest banks for these and other transgressions exceed US$128 billion. Pre-crisis, such actions would have been impossible.

Within this process, the impact of policy changes begun by the G20 and FSB can be expected to fluctuate, and they do, with a lack of consistency area to area and country to country across the globe in 2020. Policy making is a messy process after all. And viewed in isolation, individual policies promulgated as a result of the G20-led and FSB-championed shift may look more or less strong. But viewed in totality and within the wider cultural context, what we see underway is a G20-directed, central bank-designed series of concrete policies underpinned by the narrative and policy consensus paradigm shift amongst regulators and central bankers. In 2020 the consensus regulatory narrative is still in place as a new equilibrium is still being translated into first-, second- and third-order changes in coordinated international financial regulatory policies (Hall, 1993, pp. 281–287). Viewed as a whole, as one participant affirmed, 'the financial regulation agenda has been a major success' (Mackintosh, 2012, 33, p. 4). Once again, perspective matters, and a single observer may be too close to events that continue to unfold to fully appreciate the nature of the change in worldview started by the G20 and the FSB leadership in 2008–2009 and still underway. It appears, however, that the shift remains resistant to dismantlement, even though some jurisdictions are shifting emphasis (notably the US).

The type of paradigm you get depends on who leads

The creation of the G20 forum brought together old leadership from North America and Europe and the leaders of the major emerging economies in a manner not previously seen, and to an extent that will have a significant impact in the future. This change was not and is not temporary window dressing and it cannot be rescinded. Today, the leadership forum of global international economic diplomacy is permanently larger. To be sure, especially during phases one and two of the forum's evolution, the burst of activity and the reform agenda were driven by

North American and European leaders. The crisis was their fault, and weaknesses in their supervision, their regulation and their markets needed to be addressed. Emerging-market leaders agreed with this assessment and did not oppose G20 reforms and action plans which would predominantly affect regulation of markets at the core. They permitted the core in the G20, advised by their central banks, to devise the redesign and reform agenda in 2008 and 2009. Crucially, principal officials from those states directing the detailed re-regulatory programme tended to be hawks – supportive of state power reassertion and aggressive re-regulation of global finance. It will become clear in Chapter 6 that the detailed financial reform agenda, within the FSB and within the standard-setting bodies, also reflects these actors' goals and not those of a smaller grouping (from France, Germany and Japan) who sought somewhat weaker responses pressed by level-one domestic interests.

US and European powers have to an important extent moved away from a reliance on the G7 grouping in favour of a still exclusive but much more inclusive collectivist (Germain, 2001) process over which they continued to retain a pivotal degree of influence and control. In 2020 the G7 now appears to be used as a 'pre-meeting' for the G20 summitry. The leading powers have expanded and embraced the collectivism of the wider forum but also simultaneously used the G20 as an instrument of 'hegemonic incorporation' of emerging countries within a new architecture still largely designed and led by members of the G7 'as was' (Beeson and Bell, 2009, p. 67). In 2020 the G20 as the central forum is here to stay. This is the case even as the US has abandoned its leadership role, raising alarm amongst those around the table.

When a hegemon exits leadership, trouble beckons

The challenge facing the G20 forum today has a name – US President Donald Trump. While we can see the strength of the G20 process, and its permanence in 2020, we can also see the strains from 2017 caused by the abrogation of US leadership inherent in the America First approach by the US president and his administration. Since 2017 G20 summitry has been seriously affected by the (temporary?) end of US leadership. On a host of major global issues, from climate change, to trade and protectionism, to the maintenance of the rules based international order, to the non-existent COVID-19 response, America now stands alone and apart from not leading the consensus in the G20. G20 presidencies now deal with an intransigent US leader opposed to the nature of global diplomacy (in NATO, at the G7, at the UN and at the G20) – one who is unwilling to forge consensus, unwilling to lead, one who is visibly hostile to the requirements of leadership in a globalised world. The negative effects of the US abrogation of leadership underscores that, to operate effectively, the G20 still requires advanced-country, and especially US, leadership, even as emerging countries take over leadership of the summitry.

This continued dominance by those at the core has led some to suggest the G20's emergence and its leadership entrenched 'the institutional leadership of the advanced imperial powers of old' (Kirton, 2010, p. 13), or in other words, the G7 (Porter, 2000; Soederberg, 2002). Perhaps this is partially the case. The shift, reform agenda and its policy prescriptions were a Western package addressing Western failings and designed by Western leaders and their more hawkish technocrats. Emerging countries signed up to an agenda designed by the US and Europe. From the perspective of the advanced-country negotiators, it was a 'pretty damn good deal' (Mackintosh, 2012, 12, p. 11). But the emerging countries' roles and approach to the G20 process was itself evolving, and not much should be read into their relative silence at the start of the process, when they were brand new members of this still exclusive club, and they were in support of the direction of the paradigm shift. The G20 does not signify a wholesale change in power relationships, but change it is, and over time the forum has sustained its centrality to the architecture despite some such as Jim O'Neill (2019) asking, 'Does the G20 still matter?'

Emerging countries growing into their roles

This chapter has shown that from 2010 onwards, emerging-country voices were not only critical but also increasingly additive and strategic. This was the case in the talks over a Eurozone firewall in 2011 and 2012. Emerging-country leaders came to the table with solid offers, cash, and reasonable quid pro quo demands. Emerging countries actively engaged to an extent not seen in phases one and two. In doing this, emerging countries were negotiating within the new G20 process, advocating their own political and power goals. This is evidence of the G20 process fostering change and the emerging countries buying into the process and engaging in a way they would not have done in the absence of the G20 structures and summitry.

Not only were emerging-country voices easier to discern in phase three, but they took formal leadership roles in the presidency of the G20. The leaders of Korea and Mexico both acquitted themselves well. The former refereed an imbalanced shouting match between the US and China and still continued financial reform with the landmark signing of Basel III under its leadership, and the latter got a deal on the Eurozone firewall. These are not minor successes. Thus, two emerging-country powers delivered major breakthroughs even during a time of increasing public diplomatic tensions. In contrast, the Russian presidency in 2013 demonstrated the limits of the summit processes; when major members clash over irreconcilable geopolitical risks issues, summitry is of only marginal help. Both the Turkish and Chinese presidencies were relative successes as tensions amongst leaders rose for differing reasons. Argentina was hostage to external crises and dynamics largely caused by the sudden shift in the US position from engaged leadership to oppositional hostility. Such was this shift that neither Germany nor Japan could mend the widening breach between the US and the rest of the G20.

In summary, emerging countries and their leaders are now part of, and used to, the process, supportive of the framework and assertive within the structures. Within the boundaries of the power dynamics in place, the G20 is still exclusive, but the table is permanently larger. The G20 'club', founded as a leaders' state-to-state diplomatic construct, will not satisfy critics (Aslund, 2009). But it is broader and more representative than previous forums (Bradford, 2009), and it is more legitimate as a result. It is a relative improvement over the entirely unsatisfactory G7 or the large and unwieldy rigidly institutionalised United Nations and International Monetary Fund.

Inclusion does not avoid a head-on clash when populism and nationalism rise

In 2020 the shift in the US to an America First policy means the G20 forum has become a platform for the struggle between a still dominant but slowly declining hegemonic US, a rising and resistant China and American allies at odds with the shift in the US stance. As we have seen, from 2016 onwards, G20 forum leaders repeatedly tried to minimise the adverse effects of America First. The communiqués – for the first time – have specific carve-outs which note American opposition to the G20 consensus on climate change and trade. This split will likely continue and worsen from 2020 onwards if President Trump is re-elected. This clash between the new power versus the old is fuelled by populism and nationalism. This phase three dissension and American abrogation of its leadership role runs in parallel with an ongoing defence of the new equilibrium, its processes and its architecture by other states, including China. In this important manner, the clash between powers is arguably less severe because of the G20's existence than it might otherwise be.

The G20 succeeds so long as leaders view it as a productive venue for discussion, debate and (one hopes) eventual agreement. Even when agreement is not possible, discussion is nonetheless valuable. The clash between the US, China and the US' allies could be markedly worse without regular, structured discussions and a shifting agenda. The G20 processes are additive and ameliorative of tensions below the level of the leaders' meetings. Today China as a rising power is often on the same side as European powers as they both seek to defend the globalised system and common goals. This is architecture proving to be a venue that fosters new coalitions. In a multipolar world, that is an important diplomatic outcome.

Of course, the G20 processes and reforms have been constructed largely by Western leaders and their officials, albeit backed by the emerging powers and paradigmatically redesigned. Now what exists is increasingly used by the empowered leadership of emerging countries. In phase three, emerging countries increasingly took over leadership of the G20 and play a larger role, indicative of this permanent but gradual evolution in power relationships within the new architecture. North American and European voices still dominate, but the balance of power is changing within the flexible G20-led architecture. The US abrogation of its leadership role since 2017 will hasten this shift, the cementing of new coalitions and agreements across and around the summit table. America First may have the effect of diminishing US soft power as it forces erstwhile allies and competitors together.

The G20 as a flexible leadership response to crisis

The G20's success after its hasty creation and during its formative and early reformist period depends not only on the pressure of events and the urgency of action, but also on the nature of the forum itself. Part of the forum's success is due to the flexibility provided by the G20 meeting format. Leaders, face-to-face, can strike a deal when sherpas cannot. Even when a deal cannot be done, small, incremental steps can still be taken. Other more formal settings, such as the International Monetary and Financial Committee, do not replicate the tension, the degree of urgency or this action-oriented format. In essence the G20 is an updated concentration of state power designed to more closely reflect twenty-first century geopolitical realities. But critics are not assuaged by small adjustments in relative power in an exclusive forum that was admittedly nimble in the face of the crisis.

Events in 2013 and 2014, and since 2016, have shown the G20 forum cannot create comity on geopolitical goals where no win sets exist. America and its allies clashed repeatedly with Russia. The G20 cannot solve the Crimean and Ukrainian crises. It has no tools to do so. When America opposes action on climate change, on trade or on global rules, no deal is possible and carve-outs occur. Confronted by issues of foreign policy, national economic policy or populist-driven dynamics bound up with particular historical or electoral positions and beliefs, we cannot expect the G20 gatherings to provide solutions, and they have not done so.

Nonetheless, despite dissension rising at the summits as America First and populism fracture the consensus, the G20 process demonstrated that progress was still possible, on financial regulatory reform and on climate change, for instance, despite very real splits at the leadership level. Technocrats, their community insulated from the national and diplomatic disputes, continued their work constructing the regulatory architecture. Not for the first time, nor likely for the last, the G20, and the technocratic architecture and FSB-community-led process it helped create, sustained and helped ensure progress on joint policy goals. But this ongoing activism at the technocratic level also has its critics.

Legitimacy still matters

What is obviously necessary in a crisis and accepted even by those excluded in an emergency, when a great many risk almost all if nothing is done, is less appealing when the wave of the crisis dissipates and the chosen forum continues to exclude the many and the small (Vestergaard, 2011; Vestergaard and Wade, 2010). Complaints that the G20, the architecture and the process it has constructed are illegitimate continue to be heard. Critics have warned that it 'represents an extraordinary regression in international governance to Prince Metternich's concert of great powers in Vienna after the Napoleonic Wars in 1814–15' (Aslund, 2009). Aslund and other champions of universal institutions reject the 'small and flexible' defence. They retort that the G20 represents a retreat to the power politics of the past. It still excludes 150 of 192 countries and is not universal. It is condemned as a shift towards a 'plurilateralism of the big', with the smaller states still frozen out of the informal summitry processes (Vestergaard, 2011, p. 7).

The G20 is, it is said, usurping the sovereignty of those excluded from the process. Excluded national leaders, such as former Danish Prime Minister Lars Rasmussen, concur and have voiced concern about a sustained move away from universal institutions in favour of the G20, an exclusive state-power-based, informal forum (Rasmussen, 2011), even as they recognised the forum's effectiveness in 2008–2009 and its improvement over the G7 – G8 approach (Vestergaard and Wade, 2010).

The critics are right. The rise of the G20 and FSB process was and remains a reassertion of state power and authority through more informal political structures and processes in place of the universalism of the IMF. Complaints about the process of selection and the forum's lack of regional representation and balance are also reasonable. This construct was chosen in part because key actors did not want to use the IMF because of its own perceived failings and weaknesses. In addition, elevating the G20 was also a sudden move, unplanned and forced by events in 2008.

The wave of policy making and institution rebuilding and reform that results from a crisis, and the decisions that are made in such times, are never perfect and seldom please even most of those consulted, let alone all of those left outside the room. That was the case in Washington, and it remains the case in 2020. The G20 was hastily formed from a previous body and so exhibits, as most similar constructs would, its own new legitimacy gap, and small steps are being taken to increase communication amongst a wider grouping (it is now really the G20 plus five).

However, increasing membership, and its agenda of topics within the process, could undermine the G20's identified strengths. The G20 was and remains effective because of its flexible and small nature, and expansion, if excessive, would be foolish and counterproductive. Such steps could diminish its effectiveness or just drive decision makers to select other mechanisms to pursue common policy goals. The G20 will not become a permanent, free-standing resourced universal international body, as some, such as the Canadians, would wish. Decisions taken at the Cannes summit made that clear. Membership creep may still occur, via the technical bodies in particular, but universality is off the table. Given that fact, those outside the forum must find other ways of affecting an evolving process rather than simply demanding admittance.

Dissension and the dialectic of crisis response and reaction

The history of the creation and early growth of the G20 follows a trajectory similar to past national financial crises. There is a crisis response phase in 2008, a concrete reform phase in 2009 and a tension between the new consensus and dissention amongst state leaders from 2010 onwards. Eleven years on from the apogee of G20 summitry, at the political-diplomatic level, but not yet at the technical level, public disputes have become increasingly vocal and strident, sapping the forum's strength.

The issues left on the table are those that are not part of the agreed crisis-formed policy consensus. They are grounded in competing national paradigms of growth and economic policy. Still, the negotiators grapple with the issues, almost always unsuccessfully, particularly as regards global imbalances. Historical antecedents exist, with similar disputes occurring repeatedly over time – especially over currency, trade and surplus matters. With no consensus on causes, solutions and actions in these areas, no progress is possible. With the crisis behind them, G20 leaders grapple with difficult, potentially insoluble, global political economy issues. The very state power that was centripetal in the crisis and reform phases now is centrifugal in phase three because their macroeconomic and currency goals cannot be reconciled.

Thus, we have the dialectic – crisis management, reform and results – leading to a consequent return to nations pursuing their own national objectives and an increase in public disunity due to greater economic stability. Today the cycle continues. A global pandemic has forced states and central banks to again step forward and act as final guarantors of our health, security and our economies. In crises only state actors have the ability and levers to deliver. This time – in part due to the absence of US leadership – state authority has been extended even further and used even more extensively – but not utilising the G20 forum.

The G20 remains however, a permanent addition to the top of the architecture of international economic and financial diplomacy. State-to-state, power-based diplomacy is back and is here to stay. The coordinated, cooperative, impactful application of that power will have to wait until the US returns to leadership, or at least shifts from active opposition to grudging acceptance of the utility of the forum. Until then other states must work to maintain its processes below the summit level and sustain the technical architecture below the leaders' forum that does continue to operate.

At the regulatory level, the changes wrought as a result of the 2007–2008 global financial crisis are real. The severity of the crisis forced the beginning of a worldview paradigm shift amongst technocrats and in certain regulatory areas via a series of interrelated reforms that continue today. But the economy goes through boom and bust cycles, and the response by policy makers operates in cycles, as well. Behind the bluster and G20 posturing over divergent national economic policies and interests, the re-regulation of financial markets continues. Dissension at the G20 level does not translate into paralysis at the technical level. At that level, the leadership from the core continues to build out structures born in 2009. In phase three, the FSB's status was formalised. In 2020 the FSB is the permanent nexus for coordination and cooperation amongst the central banking technocratic community. This will not change. Indeed, the policy workstream (see Chapter 6) and the response of the community to emerging crises (see Chapter 7), suggests that construction continues, despite growing disputes at the G20 level fuelled by an isolationist US.

The narrative shift that commenced in 2008–2009 have now, more than a decade later, been translated into policy output. All policies are not uniformly strong. Indeed, the further away from direct control of the central banking community, the weaker they sometimes appear. But there is no doubt that in 2015, the policy actors are still engaged to a degree that prior to the crisis could not have been imagined. Today, they are working on policy formulation and on paradigm maintenance and defence as well. But that also is normal, because after a paradigm shift, a community must still defend that which it believes in and has created in its own image.

Eventually, as in previous lesser economic crises, as a crisis dissipates, the sense of urgency also evaporates, and state commitment to coordinating processes can also tend to weaken. Given this rhythm, will we see a further radical extension of the policy consensus? Perhaps not. But it is also possible that the terrible effects of the COVID-19 pandemic may result in further pressure for new mechanisms for collective action. That would require a return of US engagement and its commitment to the international architecture and the cooperative goals that they represent.

The following chapter addresses the abrogation of US leadership under President Trump and the negative effects and implications of his America First policy for the global system constructed since 2008.

References

Asian Infrastructure Investment Bank. (2019) '2019 financial statements' [Online]. Available at: www.aiib.org/en/about-aiib/financial-statements/.content/index/pdf/Q3-Financial-Statements.pdf (accessed: 4 March 2020).

Aslund, A. (2009) 'The Group of 20 must be stopped', *Financial Times*, 27 November, p. 9.

The Atlantic. (2015) 'The staggering scale of Germany's refugee project', 12 September [Online]. Available at: www.theatlantic.com/international/archive/2015/09/germany-merkel-refugee-asylum/405058/ (accessed: 31 March 2020).

BBC News. (2014) 'Forex scandal: How to rig the market', 14 November [Online]. Available at: www.bbc.com/news/business-26526905 (accessed: 22 January 2015).

———. (2016) 'Paris climate deal: US and China formally join pact', 3 September [Online]. Available at: www.bbc.com/news/world-asia-china-37265541(accessed: 31 March 2020).

Beeson, M. and Bell, S. (2009) 'The G20 and international economic governance: Hegemony, collectivism, or both?', *Global Governance*, 15, pp. 67–87.

Blackden, R. (2012) 'G20 leaders insist no more IMF cash unless Eurozone boosts financial firewall', *The Daily Telegraph*, 26 February [Online]. Available at: www.telegraph.co.uk/finance/financialcrisis/9107437/G20-leaders-insist-no-more-IMF-cash-unless-eurozone-boosts-financial-firewall.html (accessed: 25 November 2012).

Blyth, M. (2002) *Great transformations: Economic ideas and institutional change in the twentieth century*. Cambridge: Cambridge University Press.

Bradford, C.I. (2009) 'The G20 stimulus split: A false debate', *Brookings Institution*, Washington, DC, 1 April.

CBS. (2017) 'Angela Merkel: I deplore US leaving Paris Climate Accord', July 8 [Online]. Available at: www.cbsnews.com/news/angela-merkel-donald-trump-paris-agreement-i-deplore-this/ (accessed: 31 March 2020).

Center for Responsive Politics. (2010) 'Sector profile: 2010' [Online]. Available at: www.opensecrets.org/lobby/indus.php?lname=F++&year=a (accessed: 17 February 2011).

Chen, S., Stolberg, S.G., and Sanger, D.E. (2010) 'Obama's economic view is rejected on world stage', *New York Times*, 12 November, p. 1.

Cohen, B.J. (2008) 'Power and rules in the changing economic order', *International Affairs*, 84(3), pp. 455–470.

Dervis, K. (2010) 'Keep the faith: The G20 can stop the war', *Financial Times*, 9 November [Online]. Available at: www.ft.com/cms/s/0/88c24b14-eb6f-11df-b482-00144feab49a.html#axzz2cdL9WLx1 (accessed: 20 November 2010).

Dong-Hwi, L. (2010) 'Assessment of the Toronto G20 Summit and tasks ahead: In preparing for the upcoming Seoul Summit', 13 July [Online]. Available at: www.g20.utoronto.ca/biblio/LEE-4-20100713-en.pdf (accessed: 3 August 2010).

Eichengreen, B. (2009) 'The G20 and the crisis', *VoxEU.org* [Online]. Available at: www.voxeu.org/index.php?q=node/3160 (accessed: 10 November 2010).

Financial Times. (2017a) 'G20 drops vow to resist all forms of protectionism', March 18. [Online]. Available at: www.ft.com/content/241cdf2a-0be9-11e7-a88c-50ba212dce4d (accessed: 31 March 2020).

——— (2017b) 'Unanimous communique fails to hide US tensions' [Online]. Available at: www.ft.com/content/2f380e14-63ca-11e7-9a66-93fb352ba1fe.9 (accessed: 31 March 2020).

FSB (Financial Stability Board). (2012) 'The bilateral complaint handling process' [Online www.fsb.org/2015/11/total-loss-absorbing-capacity-tlac-principles-and-term-sheet/]. Available at: www.financialstabilityboard.org/publications/r_120427b.pdf (accessed: 28 February 2013).

———. (2015) 'Total loss absorbing capital principles and term sheet', 9 November [Online]. Available at: www.fsb.org/2015/11/total-loss-absorbing-capacity-tlac-principles-and-term-sheet/ (accessed: 31 March 2020).

G20 (Group of Twenty). (2010a) 'Toronto Declaration', 27 June [Online]. Available at: www.g20.utoronto.ca/2010/to-communique.html (accessed: 3 April 2011).

———. (2010b) 'Seoul Declaration' [Online]. Available at: www.g20.utoronto.ca/2010/g20seoul.html (accessed: 10 December 2010).

———. (2011) 'Cannes Declaration' [Online]. Available at: www.g20.utoronto.ca/summits/2011cannes.html (accessed: 15 December 2011).

———. (2012) 'Los Cabos Declaration' [Online]. Available at: www.g20.utoronto.ca/summits/2012loscabos.html (accessed: 20 June 2012).

———. (2013) 'St Petersburg Declaration' [Online]. Available at: www.g20.utoronto.ca/2013/2013-0906-declaration.html (accessed: 8 January 2014).

———. (2014) 'Brisbane Declaration' [Online]. Available at: www.g20.utoronto.ca/2014/2014-1116-communique.html (accessed: 8 January 2014).

———. (2015) 'G20 Anatalya Communique' [Online]. Available at: www.g20.utoronto.ca/summits/2015antalya.html (accessed: March 2020).

———. (2016) 'G20 Hangzhou Summit Communique' [online]. Available at: www.g20.utoronto.ca/summits/2016hangzhou.html (accessed: 31 March 2020).

———. (2018) 'Buenos Aires Leaders' Declaration' [Online]. Available at: www.g20.utoronto.ca/2018/2018-leaders-declaration.html (accessed: 31 March 2020).

Gamble, A. (1998) *The free economy and strong state: The politics of Thatcherism*. Durham: Duke University Press.

Germain, R. (2001) 'Global financial governance and the problem of inclusion', *Global Governance*, 4(7), pp. 411–427.

Gilpin, R. (1987) *Political economy of international relations*. Princeton: Princeton University Press.

The Guardian. (2013) 'Edward Snowden asylum case a gift for Vladimir Putin', 1 August [Online]. Available at: www.theguardian.com/world/2013/aug/01/edward-snowden-gift-vladimir-putin (accessed: 1 January 2015).

———. (2016) 'Breakthrough as China and US agree to ratify Paris climate deal', September 3. [Online]. Available at: www.theguardian.com/environment/2016/sep/03/breakthrough-us-china-agree-ratify-paris-climate-change-deal (accessed: 31 March 2020).

———. (2019) 'Trade war, tweets, and Western liberalism: G20 summit wraps up in Osaka', 29 June [Online]. Available at: www.theguardian.com/world/2019/jun/29/g20-summit-osaka-japan-trade-wars-liberalism. (accessed: 31 March 2020).

Guebert, J. (2010) 'Plans for the fourth G20 summit: Co-chaired by Canada and Korea in Toronto, June 26–27, 2010', *G20 Information Center*, 10 May [Online]. Available at: www.g20.utoronto.ca/g20plans/g20plans100510.pdf (accessed: 3 April 2011).

Hall, P.A. (1993) 'Policy paradigms, social learning, and the state: The case of economic policymaking in Britain', *Comparative Politics*, 25(3), pp. 275–296.

Hoschild, A. (2016) *Strangers in their own land: Anger and mourning on the American right*. New Press.

IMF (International Monetary Fund). (2011) 'IMF quotas', 3 March [Online]. Available at: www.imf.org/external/np/exr/facts/quotas.htm (accessed: 5 April 2011).

King, C. (2013) *Odessa: Genius and death in a city of dreams*. New York: Norton.

Kirton, J. (2010) 'The G20, the G8, the G5 and the role of ascending powers', *Revista Mexicana de Politica Exterior*, December.

Mackintosh, S. (2011) Interview 7. G20 principal supervisor, 7 December.

———. (2012) Interview 12. G20 Finance Ministry Official, 27 January.

———. (2012) Interview 17. G20 Presidential Advisor, 3 March.

———. (2012) Interview 22. Former G20 Finance Minister, Central Bank Governor, 1 May.

———. (2012) Interview 33. Senior Finance Ministry Official and G20 Lead, follow-up meeting, 14 November.

———. (2016) 'The creation of the Asian infrastructure and investment bank: America's loss and China's gain', *World Economics*, 17(3), pp. 25–38.

Malloch-Brown, M. (2010) 'How the G20 glasshouse is under attack', *Financial Times*, 12 November [Online]. Available at: www.ft.com/intl/cms/s/0/94764afe-edd2-11df-9612-00144feab49a.html#axzz2cdL9WLx1 (accessed: 14 August 2013).

Moore, J. (2011) 'Bob Diamond: No apologies. No restraint. No shame', *The Independent*, 12 January [Online]. Available at: www.independent.co.uk/news/business/news/bob-diamond-no-apologies-no-restraint-no-shame-2182231.html (accessed: 9 February 2011).

Moschella, M. and Tsingou, E. (eds.) (2013) *Great expectations slow transformations: Incremental change in post-crisis regulation*. Colchester: European Consortium for Political Research (ECPR).

The Moscow Times. (2013) 'Obama to attend G20 summit in St. Petersburg', 7 August [Online]. Available at: www.themoscowtimes.com/news/article/obama-to-attend-g20-summit-in-st-petersburg/484200.html (accessed: 1 January 2015).

NPR. (2019) 'Germany recalibrates after two years of Trump', 27 February 2019 [Online]. Available at: www.npr.org/2019/02/27/697803708/washington-has-become-much-rougher-germany-is-still-recalibrating-with-trump (accessed: 31 March 2020).

O'Neill. (2019) 'Does the G20 still matter?', *Chatham House*, 16 July [Online]. Available at: www.chathamhouse.org/expert/comment/does-g20-still-matter# (accessed: 31 March 2020).

Orwell, G. (1946) *Animal farm*. London: Penguin Books.

Padoa-Schioppa, T. (2010a) 'The ghost of Bancor: The economic crisis and the global monetary disorder', *Speech delivered in Louvain-la-Neuve*, 25 February.

———. (2010b) 'Markets and government before, during and after the 2007–20XX Crisis', *Per Jacobsen Lecture*, Basel, Switzerland, 27 June.

Palais Royale Initiative. (2011) 'Reform of the international monetary system: A cooperative approach for the twenty-first century' [Online]. Available at: http://global-currencies.org/smi/gb/telechar/news/Rapport_Camdessus-integral.pdf (accessed: 20 March 2013).

Payne, A. (2005) *The global politics of unequal development*. New York: Palgrave.

People's Bank of China. (2009) 'Notes of a meeting with officials of the People's Bank of China', 12 June, National Association for Business Economics Mission to Beijing.

Pew Research. (2015) 'Number of refugees to Europe surges to record 1.3 million in 2015', 2 August [Online]. Available at: https://www.pewresearch.org/global/2016/08/02/number-of-refugees-to-europe-surges-to-record-1-3-million-in-2015/ (accessed: 28 July 2020).

Porter, T. (2000) 'The G-7, the Financial Stability Forum, the G-20, and the politics of international financial regulation', *International Studies Association annual meeting*, Los Angeles, 15 March.

Rasmussen, L. (2011) 'Notes of a working lunch with the Prime Minister of Denmark', 15 March, Washington, DC,

Reuters. (2017) 'Merkel issues warning to Trump ahead of G20 summit', 29 June [online]. Available at: www.reuters.com/article/us-g20-germany-merkel-idUSKBN19K2B2 (accessed: 31 March 2020).

Sanger, D. (2010) 'Challenges await U.S. at group of 20 meeting', *New York Times*, 9 November [Online]. Available at: www.nytimes.com/2010/11/10/business/global/10global.html?pagewanted=all&_ (accessed: 10 July 2013).

Skidelsky, R.J.A. (2018) *Money and government*. New Haven: Yale University Press.

Soederberg, S. (2002) 'On the contradictions of the new international financial architecture: Another procrustean bed for emerging markets', *New Political Economy*, 23, pp. 607–620.

———. (2010) '"Overview" in global economic governance in transition a Bretton Woods moment? The 2007–2008 crisis and the future of global finance', *International Affairs*, 86(3), pp. 607–619.

The Telegraph. (2014) 'G20: Russia urged to stop meddling in Ukraine', 16 November [Online]. Available at: www.telegraph.co.uk/news/worldnews/11233880/G20-Russia-urged-to-stop-meddling-in-Ukraine.html (accessed: 1 January 2015).

Trump, D. (2017) 'Full text: Trump's 2017 UN speech', *Politico*, August 2019 [Online]. Available at: www.politico.com/story/2017/09/19/trump-un-speech-2017-full-text-transcript-242879 (accessed: 31 March 2020).

———. (2018) 'Full text of Trump's 2018 UN speech', *Politico*, 25 August [Online]. Available at: www.politico.com/story/2018/09/25/trump-un-speech-2018-full-text-transcript-840043 (accessed: 31 March 2020).

———. (2019) 'Decoding Trump's speech before the United Nations', *Politico* [Online]. Available at: www.politico.com/story/2019/09/24/trump-speech-at-un-1507923 (accessed: 31 March 2020).

Vestergaard, J. (2011) 'The G20 and beyond: Toward effective global economic governance', *DIIS Report*, 2011–04.

Vestergaard, J. and Wade, R. (2010) 'Overhaul the G20 for the sake of the G172', *Financial Times*, 21 October [Online]. Available at: www.ft.com/intl/cms/s/0/a2ab4716-dd45-11df-9236-00144feabdc0.html#axzz2O5LmZd3n (accessed: 20 March 2013).

The White House. (2014) 'U.S. China joint announcement on climate change', 11 November [Online]. Available at: www.whitehouse.gov/the-press-office/2014/11/11/us-china-joint-announcement-climate-change (accessed: 1 January 2015).

Wright. (2016) 'Trump's 19th century foreign policy', *Politico* [Online]. Available at: www.politico.com/magazine/story/2016/01/donald-trump-foreign-policy-213546 (accessed: 31 March 2020).

5 America First and the global architecture[1]

> From this moment on, it's going to be America First.
>
> (Trump, 2017a)

> Trump seeks nothing less than ending the U.S.-led liberal order.
>
> (Wright, 2016)

> The United States of America . . . rejects the idea of an international community.
>
> (Steinmeier, 2020)

In 2008, the global financial crisis forced G20 leaders together in a crisis-fighting endeavour the scope and breadth of which had not been seen in 70 years. Actions by governments and central banks acting collectively and individually, addressing institutional, economic, fiscal, monetary and regulatory crisis management swiftly followed by reform endeavours in 2009 and beyond assured the Great Recession of 2008–2009 would not become a second Great Depression. We witnessed a burst of action and a coordinated reform agenda from G20 leaders led by a technocratic epistemic central banking community that had itself undergone a paradigm shift in its regulatory and (to a much lesser degree) economic policy worldview. Central bankers at that juncture rejected neoliberal deregulatory norms in favor of a reassertion of state power. This crisis response and reform process resulted in a new equilibrium. Once a degree of sustained economic calm was ensured, the economic pressures dissipated, the urgency of continued action lessened and the normal peacetime dynamics of negotiations and divergent national interests reasserted themselves. As part of that process, win spaces shrank and level-one negotiators found level-two (i.e. national and local) political, regulatory and economic interests limiting the room for further deals. This return to dissention and dispute has been particularly visible at the governmental, i.e. G20, level, of the reformed global architecture, and this is to a certain extent normal.

What is abnormal is the remarkable and abrupt shift in America, away from leadership and support of the global architecture, after the 2016 upset victory of Donald J. Trump as America's populist president. This surprise election result, which was unexpected by Mr Trump himself (Wolfe, 2018, 2019),[2] upended prior long-standing assumptions about the role of America. With America engaged, a great deal was achieved in 2008–2009, and much has been secured in the years since. Mr Trump's victory signaled America would become absent, isolated and openly hostile to the norms and the international cooperative architecture collectively built with allies both post-war and in response to the global financial crisis.

President Trump made his intentions clear at the outset, declaring in his inaugural speech: 'From this moment on, it's going to be America First.' (Trump, 2017a). This was no mere boasting. The president's actions would back up his rhetoric. Just how far would President Trump go and what might it mean for the global system? Wright thought very far indeed warning, 'Trump seeks nothing less than ending the U.S.-led liberal order'(Wright, 2016). Pushed by this seismic change in American policy, the diplomatic and policy calculus would have to shift and adjust dramatically for allies and competitors, institutions, governments and regulators. In this chapter, I analyse the architectural, institutional and policy implications of the election of President Trump, a populist, isolationist, anti-intellectual, anti-technocrat to the topmost position in the global power structure. In geopolitics and diplomacy, leadership, or lack thereof, always matters.

Leadership always matters

As we approach the end of President Trump's first term in office, the impact of his 'America First' policy, with its echoes of Charles Lindbergh's pre-Second World War nationalism and isolationism, is clearly visible (Myre, 2017). Four years on from his victory, allies and competitors understand what a Trump presidency implies for the international rules-based system. The prognosis is negative and may be worsening. Initial hopes that this serially bankrupt developer-turned-primetime-television-star and now president would revert to Republican norms on policy and approach were hugely off the mark. In 2016 it was common to hear American newspaper pundits explain reassuringly that the president was a real estate developer and was transactional and that he would quickly revert to Republican norms on foreign and security policy, trade and economic policy. The president, we were assured, would turn out to be a conventional Republican operator. This was wishful thinking. To the contrary, the president has continued to act in the same manner he has in decades past, repeating the same bad behaviours and questionable approaches to business, ethics (or lack thereof) and personal conduct. As David Runciman makes clear, election to high office doesn't change the actors who win; rather, it amplifies their existing traits and behaviours, for good or ill (Runciman, 2019).

As Runciman's analysis suggests, and Paul MacDonald observes, President Trump's views on America's power and foreign policy have 'proven remarkably clear and consistent' (MacDonald, 2018), in line with past statements and beliefs. Indeed, as Colin Khan and Hal Brands note, the 'Trumpian view of the world goes back decades' (Kahl and Brands, 2017). President Trump's America First policy is highly disruptive but has elements of consistency across time. The president has, according to Joe Klein, 'created a coherent, if dangerously myopic, populist platform that borrows from the shattered remains of 20th-century liberalism and conservatism' (Klein, 2020).

The president has maintained his long-standing distrust of exterior military commitments and entanglements. NATO is declared 'obsolete' (*New York Times*, 2017). Commitments in Syria, Iraq and Afghanistan are altered. The president repeatedly proclaims his disdain for globalisation and cooperation. He engages in disputes and conflicts with allies (at the United Nations, with Europe, with Mexico, with Turkey and others) and competitors (China), and enemies (Iran). And the president is open in his public disparagement of international institutions, preferring populist, nativist, nationalist jingoism over leadership and cooperation with allies.

Seventy-five years on from the creation of the Bretton Woods system and international financial organisations that form its superstructure, America, under President Trump is abandoning its leadership role (Park and Stangarone, 2019). This heralds the return to an old type of American nationalist isolationist populism, previously seen in the campaigns of William Jennings Bryan, Huey Long and Pat Buchanan (see Box 5.1). This American form of nationalist populism is the narrative force behind Trump's foreign and economic policy decision making (Eichengreen, 2018).

Box 5.1 American populism

Populism is not a new phenomenon in America. America's voters rally behind populists when they see rising inequality, wage stagnation, and industrial concentration and when they feel they are strangers in their own land (Hochschild, 2016). Anger can rise when new groups of immigrants arrive, competing for scarce resources with the working people just above them. Identity politics, 'us' versus 'them', and cultural splits also occur, between the current inhabitants and the newcomers, between working Americans and the elite, and between urban and rural voters. American populists can come from the left or the right, depending on the political circumstances of the day.

William Jennings Bryan (1860–1925) was the 19th century archetype of an American populist. He ran three times for president as the Democratic Party's nominee. He also ran as nominee for the American Populist Party. A famed orator, he used those skills in his famous 'Cross of Gold' speech in 1896 to call for a switch to silver coinage from gold (to stimulate the economy). Bryan's campaigns also included themes of anti-imperialism and attacks on the power of the 'trusts', that era's corporate behemoths (McGerr, 2005).

In the twentieth century, **Huey P. Long** (1893–1935), governor of Louisiana and then a member of the US Senate, took up the populist banner, campaigning for poor southern farmers against the monied elite, the bankers and the railway barons who dominated the Gilded Age. Long supported an asset tax, and he believed that President Franklin Delano Roosevelt's proposed 'New Deal' did not go far enough. Long ran on a record of delivering for the poor with better infrastructure, education spending and health-care provision. Long's campaign was not race-based; instead, it championed the poor against the rich, the working against the rentiers, the honest against the corrupt. He ran on a 'Share Our Wealth Plan'. Long never saw the outcome of his campaign. He was assassinated by a political rival on the floor of the Louisiana State Capitol on 8 September 1935 (White, 2006).

In the modern era, **Pat Buchanan** (1938–) took up the populist pitchfork from the right-of-center, campaigning for the Republican nomination for president against the incumbent George H. W. Bush. Buchanan, founder of the *American Conservative* magazine and a well-known public figure with a firebrand style of delivery, was the antithesis of President Bush. Buchanan went after the president declaring, 'Read our lips – no new taxes', a direct attack on the president, who had prudently marginally raised taxes to close the federal deficit. Buchanan's campaign was anti-establishment, anti-insider and anti-immigrant, and he railed against multiculturalism, gay rights and women's rights. He garnered 23 per cent of the vote. Buchanan's campaign is perhaps closest, in its cultural and thematic terms, to that of Trump's in 2016 (*New York Times*, 2012).

The key difference between these earlier instances of American nationalist populism and the current era is that Trump was elected on the back of an even larger wave of voter anger against the center-left and center-right establishment. That establishment had for too long failed to address the real and economically painful effects of globalisation on the working class of America, whose wages stagnated, and for whom health-care and education costs rose, while the rich got richer as the dream of America's equality of opportunity evaporated for the many (Chetty, 2020).[3]

President Trump views geopolitics as a zero-sum proposition. Leadership based on compromise and consensus is rejected as a first, best option. Instead, aggressive unilateralism is in, accompanied by barely concealed hostility to allies and existing norms and institutions, with implications for diplomacy as well as American democracy (Levitsky and Ziblatt, 2018).[4] As Gary Cohn, then-chairman of the President's National Economic Council, and H. R. McMaster, then-director of the National Security Council, put it starkly in 2017:

> The world is not a "global community" but an arena where nations, nongovernmental actors and businesses engage and compete for advantage. We bring to this forum unmatched military, political, economic, cultural and moral strength. Rather than deny this elemental nature of international affairs, we embrace it.

I hear echoes of Margaret Thatcher's 1987 'no such thing as society' interview for *Women's Own* (Thatcher, 1987). But this American iteration is even more alarming coming from the leaders of the remaining global hegemon. The president's clearest repeated expression of his America First worldview is seen and heard in his speeches delivered at the United Nations. They are a disjunctive break from past presidential messaging in the UN.

The US president's discordant voice

President Trump's voice and language at the United Nations has been consistent. In 2017 he stated, 'As President of the United States, I will always put America first' The president continued, 'The United States will forever be a great friend to the world, and especially to its allies. But we can no longer be taken advantage of, or enter into a one-sided deal where the United States gets nothing in return. As long as I hold this office, I will defend America's interests above all else' (Trump, 2017b). We were being told not to expect America to compromise in order to lead.

President Trump has made clear that he will not defer to technocrats and experts. In 2018 he stated, 'America's policy of principled realism means we will not be held hostage to old dogmas, discredited ideologies, and so-called experts who have been proven wrong over the years, time and time again'. The president continued, with a wolf whistle to extreme right American nationalists, 'America is governed by Americans. We reject the ideology of globalism, and we embrace the doctrine of patriotism' (Trump, 2018). In his speeches at the UN (and elsewhere), the president stresses the centrality of national sovereignty, of ensuring America succeeds and is first above others. And just in case there was any remaining doubt about President Trump's rejection of America's historic defense of a globalised rules-based world, he stated in 2019, 'The future does not belong to globalists; it belongs to patriots' (Trump, 2019).

This message alarmed allies and competitors who have invested a great deal politically and diplomatically in the interlinked structures that help girder the global geopolitical, economic and financial architecture and provide it with strength under pressure. But to what extent are these public statements mirrored in policy outcomes?

Rhetoric and action – divergence between statements and policy

Since 2017, policy makers and diplomats have been recalibrating their expectations of American leadership, absence of leadership or open hostility. Nearing the end of the first term of the Trump presidency, we can see varying degrees to which aggressive public statements of hostility towards the global rules-based system translate into action that could begin to dismantle, undermine and stymie long-standing and newer processes of international cooperation and coordination – what I observe is a sliding scale of damage to the architecture of global coordination. This is visualised in the matrix presented in Figure 5.1. This matrix could, in fact, be applied in numerous policy implementation assessment exercises.

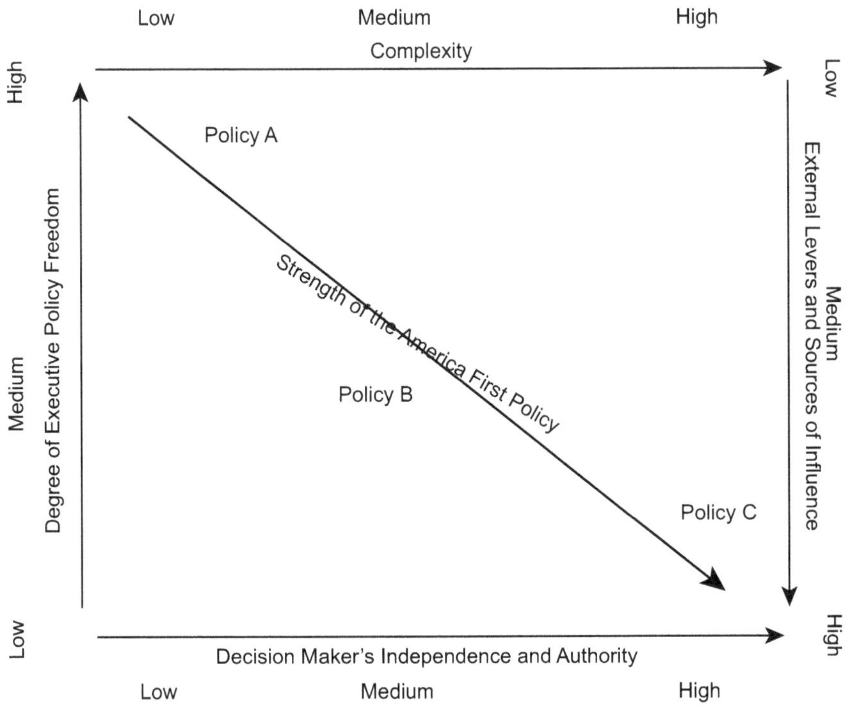

Figure 5.1 Nationalist populist policy matrix

Note: The **left-hand Y axis** shows the 'degree of executive policy freedom' from low to high, running up the page. The greater the extent of policy manoeuvrability the more impactful the populist policy can be. The **right-hand Y axis** shows the 'external levers and sources of influence' from low to high, running down the figure. With few external levers and little influence affecting presidential or executive power, the likelihood of a populist policy outcome is higher; with greater external (i.e. level-one and level-two interests involved), the policy outcome weakens. The **top X axis** denotes the degree of policy complexity from low to high, left to right. As policy complexity increases, the probability of the swift execution of a populist outcome decreases. The **bottom X axis** shows the decision makers' independence and authority from the executive or presidency, from low to high, left to right. A greater degree of independence lessens the impact of a populist policy insofar as the decision makers are institutionally resistant to sudden shifts. Under **Policy A,** the executive has maximum room to manoeuvre. The policy is relatively simple to execute, there are few sources of external leverage, and the institutional decision makers are not independent of the executive. In this quadfecta circumstance, a populist policy can be articulated and rolled out relatively quickly, to maximum effect. Under **Policy B,** the executive freedom to act is somewhat more limited, the policy complexity is higher, external level-one and level-two actors have some (often directionally different) influence, and the decision makers, upon appointment, have a degree of independence but are mindful of executive demands. In this instance, differing pressures and dynamics from all sides mitigate and moderate populist changes, but policy shift is nonetheless clearly visible. Under **Policy C,** the executive has quite limited freedom to act (perhaps due to existing commitments), the policy is highly complex, the decision makers are at arm's length institutionally from the executive and external levers and influence are seen. In this instance, a populist outcome can be stymied to a greater extent, notwithstanding a general desire by the president to act.

The strength of the US president's America First policy outcome varies depending on where the policy lies within the matrix. Note that the matrix is a stylised representation of the policy process dynamics and should be viewed as such.

At the one extreme, where President Trump and his immediate, most trusted advisers are in control of the levers of policy and can largely independently act without US congressional or other brakes on his actions, the damage to long-standing systems, structures and norms is considerable and potentially long-lasting. In the middle, we find policies that the administration pursues aiming at significant changes, but in areas which are complex and subject to congressional and diplomatic interventions. Here, presidential rhetoric does not fully match policy outcomes. At other end of the scale are policy decisions not directly controlled by the administration after the selection of key appointees. In those cases, existing institutional independence (within the G20 process or within the central banking community) significantly slows the momentum desired by the US president. But even at this end of the scale, this does not mean the effects of Trumpism are nonexistent.

The US president's impact on G20 summitry and communiqués is a maximal example of his room to manoeuvre.

The G20 adjusts to Trumpism

In the G20 leaders' forum, the American voice is important to the forum's diplomatic effectiveness – or lack of effectiveness. Leadership always matters in its presence and in its absence. As discussed in Chapter 4, since 2017, G20 summitry has been much more contentious, with the US demanding changes in language in the communiqués and signaling a break with past norms, US leadership and approach. President Trump's election caused consternation within the G20. Leaders struggled to minimise the effect of America's intransigence and its embrace of populist stances at odds with the consensus on climate change, trade and economic globalisation issues. Even dominant leaders such as Germany's Chancellor Merkel have been unable to repair the tears in the G20 consensus, and the strains in the personal relationship between the two were visibly on display.[5] Lesser leaders, from Argentina and Japan, were unable to counteract the hostility of the Trump administration and could do little but watch as America clashed with allies and a rising China.

Recent summits have shown that the G20 modus operandi and flexibility in approach and structure work in crises under strong leadership but can instead result in stalling and slower progress if a key actor baulks at compromise. In such cases, G20 leaders instead opt for agreement in fewer areas. As a result, the G20 impact has shrunk, leading a Chinese commentator to ask, 'Is the G20 destined to fade into irrelevance in a leaderless world – courtesy of Donald Trump?' (*South China Morning Post*, 2019). This is perhaps too hyperbolic. But major diplomatic and economic issues are put aside, unresolved, with the loss of American leadership.

Bend but don't break

Confronted by Mr Trump, the G20 process has shrunk the level of its ambition. We see a more defensive posture by other actors; shorter summit communiqués; disputes over key language, from 'rules-based international order' to climate change references; and a willingness to bend when faced by US intransigence. This is the right strategy. Since other G20 members view the leadership forum and its processes as important in and of themselves, they are trading loses now (in the communiqués) for the maintenance of the forum until a new leadership takes over in the US, preserving a forum that has worked better in the past for the next crisis, when, not if, it occurs. This approach means the G20 process is sustained, although shrunken in ambition, a reasonable compromise when confronted by Trumpism and America First.

The effect of America First on close allies of the US is real and requires an ongoing reappraisal of alliances and the role of America. This is clearly seen in Germany (see Box 5.2). A similar reassessment is underway in all capitals. Because of this, observers worry about the 'danger to America's superpower standing' posed by Trump's lack of understanding of history, foreign policy and diplomacy (*Washington Post*, 2020). Robert Kagan (2020) finds that 'overall, we have weakened the fabric of the international order that we created after World War II and that served us and others well during innumerable crises'.

Box 5.2 Germany and the Trump era

US relations with Germany are an example of the repositioning and reappraisal underway in G20 capitals since 2016. The US president has been audibly and visibly hostile to Germany and its chancellor. In 2017 President Trump said that 'Germans are bad, very bad' (Muller, 2017). The president has also claimed that 'Germany is captive to Russia' due to its gas imports (McBride, 2018). By 2018 German Chancellor Merkel was clear that the alliance could no longer be relied upon, stating, 'The times in which we could fully count on others are somewhat over. . . . We Europeans truly have to take our fate into our own hands' (Schulz, 2018). Or as Frank Walter Steinmeier, the president of Germany, noted ruefully, 'The United States of America, . . . rejects the idea of an international community' (Steinmeier, 2020).

Germany has been a pivotal European ally of America since immediately after World War II. The US Marshall Plan reconstructed Europe and Germany. The US backed NATO and the creation of the European Economic Community (now European Union). The Atlantic alliance grew as the European Union matured. Both have been remarkable successes, supported by Germany and the US, ensuring peace, democracy and prosperity took root in Europe over 70-plus years. Unfortunately, America First rejects this common narrative and political history and what it represents. For Trump, reading is for fools (Wolfe, 2018; Woodward, 2018), and for him, it appears that 'history is just one fucking thing after another' (Bennett, 2006). What matters above all is winning (Rucker and Leonnig, 2020).[1]

Chancellor Merkel's dim view of the US president mirrors that of German voters. Fully three-in-four or more lack confidence in Trump in Germany, Sweden, France, Spain and the Netherlands (Wike *et al*., 2020). The next German chancellor will have to continue to assume a lack of American leadership and plan for that eventuality. An especially close alliance has been damaged, not irreparably, but seriously. Other G20 allies are undertaking a similar strategic reassessment, both inside the G20 process, and in other forums, institutions and contexts.

Note: 1 Philip Rucker and Carol Leonnig describe a meeting with Defense Secretary James Mattis, National Security Council Chair H. R. McMaster and Secretary of State Rex Tillerson. The meeting was designed to give the president historical background to the policy process. The president became enraged and accused the chiefs of staff of being 'losers'. Secretary Tillerson intervened, defending the military. After the meeting Tillerson apologised to the military leaders, allegedly calling the president 'a fucking moron'. Within weeks, Tillerson would be fired by tweet, as would McMaster. Secretary Mattis held on longest but resigned when the president abandoned US allies to their foes in the Syrian desert.

Strategy? What strategy?

The policy reappraisal exercise and calculus is all the more difficult because, whilst the president's opinions (opposition to anything enacted by President Obama, for instance) and tactics (the use of tariffs to extort concessions from your opponent) may have certain consistent elements, there is a strategic conundrum, or black hole, at the very center. To put it bluntly, there is no overarching Trumpian master strategy, no equivalent of the Marshall Plan, no Powell Doctrine. Decisions are constantly made without proper consideration of the strategic implications (Sanger and Broad, 2019).[6] What we see instead is quasi-monarchical decision making, not a normal 'agency process', as the Ukrainian scandal, which led to the president's impeachment, illuminated (LaFraniere, Kramer, and Halin, 2019).[7] Analysts repeatedly try to divine the administration strategy in a specific sphere. But whilst there are short-term tactics, there is no long-term strategy (Cohen, 2020), and the normal policy processes are not operating (Seligman, 2020). This clearly complicates negotiations at the G20 level.

Placed in the matrix, G20 summit outcomes since 2017 are in the upper-left-hand quadrant. The US administration has veto power over summit declarations. They can insist on textual changes or deletions. If the US is opposed, a consensus cannot be reached, and carve-outs then occur. Of course, considerable complexity exists in the G20 summit process, and others are engaged seeking to ameliorate US actions, more often unsuccessfully. A 'no' from the US administration undermines and halts the G20 consensus-based processes. Whilst the G20 can bend, bide their time and continue to operate, the World Trade Organization (WTO) does not have that luxury. In 2020 the WTO faces its worst crisis since creation as Trump takes direct aim at this central pillar of liberalised globalisation.

A World Trade Organization in crisis

The WTO is today on the brink of collapse and is crippled (*Reuters*, 2019). The current crisis in the functioning of the WTO and its dispute settlement procedures (DSPs) demonstrates Trumpian populism at its maximal effect, and I place this Trumpian attack on the rules-based architecture in 'Policy A' position in the matrix. The US president has taken a hard line opposing the appointment of new judges to the dispute settlement process, causing the system to seize up (Swanson, 2019). In taking this stance, the president has a wide degree of policy freedom. The decision to refuse to allow appointments to the WTO DSP Appellate Body is entirely within his control; he is the sole decision maker, advised by a supportive team in the White House at the United States Trade Representative (Behsudi, 2017).[8] This decision is a simple one, with very significant implications. No other power can pull levers to counteract the US decision, given the need for a consensus.

The DSP is the key enforcement pillar of the WTO. By refusing to allow appointment of judges to the Appellate Body, the US administration has brought the WTO system to a standstill and to the brink of collapse, as there are no longer enough judges for it to operate.[9] Over 100 trade disputes before the court are in limbo, and the WTO rules-based system is directly undermined, perhaps fundamentally. With this US move, the WTO as a consensus-based body cannot resolve the impasse. And with the WTO norms undermined, anti-free-trade measures that breach WTO norms and rules (a majority enacted by the US) are on the upswing. In the year ending October 2019, import tariffs enacted by WTO members hit US$747 billion, an all-time high and up 27 per cent over 2018 (WTO, 2019).

This crisis in the WTO shows the maximal effect of the America First doctrine on the global architecture, that is a freezing of the rules-based consensual and judicial system of global trade. This heralds a return to mercantilism. A new period of great power competition has begun, unconstrained by existing rules (Steinmeier, 2020). The Trump administration move demonstrates that where the policy room to manoeuvre is maximal, where they have direct levers of control, where decisions are simple and where external influences are muted, the US will act against allies and existing institutions in pursuit of nationalist populist goals. Although trade policy is not the principal focus of this book, the president's assault on the WTO, the DSP and the global trading system is *the* poster child for the Trump presidency's America First policy and an important element of the end of Pax Americana (Mackintosh, 2018). The destruction of rules and a rejection of established norms that this attack represents may have a long-term corrosive effect, unless other state actors can better defend the global system of trade. Not all outcomes of America First are as shocking. When external and domestic complexities and constraints exist, America First's effects can be somewhat more nuanced.

Leadership of international financial institutions

A moderation of the effects of America First can been seen in the picks to lead key international institutions, specifically the World Bank and Financial Stability

Board. Here, external dynamics and institutional politics resulted in somewhat more mainstream selections and therefore outcomes.

A Trump loyalist at the World Bank

The US administration, as per a long-standing agreement that has been also been a matter of dispute and disagreement, still selects the president of the World Bank. President Trump selected a loyalist, David Malpass, an economist and political appointee of the Trump administration from the US Treasury. This alarmed observers. Mr Malpass is a longtime controversial critic of the World Bank and International Monetary Fund and was known to view their work with scepticism. Mr Malpass had previously maintained these institutions should do less and the private sector should do much more to ensure the stability of the global financial system – essentially that market mechanisms should provide more stability.

This argument is not new and is usually raised during periods of calm in the global system. As we saw in Chapter 1, prior to the global financial crisis during the great moderation, the IMF and World Bank were increasingly viewed as unnecessary, with the former almost running out of resources as it had practically no paying borrowers. When things are calm, who needs the financial fire brigade? But when financial crisis strikes, credit freezes, trade stops, banks teeter and economies wobble dangerously, the private sector, riven by panic, itself in disarray, cannot and will not support the stability of the system as a whole.

As I have shown, *in extremis*, the only actors capable of stopping a runaway crisis and restoring calm are major states, their central banks and the international institutions they support, including the IMF and World Bank. It is at best naive and at worst a fundamental misunderstanding of the dynamics of crisis management and the history of crises to suppose markets can offer the solution. They cannot. So how has Mr Malpass led the World Bank so far? Critics warned he would do damage. This has turned out not to be the case.

Where you stand depends on where you sit

Positional dynamics and bureaucratic politics mean that more often, as Miles' Law states, 'where you stand depends on where you sit' (Miles, 1978). Mr Malpass has been affected by the shift in his position, from US administration official to leader of an international financial institution, with scores of shareholders and different dynamics, demands and drivers. He has undergone an apparent rapid conversion to support of multilateralism and the collaborative style it requires. Mr Malpass has walked back from being a harsh critic to become a supporter of the bank's aims and mission. His leadership has been marked by a clear effort to reassure the staff that he no longer works for Mr Trump. A smart move. To be effective, Mr Malpass cannot oppose his own officials and staff; he needs them behind him, not fighting against him. Mr Malpass's success rests on how he leads the Executive Board, which is consensual in nature, not confrontational. Of course, he must maintain good links with the US administration. But this requirement is balanced by bureaucratic institutional dynamics and his separation and distance from the tweetstorm in the White House. This demonstrates that when the decision maker is separate from the executive (after appointment), is independent in their decisions, when policy complexities exist and external levers and influence can be applied (i.e. within the Executive Board), the America First approach is watered down. Placing the outcome of Mr Malpass's appointment within the policy matrix, it would be towards the right in the lower quadrant of the matrix.

The change in FSB leadership also shows that where you stand depends on where you sit, and the limits to Trumpian actions within external independent institutions that are some distance from the president.

Hold your opponent closest to you

Political analysts observe that one of the best ways to co-opt and thus neutralise a possible opponent is to draw them into your orbit – to place them in a leadership role – and thus ensure they have a vested interest in supporting and not attacking you (for instance, US President Barack Obama did this by appointing Hillary Clinton as secretary of state). This is solid advice and it was followed by the FSB leadership when responding to the Trump election victory. As Mark Carney, then-governor of the Bank of England and chair of the FSB, was considering who should replace him, the 2016 US election result shook the global architecture. What to do? How should the FSB react? Mr Carney decided to pull the leadership of the Federal Reserve Board closer to the FSB. He did this by selecting Randal Quarles, the Trump-appointed vice chair of America's central bank, to be chair of the FSB from December 2018 for half of a full term, after which time Quarles would hand over to Klaas Knot, governor of the central bank of the Netherlands. Mr Carney is nothing if not strategically astute, and this was another master stroke. In making the appointment, which was agreed by other FSB principals, Mr Carney ensured engagement and support from the FSB at a crucial time of heightened uncertainty. In doing so, he drew Mr Quarles into close support and leadership of the FSB. Just like Mr Malpass, once in place Mr Quarles's success would rest on different dynamics and political calculations. As chair, Mr Quarles was co-opted into a defense of existing structures, in support of the FSB's mission to address current and future risks, and in support of the mechanisms of cooperation, coordination and monitoring work. As chair, Mr Quarles will not want his time in office to be a failure. Mr Quarles now leads the key institution he might otherwise attack and undermine from the outside. But what of the policy output of the FSB under new management?

Policy construction and maintenance are still underway

The institutionally and politically astute selection of Mr Quarles followed by Mr Knot to lead the FSB within the international regulatory architecture is not the only evidence of the limits of America First at that reach and distance. The FSB has continued to work on shoring up processes and workstreams designed to strengthen the systemic resilience of the global financial system and the world's largest banks when and if faced by a new crisis. The speed of the work is slower, the steps somewhat more incremental and the shock and awe are gone, replaced by the grind of ongoing workstreams and processes designed to operate in peacetime as well and financial regulatory wartime.

These processes and the workstreams – on Basel III, on derivatives, on shadow banking, on digital transformation, on emerging risks – all occur shepherded by a community of central banks still jealous of their operational independence. This community's continued independence from governments (ministries of finance sit in the FSB but are not dominant) ensures process and some progress can continue even when America abandons a leadership role at the G20 because the FSB chair and other principals have room to manoeuvre and continue the organisation's mission. Moreover, the institution and the community that drives it are protected by their relative obscurity. What do I mean? What are the odds that President Trump knows what the FSB is and does? He is unlikely to be aware that the FSB is beavering away in the background, a group of elite, mostly foreign, unelected experts constructing a globalist architecture in Basel unencumbered by the direct effect of America First. Should President Trump suddenly become aware and angry, this could change. But for now, the FSB's relative obscurity is to be prized and coveted, and tweets avoided (see Box 5.3).

Box 5.3 Trumpian tweets – the stuff of technocratic nightmares

The central banking and FSB technocratic nightmare of today is 'assault by tweet'. The tweets come suddenly from left field; they cannot be anticipated. Yet presidential tweets make policy, shake markets, unnerve investors and alarm allies (Mackintosh, 2017),[1] whilst causing consternation in the US Congress. The tweets have a wide readership – the president has more than 69 million Twitter followers. Being a target terrifies the technocrati. Take only one example of thousands issuing from the president's callused but practiced thumbs.[2]

On 23 August 2019, the president responded angrily to a decision by Federal Reserve Board Chair Jerome Powell not to lower interest rates at a time when a Trumpian trade war with China was raging by asking, 'My only question is, who is our bigger enemy, Jay Powell or Chairman Xi?' (Smialek, 2019). Presidents have clashed with past Federal Reserve chairs before (Mackintosh, 2019).[3] But the attack on Chair Powell was an unheard of degree of vitriol directed at a Fed chair. The tweet stream is constant: from inauguration until the beginning of November 2019, the president sent more than 11,000 tweets (*New York Times*, 2019), many of them in anger, and many littered with falsehoods. And there is no recourse, no avoidance – except to keep your technocratic head down and hope the presidential gaze does not land on you but instead roves elsewhere.

As of 1 February 2020, the FSB's leadership and regulatory work have not been the focus of any tweets from the US president. One must assume the organisation is just too obscure, the work too uninteresting for the president. This obscurity is to be cherished. But it could all change in an instant if an industry lobbyist got on Fox News (the president's preferred network) in the morning and lambasted its work.

Note:

1 The author asked a senior UK diplomat in the US how they handled the constant tweets from the president, and if they had to monitor matters overnight. His reply was in the affirmative – a diplomat is tasked with reading and preparing memos on tweets for the ambassador and as necessary, 10 Downing Street, often at night, a tough and never-ending job.

2 President Trump, according to his tweet output, appears to spend too much time alone. One suggestion would be to import the approach first institutionalised by Henry VII and used by monarchs in Britain – the Privy Chamber. In this, the British monarch was surrounded by senior aides, including the Gentlemen of the Bedchamber, and at night, by the Groom of the Stool (See Penry (1995). Perhaps the American president needs a similar figure. One might call them the 'Special Assistant of the Tweet'. This individual would be tasked with asking the president, when he feels the urge to tweet alone at 3:00 a.m., "Perhaps the president sir should wait to speak to [insert relevant official's name here] first before acting?' A great many senior figures would sleep more soundly if such a process were put in place.

3 In his memoir, Chairman Volcker recounts how in 1984 he was called to the White House by Jim Baker, then Ronald Reagan's chief of staff. President Reagan was present but remained uneasily silent. Baker, speaking for the president, told Volcker he opposed any interest rate rises in advance of the upcoming elections. Volcker, thought to himself "What to say? What to do?" His response? He got up and walked out without saying a word. That is how you send a signal on the Federal Reserve System's independence.

The FSB leadership handover and outcome shows both the political manoeuvring skills of the FSB leaders and the limits faced by those seeking an international institutional and policy extension of America First. This example would be placed in the Policy C position in the matrix. If America First is harder to pursue and implement in institutions at arm's length, independent from the US administration and subject to different influences and internal dynamics, this is not the case to the same degree for domestic regulatory policies, where administration officials and the Congress can chip away at the re-regulation of banking and finance achieved post-global financial crisis.

Chipping away at the domestic regulatory architecture

International institutions and their leaders can resist America First demands. Domestic US policy dynamics are a different matter. Political appointees pursue the party line. Even those in independent institutions (such as the Federal Reserve) change their focus and direction in response to a change in political leadership. This has been the case since 2016 and reflects a White House de-regulatory mind-set affected by a US Congress with its own goals and shifts in the balance of power (the 2018 midterm elections gave Democrats a large majority in the House of Representatives, while Senate was placed more securely in the hands of the Republicans). What is visible is a chipping away at aspects of the re-regulatory architecture constructed by the Obama administration; the current president opposes almost all policies enacted by his predecessor[10] and supports weakening post-global financial crisis regulatory reforms. This deregulatory approach is visible across the entire US government; from environmental policy, to energy policy, to educational policy, to school meals, to financial regulation, the rollback is underway. Regulations are being reversed. Supervisory approaches changed. Loopholes in existing regulations widened. The details of these regulatory shifts are discussed in Chapter 6. What the regulatory rollback and other changes demonstrate is not only the shift in the administration mind-set, but also the increased power and influence of level-two interests and domestic banking lobbies. Bank CEOs are almost always closer to the Republicans than to the Democrats, and they have been vocally critical of the regulatory reforms put in place since 2008, even as the firms grudgingly implemented them.

The Trump administration has pursued deregulation mainly via agency regulatory decisions – i.e. steps that do not require congressional action. Agencies have adjusted existing definitions and shifted regulatory boundaries in implementation and interpretation. The Trump administration knows it cannot get a wholesale legislative reversal (House Democrats would stop it); instead there is an erosion of the rules' application. And there are shifts in supervisory tone and approach. What was previously a hardline has become much more accommodative.

As Chapter 7 shows, even as the G20 saw a rise in dissension, the general direction of regulatory action was a 'gold plating' of agreed FSB standards, i.e. national regulators adding to norms and rules. But since 2017 we have witnessed a marked US rollback of those standards and a weakening of rules. In 2020 external level-one pressure to sustain rules is weakening, and Mr Quarles and other Trump appointees are closer to the industry and are more likely to listen to complaints about regulatory overreach and to act. Level-two interests are growing in influence 11 years on from the last global financial crisis. When an administration shifts from one political party to another, such a change in emphasis is normal. There is also an element of regulatory amnesia developing as institutions' leaders change and memories fade.

In 2020 almost all the officials who led the crisis response and the re-regulatory reform phase have left the stage. They have been replaced by many who did not personally experience the heat of the fire and the comradery of the lifeboat. And if you don't experience something, you can't remember it. You can be told of the disaster and the terror and lessons learned, but such stories are a poor substitute for staring into the abyss of collapse and stepping back. As a result, today many bankers and regulators have begun to fall back into old habits and beliefs about the safety and stability of the system. In this manner, the strength of the domestic architecture is weakened – perhaps not fatally, but certainly incrementally.

America First versus an expert-led process

The Trumpian America First policy drive is troubling because the superstructure of international institutions and their functioning and processes are of necessity technocratic, expert-driven, consensus-based, internationalist, and globalist (in the nonpejorative sense). This is essentially a list of things the American president says he opposes and rejects. Yet for American leadership to succeed the global international architecture requires compromise, a search for consensus, flexibility and general agreement on goals, with considerable give and take. The history of the response to the global financial crisis in 2008–2009 demonstrates this.

Resistance may not be entirely futile

This chapter has shown that, to some degree, institutional structures, once strong and self-reinforcing, can resist active US opposition and efforts to undermine them. However, these structures are not impervious to repeated assaults. A major unwanted and unplanned-for test is now underway. Can the global architecture withstand the active opposition of the dominant but declining hegemon? Are the foundations strong enough? Can the G20 led structure operate in a crisis when America is absent – such as the COVID-19 global health and economic catastrophe? (see Chapter 8). The early indications are highly mixed. Thankfully, resistance is not futile in all cases.

The WTO case suggests that when the policy dynamics are favorable to the White House, resistance is ineffective and you end up with institutional paralysis in the WTO and a potential collapse of the rules-based trading system. When we assess G20 summitry from 2017 onwards, (see Chapter 4), you also see a consensus-based process partially stymied by aggressive American opposition. Communiqués are shortened. Language is omitted. Carve-outs are seen. The forum's effectiveness is compromised but not entirely undermined.

Leadership and context matter. So, when we assess the actions of Trump officials now in leadership roles, including Mr Malpass and Mr Quarles, we can see their positions shifting due to institutional power dynamics outside of the control of the White House.

In the domestic US sphere, the White House has greater leverage, even as it faces domestic pressures, political and otherwise, and so deregulation commences, piece by piece – not wholesale dismantlement, but a chipping away at existing rules and standards.

At the FSB level we see Mr Quarles leading the effort to identify future risks, notwithstanding the deregulatory moves he supports within the US. To some extent, the FSB process can substitute for explicit political US leadership. The review and monitoring functions can continue. New areas of focus are added (on digital currencies, on cloud computing, on AI).

The technocrats can keep busy looking towards the risk horizon. But is this sufficient? I do not believe technocrats in the central banking community can alone grapple with future risks. They can do a great deal, more than most, but they are not macroeconomic or supervisory supermen, despite what some of them may appear to think.

When the next crisis strikes . . .

Perhaps the singular and most important lesson from the crisis management response to the global financial crisis was that when crisis strikes, the state, in the form of national governments *and* central banks acting in coordination, is the final bulwark against disaster, the lender of last resort, the only rescuer still able to step into action and shore up the economy, commit resources and stimulate frozen markets when the private sector actors have run for cover. State authority, collectively and decisively wielded, is the final guarantee of stability in the national and the global financial system. That is what we saw unfold in 2008–2009; G20 states and central banks acted collectively and swiftly to calm markets, jumpstart economies and begin reforms to strengthen the system.

Recall that in the autumn of 2007, Timothy Geithner, then-president of the Federal Reserve Bank of New York; Ben Bernanke, then-chair of the Federal Reserve; and Hank Paulson, then-secretary of the US Treasury convened an emergency meeting with President George W. Bush. They told the president they must have his backing to do whatever was necessary to arrest the collapse in the markets. The president was decisive; he backed the team unambiguously. This clarity of leadership and flexibility allowed both arms of government and the central bank to move as swiftly as possible. There was no gap between the actors *in extremis*.

COVID-19 – a global public health and economic disaster

The COVID-19 crisis is a tragedy of staggering proportions, dwarfing all previous crisis events in our collective memory. Nothing of this scale had occurred since the 1918 flu pandemic that killed at least 50 million across the world. Billions of workers are being told to stay at home. Millions of people are being laid off every week. Millions of people are being infected. A great many are dying as health systems struggle to treat those gasping for breath. Economies are stopped in their tracks and a global recession begins. What can we conclude from the initial response in the COVID-19 pandemic? Did we see crisis dynamics and reactions that mirrored those seen in 2008–2009?

Many observers had worried that President Trump was incapable of handling a real as opposed to imaginary foe of any scale. How would a man who distrusts experts; who surrounds himself with family, corrupt sycophants, second-rate advisers and hangers on; who is quick to anger and slow to forget slights, react? Chapter 8 analyses the preliminary evidence available as this crisis unfolded in the spring and summer of 2020. If Mr Trump's style of presidential power causes nightmares for crisis managers in America, it is nonetheless a boon for those who want to see America's soft power weaken and fade.[11]

What of American soft power?

The Trump presidency's America First policy appears to be weakening the country's soft power and influence globally. If we define soft power as 'the ability to achieve objectives through attraction and persuasion' (Softpower30, 2020), it is clear this is almost the reverse of what the Trump presidency and America First is about. A 2017 Pew Research Poll found 70 per cent of those asked had no confidence in President Trump, with the same number saying the US does not consider the views of other countries. A majority still desire continued American leadership (rather than China). Many of those questioned now view the US as the main risk factor, not a pillar of strength. Populations are beginning to reorient and reconsider alternatives. When asked 'who is the world's leading economic power?', China now lags American by only 5 per cent.[12] America's standing in the world is slipping and China's is rising. American isolationism, its rejection of allies and the president's zero-sum policy stances are hastening America's relative decline as the global hegemon, speeding China's diplomatic and soft power rise, as well as forcing the creation of new alliances.

Even relatively weak powers, such as Russia, are benefitting significantly from the lack of cohesive strategic clarity in the US. President Putin has actively sowed discord and confusion in the US electoral process, with hacking, election meddling and social media misinformation. In this he has been aided by a White House unwilling to listen to its own advisers and intelligence agencies. The chaos and confusion further weaken American soft power, making its model and approach less appealing to others. America's soft power is being neglected by a president who sees no need for it (Nye, 2019).

President Trump's America First policy and the related tactics gain short-term 'wins', but at the cost of future trust, stability and the long-term strength of American diplomacy and soft power. Thus, the 'phase one' deal with China in trade and tariffs can be forced through, with China clearly getting the losing hand. This is a US Trump-generated win – for now. But the message received in Beijing is different from the tweets coming from the White House. The Chinese leadership understand they must do more to shore up their unilateral and multilateral position to resist further US pressure. They must create additional alliances (excluding the US as needed) to achieve their strategic and economic goals. In this manner, Trump's policy speeds the day when China can and will say 'no' to US demands, from a position of even greater strength.

Additionally, the alienation of America's natural allies, in Germany, in France, in Canada, in Mexico and elsewhere, further saps American standing and undermines the cooperative system America itself created from 1944 onwards. It forces those allies to look elsewhere and construct new routes to solve massive collective action problems such as climate change.

American populism . . . four more years . . .

Mr Trump and America First have yet to fatally undermine the foundations of international cooperation and coordination, the institutions that support the rules-based system upon which our future global economic sustainability, stability and prosperity relies. But make no mistake – a second four-year term – which is possible – would be potentially disastrous for the efficacy, strength and operation of the global architecture. The G20 would continue to flounder. The WTO would be dormant or dead. Collective solutions to common problems would be further neglected, from climate change, to the management of the digital transformation, to rising income inequality, to falling tax revenues, and the concentration of economic power among global tech giants. The regulatory rollback in the US would continue, possibly setting the stage for future systemic crises. The world can ill afford another four years of Mr Trump.

Perhaps, Mr. Trump's almost complete failure to arrest COVID-19 will lead to his defeat in 2020; the polls appear to be signalling as much. But nothing is certain. And even if Mr Biden is elected and beats Mr. Trump, he will have great deal to do to restore America's economy and her position of global leadership.

Notes

1 This chapter further develops analyses published in Mackintosh (2017).

2 Wolf (2018) recounts astonishment in the Trump camp as it gradually became clear on election night that Trump was going to win. The president's wife, Melania, is said to have wept at the outcome, distraught at the result.

3 Professor Raj Chetty's seminal and striking work on the atrophy of equality of opportunity in America has laid bare the end of the 'American dream' of upward mobility for the poor. The idea that if you work hard you can succeed and become rich yourself is an essential part of the American myth. Today, as Professor Chetty notes, 'If you believe in equality of opportunity move to Canada' (Chetty, 2020). The work draws on anonymised IRS records that allow Professor Chetty to follow the lifetime trajectory for thousands of children from rich and poor families across America. Professor Chetty may win a Nobel Prize for his work.

4 Steven Levitsky and Daniel Ziblatt (2018) make clear that the erosion of rules, but also norms, is very damaging to democracies that rest on a series of often unwritten assumptions about behaviour and approach to political engagement. They argue that President Trump exhibits all the traits of an autocrat, and they furthermore warn the reader to remember that most autocrats in recent history were elected first and then began dismantling the norms that underpinned their democracies.

5 David McHugh (2018) discusses a now famous photograph by the Associated Press. The image more than others captures the tension between Merkel, her allies, and President Trump. The president does not like to be told he is wrong. In this case he is at the Hamburg G20 summit in a room of leaders who are visibly in opposition to the president.

6 Cobbs and Field (2020) discuss the assassination of the Iranian General Qassim Suleimani on 2 January 2020 by a US drone strike is an example of this lack of strategic forethought, likely leading to a series unintended and increasingly dangerous outcomes.

7 In the impeachment hearings before the US Congress, witnesses testified that the normal agency process of review was sidestepped by the president seeking dirt on his opponent. Officials opposed the steps and sought to raise concerns. The decision to

pressure Ukraine does not appear to have grown out of a strategic review of the president's foreign policy goals in the region, let alone an assessment of how that tactical end-run around normal processes might result in a strategic failure and the impeachment of the president.

8 Mr Lighthizer, the United States Trade Representative, spent the last three decades representing steel producers in the US and seeking anti-dumping remedies against WTO allies – with some success – and he views the current WTO and dispute settlement system with considerable hostility. Observers point to 2003 for an explanation. That year, Lighthizer was nominated to fill a vacancy on the WTO Appellate Body by then-US Trade Representative Robert Zoellick. But Lighthizer was not appointed to the WTO; other member states blocked him as too hostile to the institution. Perhaps some snubs are never forgotten.

9 Normally, the WTO DSP and Appellate Body operate with seven judges. The judges serve for fixed terms so there are regular retirements and a need for new – usually uncontroversial – replacements, from amongst a small community of international lawyers. The Appellate Body requires a minimum of three judges to operate. Two of the last three judges on the body retired in December 2019.

10 A standard joke doing the rounds in Washington reflects this. 'How do you get President Trump to change a light bulb?' – 'Tell him President Obama put it in.' Indeed, President Trump regularly rails against President Obama's environmental standards at his rallies, particularly the regulation that required LED lighting replace incandescent bulbs. President Trump is rescinding this regulation.

11 Dunn Tenpas (2020) discusses President Trump's 'churn rate' of senior advisers; i.e. the rate at which they are fired or leave is far higher than previous administrations. At the time of writing, the key remaining actors of real influence on the president are Mike Pompeo, secretary of state; Stephen Miller, senior advisor; Peter Navarro, assistant to the president (for trade) who has driven the anti-China policy and has written vituperatively on it – penning *Death by China: Confronting the dragon – A call to action* (Navarro, 2011) the reason he got his role in the first place; Robert Lighthizer, United States Trade Representative; and Steven Mnuchin, secretary of the Treasury.

12 Historically sitting US presidents win a second term in office. In the modern era only two presidents failed to win a second term – Jimmy Carter and George H. W. Bush – both who ran for a second term during a period of economic crisis or recession. Until the COVID-19 crisis erupted in January 2020 it was generally expected that Mr Trump would win a second term. The pandemic and ensuing global recession would normally result in an electoral loss for an incumbent. However, as of spring 2020 the president's approval ratings have been rising – as he was seen to be performing better than in the last three years and as the country pulled together to get through the crisis. If Mr Trump's approval ratings are running consistently above 50 per cent at the time of the election, he would be normally expected to win, even of the economy is in recession.

References

Behsudi, A. (2017) 'The man getting ready to take on the WTO', *Politico*, 15 February [Online]. Available at: www.politico.com/agenda/story/2017/02/robert-lighthizer-wto-000304 (accessed: 6 January 2020).

Bennett, A. (2006) *The History Boys*. London, UK: Faber Drama.

Chetty, R. (2020) 'Income segregation and intergenerational mobility across colleges in the United States', *Opportunity Insights* [Online]. Available at: https://opportunityinsights.org/ (accessed: 2 March 2020).

Cobbs, E. and Field, K. (2020) 'Why did the US kill Suleimani?', *New York Times*, 7 January [Online]. Available at: www.nytimes.com/2020/01/07/opinion/soleimani-killed-us.html?action=click&module=Opinion&pgtype=Homepage (accessed: 7 January 2020).

Cohen, E. (2020) 'Trump is playing chess one turn at a time', *The Atlantic*, 4 January [Online]. Available at: www.theatlantic.com/ideas/archive/2020/01/does-trump-have-strategy-confronting-iran/604414/ (accessed: 6 January 2020).

Cohn, G. and McMaster, H.R. (2017) 'America First doesn't mean America alone', *Wall Street Journal*, 30 May [Online]. Available at: www.wsj.com/articles/america-first-doesnt-mean-america-alone-1496187426. (accessed: 12 December 2019).

Dunn Tenpas, K. (2020) 'Tracking turnover in the Trump administration', *Brookings Institution*, Washington, DC, January [Online]. Available at: www.brookings.edu/research/tracking-turnover-in-the-trump-administration/ (accessed: 19 January 2020).

Eichengreen, B. (2018) *The populist temptation: Economic grievance and political reaction in the modern era*. Oxford: Oxford University Press.

Hochschild, A. (2016) *Strangers on their own land*. New York: New Press.

Kahl, C. and Brands, H. (2017) 'Trump's grand strategic train wreck', *Foreign Policy*, 31 January [Online]. Available at: https://foreignpolicy.com/2017/01/31/trumps-grand-strategic-train-wreck/ (accessed: 4 January 2020).

Kagan, R. (2020) 'We're a national all too ripe for another shock', *Brookings*, 29 March [Online]. Available at: https://www.brookings.edu/blog/order-from-chaos/2020/03/29/were-a-nation-all-too-ripe-for-another-shock/ (accessed: 28 July 2020).

Klein, J. (2020) 'How Trump won his war against his own advisers', *Washington Post*, 19 January.

LaFraniere, S., Kramer, A., and Hakim, D. (2019) 'Trump, Ukraine and impeachment: The inside story of how we got here', *The New York Times*, 11 November. Available at: www.nytimes.com/2019/11/11/us/ukraine-trump.html (accessed: 6 January 2020).

Levitsky, S. and Ziblatt, D. (2018) *How democracies die*. New York: Random House.

MacDonald, P. (2018) 'America first? Explaining continuity and change in Trump's foreign policy', *Political Science Quarterly*, 133(3), p. 409.

Mackintosh, S. (2017) 'Will "America First" Trump international cooperation and coordination?', *World Economics Journal*, 18(4), pp. 59–73.

———. (2018) 'America First and the end of Pax Americana', *EuropeNow*, 7 November [Online]. Available at: www.europenowjournal.org/2018/11/07/america-first-and-the-end-of-pax-americana/ (accessed: 6 January 2020).

———. (2019) 'Volcker and de Larosiere: The end of giants?', *Business Economics Journal*, 54(1), pp. 151–154. A review of *Keeping at It*, Paul A. Volcker (2018). Public Affairs Books, and *50 Years of Financial Crises*, Jacques de Larosiere (2018). Odile Jacob Publishing.

McBride J. (2018) 'Nord Stream 2: Is Germany captive to Russia?', *Council on Foreign Relations*, 16 August [Online]. Available at: www.cfr.org/in-brief/nord-stream-2-germany-captive-russian-energy (accessed: 5 January 2020).

McGerr, M. (2005) *A fierce discontent: The rise and fall of the progressive movement in America 1870–1920*. Oxford: Oxford University Press.

McHugh, D. (2018) 'Body language: Photo of Merkel, Trump captured G7 tensions', *Associated Press*, 10 June [Online]. Available at: https://apnews.com/ea58db1f82c24a9aa48985002a55d948/Body-language:-Photo-of-Merkel,-Trump-captures-G-7-tensions (accessed: 5 January 2020).

Miles, R. (1978) 'The origin and meaning of Miles' Law', Public Administration Review, 38(5), pp. 399–403.

Muller, P. (2017) 'The Germans are bad, very bad', *Der Spiegel*, 27 May [Online]. Available at: www.spiegel.de/international/world/trump-in-brussels-the-germans-are-bad-very-bad-a-1149330.html (accessed: 5 January 2020).

Myre, G. (2017) '"America First": From Charles Lindbergh to President Trump', *All Things Considered*, 6 February [Online]. Available at: www.npr.org/sections/parallels/2017/02/06/513240634/america-first-from-charles-lindbergh-to-president-trump (accessed: 4 January 2020).

Navarro, P. (2011) *Death by China: Confronting the dragon – A call to action*. London: Pearson Press.

New York Times. (2012) 'Cultural war of 1992 moves in from the fringe', 29 August [Online]. Available at: www.nytimes.com/2012/08/30/us/politics/from-the-fringe-in-1992-patrick-j-buchanans-words-now-seem-mainstream.html (accessed: 23 January 2020).

———. (2017) 'Trump criticizes NATO and hopes for "good deals" with Russia', 15 January [Online]. Available at: www.nytimes.com/2017/01/15/world/europe/donald-trump-nato.html (accessed: 19 January 2020).

———. (2019) 'The Twitter presidency', 2 November [Online]. Available at: www.nytimes.com/interactive/2019/11/02/us/politics/trump-twitter-presidency.html (accessed: 3 January 2020).

Nye, J. (2019) 'American soft power in the age of Trump', *Project Syndicate*, 6 May [Online]. Available at: www.project-syndicate.org/commentary/american-soft-power-decline-under-trump-by-joseph-s-nye-2019-05?barrier=accesspaylog (accessed: 2 March 2020).

Park, J. and Stangarone, T. (2019) 'Trump's America First policy in global and historical perspectives: Implications for US – East Asian trade', *Asian Perspectives*, 41(1), pp. 1–34.

Penry, W. (1995) *The later Tudors: England 1547–1603*. Oxford: Oxford University Press.

Reuters. (2019) 'U.S. brings World Trade Organization's top court to brink of collapse', 9 December [Online]. Available at: www.cbc.ca/news/business/u-s-seals-demise-wto-s-appeals-bench-1.5389276 (accessed: 7 January 2020).

Rucker, P. and Leonnig, C. (2020) *A very stable genius: Donald J. Trump's testing of America*. London: Penguin.

Runciman, D. (2019) *Where power stops: The making and unmaking of presidents and prime ministers*. London: Profile Books.

Sanger, D. and Broad, W. (2019) 'Iran Challenges Trump, announcing end of nuclear restrictions', *The New York Times*, 6 January [Online]. Available at: www.nytimes.com/2020/01/05/world/middleeast/trump-iran-nuclear-agreement.html?action=click&module=Top%20Stories&pgtype=Homepage (accessed: 6 January 2020).

Schutz, S. (2019) '"Washington has become much rougher": Germany is still recalibrating with Trump', *National Public Radio*, 27 February [Online]. Available at: www.npr.org/2019/02/27/697803708/washington-has-become-much-rougher-germany-is-still-recalibrating-with-trump (accessed: 5 January 2020).

Seligman, L. (2020) 'Pentagon chief kept tight circle on Suleimani strike', *Foreign Policy*, 5 January [Online]. Available at: https://foreignpolicy.com/2020/01/05/pentagon-chief-kept-tight-circle-on-suleimani-strike/ (accessed: 5 January 2020).

Smialek, J. (2019) 'Powell highlights Fed's limits. Trump labels him an "enemy"', *New York Times*, 23 August [Online]. Available at: www.nytimes.com/2019/08/23/business/powell-fed-interest-rates-trump.html (accessed: 4 January 2020).

Softpower. (2020) 'What is soft power?' [Online]. Available at: https://softpower30.com/what-is-soft-power/#:~:text=In%20contrast%20to%20the%20coercive,to%20 achieve%20foreign%20policy%20objectives.&text=Joseph%20Nye%2C%20the%20originator%20of,as%20he%20developed%20the%20concept (accessed: 28 July 2020).

South China Morning Post. (2019) 'Is the G20 destined to fade into irrelevance – Courtesy of Donald Trump?', 23 June [Online]. Available at: www.scmp.com/news/china/diplomacy/article/3015447/g20-destined-fade-irrelevance-leaderless-world-courtesy-donald (accessed: 21 January 2020).

Steinmeier, W. (2020) 'German President takes swipe at global powers as Munich conference opens', *Radio Free Europe*, 14 February [Online]. Available at: www.rferl.org/a/global-officials-meet-at-munich-security-conference-afghanistan-pompeo/30433691.html (accessed: 29 February 2020).

Swanson, A. (2019) 'Trump cripples W.T.O. as trade war rages', *The New York Times*, 8 December [Online]. Available at: www.nytimes.com/2019/12/08/business/trump-trade-war-wto.html (accessed: 6 January 2020).

Thatcher, M. (1987) 'Interview for *Women's Own*', *Margaret Thatcher Foundation*, 23 September [Online]. Available at: www.margaretthatcher.org/document/106689 (accessed: 20 December 2019).

Trump, D. (2017a) 'The inaugural address', 20 January [Online]. Available at: www.whitehouse.gov/briefings-statements/the-inaugural-address/ (accessed: 23 April 2020).

———. (2017b) 'Remarks of President Trump at the 72nd session of the United Nations General Assembly', *United Nations*, 19 September [Online]. Available at: www.whitehouse.gov/briefings-statements/remarks-president-trump-72nd-session-united-nations-general-assembly/ (accessed: 18 December 2019).

———. (2018) 'Remarks of President Trump at the 73rd session of the United Nations General Assembly', *United Nations*, 25 September [Online]. Available at: www.whitehouse.gov/briefings-statements/remarks-president-trump-73rd-session-united-nations-general-assembly-new-york-ny/ (accessed: 18 December 2019).

———. (2019) 'Remarks by President Trump to the 74th session of the United Nations General Assembly', *United Nations*, 25 September [Online]. Available at: www.whitehouse.gov/briefings-statements/remarks-president-trump-74th-session-united-nations-general-assembly/ (accessed: 18 December 2019).

Washington Post. (2020) 'You're a bunch of dopes and babies': Inside Trump's stunning tirade against generals', 19 January [Online]. Available at: www.washingtonpost.com/politics/youre-a-bunch-of-dopes-and-babies-inside-trumps-stunning-tirade-against-generals/2020/01/16/d6dbb8a6-387e-11ea-bb7b-265f4554af6d_story.html (accessed: 21 January 2020).

White, R. (2006) *Kingfish: The reign of Huey P. Long*. New York: Random House.

Wike, R., Stokes, B., Poushter, J., Silver, L., Fetterolf, J., and Devlin, K. (2020) 'Trump's international ratings remain low, especially among key allies', *Pew Research Center*, 1 October [Online]. Available at: www.pewresearch.org/global/2018/10/01/trumps-international-ratings-remain-low-especially-among-key-allies/ (accessed: 5 January 2020).

Wolfe, M. (2018) *Fire and fury*. New York: Holt and Co.

———. (2019) *Siege: Trump under fire*. New York: Holt and Co.

Woodward, B. (2018) *Fear: Trump and the White House*. New York: Simon and Schuster.

Wright, T. (2016) 'Trump's 19th century foreign policy', *Politico*, 21 January [Online]. Available at: www.politico.com/magazine/story/2016/01/donald-trump-foreign-policy-213546 (accessed: 3 January 2019).

WTO (World Trade Organization). (2019) 'Report shows trade restrictions at historically high level', 21 December 2019.

6 The Financial Stability Board

Its creation, structure, and processes[1]

> Institutional change only makes sense by reference to the ideas that inform agents' responses to moments of uncertainty and crisis.
>
> (Blyth, 2002)

Introduction

Crises tend to force actors together and to clarify common goals. When actors collectively face possible disaster, the failures of the past become clear, as does the necessity for change, and the search for solutions must include the broadest actions possible. In this way, financial and economic crises increase possible policy options, and actions thought impossible in normal times become possible in the face of unprecedented shocks.

The global economic and financial crisis of 2007–2008 was such an event. The world's political and central banking leadership knew they had to act, and act fast, to arrest the worst global economic slump since 1929. Together, a small number of actors seized the crisis as a pivotal moment for institutional and policy activism. They began a paradigm shift in international regulatory reform and coordination, from the previous, now discredited, deregulatory mind-set, towards the reassertion of state power over financial markets and firms and the globally coordinated re-regulation that this new worldview required.

As Joseph Stiglitz has rightly noted, however, 'changing paradigms is not easy' (Stiglitz, 2010). These rare shifts in an ideological and regulatory worldview do not occur instantaneously, but once the break point for the prior worldview is reached, they unfold over years, involving many individual actions, which, viewed together, constitute meaningful change. To successfully execute a series of complex multiyear interconnected reforms – from addressing systemic risks, to raising bank capital, to derivatives regulation, to bankers' bonuses, to addressing too-big-to-fail and more – an elite 'swat team' (Mackintosh, 2012, 24, p. 9), in the words of one principal present, called the Financial Stability Board (FSB) – was created in April 2009. Yet, more than a decade later, outside of a small number of cognoscenti, this entity is largely unknown. The importance of this ideological and policy shift and of the FSB's centrality to the reform process in the years since the apogee of the crisis in 2008 should not be underestimated. The G20-led central-banker-backed crisis response saw a new institution created that in 2015 is still growing in influence and authority, but with few paying attention. Without this new forum, the financial reform drive would not be as effective or as durable. It is the FSB that coordinates and often determines international financial rules and boundaries within which global markets and firms must operate. And as the de facto global regulatory coordinator and arbiter, the FSB deserves to be better understood and scrutinised more closely.

An elite, expert, tight-knit epistemic community composed of central bankers (Haas, 1992a), primarily principals from a few Western states, played a crucial role at the FSB's creation and in delineating its structure and the scope of its activities. Members of this FSB community were recipients of the G20's political capital, and they played a highly influential role in fashioning the reform mandate that the G20 agreed to. This community of officials was and still is essential to the creation and maintenance of the paradigm shift focused on state regulation of financial markets firms and to the diffusion of policy (Lazer, 2005; Levi-Faur, 2005) from 2008 to 2009 onwards. That shift was strengthened even during phase three of the G20's existence, i.e. after 2009. A community that largely failed to anticipate the financial crisis in advance seized control over the reform and redesign via the FSB and came out of the process reinvigorated and more powerful than before the crisis. That is quite an achievement. As one participant recalled:

> You have got to see this also in terms of power, you've got to see this as central bankers retaining their authority in the face of a major crisis which could [otherwise] lead to a different structure. . . . Through the FSB internationally and nationally, more power has been given to the central banks.
>
> (Mackintosh, 2011, 9, pp. 23–30)

From its birth in 2009, the leadership of the FSB rapidly evolved into the dominant coordinating forum, backed by the G20 above it and underpinned by the power and authority of its own central banking community. The organisational impact of the FSB was considerable in terms of increasing the intensity and efficacy of international cooperation and the coordination of the policy output of the actors and standard-setting bodies involved.

The FSB's creation increased by at least an order of magnitude the level and intensity of the international technical state-level agency-to-agency coordination and cooperation amongst central banking and supervisory communities. The G20 move to create the FSB and the processes it oversees was a third-order change (Hall, 1993) and constitutes part of the concrete realisation of the paradigm shift begun by the G20 in 2008. Then US Treasury Secretary Timothy Geithner called the FSB 'in effect, the fourth pillar in the system of global governance' (in Helleiner, 2010, p. 6). The financial regulatory reforms agreed to by the G20 were overseen and directed by the FSB. The FSB's members and its processes made the narrative jump together. They were key to the paradigm shift and led the policy reforms that flowed from the change in worldview and which are still underway in 2015.

Who designs and controls an institution matters. The FSB would be stronger, more dynamic, more inclusive and more activist than its predecessor. The FSB was created by predominantly hawkish officials from a small group of key advanced economies who from 2009 to 2012 led the organisation, chaired many of the committees and working groups and determined key work streams. A relatively small number of European and North American central banking and supervisory technocrats retained significant power even as the leadership roles changed marginally from 2012. In essence key actors responsible for major markets in leading G20 states continued to dominate the reform deliberations, and they will likely do so going forward.

Emerging-economy voices were heard, for instance, at the outset in support of the new re-regulatory paradigm. These actors participated in the FSB, and their engagement is quantitatively and qualitatively greater than in the previous exclusionary structure. On occasion, their input could tip the balance in favour of a particular policy solution. But in the key formative years, the FSB's organs and policy levers remained in the hands of a few from the core. In 2015 emerging-economy members have an enhanced role but are not yet central actors.

Eleven years on, the FSB has dedicated resources, a distinct identity, and a much enlarged staff. After its initial creation, the FSB was built by stealth, brick by brick. Ultimately, its success is dependent in part on the efficacy and strength of the G20 and also on the cohesiveness of the policy consensus of its dominant community. The FSB is an institutional tween, albeit a precocious one carefully nurtured by its central banking parents. The FSB's precise role and *modus operandi* are still today obscure to outsiders. It is far less transparent or open to civil society than the International Monetary Fund (IMF) or World Bank, for instance. This is despite its position at the very centre of the post-crisis redesign of the global financial regulatory architecture. In 2020 in comparison to the existing international financial institutions (such as the IMF), it is a black box.

This chapter highlights the paradigm shift that the FSB's creation, structure and operation represent. The FSB was and is a crucial part of, and its leaders were key actors in, the paradigm shift and altered policy consensus. The FSB's creation and its operation were a third-order change in the mechanisms of international regulatory coordination and cooperation. What was seen was a burst of rapid institutional creation followed by additional, more incremental steps to strengthen the new FSB. This rhythm in the construction, strengthening, paradigm maintenance and 'resilience' (Skogstad, 2008, p. 16) of the FSB was in part matched by, but extended and deepened, the more modest and less resilient shift seen at the political level of the G20 summits. This was because the FSB's leadership and community were more cohesive and had a unique influence over and role in the G20 policy reform process as a whole. The two processes are linked, and the FSB, its *modus operandi* and processes were and are important to the creation of the re-regulatory paradigm shift and to its maintenance.

The creation of the Financial Stability Board

G20 summitry shows that for the decision makers, 'it often takes a crisis or shock to overcome the institutional inertia and habit and spur them to seek help from an epistemic community' (Haas, 1992a, p. 14). Blyth adds that 'institutional change only makes sense by reference to the ideas that inform agents' responses to moments of uncertainty and crisis' (Blyth, 2002, p. 251). Through the creation of the FSB, a central banking community joined by common experience and beliefs rapidly evolved during the crisis and acted internationally in support of a re-regulatory collective state-power-based paradigm shift. In 2008 the central banking and regulatory community rushed to support the G20 and to provide an outline of a consensus view about the causes and effects of the crisis, and of its failurcs and solutions. This developing consensus reduced uncertainty and facilitated the paradigm shift in worldview and policy prescriptions. The group advised and directly affected the shape of the G20-backed reforms, policy process and options going forward. This gathering of principal central bankers and supervisors was a distinct epistemic community (Haas, 1992a), and they devised their own institutional creation to match the reform impulse. The G20 set the process of reform going, with an investment of collective political capital in the crisis management and reform phases. As one participant recalled, there was an 'alignment of leaders and technocrats' and, on the actual policy prescriptions, 'technical professionals were allowed to figure it out' (Mackintosh, 2012, 22, p. 12). Another recalled, 'the intellectual heft came from the core' (Mackintosh, 2012, 24, p. 10), i.e. a small number of advanced-country principals.

This central banking and supervisory community identified the proximate causes of the crisis and possible policy solutions. The causes of the crisis included global imbalances driving a credit boom in deficit countries (Smaghi, 2008); unintended consequences of the great moderation (that is the reduction in the volatility of the business cycle) (Gudmundsson, 2008); excess leverage in banks (King, 2010; Turner, 2009); poor risk management and excessive risk taking (King, 2009); opacity in complex interconnected global securities markets, which acted as a risk and panic transmission mechanism for the crisis (Buchanan, 2013, p. 20; Gudmundsson, 2008; Weber, 2008); and a failure of supervision and oversight of markets and firms (G30, 2009). Having a common crisis-driven conception of the nature of the failures, it was then possible for the community to coalesce relatively quickly around a new paradigm, and as a key part of that, the institutional reforms needed in response to the crisis.

The community's move towards financial market reform and stronger global regulation during this crisis period is explicitly characterised as a new 'consensus' by various sources (Blanchard *et al.*, 2012; Constancio, 2010; Smaghi, 2008, p. 3). What is being constructed is a policy 'consensus amongst the elite that operates, in the first instance, above the fray of domestic politics' (Bennett, 1991, p. 225). All this required 'greater international coordination, requiring concerted efforts by international organizations' (Watanagase, 2008, p. 3) and a strengthening of the international architecture (Noyer, 2008). Hence the need for the FSB.

Central bankers as an epistemic community

Central banker and supervisory responses in crisis show the individuals acting as an epistemic community. The group exhibited a shared set of causal and principled beliefs and notions of validity. From 2008 onwards the community rapidly developed a common policy consensus and a series of policy responses to the crisis and internationally coordinated reforms. As with other communities, the actors knew each other well and tended to trust one another (Adler, 1992, pp. 111–112). They operated as a 'network of professionals with recognized expertise and competence' (Haas, 1992a, p. 3). They were deferred to for technical expertise by political leaders, and they, also unlike some other communities of experts, retained the independent regulatory authority to make policy changes in many key areas they identified for reform.

This elite community facilitated policy convergence, bound by knowledge and expertise and experience of common policy problems and solutions (Bennett, 1991). Once policy options became clear they assisted in efficient top-down information diffusion (Levi-Faur, 2005) via ties that connected otherwise unconnected communities across geography, culture and political and economic factors (Lazer, 2005, p. 56). The community prepared the ground for international policy harmonisation (Holzinger and Knill, 2005). As early as late 2008 and spring 2009, the outline of a new policy narrative was taking shape.

The community was a knowledge elite to whom the leaders deferred in the crisis and reform phases. The regulatory issues were technical in nature, and this required G20 leaders to turn to the community for advice, as has happened in negotiation of the Montreal Protocol (Haas, 1992b). The central banking community, as have other specialist communities, influenced the debate, provided the technical knowledge, identified cooperative options (Adler, 1992) and at the very outset, pushed for the creation of an institutional structure that could build collective vested interests in the international reform process – i.e. the FSB itself.

Crucially, it is the combination of relative clarity on external anomalies and causes amongst a strong central banking epistemic community, the coalescence around a common macroprudential policy consensus and the control this one community had over many of the policy levers, which increased the probability of a paradigm shift in worldview and linked policy outcomes (as pictured in Figure 1.2). Because this combination was present in the economic and financial crisis, the re-regulatory shift began, and the community proved to be the most influential operator below the G20 level.

Seizing the crisis and reasserting collective state and central bank control

Two officials in particular, Tim Geithner and Mario Draghi, were instrumental in the FSB's creation. As the crisis grew during 2007–2008, they consulted with an ad hoc grouping of senior central bankers and supervisors, at discussions at the margins of other official IMF and G7 gatherings to consider the options. The central banking community leadership dominated these informal discussions (Geithner at that time was a central banker and subsequently became US Treasury secretary).

The meetings included a who's who list of the world of central banking: The two leaders – Mario Draghi (as Financial Stability Forum (FSF) chair) and Tim Geithner – were joined by Mark Carney, governor of the Bank of Canada; Jaime Caruana, general manager of the Bank for International Settlements (BIS); Philipp Hildebrand, governor of Swiss National Bank; Mervyn King, governor of the Bank of England; Jean-Claude Trichet, president of the European Central Bank; Adair Turner, chair of the UK Financial Services Authority; Axel Weber, president of the Deutche Bundesbank; and a few others. The group was almost all central bank governors, and many of them post-crisis tended to lean in favour of greater international regulatory discipline, higher capital, less leverage, more liquidity and other solutions that, taken together, signalled a possible re-regulatory paradigm shift. It is from these deliberations that the FSB concept emerged.

These actors saw the crisis as an opportunity for institutional re-creation and international and national re-regulatory action, a reassertion of their power and authority over markets and firms. A failure to seize control of the reform agenda could have led to an alternative structure, with the IMF taking a larger role in crisis response matters, as occurred in response to the Mexican and Asian crises of the 1990s. Instead by championing the more exclusive FSB led by central bankers, the community's members kept the regulatory policy-making response within their control, as the functional exclusion of finance ministries from the leadership decision-making process from 2009 to 2011 underscores. This technocratic elite community was to be pivotal at the outset and throughout the technical policy responses from that point onwards.

During autumn 2008 and until creation of the Financial Stability Board by the action of the G20 leaders in London in spring 2009, the central banking community, and predominantly this small, largely Western, subsegment of it, discussed options. It was clear to many of the actors that 'there needed to be an international group whose remit was to take a top-down view of the entire financial system' (Mackintosh, 2012, 15, p. 2). The solution: a renamed, enlarged, empowered FSF to mirror the leadership forum above it. Thus, the central banking epistemic community met informally and formed a consensus on how to proceed institutionally and in terms of policy choices. In doing so, they would 'attempt to select the forum that best suited their interests' (Raustiala and Victor, 2004, p. 299). The forum was a reformed, enlarged and renamed FSF, which itself had been created in 1997 by a former grouping, the G22, in reaction to a previous, less severe financial crisis cycle (Blustein, 2012; Cartapanis and Herland, 2002, pp. 26–265) of crisis, response, reform and relapse.

Why the new name? Because 'a forum sounds like you are discussing things, a board sounds like you are deciding things' (Mackintosh, 2011, 9, p. 4). The central banking community, largely from advanced economies, duplicated and slightly expanded the G20 diplomatic structure via creation of the overarching

FSB to stand between the G20 leaders, deputies and sherpas (political operatives) and the standard-setting body (SSB) members (second-rank technicians and officials). The government officials faced political constraints and lacked the technical know-how, and lower-level technocrats lacked the authority to take robust action. Inserting in the middle an authoritative leadership body composed only of central banking and supervisory principals could provide the requisite direction, cohesion and authority to national agencies and technocrats in the reform responses and policy output.

European and North American principal central bankers and supervisors who conceived of the FSB went on to serve and lead this new entity at the outset. They oversaw a broader, deeper work stream. With a new name and enlarged membership to reflect the composition of the G20 leaders' forum, the chairman of the FSB, Mario Draghi, who also chaired the predecessor FSF, swiftly pressed regulatory changes and reforms. Many of the solutions the FSB proposed had been identified by the FSF in 2008 (Smaghi, 2008). But post-crisis the reforms were pursued with greater international and institutional vigour and success, with explicit political backing provided by the G20 summit process. Draghi, an accomplished political operator, designed an entity that has many of the characteristics of an institution. From its inception in 2009 the FSB was further strengthened, and it became the central new actor in the coordination of international financial and regulatory diplomacy.

The FSB's mandate

The FSB's mandate contains a series of broad objectives which fall into six main categories: 1 assessing vulnerabilities affecting the global financial system and identifying the required regulatory, supervisory and related actions (i.e. directing global financial macroprudential and other reforms); 2 overseeing coordination and information exchange amongst authorities responsible for financial stability; 3 vigilance on future market risks; 4 monitoring application of agreed regulatory standards; 5 overseeing the work of the SSBs; and 6 addressing systemic risk and crisis management as applied in particular to the world's largest banks and financial firms (FSB, 2012, Art. 1(2 a-i)).

In essence the FSB stands at the centre of the regulatory redesign, as the designer, coordinator, facilitator and reform monitor for the central bank community, reporting to the G20. The FSB has considerable authority because of its composition, which is underpinned by a cohesive re-regulatory narrative and post-crisis macroprudential consensus. But its mandate does not include enforcement powers, i.e. the ability to coerce agencies or individuals to do that which they do not wish to do. This weakness should not be overplayed. The evidence in this chapter and in Chapter 7 demonstrates that this lead community, with a strong consensus, which controls the levers of policy making, can produce third-order change. Moreover the FSB coordinating process and institutional processes also themselves constitute a third-order change in the apparatus of international regulatory coordination, communication and cooperation.

The FSB, coordination and international regulatory cooperation

Before the 2007–2008 global economic and financial crisis leaders, central bankers, and regulators often paid lip service to collaboration and coordination. Serious reports on the subject were considered incomplete without an obligatory paragraph stressing the importance of greater collaboration and coordination. Clearly everyone agreed about it, but no one did anything about it. Why? Because in non-crisis times, centrifugal forces dominate, and national leaders and their regulators bicker amongst themselves. Prior to 2009 there was no effective mechanism to overcome (or at least mitigate) the tendency to diverge from, instead of converge on, common goals. The financial crisis changed all that, and the FSB was tasked as 'a general contractor for financial reform'. By 2012 at the Los Cabos summit, G20 leaders claimed that 'the G20 has led to a new paradigm in multilateral cooperation' (G20, 2012).

The FSB's main task is coordinating and improving the information exchange and dialogue amongst SSBs, member finance ministry officials, central bankers and supervisors on the policy reforms identified by the G20. The FSB plays the key role in facilitating, monitoring and reporting on all work streams resulting from the G20 process. The FSB leadership does not in all cases produce the regulatory recommendations themselves. SSB representatives also produce deliverables under the aegis of the FSB, its standing committees and working groups. The FSB leadership then monitors progress, reports on outcomes upwards to the G20, agrees to next steps and provides a venue for discussion of the continuing work streams.

The G20-FSB-SSB process has a multitier reporting and monitoring superstructure. This is new and significant because the FSB can pressure SSBs and national regulators to complete the G20 tasks assigned to them and to monitor adherence to agreed standards. The FSB's leadership can, as one participant notes, 'use the bully pulpit of the FSB and the G20 reporting' process to push recalcitrant members to adhere to standards and timetables (Mackintosh, 2012, 24, p. 21). In return for inclusion the SSBs and their memberships get elevated status; they play a bigger role in the policy process and are more closely connected to decision-making processes. This is binding together disparate actors and pressing for uniformity and accountability in the application of agreed rules, standards, best practices and principles.

As Figure 6.1 indicates the G20 provides political capital and agreed policies and supplies political pressure to the process. The G20 is a level-one decision maker, providing directional, nontechnical input downward to the FSB and SSBs.

The FSB engages in policy design, oversight and monitoring; reports upwards to the G20; and provides direction and oversight to SSB participants. It is a level-one decision maker composed of a cohesive community with a common policy narrative. Its decisions are both directional (i.e. on policy goals) and detailed (i.e. it can determine actual policy rules). This is in part because, as one participant said, 'it's the principals there' and 'discussions are quite rich and technical' (Mackintosh, 2012, 24, pp. 12–13). In this manner the 'experts, the

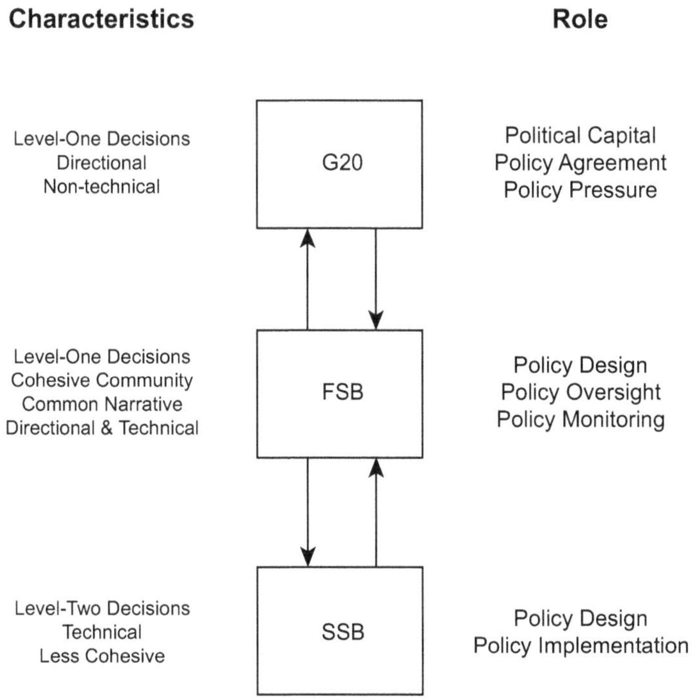

Figure 6.1 The G20-FSB-SSB coordination process

central bank governors, the principal supervisors, can hammer it out" (Mackintosh, 2012, 22, p. 11).

The SSBs in this structure are engaged in policy design and implementation at the direction of the FSB, with an upward reporting process through the FSB to the G20. The SSBs are level-two decision makers, technically focused and composed of national actors that may exhibit a less cohesive community narrative and thus weaker processes. Some SSBs, such as the Basel Committee on Banking Supervision (BCBS) (predominantly deputies of the FSB leaders above them), are cohesive and quite strong. Others, such as the International Organization of Securities Commissions (IOSCO), are weaker institutionally, outside the direct control of the leading reformers and may not have experienced such a marked collective narrative shift.

What is notable in this process is the qualitative and quantitative improvements in the level of engagement and integration of the FSB and SSB participants into this coordinated policy process led and backed by G20 political leaders at the summits. The upward reporting through the FSB to G20 leaders in the structure is an important innovation missing from the previous architecture, because the pressure of (FSB-imposed) reporting to the G20 on deadlines and policy reform goals provides impetus to the reform dynamic, strengthening the momentum towards common goals. Where necessary the G20 has intervened to press progress forward. There is policy development, monitoring and reporting pressure on FSB members and SSB leaders and national agencies from multiple FSB actors (such as the Chair, Steering Committee, Standing Committees or Working Groups). Deadlines that are agreed to by the FSB and G20 are pressed forward. Today SSBs are under pressure and they have been 'raising their game' (Mackintosh, 2012, 22, p. 15).

The previous weak, fractured and disparate structure was much less effective. SSBs operated independently. They were linked to other SSBs via a 'Joint Forum', but this body had a weak mandate and no power or authority. SSBs did not feel pressure to deliver or coordinate in this structure, did not report via a direct chain to a body composed of principals and did not report to national political leaders at summits.

The current structure is qualitatively stronger and exerts coordinating and cooperative pressure and direction on the collective G20-led FSB-SSB output. In this construct the SSBs are 'half independent and half taking direction from the FSB' (Mackintosh, 2011, 7, p. 25). The structure acts 'to provide a kick in the butt to the standard setters' (Mackintosh, 2012, 15, p. 3).

The FSB sits as the centre of the post-crisis regulatory reform, which it coordinates and directs. The FSB and the processes it oversees constitute a third-order shift, a paradigm shift in international regulatory coordination. The principals engaged in the FSB see these processes as a significant innovation and an increase in intensity of the dialogue. A senior US participant observed that the FSB has been 'invaluable in coordinating and urging SSBs to move forward with their work' (Bretton Woods Committee, 2010). An EU commissioner applauds the G20-FSB process for facilitating a 'constant dialogue at the technical level' (Barnier, 2011). Former European Central Bank President Trichet stressed that the process ensures 'an unprecedented degree of international cooperation in regulatory matters' (Trichet, 2010, p. 5). The intensity of the dialogue, the number of actors involved and the multifaceted nature of the discussions are quantitatively greater and qualitatively better, something not seen pre-crisis. By backing the creation of the FSB the G20 got an enhanced, institutionalised and regularised system of international coordination and cooperation on both financial regulation amongst a much larger grouping of regulators than hitherto existed, building networks and on SSB processes. This coordination and cooperation infrastructure was essential to the reform project.

In 2020 the FSB continues to foster closer state-to-state international cooperation and coordination than existed in the past. The prior perfunctory genuflection towards the importance of international coordination and cooperation has been replaced by authoritative deep, broad and robust policy processes coordinated by the FSB and its leaders. The FSB grasped the opportunity to closely coordinate the G20 financial reform agenda in 2009, and it has yet to let go. The effectiveness of the FSB at the centre of the reassertion of state authority over markets is due not only to position in the architecture, but also to its internal structure and operation.

The institutional structure of the FSB

Architecturally the FSB was to be a process-driven organisation and required 'an institutional structure commensurate with its expanded tasks' (Draghi, 2009, p. 2). Its supporters expected it to become a 'fully-fledged international body' (Noyer, 2009, p. 4). Indeed its structure projects solidity and includes five levels of organisation (Chair, Steering Committee, Plenary, Standing Committees, and Working Groups; see Figure 6.2). The FSB has a larger membership than the FSF, more than triple the staff, and a considerable increase in time commitment and resources from scores of agencies, many principal-level officials, and hundreds of lower-level officials, backed by a G20 commitment to its common goals. The following sections outline the structure of the FSB and discuss its strengths and limitations.

Membership: FSB membership includes 36 states, institutions and agencies.[2] The FSB is larger than the G20 leadership grouping and has 25 membership jurisdictions (i.e. states within which regulatory decisions made by the FSB may be implemented nationally by national regulatory agencies. It was designed to include key financial markets, states and standard-setters that play a role in global financial regulation and supervision. Thus Hong Kong SAR, China; the Netherlands; Singapore; and Switzerland are included because they each have major regional or global financial centres.

Chair: The FSB Chair is appointed by the plenary for a three-year renewable term. The individual chairs the Plenary and the Steering Committee and oversees the Secretariat. Mark Carney was selected via an informal 'sounding out' of key constituencies (Brookings Institution, 2011a). As of 2013 there is a more formal process (FSB, 2013), but the process still allows the most influential states to retain control of this post, since the person proposed must be the consensus choice of the key states and their central banks.

The Chair is a central figure and in practice has wide discretion in the running of the organisation, its Plenary, and its meetings. The first chairman was Mario Draghi, governor of the Banca d'Italia. Draghi moulded the FSF into the FSB and led the organisation in its formative period until 2011. The FSB is viewed by participants as Draghi's creation and shows Draghi's diplomatic skill in institutional transformation, turning a subpar FSF into a turbocharged FSB, demonstrating his ability to seize the crisis and press for an architectural solution that benefited his personal and community standpoint. Mark Carney, then-governor of the Bank of England, replaced Mario Draghi in 2011, and served until 2018. Carney was a very strong influential Chair and a champion of the re-regulatory agenda.

US leadership at a key juncture: The American Randal Quarles, took over as Chair in 2019. Mr Quarles is vice chair of the US Federal Reserve System. By appointing Quarles to lead the FSB Carney and his allies drew the American central banker into the leadership of the architecture. By taking this step they hoped to secure American defence of the FSB, its cooperative mission and convening function. And they have in large part succeeded. Mr Quarles is mainstream (i.e. not especially Trumpian) economist and lawyer. Although more sceptical of

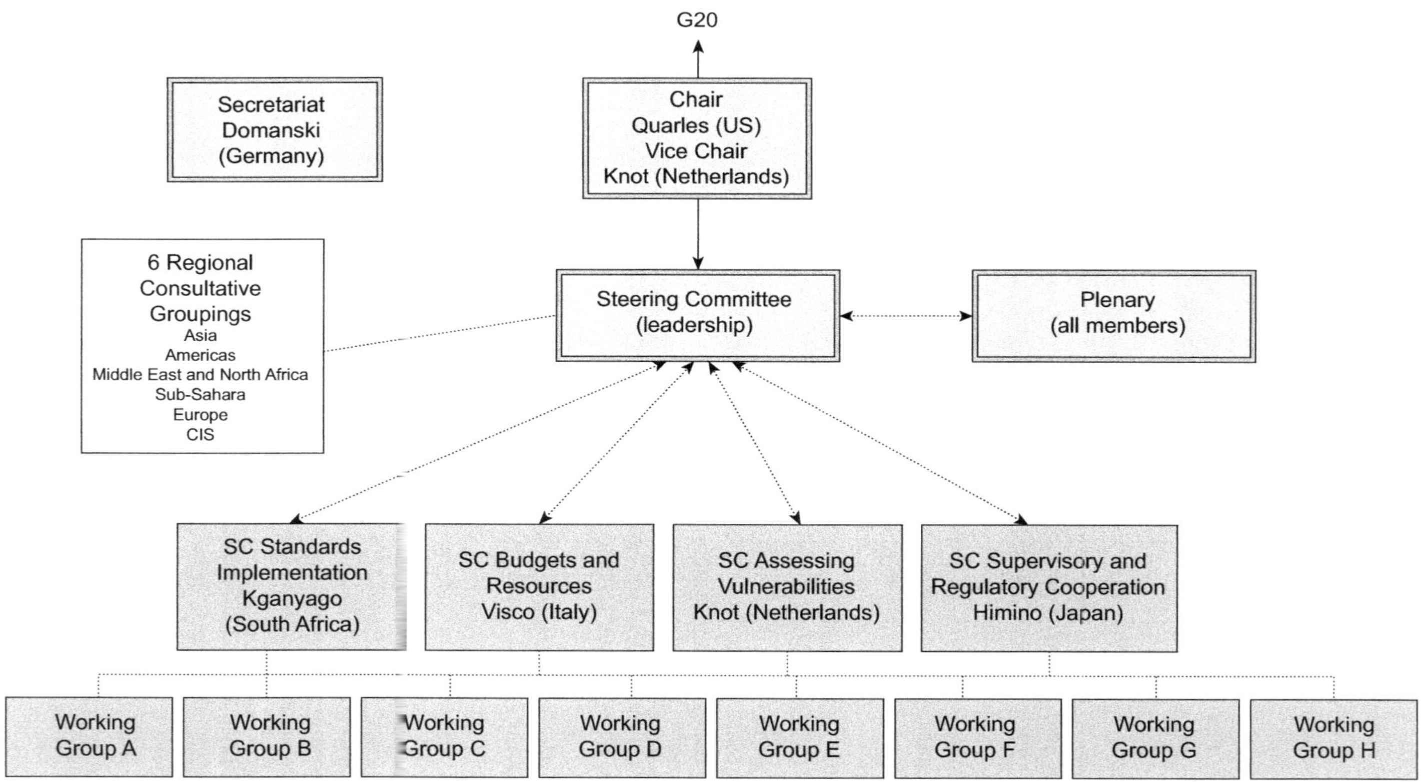

Figure 6.2 The structure of the Financial Stability Board

Source: FSB and Mackintosh 2020.

Note: The FSB process reports directly to the G20 summits; it does not report via finance ministries. FSB leadership roles changed in 2013 and now include additional emerging-market leaders. During the FSB's formative period, 2009–2012, it was led exclusively by North American and European central bankers and supervisors.

regulation than his predecessor Mr Quarles now leads a consensual international body of his peers. He cannot do so by aping Mr Trump. To the contrary he must defend the community against emerging risks and ensure existing standards are not severely watered down. His success or failure is now linked to the FSB's success or failure. The buck stops on his desk. This leadership change was a masterstroke by the FSB community. At the very point of maximum danger they have drawn the US central bank closer, its leadership closer, to defend the FSB's mission against potential American political attacks.

Steering Committee: The Steering Committee is appointed by the Plenary, but members are in practice recommended, that is to say, selected, by the Chair. This is where the real power lies and where the Chair focuses his or her attention. The Steering Committee meets at least four times a year. The size of the Steering Committee has grown, and in 2020 it had 38 members (FSB, 2020).

Chairman Draghi created the Steering Committee because he wanted a more select grouping to direct and coordinate the work stream. The Steering Committee is the key decision-making body in the structure and its formal duties are to promote coordination amongst FSB bodies, review progress in policy development and carry out the work of the FSB. As the committee's leadership role became clear, more and more FSB members began to demand admittance; like any popular club, those outside want in.

From 2009 until the Cannes summit in 2011 the Steering Committee had no ministry of finance representatives. At Draghi's insistence it was technocrats only. From the first burst of institutional creation and for three key formative years of the G20-led process the leadership of the forum was completely in the hands of the central banking regulators and was dominated by European and North Americans supportive of the re-regulatory shift in worldview.

The Steering Committee in 2020 has as many members as the original FSB had in 2009 and is the organ through which the FSB is run on a day-to-day basis. Since 2011 it has included finance ministry officials from the leading G20 states, which has changed its nature away from a technocratic club to one that also now considers national political factors. Political considerations were not uppermost during the first years of FSB operation, when only central bankers and supervisors were in the room.

Plenary: The Plenary is the final decision making body of the FSB and operates by consensus, although each person has one vote. Its membership is limited to 70 individuals (FSB, 2014). The FSB Charter does not state how consensus is achieved. All members have equal rights, but, as in *Animal Farm*, all are equal but some are more equal than others (Orwell, 1946). The Plenary approves the work programme of the FSB, adopts FSB reports and recommendations, appoints the Chairperson and decides on FSB membership matters. The Plenary takes place twice a year. The number of seats a country has in the Plenary depends on the size of its national economy and financial market. Large powers and emerging economies have three seats, the middling powers two seats, and the rest a single seat at the table (FSB, 2009, p. 4, as amended; see also FSB, 2014, 2015). In the case of the large states each state actor is permitted to send a representative from its finance ministry, its central bank and its regulatory agency responsible for financial stability. This ensures that the US and the Europeans have what some view as disproportionate representation.

In practice the Plenary normally confirms decisions taken by the Chairman and Steering Committee. It is characterised by participants as a rubber stamp of the Steering Committee and decisions already agreed by FSB committee chairs – i.e. decisions taken by the core group driving the FSB. Plenary members know their position in the pecking order and generally defer to Steering Committee views, especially if they reflect the views of a plurality of key central bankers and supervisors.

Standing Committees: The FSB has Standing Committees that oversee its regulatory goals. The Chair recommends, based on soundings, and the Plenary appoints, the committee chairs, and the chosen chairs then determine who sits on each committee. The make-up of the membership of the standing committees is not publicly disclosed. The committees address topics including financial stability, systemic risks and early warning exercises; supervisory and regulatory coordination; standards implementation; and resources.

Working Groups: The FSB Working Groups operate below the Standing Committees, reporting upwards on particular work streams. Subjects covered in this way include shadow banking, implementation monitoring, peer review, non-cooperative jurisdictions, compensation monitoring (i.e. bankers, bonuses), OTC derivatives, data gaps and credit rating agencies.

Standard-Setting Bodies (SSBs): The leadership of key SSBs are included in the FSB. This is an important innovation because it brings under FSB auspices independent substate-level organisations that until 2009 tended to operate largely in isolation from one another, each guarding its prerogatives. To put it bluntly these obscure technical bodies hitherto had not been coordinated across sectors by powerful principal state actors working collectively. With the creation of the FSB that changed. The FSB monitors the G20 work delegated to the SSBs, drawing these substate bodies into coordination and collaboration driven by the G20 agenda as identified by the FSB leadership. SSBs are independent international substate forums, but in practice, much of their workload, deliverables and their enhanced relevance was affected by the G20 tasks they were asked to perform. In 2015, the SSBs are, because of the FSB, under much greater pressure to deliver and effectively collaborate, according to participants.

Regional Consultative Groupings (RCGs): In response to complaints by non-member countries that the FSB was too exclusive and exclusionary the FSB at the Cannes summit in 2011 created six regional consultative groupings. Each consists of 12 non-FSB countries (reminiscent of the constituency approach within the IMF Executive Board) and is co-chaired by one current FSB member and one non-member. The latter 'may' be invited to attend FSB Plenary meetings. The groupings set their own agendas, but in general they mirror topics being considered within the FSB (Thorne, 2012).

The RCGs have no formal role in FSB decision making, and in 2015 they appear to have little impact on the FSB. The RCGs and their chairs lack influence, and this is reflected when they are allowed to voice views, which is at the very end of plenary proceedings, when few are paying attention. However, once created, such bodies tend to ask for greater input. And even if they continue to prove to be ineffectual they cannot be easily dismantled. From a more positive standpoint the RCGs show the FSB leadership is listening to external complaints about its legitimacy and exclusivity, regardless of their current utility.

Institutional and legal basis for the FSB: The FSB is an institution without a strong legal foundation, a compromise necessary to get G20 leaders to agree to its creation in 2009. The FSB operates as a Swiss-registered nongovernmental organisation. It has no capacity to enter into agreements and no privileges or immunities, unlike formal treaty-based institutions such as the IMF or the World Bank. In 2015 the FSB has a complex organisational superstructure, but it rests on a weak legal foundation compared to the IMF or the World Bank. But this is the norm for non-treaty-based substate financial regulatory organisations. Compared to other SSBs, the FSB is institutionally strong and getting stronger.

Secretariat and Resources: The Secretariat of the FSB is headed by a Secretary General. The FSB is funded by and located in the BIS (G20, 2012). The central banker's bank has put its resources behind the FSB. The Secretariat was not influential at the beginning, but there are signs that as the FSB evolves, the Secretary General, and their team are gradually taking a more assertive tone, insofar as they are actively pursuing the goals of the Chair.

Policy coordination at a new level: an institutional structure that reflects permanence

A key output of the G20-FSB reforms is a process with policy implications: the creation within the FSB of a more effective means of policy coordination and cooperation. The FSB is the general contractor for regulatory reform and is central to the policy output. Compared with its predecessor, the FSF, the FSB's coordination was and still is more effective, multilayered, deeper, broader and more dynamic. Its creation amounts to a third-order change in policy coordination at the international level, a paradigm shift in international financial regulatory coordination.

The FSB permanently strengthened qualitative and quantitative international cooperation and coordination on financial regulation. As the locus of global financial regulatory policy, it is the concrete expression of the return of state authority. In 2020 the FSB is a permanent addition, a growing international organisation, with a growing staff, resources and a legal basis. It facilitates coordination and cooperation and supports policy convergence. The FSB is the principal venue for intensive engagement by key central bank governors, supervisors and finance ministry officials. Below the leadership strata the FSB demands the commitment of hundreds of other officials through its working groups, work streams and in national policy implementation.

The detailed and complex institutional structure of the FSB is not associated with flimsy, ephemeral, temporary institutions. It signals solidity and structural permanence. The FSB has strong leadership, four tiers of committee structures, a direct reporting line up to the G20 leadership summits and a supervisory and oversight line through to the SSBs below. Western leaders of the central bank community wanted an FSB with institutional weight, and they got what they wanted: Mario Draghi created the FSB. He ensured a strong role for the chair; he formed the steering group and chose its membership, He selected the chairs of committees and working groups from within a small community group. The legal foundation and resource issues were dealt with formally. Some years later, G20 summits have built incrementally on the initial structure and strengthened and filled in the gaps in the foundations, both legal and resource. Mario Draghi, Mark Carney and their allies were behind these incremental institutional steps. In 2020 the FSB is a permanent international institutional addition to the regulatory architecture, as Christian Noyer predicted would occur (Noyer, 2009).

Lack of formal state obligations not insurmountable

The lack of a 'hard law' international treaty base for the FSB has not been an impediment to effectiveness. The policy makers established the FSB and launched the regulatory reform agenda in 2009. Legal matters were addressed later. Other institutions have been born in this 'lumpy' fashion. The World Trade Organization (WTO) did not start as a strong organisation with a judicial arm capable of binding all member states to its rulings. The rules-based global trading system became stronger only after the WTO superseded the General Agreement on Tariffs and Trade (GATT) (Jackson, 2008). We know that institutional birth and evolution take time. Not all bodies emerge fully formed. The Bretton Woods institutions were created as part of a process, not a single event. The FSB's birth follows a similar trajectory.

Whether the institutional weakness may prove troublesome in the future, as memories of the crisis abate, as they are doing in part due to the work of the G20 and FSB, remains to be seen. The pressure for collective action and demands for tough policy implementation could fade. Level-one win sets are sure to shrink, even amongst the members of the cohesive technical community; national level-two domestic differences can become more divisive. At that point the activism and strength of the FSB, as a locus for action, driven by membership demands could be problematic.

This is not happening yet. In 2020 the FSB is still being built and central bankers are engaged in paradigm maintenance and defence, and it is proving resilient. How the FSB will evolve in the coming years is uncertain, but if the first seven years are any guide, it will not rapidly lose momentum. Instead, it may, if the paradigm shift is successfully defended by the community, become progressively stronger, with additions to the foundations and superstructure.

Initial dominance of European and North American principals

As has been observed the FSB is driven by its chair and committee leaderships operating in the Steering Committee. In its early evolution, almost all the key roles (Chair, Standing Committee Chairs, Working Group Chairs, etc.) were held by senior central banking and supervisory principal figures from Europe and North America. And almost all the main decision-making roles were held by those who were supportive of the construction and maintenance of the new re-regulatory paradigm (from Canada, Italy, Norway, Spain, the UK and the US). Those less supportive of reform (from France, Germany and Japan, for instance) did not hold leadership positions. Draghi and Carney were pushing difficult reforms: they ensured their own allies held the levers of policy-making power.

Those leadership roles are not titular. As one participant noted, 'the senior people do the work and that is what is remarkable about it' (Mackintosh, 2011, 10, p. 9). Decision making is also more effective because 'you have all the principals at the table and so buy-in is much more readily available' (Mackintosh, 2012, 24, p. 7). As a result especially at the outset, the FSB's end product bore the personal imprint of the principals themselves. This contrasts sharply with the methods in larger institutions like the IMF. Inside the FSB the chairs of the committees individually drive the processes and shape the outcomes. In 2020 the leadership is slightly more balanced.

Does this early geographic bias matter? The dominance by European and North American leaders was in part due to their institutional and personal intellectual heft. All were and are heavyweights within the small community. But the leadership imbalance, justifiable on an expert-to-expert level, is obscured, and the FSB structure and membership of committees are not made publicly available. This lack of transparency is said to spare the blushes of the G20 states without key roles and assignments (Wright, 2011). But it could be the reverse: the nature of the FSB's leadership could have required a lack of transparency 'precisely because the composition is inappropriate' (Mackintosh, 2011, 11, p. 24). This underscores important issues of balance and legitimacy, regardless of the talents of the leadership selected.

Leadership matters, but the evolution of the leadership in the FSB in 2020 does not appear to have changed the dynamics within the FSB, since the emerging and developing market players must still have the agreement of key market regulators for the process to function. That is to say significant influence still accrues to the largest players, even if they no longer formally occupy all the leadership positions.

Decision making within the FSB

In the FSB participants know whose views really count, and decision making reflects this reality. While each member of the FSB has a vote in practice there is no voting and decisions are taken by consensus, with an implicit understanding of who carries the most weight economically and in terms of the importance of their financial markets, and their leadership roles in the FSB. The US and Europeans maintain a disproportionate representation and influence on decision making, in addition to their already dominant leadership roles in the forum. Practically all substantive decision making takes place within the Steering Committee, in the Standing Committees, and in Working Groups between the meetings of the full Plenary (Helleiner, 2010, p. 8). A consensus ideally emerges before proceeding to the Plenary meeting for formal decisions.

Developing customary practices within the FSB provide additional room for manoeuvre for the chair and his or her senior colleagues, and the absence of a clear definition of how consensus must be reached provides flexibility and facilitates the decision-making process as they seek to secure agreement. For example when a standing committee chair finds consensus elusive in committee discussions, he or she can undertake further bilateral consultations and review. In practice the chair is at liberty to construct a consensus drawing on various bilateral approaches and building on the positions of key G20 representatives before returning to the committee as a whole.

As a practical matter informal subgroups of the key member states operate in the FSB. This decision-making reality ensures key state representatives retain yet more influence over deliberative outcomes as those informal subgroupings deliberate to reach deals. This may be a negative. In terms of legitimacy such side-stepping of full committee or FSB discussions short-circuits the formal structures of deliberation and further concentrates influence. But since no consensus is possible without agreement amongst the representatives from the most powerful G20 states, and often this requires some additional diplomacy on the sidelines, this is the price participants are willing to accept. These types of negotiating tactics and mechanisms, that is ad hoc informal bilaterals, are used in the much larger consensus-based World Trade Organization. They are also seen in the informal soundings used within the Executive Board of the IMF. It is not surprising that similar practices are evolving within the FSB as ways to advance decision making.

The evolving Steering Committee membership: how big is too big?

The Steering Committee is the key power centre within the FSB. The membership was first determined by Chairman Draghi, and until late 2011 it was composed exclusively of key central bank governors and supervisors, the majority of whom came from Europe and North America. Until the Cannes summit in 2011 there were no finance ministry members on the Steering Committee, and thus no explicitly national political voices, a factor that participants report was central to its early effectiveness as the engine of reform. A Steering Committee composed purely of technocrats, which was insulated from national political voices, was pressed to change by G20 finance ministry officials alarmed by the scope of deals (especially the Basel III Accord) that were being crafted. Those officials felt bounced into these deals:

> The central bankers did their secret handshakes, we had a global crisis, and we, the treasuries, had to take the political heat, . . . [and] provide the money.
> (Mackintosh, 2012, 12, pp. 19–20)

Draghi's defence of his technocrat-only Steering Committee was affected by the dual role and diplomatic game he played in 2011 as chair of the FSB and then prospective candidate for presidency of the European Central Bank: his need for German and French political support for the latter may have affected his willingness to admit finance ministry officials to the former. Even if this was the case demands for inclusion from the ministries was such that it is unlikely Draghi could have resisted. Had he refused the influence of the FSB would have faced a challenge and a possible downgrading by G20 political leaders.

Finance ministry inclusion within the membership of the Steering Committee changed the tone and form of discussion, from technocratic towards more national political matters and calculations. Finance ministry officials have less room to deviate from agreed positions than independent central bank governors and principal supervisors, who answer to no one above them. Finance ministers reflect their governments and are subject to electoral pressures. Ministerial motivations and positioning are likely, therefore. In some G20 states (such as the US) ministries are explicitly prohibited from determining regulatory decisions. By securing a seat on the Steering Committee finance ministry leaders have an avenue through which to influence regulations within their own borders. This political influence is viewed with concern by some on the FSB. Others are less worried. The latter believe that given how important national actions are to continued implementation of FSB financial reforms, inclusion of political actors is not negative, because governments and legislatures must be supportive of FSB policy goals and willing to legislate to ensure proper national implementation of G20-FSB reforms. The enlarged institutionally dominant Steering Committee changed the dynamics of decision making. As one participant noted:

> You have too big a group. In order to be effective, you have to have a smaller group. You create the smaller group. It's effective. All the people in the bigger group want to be in the smaller group; now that you've moved them into the smaller group, it cannot be effective anymore.
>
> (Mackintosh, 2012, 15, p. 8)

The Steering Committee's size has made it more cumbersome. It appears that the chair now has to take decision making into other informal groupings outside the Steering Committee. Indeed the reliance on informal subgroups within the membership and organs of the FSB to thrash out deals is indicative of the effect of expansion in the key decision-making organs and committees of the entity; as the size of the formal committees and organs increases, leaders have adopted coping strategies that operate outside or parallel to the formal processes. It is probable such informal practices are here to stay.

Legitimacy and the FSB

The initial and continued dominance of the FSB by North American and European leaders of the central banking community who were instrumental in its creation also raises legitimacy concerns. But compared to the FSF structure the FSB is an improvement in legitimacy and authority. Legitimacy was and is necessary for the FSB to wield authority amongst and beyond its membership, and this is essential if the FSB is to be an effective central component of the new global architecture. If the FSB is to be effective, post-crisis and in the years ahead, it needs to command broad legitimacy, respect or authority from non-member states; the system should not be divided into rule takers and rule makers (Helleiner, Pagliari, and Zimmermann, 2009, p. 4). Although the FSB is still an exclusive entity its membership represents 85 per cent of global GDP, and it includes practically all the major financial market regulators. Rules agreed to by the FSB now have the practical effect of being global standards. FSB-endorsed standards fashioned by expanded SSBs, under the FSB rubric, have greater weight because the FSB ties all member states and their agency heads into the standard-setting process and by extension places pressure on all officials involved to adhere to standards they jointly endorse.

The make-up of the leadership of the FSB organs shows the dominance of the advanced core economies in the FSB despite the inclusion of emerging-economy representatives. This is in part a recognition by emerging-economy members that those actors have more at stake, that their firms and markets are more developed and interconnected and that these states should of necessity play a larger role in the FSB in repairing the system. Certainly in the crisis management and reform phases, the FSB was driven by the Western powers, whose markets and failures caused the crisis, with emerging countries playing a supportive but not visible leadership role within the new formal structure.

Critics are right to demand a larger role for officials from emerging economies. Otherwise, the FSB will continue to focus on Western rules applied across the globe, without consideration of other models or levels of development. As emerging countries take leadership of the G20 summits this is beginning to translate into a larger role within the FSB. Despite some bias in the leadership roster emerging-country representatives are today more engaged and assertive, and this trend will continue. While leadership make-up matters it is not the only measure of further evolution within the FSB. A once small and nimble FSB is evolving into a larger organisation.

Since its creation the FSB's evolution, and specifically its leadership grouping, has grown significantly, and the extent to which this is a real answer to the legitimacy issue is unclear. It is true that one way to address the current legitimacy gap faced by FSB could be to further enlarge the institutional membership. Paul Martin, creator of the finance ministry G20 process in the 1990s, suggests opening membership to all 187 members of the IMF and World Bank (Helleiner, 2009; others expect it to be the 'hub' of a network of actors and institutions (Cooper and Thakur, 2013, p. 125). Calls to make the G20-FSB structures and process universal may be misguided, and they are opposed by leading central banking powers, who view such slow-moving bodies (such as the IMF) with scorn. Continued expansion negates key reasons for opting for the FSB over the universal IMF: its nimbleness, flexibility and small size. Global governance and collective decision making in general often 'faces a trade-off between efficiency and legitimacy'

(Trichet, 2010, p. 5). Striking that balance is not easy. If being relatively small and flexible are important goals then expansion undermines why the FSB was created in the first place: a desire to create a faster-moving, more effective policy-making forum than the slow, bureaucratic IMF. If one accepts this then the FSB should not be pressed to expand further and further, perhaps stretching to the breaking point the very features that have made it effective thus far. Regardless of these considerations membership creep is seen.

A constant pressure for enlargement by those clamouring outside to get in has been partially successful, with the FSB's agreement on six RCGs. Will these bodies address the complaints of outsiders? The RCGs are a small step towards opening to a wider constituency. But participants in the FSB Plenary indicate the RCGs remain ineffectual, are not listened to and are viewed negatively by those actually leading the FSB; if this continues to be the case, then the RCGs will not solve complaints of illegitimacy.

Unfortunately it is probable that the FSB's creation and its slow membership enlargement will never assuage those that remain on the outside looking in. States excluded from the process resent demands that they apply G20-FSB standards over which they have no control or input. This will not change. Certainly legitimacy matters – it affects the authority of the decisions agreed to and their reach. Compared against its predecessor the FSB is a significant improvement over the ineffectual and closed FSF. Many more emerging-country leaders now sit on the FSB, on the steering group and in the various committees. The visible authority of the FSB process since its 2009 creation reflects this; the FSB is more inclusive, better structured, more effective. However it is not and will never become a universal organisation; the G20 and FSB leaders will not permit it. It is perhaps precisely because the FSB has proven effective that we hear loud criticisms of its legitimacy and accusation of opacity.

Transparency: a real weakness in the new structure

The FSB is the dominant arbiter of global financial rules and reform endeavours, but it remains opaque. In 2020, however, the functioning and processes of the FSB are gradually becoming more transparent, although they remain obscure to outsiders. The committee membership rosters are published. The meetings remain closed. The organisational procedure and structure are now public (FSB, 2013, 2014). The FSB in 2020 publishes documents in advance of their formal adoption by the FSB.

Further steps to improve the public understanding of the FSB should be encouraged. A body that is overseeing the implementation of financial market and firm-level rules that apply as the de facto norm for the entire world, developed and developing, North and South, East and West, should be visible and subject to informed scrutiny. The gradual steps in this regard are an improvement over past crisis-focused operations. But the FSB's communications approaches still make the IMF and World Bank public outreach efforts look like first-rate public relations campaigns by comparison.

In 2020 that transparency also includes a three-stage consultation process.

- *Consultations:* lasting 60 days as announced by the FSB. The FSB issues alerts when new publications, including consultations, are published on its website.
- *Public responses to consultations:* published by the FSB within 15 days of the consultation closing.
- *Overview of responses:* when a final policy document is published, following agreement by the FSB Plenary, a report providing an overview of comments and responses to the issues raised in the consultation is published by the FSB on the web.

The format is in line with other governmental approaches. It signals the maturation of the FSB consultation process, from non-existent in 2010, to theoretical in 2012, to standardised and normalised in 2020. This is generally good practice and it is operating smoothly, although how impactful to the consultative responses are merits further research.

As a matter of practice a relatively small number of 'insider outsiders' participate in peer reviews and other consultative processes.

The FSB's approach in 2020 reflects the particular biases of its central banking parents. Participants come from organisations that prefer confidentiality to openness. Members believe it is required to get results. Those inside the FSB prefer to operate in a small 'club like' setting (Tsingou, 2014). But those lucky enough to be inside such elite groups always say that. The FSB is too important to operate in obscurity. Keeping the organisation relatively small with deliberation and disputes private permits better decision-making outcomes. But while it is certainly less complicated that way, legitimacy suffers if policy is made in back rooms (Alston, 1997, pp. 440–441).

Institutional secrecy could undermine broader support of the new paradigm

The FSB is tasked with developing and promoting the implementation of effective regulatory, supervisory and other financial sector policies in the interest of global financial stability. To do that you need public support that can resist the false narratives of the lobbies for the banks and major financial firms that would dismantle the new normal. These firms have huge resources and they will deploy them for private gain against the purported public good being pursued by the FSB in the new paradigm. To counteract the critics the FSB's mission needs to be defended publicly and explained effectively, and the process of decision making needs to be improved and made visibly more legitimate. If this is not done opponents can portray what is going on 'over there in Basel' as wrongheaded, damaging and an affront to national prerogatives. To suspicious outsiders this lack of transparency and accountability, this type of elite closed network can have the smell of 'a vast technocratic conspiracy' (Slaughter, 2001, p. 347).

During a crisis all are affected and need relief, so a lack of consultative processes and the small club-like operation of the FSB was not an issue for many outside the club. But six years on, legitimacy and transparency issues loom larger. Policy making may be easier in small private groups, but the output can be harder to defend from external critics. It is difficult to build coalitions in support of global standards when the process of arriving at those standards is exclusive and not properly understood. A process controlled by the few, even one, ostensibly engaged in furthering the general public good – supporting systemic financial and economic stability – may be weakened by its own limited nature.

International forums as they evolve and mature need to build support from the general populace, and to do this they need to be reasonably transparent and open to public understanding, scrutiny, analysis, critique and cross-examination. In 2020 the FSB needs to continue to articulate its role and mission to the wider public, market participants and voters. As the nexus for global regulatory coordination and monitoring, driven by technocrats, the FSB should become better understood by external observers. If the mission is not properly understood it is all the more easy to undermine. If policy makers do not properly articulate the reasons behind policies, even if they are perhaps rightly thought necessary for future financial stability by those charged with taking action, they will be vulnerable to attack from national and international lobbies that may have little interest in stability and more interest in private profit over public good.

These issues of legitimacy and transparency will continue to arise and remain to be addressed in a manner that partially satisfies critics. The FSB has addressed complaints over legitimacy via gradual membership creep. But this expansionary impulse must balance a desire for greater inclusiveness with the need to retain the effectiveness which comes with a smaller size and more flexible mode of operation. On transparency small steps are being taken to tackle the FSB's relative obscurity, but it is not enough, and this obscurity could undermine necessary support from the stakeholders, actors and the public.

The FSB: the institutional achievement of central bank post-crisis activism

The creation of the FSB is the singular institutional triumph of the G20-led process. From out of that crisis a new coordinating body was born, an institution in outline and form which has been strengthened progressively from 2009 onwards. The process was not solely the masterstroke of the G20 leaders who backed the move. It was 'absolutely [Mario] Draghi's baby' (Mackintosh, 2011, 9, p. 7). He quickly understood the need to enlarge the FSF (which he chaired). Supported by his own community of like-minded central bank governors and principal supervisors, he seized the opportunity that the crisis offered to pursue his community's reform agenda and to defend their centrality in the reappraisal and reforms that began in 2008. At the outset 'the intellectual heft came from the core' (Mackintosh, 2012, 24, p. 10), and the contours of the reforms the FSB began reflected this.

In doing so Draghi, Carney and their community made a power play to defend its position in the reform response. The very same bankers who had not seen the dangers of the 'great moderation', those from the core of the advanced economies, grasped control. The central bankers were deferred to by G20 leaders as experts. The community constructed a coordinating mechanism that reflected their goals and their biases. In taking charge this 'consolidated the position of central banks as leaders of the regulatory agenda as well as the monetary agenda' (Mackintosh, 2011, 9, p. 9). By creating the Financial Stability Board Draghi pushed aside the IMF and took control of the re-regulatory policy agenda and of the paradigm shift he supported. Today much more power is in the hands of the central banking community than before the crisis. The FSB is an institutional triumph for Draghi, Carney and their collaborators. As one participant recalled:

> It lies between two worlds and I think, very largely due to Mario [Draghi]'s skill and Svein [Andresen – the FSB Secretary General]. It has been a transmission of the political imperative but has kept at bay political interference. . . . It has been – it's led by senior technocrats.
>
> (Mackintosh, 2011, 10, p. 5)

The institutional processes within the FSB show it was structured in a way to ensure maximum speed and control by its leadership, who were and are highly supportive of the move to re-regulate, of the macroprudential policies and of this paradigm shift that the community adopted as their common project.

The FSB as a coordinating forum is a considerable structural and institutional improvement over its predecessor. Its creation forms part of the concrete re-regulatory paradigm shift seen after the crisis. The FSB's increased size and greater structural complexity indicates a rapid crisis-driven metamorphosis from a small talking shop to an established international institution at the centre of the new architecture of international financial diplomacy. There has been a durable shift from empty platitudes pre-crisis to a deep and complex coordination and cooperation process which has been institutionalised, with the FSB at the centre.

The crisis response resulted in a technocratic consensus, a new re-regulatory narrative and paradigm shift and a concomitant burst of institutional creation and policy making followed by more gradual steps. Since the FSB's creation in 2009 the structure has been built upon with progressive incremental changes addressing functions, standing, transparency and resources. Its creation as the central coordinating body for global financial regulatory reform amounts to a third order change (Hall, 1993). In 2020 the FSB is maturing and is a permanent and increasingly solid addition at the centre of the new global financial architecture. The reassertion of state authority over markets and firms led by the FSB and its community continues in 2020 and gathers strength, as Chapters 7 and 8 will make clear.

Notes

1 This chapter draws in part on material contained in an article by the author, Stuart Mackintosh, titled "The global financial and economic crisis, and the creation of the Financial Stability Board," published in 2014 in *World Economics*, 15 (3), pp. 103–119.

2 FSB members are Argentina; Australia; Brazil; Canada; China; France; Germany; Hong Kong SAR, China; India; Indonesia; Italy; Japan; Mexico; the Netherlands; the Republic of Korea; Russia; Saudi Arabia; Singapore; South Africa; Spain; Switzerland;

Turkey; the UK; the US; the International Monetary Fund; the World Bank; the Bank of International Settlements; the European Commission; the European Central Bank; the Organization for Economic Co-operation and Development; the Committee on the Global Financial System; the Committee on Payment Settlement Systems; the International Organization of Security Commissions; the International Association of Insurance Supervisors; the International Accounting Standards Board; and the Basel Committee on Banking Supervision.

References

Adler, E. (1992) 'The emergence of cooperation: National epistemic communities and the international evolution of the idea of nuclear arms control', *International Organization*, 46(1), pp. 105–145.

Alston, P. (1997) 'The myopia of handmaidens: International lawyers and globalization', *European Journal of International Law*, 8(3) pp. 437–448.

Barnier, M. (2011) *Presentation at the Brookings Institution*, Washington, DC, 3 June.

Bennett, C.J. (1991) 'What is policy convergence and what causes it?', *British Journal of Political Science*, 21(2), pp. 215–233.

Blanchard, O., Romer, D., Spence, M., and Stiglitz, J. (eds.) (2012) *In the wake of the crisis: Leading economists reassess economic policy*. Boston: MIT Press.

Blustein, P. (2012) 'How global watchdogs missed a world of trouble', *CIGI Papers* 5(7) [Online]. Available at: www.cigionline.org/publications/2012/7/how-global-watchdogs-missed-world-of-trouble (accessed: 1 May 2013).

Blyth, M. (2002) *Great transformations: Economic ideas and institutional change in the twentieth century*. Cambridge: Cambridge University Press.

Bretton Woods Committee. (2010) *International council meeting*, Washington, DC, 8 October. Transcript.

Brookings Institution. (2011a) 'The governance of the Financial Stability Board', *Issues Paper*, September [Online]. Available at: www.brookings.edu/~/media/research/files/papers/2011/9/23%20financial%20stability%20board%20lombardi/fsb_issues_paper_lombardi.pdf (accessed: 25 September 2011).

Buchanan, M. (2013) *Forecast: What physics, meteorology, and the natural sciences can teach us about economics*. New York: Bloomsbury.

Cartapanis, A. and Herland, M. (2002) 'The reconstruction of the international financial architecture: Keynes' revenge?', *Review of International Political Economy*, 9(2), pp. 257–283.

Constancio, V. (2010) 'The future of economic governance in Europe in a global perspective', *Speech delivered at the Centre Culturel Calouste Gulbenkian*, Paris, 7 December.

Cooper, A. and Thakur, R. (2013) *The Group of Twenty (G20)*. New York. Routledge.

Draghi, M. (2009) 'Financial stability in the global environment? Learning the lessons from the market crisis' [Online]. Available at: www.bis.org/review/r090615a.pdf?frames=0 (accessed: 11 June 2011).

FSB (Financial Stability Board). (2009) 'Charter, as amended in 2011 and 2012' [Online]. Available at: www.financialstabilityboard.org/wp-content/uploads/r_090925d.pdf?page_moved=1 (accessed: 26 January 2015).

———. (2012) 'Charter (as amended)' [Online]. Available at: www.financialstability-board.org/wp-content/uploads/r_120809.pdf (accessed: 14 February 2015).

———. (2013) 'Procedural guidelines' [Online]. Available at: www.financialstability-board.org/wp-content/uploads/FSB-Procedural-Guidelines-31.1.13.pdf (accessed: 26 January 2015).

———. (2014) 'Organisation chart' [Online]. Available at: www.financialstabilityboard.org/wp-content/uploads/FSB-Organisation-Chart-as-of-15-Oct-2014.pdf (accessed: 26 January 2015).

———. (2015) 'Organisational structure and governance' [Online]. Available at: www.financialstabilityboard.org/about/organisation-and-governance/ (accessed: 26 January 2015).

_______. (2020) 'FSB members' [Online]. Available at: https://www.fsb.org/about/fsb-members/ (accessed: 27 July 2020).

G20 (Group of Twenty). (2012) 'Los Cabos Declaration' [Online]. Available at: www.g20.utoronto.ca/summits/2012loscabos.html (accessed: 20 June 2012).

G30 (Group of Thirty). (2009) *The reform of the International Monetary Fund*. Washington, DC: Group of Thirty.

Gudmundsson, M. (2008) 'How might the current financial crisis shape financial sector regulation and structure?', Speech delivered *Financial Technology Congress 2008*, Boston, 23 September [Online]. Available at: www.bis.org/speeches/sp081119.htm (accessed: 31 January 2013).

Haas, P.M. (1992a) 'Introduction: Epistemic communities and international policy coordination', *International Organization*, 46(1), pp. 1–35.

———. (1992b) 'Banning chlorofluorocarbons: Epistemic community efforts to protect stratospheric ozone', *International Organization*, 46(1), pp. 187–224.

Hall, P.A. (1993) 'Policy paradigms, social learning, and the state: The case of economic policymaking in Britain', *Comparative Politics*, 25(3), pp. 275–296.

Helleiner, E. (2010) 'A Bretton Woods moment? The 2007–2008 crisis and the future of global finance', *International Affairs*, 86(3), pp. 619–636.

Helleiner, E., Pagliari, S., and Zimmermann, H. (eds.) (2009) *Global finance in crisis: The politics of international regulatory change*. Abingdon: Routledge.

Holzinger, K. and Knill, C. (2005) 'Causes and conditions of cross-national policy convergence', *Journal of European Public Policy*, 12(5), pp. 775–796.

Jackson, J. (2008) 'The case of the World Trade Organization', *International Affairs*, 84(3), pp. 437–454.

King, M. (2009) 'Finance a return from risk', *Speech delivered to the Company of International Bankers*, London, 17 March.

———. (2010) 'Banking – from Bagehot to Basel, and back again', *Second Bagehot Lecture, Buttonwood Gathering*, New York, 25 October [Online]. Available at: www.bis.org/review/r101028a.pdf (accessed: 7 March 2011).

Lazer, D. (2005) 'Regulatory capitalism as networked order: The international system as an informational network', *Annals of the American Society of Political Science*, pp. 52–66.

Levi-Faur, D. (2005) 'The global diffusion of regulatory capitalism', *Annals of the American Academy of Political and Social Science*, 598, pp. 12–32.

Mackintosh, S. (2011) Interview 7. G20 Principal Supervisor, 7 December.

———. (2011) Interview 9. G20 Central Bank, Former Deputy Governor, 9 December.

———. (2011) Interview 10. G20 Central Bank, Former Deputy Governor, 9 December.

———. (2011) Interview 11. Advisor G20 Central Bank, 9 December.

———. (2012) Interview 12. G20 Finance Ministry Official, 27 January.

———. (2012) Interview 15. G20 Central Bank Governor, 16 February.

———. (2012) Interview 22. Former G20 Finance Minister, Central Bank Governor, 1 May.

———. (2012) Interview 24. G20 Central Bank Governor, 2 July.

Noyer, C. (2008) 'A new regulatory framework for a new financial system', *Speech delivered at the University of Dauphine*, Paris, 11 December.

———. (2009) 'Economic and financial crisis – The post-G20 outlook', *Speech delivered to the Hong Kong Chamber of Commerce*, Hong Kong, 11 June.

Orwell, G. (1946) *Animal farm*. New York: Signet.

Raustiala, K. and Victor, D.G. (2004) 'The regime complex for plant genetic resources', *International Organization*, 58(2), pp. 277–309.

Skogstad, G. (2008) *Internationalization and Canadian agriculture: Policy and governing paradigms*. Toronto: University of Toronto Press.

Slaughter, A.M. (2001) 'The accountability of government networks', *Indiana Journal of Global Legal Studies*, 8(2), pp. 347–367.

Smaghi, L.B. (2008) 'The financial crisis and global imbalances – Two sides of the same coin', *Speech delivered to the Asia Europe Economic Forum*, Beijing, 9 December.

Stiglitz, J. (2010) 'Needed: A new economic paradigm', *Financial Times*, 19 August [Online]. Available at: www.ft.com/intl/cms/s/0/d5108f90-abc2-11df-9f02-00144feabdc0.html#axzz1yGalnhcI (accessed: 19 June 2012).

Thorne, R. (2012) 'Letter from Rupert Thorne, Deputy Secretary General of the FSB to Jo Marie Grunseigger', of *FSB Watch*, 11 January.

Trichet, J.C. (2010) Speech at the *World Policy Conference*, Marrakech, 16 October [Online]. Available at: www.ecb.int/press/key/date/2010/html/sp101016.en.html (accessed: 4 June 2012).

Tsingou, E. (2014) 'The club rules in global financial governance', *The Political Quarterly*, 85(4), pp. 417–419.

Turner, A. (2009) *The Turner review: A regulatory response to the global banking crisis*. London: Financial Services Authority.

Watanagase, T. (2008) 'Combating the global financial crisis – Role of international coordination', *Speech delivered at the Hong Kong Monetary Authority*, Hong Kong, 16 December [Online]. Available at: www.bis.org/review/r081223b.pdf (accessed: 12 July 2013).

Weber, A. (2008) 'Risk transfer – Challenges for financial institutions and markets', *Speech delivered at Risk Transfer: Challenges for Financial Institutions and Markets conference*, Frankfurt, 11 December [Online]. Available at: www.bis.org/review/r081216a.pdf (accessed: 21 August 2013).

Wright, W. (2011) 'Why all the secrecy at the FSB?', *Financial News*, 2 May [Online]. Available at: http://blogs.wsj.com/source/2011/05/03/why-all-the-secrecy-at-the-fsb/ (accessed: 21 August 2013).

7 Making the paradigm real

The FSB's key policy outcomes

'[The FSB is] the general contractor of the reform process'.
(Mackintosh, 2012, 22, p. 8)

Introduction

For a paradigm shift to occur there needs to be a wide recognition of growing unexplained anomalies. This precipitates a narrative shift of a majority of the policy-making community, resulting in a series of external policy changes that are first, second, and third order in nature, which are designed to realise and implement the narrative shift. Ardent Thatcherites in the 1970s and 1980s held to a clear ideological narrative that informed their actions and helped shape the nature of policies they sought to construct. Central bankers from the core states of the global economy went through the same process in 2008. This community recognised failings in the past deregulatory laissez-faire neoliberal model. The central bankers were determined to reassert state power and authority over global financial markets and firms, and they created a new institution to coordinate the policy process: the Financial Stability Board (FSB).

In the end a paradigm shift must be measured by its policy outcomes. For a shift to become tangible and durable it must move from the theoretical and ideological to the concrete and actual. This chapter addresses the major policy outcomes of the FSB-led reform process and makes a judgement of their relative strength and effectiveness. The chapter looks at the apparent policy outcomes, individually and as a whole within the shifting cultural context in which they have been fashioned and in which they reside.

The FSB's particular policy successes were and are driven by a stronger, consensual paradigm and narrative, and by a policy consensus agreed to after rapid policy convergence (Bennett, 1991) by key state actors, and within a relatively small group of North American and European central banking technocrats leading the reform process who form part of a cohesive epistemic community (Haas, 1992) and who acted as the vanguard of the reform movement. From 2009 the community leading the FSB moved to implement a complex, multitiered, internationally coordinated financial reform agenda that they fashioned or alternatively tasked to other standard-setting bodies (SSBs). These policies formed the concrete realisation of the paradigm shift in the policy consensus embarked upon in reaction to the economic and financial crisis of 2007–2008.

Policy making and implementation is where the FSB regulatory heft is measured, where G20 political capital matters and where the existence or absence of a common narrative amongst the community of technical actors has a direct impact on policy outcomes. Where reforms were led by this elite expert community they were markedly stronger, strengthened by a common policy consensus and convergence within the FSB, backed by the G20 and by the regulatory power of the FSB in key processes of implementation and oversight. The central banking community's control was essential to the FSB's most successful reforms, and those policy changes indicate a rejection of the previous laissez-faire neoliberal financial deregulatory paradigm and the adoption of a new worldview in which financial markets and firms would be internationally and nationally re-regulated, principally by national agencies overseen by the leadership within the small FSB community.

In two specific policy areas there has been a third-order change (Hall, 1993), a paradigm shift in approach by the central banking community. These areas are

1 the coordinating function of the FSB itself as an institution in the making; and
2 the adoption and implementation of a macroprudential approach (via the Basel III Accord) to the supervision and oversight of the financial system as a whole, and of major banks and systemically important financial institutions, in particular.

The creation and functioning of the FSB was the institutional masterstroke of the G20 and the central banking community. It provided both a qualitative and a quantitative improvement over past practices, when lip service was paid to the need for coordination, but no institution existed that had the collective authority and ability to pursue joint goals.

The macroprudential policy consensus shift was based on a consensus that central bankers should oversee the financial stability of the system as whole and concentrate on systemic risk potentially posed by the world's largest and most interconnected banks and financial firms. Those firms, it was agreed, should be forced to endogenise exogeneity, i.e. internalise the potential systemic costs the firms could pose to the financial system as a whole. The FSB and its community insisted in capital and a lot more of it, buttressed by lower leverage, greater liquidity, other anticyclical rules and resolution tools.

The FSB policy output is potentially significant in other related areas. Thus the proposed total loss-absorbing capacity rules, which seek to ensure no bank is too big to resolve, is a high second-order facet of the new re-regulatory normal, if and when implemented. FSB-coordinated derivatives regulation is also a high second-order, borderline third-order, shift, which is progressively bringing markets, actors and instruments hitherto completely unregulated within the globally coordinated regulated space.

In other policy areas the output has been more mixed and less substantial because the policy process is affected by a number of factors. The policy process can be negatively affected by disagreement within the G20 and the FSB membership over the narrative in a policy space, the inherent complexity of the policy area, a lack of existing control mechanisms over national legislative and regulatory levers or failure of the FSB to press existing SSBs to depart from historically obstructionist stances. In general the further the FSB leadership is from actual policy design and regulatory responsibility, the more limited its ability to counteract domestic-policy-driven centrifugal forces propelling the G20-FSB consensus apart, adversely affecting level-one and level-two win sets, particularly from 2010 onwards when greater divergence amongst state actors is seen.

This chapter will show that, on balance, the policy output of the FSB has been effective in a number of reform areas. Viewed individually the height and breadth of a particular discrete policy reform or wave fluctuates from substantial, to moderate, to minimal. But viewed as a single ongoing international project, the FSB epistemic community increased the amplitude of international and national regulation of financial markets and firms. Taken as a whole the FSB's policy actions are indicative of the paradigm shift signalled by the G20 in 2008–2009 that continues to reassert state authority over markets in 2015.

Coupled to FSB policy activism additional national actions by major jurisdictions (in the US, the UK and Switzerland, for instance) initially buttressed the new paradigm, such as 'Basel Plus' or 'gold plating' of FSB standards (on capital, compensation and other areas). This demonstrated that regulators retain the initiative and the upper hand. However, politics and elections matter, and new governments in the US and UK have begun to chip away at post-global financial crisis regulatory standards. So the strength of certain aspects of the domestic application of the regulatory response are weakening.

Analysing the FSB outcomes means judging the efficacy and success of the FSB policy-making process, which requires defining what success is. Success is the accomplishment of an aim or purpose. Here, success is defined as the extent to which G20-FSB-directed policies result in stronger globally agreed policies that may increase financial stability and market resilience, and mitigate future systemic risks potentially caused by the world's largest financial firms to the global economy. Gauging the success or failure of FSB policies is ultimately a subjective judgement viewed against agreed timelines on the current state of implementation, the possible future effectiveness of the reforms and how the reforms promote financial stability.

This chapter briefly lays out the FSB's approach to financial reform, addresses the approach to enforcement and analyses areas of relative success and contrasts those successes with weaker outcomes where less progress is evident.

The FSB approach to international financial regulation

The FSB, as the G20's financial reform coordinator and facilitator, collectively strives to secure the goals agreed on by the G20 leadership. The options available to policy makers depend on the approach they adopt. At one end of the spectrum are binding legal treaties between sovereign states that result in specific obligations for each state signatory. Examples of this type of agreement include the Montreal Protocol, the Kyoto Agreement and the World Trade Organization agreement. In such cases states bind one another via legally enforceable treaties, with the state leaders signing and committing their governments to specific obligations contained therein. These documents are recognised as international law. The agreements are viewed as contracts (Raustiala, 2005) between state parties.

Non-state parties (such as the FSB or SSBs) cannot commit their governments to treaties; they have no standing to do so. None of the policy output produced by the FSB on behalf of the G20 has the force of international law. The FSB operates by securing agreements based on pledges from participants. The pledges are not binding. Pledges are the default mechanism of international agreements across the globe, from regulatory agreements to human rights accords (Brilmayer, 2006), and are 'most common in areas of technocratic cooperation' (Raustiala, 2005, p. 600). The substance addressed by such agreements varies from deep to shallow. Generally, agreements composed of pledges tend to have greater depth and complexity than binding treaties that are limited and declaratory in nature. When faced with uncertainty state negotiators create more win sets and greater depth (i.e. content) by committing to non-binding pledges. But not all pledges are deep in content or successful in their goals. The Copenhagen Accord on climate change is an example of weakness and is a pledge-based agreement (Rogelj *et al.*, 2010).

The pledge-based approach seen in the FSB process sees substate actors grappling with complex policy issues backed by a fluctuating policy consensus, seeking broad-based internationally coordinated, nationally implemented accords. Some FSB pledge-based agreements are strong, others much less so.

The FSB community, where they control the levers of policy making and implementation, and when this is underpinned by a particularly strong internal policy consensus and narrative, can secure qualitatively more robust, stronger agreements with greater impact. Such agreements can usefully be described as pledge-based 'rules' to which all participating states and substate actors commit. These rules-based accords can have a major impact on international markets and actors. Within the FSB context a more robust rules-based approach is seen in third-order and high second-order policy areas. It requires a strong consensual narrative policy consensus. Where the policy consensus is less robust, when the FSB does not control implementation or where national level-two processes and legislative negotiations affect negotiations, the output may instead utilise principles (sometimes also called best practices, standards or attributes).

A principles-based approach is one in which the policy makers refrain from prescriptive rules. Despite their weakness, this approach can be the best alternative option policy makers have in certain cases. Principles-based approaches allow reforms to be identified, agreed and pursued within divergent national legal and cultural settings. This approach avoids trying to determine detailed rules *ex ante*, permitting further negotiation and trial and error in implementation (Raustiala and Victor, 2004, p. 280). National agencies can then determine how to achieve the goals set.

In the FSB policy output there is tension between a rules versus a principles approach. The particular regulatory form chosen depends on the extent to which the common anomalies are recognised and a new narrative has been adopted. It depends on the strength of the epistemic community in the policy-making space. And it depends on the degree to which a community or clashing communities defend or shift the policy consensus, assuming there is a consensus.

Both strong pledge-based agreements, which function as rules for the community, and principles-based agreements, rest on mutual trust (Black, 2008, p. 8) and on a perception by parties to the agreement that similar state-to-state reputational damage may occur if they fail to comply (Downs and Jones, 2002, p. 109). This is what we see occurring in the FSB. 'You have all the principals at the table', and pressure to conform to agreed norms is greater than in previous processes; 'we look across the table and say, why don't you do what you have just agreed to?' (Mackintosh, 2012, 34, p. 7).

Enforcement and compliance

The FSB Charter is silent on the enforcement of agreed common standards. The FSB is meant to 'promote members' jurisdictions' implementation of agreed commitments, standards and policy recommendations through monitoring, peer review and disclosure' (FSB, 2012a; Art. 2.(i)). Overall, enforcement and compliance under the FSB are limited and fluctuate depending on the degree of consensus and control by the lead community. Moreover, as substate actors, the mechanisms used fall short of binding transnational obligations.

There are three types of compliance activity by the FSB community.

First, at the upper end there are joint accords viewed by the community as 'rules', which are pursued via multilayered monitoring that makes judgements on compliance. To be sure these are not legal opinions, and jurisdictions could disregard them, but when the community has a strong consensus, the pressure for compliance is meaningful and is reflected in their own actions and in market responses in which investors accept the rules as effective and applicable across national boundaries.

Second, where the community consensus is less marked, the FSB uses peer review, or a Mutual Assessment Process (MAP), which is less robust in that the reporting does not make as clear determinations on compliance or consistency, but which can, over time, still result in progress. This is because the process itself presses actors to move forward, to adhere to their commitments even as it does not make decisions on relative robustness. In these processes, substate actors self-report on implementation.

Peer review and the MAP processes are evolving. Reports which in 2010 simply recorded, without indications of compliance, now include indications of weakness and gaps, i.e. the peer review and the MAP are becoming more valuable. 'Today everybody is a little nervous [thinking] damn, we don't look so good'. The FSB is now 'moving beyond assessing implementation to assessing effectiveness' (Mackintosh, 2012, 22, pp. 22–29).

Third, in areas where there is no consensus, or where extreme complexity (legal, political or economic) stymies action, the FSB community opts for advisory documents that stop short of creating obligations, except insofar as the cooperative process is a positive influence on practice and approach.

Champions of legally binding rules disparage all the 'soft' approaches described earlier that stop short of legally binding, enforceable treaties. To do so is to imply almost all international regulation is valueless. This is foolish. The FSB actors are working within proscribed limits. They are not states and cannot create binding international rules of law. But the FSB and its community can and does create rules, obligations, institutional processes and customs of approach that move towards desired collective objectives, based on the strength of the policy narrative and consensus. FSB policy making has a clearly observable impact on global financial markets and firms, despite the non-binding nature of the agreements that are struck. The macroprudential narrative made real via the Basel III Accord and related mechanisms is a third-order instance of the effectiveness of pledge-based regulatory accords.

'We are all macroprudentialists now'

A paradigm shift, to become real, requires a recognition of unexplainable anomalies; change in the underlying community narrative and theory; and a jump from one worldview to another, a third-order change in policy. The G20 and the central banking community experienced this type of event, a disjunctive shift from the old laissez-faire deregulatory worldview of the last decades to a new state-authority-based re-regulatory worldview underpinned by the adoption of a macroprudential policy approach and associated policies. Macroprudential policy '[s] eeks to develop, oversee, and deliver appropriate policy response to the financial system as a whole rather than focusing on individual institutions or certain economic measures in isolation. Macroprudential policy aims to enhance the resilience of the financial system and to dampen systemic risks that spread through the financial system' (G30, 2010, p. 13). This shift was a 'radical intellectual change' (Baker, 2013, p. 39). Viewing this change in policy narrative Claudio Borio (2009, p. 32) concluded that 'we are all macroprudentialists now'. The G20 signalled this shift, and the policy process moved swiftly, by historical standards.

In London in April 2009, the G20 leaders called on the FSB, the Basel Committee on Banking Supervision and other SSBs to 'reshape our regulatory systems so that our authorities are able to identify and take account of macroprudential risks' (G20, 2009a, p. 4). At the Pittsburgh summit the leaders added that macroprudential policy must 'help prevent credit and asset price cycles from becoming forces of destabilization' and that, moreover, there must be 'an adequate balance between macroprudential and microprudential regulation to control risks, and to develop the tools necessary to monitor and assess the build-up of macroprudential risks in the financial system' (G20, 2009b).

Prior to the financial crisis of 2007–2008 the term 'macroprudential' was largely absent from central banking literature in Europe and North America. Since then the concept has signalled a new policy approach to financial stability and global markets. The adoption of macroprudential policy was a paradigm shift in the Western central banking supervisory approach, from one predominantly focused on the stability of *individual* institutions (so-called microprudential oversight) towards a focus on the stability of the financial system *as a whole.*

Until the economic and financial crisis in 2007–2008 there was resistance amongst central banks and supervisors from advanced Western economies to such a system-wide role. A wilful blindness existed despite strong historical evidence that banking crises had become progressively more frequent and severe (Allen and Gale, 2007; King, 2011). If and when actual busts occurred then and only then might actions be taken to halt a resulting recession. Alan Greenspan, former chair of the US Federal Reserve System and a disciple of Ayn Rand, author of *Atlas Shrugged*, a controversial economic libertarian work of fiction (see MarketWatch, 2010), infamously refused to intervene during the upswing of the credit boom cycles. Unlike other US Federal Reserve chairs of the past, such as William McChesney Martin or Paul A. Volcker, Greenspan refused to 'take the punchbowl away just as the party gets going' (Mankiw, 2007). Even Greenspan's successor, Ben Bernanke, failed to fully comprehend or see the crisis as it developed and thus had to clean up after the party was over and everyone awoke suffering from terrible global hangovers. But there was a key difference. Bernanke understood the dangers of market panic and depression and moved swiftly in coordination with his finance ministry and central banking allies across the globe to intervene and support the global economy and financial markets.

Post-crisis, central bankers swiftly in 2009–2010 adopted the macroprudential approach, which viewed asymmetric supervisory and monetary policy as exacerbating booms and busts and as excessively procyclical. Post-crisis, a plurality in the community subscribed to the belief that central banks should have a new job – i.e. restraining inflation *and* helping ensure financial stability through the application policy tools to enhance financial system stability and the resilience of individual institutions, all the while being alert to the potential risks associated with the destructive extremes of asset price booms and busts (Cooper, 2008).

Building on this narrative consensus the FSB sought to design and agree on macroprudential tools to be applied consistently throughout the economic cycle (such as higher capital, liquidity and leverage standards) and variable tools that could be triggered during the cycle as asset bubbles begin to develop (such as countercyclical buffers), a demand made by critics of the pre-crisis excesses (Rajan, 2010, pp. 161–162). In recognising and constructing policies to deal with booms, busts, major market failures and potential future systemic risks and excesses the central banking community was ipso facto rejecting the prior laissez-faire neoliberal deregulatory worldview. The policy is the reverse of the prior hands-off deregulatory norm to put far too much faith in the efficient markets theory and other dubious economic beliefs. The macroprudential response was a multifaceted re-regulatory stance and series of policy solutions that were new to many but not all in the community.

The recognition of the importance of systemic macroprudential oversight was new in London and Washington, but it was old news in Asia. Asian states had been using these tools since the crisis in the 1990s (Kawai, 2011). But in the West macroprudential policy remained, warned its critics, 'a theory yet to be proven in practice' (Bretton Woods Committee, 2010). The Basel III Accord is the product of this shift in the West. It is the most important financial regulatory reform in the post-crisis period produced by the G20-FSB process and is of a third order of magnitude. The accord is the clearest, strongest policy expression of the new re-regulatory paradigm, in which financial markets and systemically important firms (especially large banks) are constrained by tougher rules and limits on risk taking.

Basel III – the high point of the regulatory reform wave

The central banking and supervisory community, led by the FSB, exited the crisis with a macroprudential consensus that meant higher capital of a more liquid and tangible form was essential to successful reform. A new Basel Accord was pursued that would prove to be the most important piece of financial regulatory reform post-crisis. The negotiations were commenced in London in April 2009 and completed by the Seoul summit in November 2010. This was 'lighting speed' (Mackintosh, 2012, 22, p. 10) compared to Basel II, which took 15 years to complete and was never implemented by all signatory states. FSB leaders were in relative accord on the necessity of this paradigm shift on capital and supervision, but they argued over the precise amount and magnitude of capital required.

Capital: How much is enough?

Because there was little internal debate within the central banking FSB and Basel Committee on Banking Supervision (BCBS) membership over the need for increased capital minimums, due to the common policy narrative, the reform debate in 2009–2010 centred instead on metrics, on the level and type of capital required and on the length of the phase-in period, not on whether higher capital was required. The Basel III Accord resulted from intensive FSB-BCBS negotiations and pitted those arguing for a tough approach (higher capital, tougher definitions and a short phase-in) against those in favour of a weaker response (lower base capital levels and a long phase-in). The battle was one of hawks versus doves. Negotiations and discussions took place in the FSB, in the Global Heads of Supervision meeting, in BCBS formal processes and in informal discussions at the margins of other international meetings in 2009 and 2010. Just as the conceptualisation of the FSB occurred in informal and formal meetings, so too, agreement on the Basel Accord was facilitated by a series of informal gatherings supporting the formal process.

On one side of the debate were the hawks, including central bankers from Switzerland, the UK, Spain, the US and emerging markets. Philipp Hildebrand, then-chairman of the Swiss National Bank, pushed for high base capital levels. UK regulators at that time, including Adair Turner, Paul Tucker and Mervyn King, were also unambiguous in their support of higher capital standards. Spanish central bankers, who already applied relatively strict prudential oversight and banking regulations domestically on big banks, also pressed for a strong accord, joined by Jaime Caruana, general manager of the Bank for International Settlements (BIS). Canada's Mark Carney was also supportive of tough core standards.

Within the US the view was more complicated. Leaders in the US Treasury, the Federal Reserve and the Federal Deposit Insurance Corporation (FDIC) all strongly supported higher capital standards (Bair, 2012, pp. 257–264; Geithner, 2011; Tarullo, 2011, pp. 2–3). But the Office of the Comptroller of the Currency sided with banks and resisted higher standards.

On the other side of the debate were the doves, arguing for a weaker accord, including German, French and Japanese central bankers and supervisors (Bair, 2012, p. 260). Each country had its own reasons. German supervisors worried that too strict a Basel III deal on capital could adversely affect German Landesbanks, which could need major capital infusions to comply with a new accord. French regulators, meanwhile, viewed the financial crisis as an American disease and feared the impact on their large universal banks. The Germans and French argued in favour of lower capital minimums. Japan, although its banks weathered the storm well, sided with the doves.

Importantly emerging-market voices were strongly in favour of higher capital. European and North American hawks were backed by tough stances from China; India; Singapore; and Hong Kong SAR, China (Bair, 2012, p. 263). Emerging-country FSB members were in agreement with the general aims of the Basel III Accord. In fact, Asian states had been implementing similar policies for years; China and key Asia G20 emerging countries saw the new accord as a move towards, not away from, their own policy proscriptions (and national regulatory approaches) of tighter state control over the financial sector, and they were content to support standards that were in many cases lower than their own domestic position. In this manner, the new Western paradigm and consensus moved towards the emerging countries' position on capital and liquidity.

The end result was a multifaceted accord with a significant increase in minimum (core equity and risk-weighted) capital levels coupled to a long phase-in period. It was a compromise which gave something to both sides. The agreement finally unveiled was, according to Geithner, 'critical to making the financial system more stable and more resilient' (Geithner, 2011, p. 4). Trichet called it 'a cornerstone of the new regulatory system' (Trichet, 2010, p. 3). Caruana lauded its 'fundamental strengthening – in some cases, a radical overhaul – of global capital standards . . . [which] deliver on the core of the global financial reform agenda' (Caruana, 2010, p. 6).

The Basel III components are as follows and are summarised in Figure 7.1:

- A qualitatively strengthened definition of risk-based capital and an increase in the minimum level of core equity capital from 2 per cent to 4.5 per cent.
- A conservation buffer, to absorb losses in periods of stress, of 2.5 per cent of risk-based capital, for a total minimum of 7 per cent.
- The adoption of a countercyclical buffer of zero to 2.5 per cent, to be increased when an economy is booming and drawn down when an economy contracts.

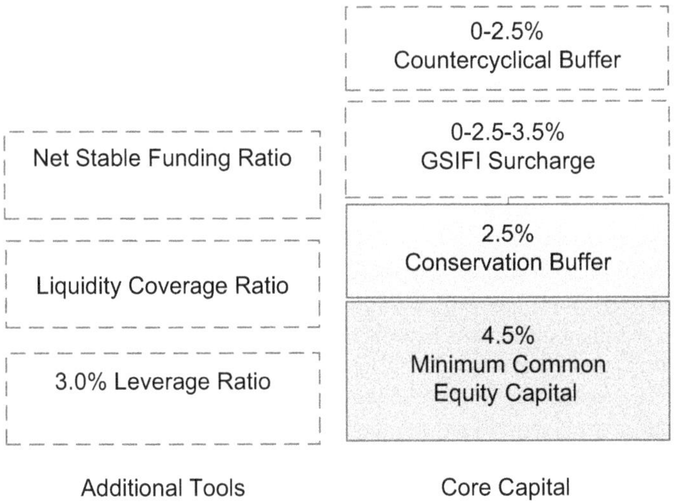

Figure 7.1 Basel III elements

Source: FSB/BIS

Note: GSIFI = Global Systemically Important Financial Institution.

- A capital surcharge (of zero to 2.5 per cent) levied against the world's largest banks (so-called Global Systemically Important Financial Institutions (GSIFIs)). The capital used will be common equity capital (BIS, 2011).
- A leverage ratio of 3 per cent to capture risk behaviour and to monitor and limit it.
- A liquidity coverage ratio to address the need for highly liquid assets in times of credit shortage.
- A net stable funding ratio to provide further strength to the institutions when they face stress.

The Basel III Accord resulted in increases in capital over the previous regime up to a 7 per cent base (a 4.5 per cent common equity and a 2.5 per cent capital conservation buffer), and the countercyclical buffer and GSIFI surcharge adding up to an order-of-magnitude increase in required capital, up from a 1 per cent functional level pre-crisis (Carney, 2011; Caruana, 2010). It was hoped that this more than tenfold increase in base capital would strengthen firms and reduce risk taking, as well as reduce the severity of boom and bust cycles in the future.

The accord included further capital requirements such as the countercyclical buffer, to be built up during periods of excess credit growth associated with increases in system-wide risk and drawn down in periods of stress. It includes a 'GSIFI surcharge', requiring the largest firms to hold more core equity capital, up to 2.5 per cent extra normally, with an additional 1 per cent for firms that grow excessively large despite supervisory warnings. Total risk-based and common equity capital could amount to more than 10.5 per cent by 1 January 2019.

Other mechanisms to provide further stability and resilience against firm-level risk-taking behaviour include a leverage ratio, a liquidity coverage ratio and a net stable funding ratio. These tools are designed to complement the effect of higher capital. Limits on leverage adds a brake on risk taking. Liquidity and funding ratios are designed to ensure that when a credit crunch occurs, banks have resources available to continue to operate and fund themselves.

Taken together the provisions of Basel III recognise that the largest interconnected and complex banks inherently pose more systemic risk to the global economy (Drehmann and Tarashev, 2011; Haldane, 2010; Haldane and May, 2011). This view amongst politicians and regulators solidified initially and strengthened (Bair, Brown, and Huntsman, 2012; Federal Reserve Bank of Dallas, 2012; Haldane, 2012a), as leading central bankers have pressed for more capital, and the higher quality the better, in subsequent actions supportive of the new regulatory normal.

A paradigm shift takes shape

The Basel III Accord's provisions are concrete evidence of the qualitative (type of capital) and quantitative (an order of magnitude of capital) shift in the re-regulatory paradigm led by the hawks in the FSB leadership. The deal is not incremental tinkering at the margins, as Helleiner (2014) and Moschella and Tsingou (2013) suggest. It is a paradigm shift in regulatory policy by the community in the FSB. The accord marks the reassertion of state power over regulation of global financial markets and firms. It shows a rejection by FSB technocrats of the extremes of laissez-faire neoliberalism. It signals the end of the deregulatory and self-regulatory era for large financial markets and the regulation of the world's largest systemically important banks. For the G20, but especially for the FSB, the accord is *the* major policy component of the reformist wave and paradigm shift.

The accord and its completion (by 2019) were possible because the central banking community rapidly came to a common understanding of the failings and anomalies of the previous worldview. The community then made a jump to a new common macroprudential policy consensus. Based on this shift the Basel Accord was agreed on. The combination of recognised anomalies, a strong epistemic community with control of policy levers and a shift in the policy consensus permits this third-order policy shift (Hall, 1993) (see Figure 1.2 on p. 16).

The negotiation required elite policy convergence (Bennett, 1991), followed by coordinated top-down policy diffusion (Levi-Faur, 2005). Negotiations were led by officials from Europe and North America supported by leading emerging-countries' representatives. The accord and its implementation mechanisms are potentially stronger and more robust because the policy actors are independent regulators.

Pledges with international reach

The central banking community committed to an agreement whose form and structure is a relatively robust pledge-based agreement, one that was then backed by the G20 leaders at the Seoul summit. It is not a treaty and does not result in binding state-to-state obligations. It is a pledge-based agreement and its depth, breadth and complexity are clearly visible, factors not seen in binding treaties of lesser complexity. Nonetheless the accord has some of the effects of a binding text. Critics of 'soft law' suggest this type of agreement has a minimal effect on states (Raustiala, 2005, p. 581). This is not convincing. FSB and BCBS actors clearly view the accord's obligations as requirements, hence, the heated arguments and the raised voices when one or another state is alleged to be failing in its obligations.

Markets and investors take the Basel III Accord seriously. They did not wait for full implementation before reacting to the accord. Banks that fail to reach the accord's capital standards even years in advance of deadlines are being hit hard negatively by investors (i.e. raising capital for these firms is more costly, as is borrowing). Gradually a hard law effect via national domestic rules and regulations has taken place. In Basel III negotiators constructed the strongest agreement possible given their limitations as substate actors, drawing on the community's worldview and narrative, their strength as the dominant transnational expert network and epistemic community in global finance and their roles as independent national regulators.

The cost of Basel III

After 2010 following on from the deal on Basel III, re-emerging domestic lobbies began to attack the policies being enacted to implement the paradigm shift, seeking to weaken Basel III's application. Domestic interests, especially the banks, did not affect the level-one talks in 2008 and had only marginal influence in 2009 and through 2010. These lobbies have taken up arms against Basel III implementation. Efforts to weaken its provisions and impact on the ground began. Critics warned that banks faced a huge capital shortfall (Masters and Baer, 2010). Banks needed to raise capital and complained about the burden; but constraining leverage and dangerous risk taking was precisely the point of the FSB leadership. Bankers' claims that the standards were too high and that the capital requirements were too onerous, too restrictive and too costly for the global economy were self-interested; the lower the capital standards, the higher the permitted leverage, the greater the risk, and the larger the compensation packages of CEOs.

Just how costly Basel III was from a macroeconomic perspective relies on Miles' Law: "Where you stand depends on where you sit" (Miles, 1978). Central bankers and regulators did not see the standards as onerous. According to the BIS each percentage point increase in the capital ratio causes a median 0.03 per cent decline in GDP, relative to the baseline (BIS, 2010) – a small price to pay for increased economic stability. Turner took a similar view, underscoring that 'the adverse costs of even very rare banking crises are so great as to outweigh any marginal growth penalty resulting from higher equity ratios' (Turner, 2011, p. 6). Anat Admati and others backed the central bankers, maintaining that increasing bank equity is not expensive, suggesting that much is 'fallacious, irrelevant, or very weak' because the risk premium paid (i.e. the cost of capital) must go down, not up, if banks have more equity (Admati *et al.*, 2011, p. 1), with even more equity capital – as much as 25 per cent non-risk-adjusted capital – being ideal (Admati and Hellwig, 2013).

Key policy makers predicted large economic gains from the Basel III deal from future crises that might be averted. Mark Carney estimated that the new standards would be worth savings of US$10 trillion in global output due to the avoidance of future financial crises (AFP, 2010). So while bank CEOs bewailed the supposed burdens on their bloated institutions central bankers and regulators viewed Basel III as a major and relatively cost-free improvement. But to be effective would require consistent application of the Basel III rules, and the FSB monitoring process underscores the seriousness with which they view compliance.

Using the 'bully pulpit of the FSB' on compliance

The full effect of Basel III cannot be achieved unless G20 and FSB member countries and regions work within the global process and fully implement the minimum standards (Walter, 2011). Consistent implementation of the accord's minimums is key. Ideally the rules should be nondiscretionary and clearly enforced (Rajan, 2010). The medium-to-long-term efficacy of Basel III, and by extension the strength of this main facet of the paradigm shift, depends on monitoring implementation and national enforcement so as to minimise regulatory arbitrage opportunities.

Leaders inside the FSB understand the importance of monitoring and reporting of implementation and have put in place a three-tier compliance monitoring regime. Historically the BCBS did not make judgements on national compliance with past accords. There could be harping and *sotto voce* complaints but no upfront naming and shaming of fellow regulators. The pre-crisis review process was thus quite weak. Not anymore. Post-crisis the FSB and the BCBS implemented a meaningful reporting and compliance process, making judgements on national regulatory actions, pro or con. This was a significant change.

To achieve this the FSB and BCBS constructed a three-tier reporting process: level one, timeliness of adoption; level two, regulatory consistency observed; and level three, ensuring consistency of outcomes. The reporting, paid for by the BIS, goes through the FSB to the G20 summits. As one principal notes, 'we used the bully pulpit of the FSB' to pressure countries to apply the standards (Mackintosh, 2012, 24, p. 21). Compliance reporting has taken aim at failures in consistency in implementation in the EU, the US and Japan (BIS, 2012), pressing for changes on all sides. These judgements do put pressure on the miscreants to act; they also, not incidentally, empower the regulators themselves against domestic opponents, as the former can use complaints from the FSB to strengthen their position against the latter. The detailed monitoring and the naming and shaming of those states that do not measure up was 'unprecedented' (Mackintosh, 2012, 27, p. 13). It had not been attempted pre-crisis by the regulatory community, because the community lacked a cohesive and agreed narrative and the related consensus on action that was seen post-crisis. The new process signalled the commitment of the FSB and central banking community to make the rules work.

The Basel III enforcement processes are policy paradigm implementation and maintenance in action. They demonstrate paradigm resilience. The compliance and monitoring processes are better than the previous non-judgemental non-enforcement regime. Findings in the FSB reporting process ensure not only the naming and shaming of laggards, but also may move towards the gradual establishment of norms and customs of adherence and, ultimately, potentially stronger compliance with the rules over time, which through repeated reporting may become widely understood and better applied.

In this process the FSB community leaders are defending the agreed policy paradigm shift and the macroprudential approach codified in the Basel III Accord. The stronger compliance structure is evidence of the strength of the FSB-BCBS expert epistemic community, its policy consensus and its ability to bind and press its own membership in a way not seen in other policy areas. Failures are not being swept under the supervisory carpet in Basel. In addition national actions since 2010 have strengthened the new paradigm, adding capital requirements on top of the Basel III minimums, as the consensus (on the centrality of capital) has hardened. These additional moves show the paradigm being built upon, supported by shifts in the political and public narratives.

Since 2010 more hawkish central bankers have moved towards 'Basel Plus' arrangements, which add to the standards agreed to by the G20 and FSB. These actors viewed the accord as the minimum, believing capital levels should be still higher. David Miles, Jing Yang and Gilberto Marcheggiano (2011) argued that a 19 per cent capital requirement would be optimal. Then-governor of the Bank of England Mervyn King warned that 'even the new levels of capital are insufficient to prevent another crisis' (King, 2010, p. 12), suggesting only much higher levels of capital, which would be seen by the industry as wildly excessive most of the time, would prevent the next crisis (Guerrera and Pimlott, 2010). Adair Turner observed, 'in an ideal world, equity ratios would be set much higher' (Turner, 2011, p. 16). Some US regulators also agreed, underscoring that 'repairing the capital strength of our banking industry is the most import task facing regulators and a pre-condition for restoring a healthy and competitive economy (Bair, 2011, p. 30).

The global compromise contained in the Basel III Accord saw many hawkish central bankers and supervisors reaching for more capital. The Vickers Commission Report for the Bank of England recommended a higher capital requirement for the largest British banks of 10 per cent minimum (Vickers, 2011). The Swiss National Bank added on its own gold plating, the so-called 'Swiss finish' (Swiss National Bank, 2010). Chinese authorities set varying capital levels as high as 11.5 per cent (*China Daily*, 2011). The US Federal Reserve also acted, implementing its own Basel-plus leverage requirements.

However, this gold-plating exercise was not sustained in major markets in the longer run, as the policy makers who lived through the crisis together left and were replaced by others without that terrible memory. Institutional positions adjusted. Domestic interests and politics reasserted influence on the regulatory process. Level-two interests affected win sets and the application of agreed norms in the domestic context.

US central bankers and supervisors, appointed by Mr Trump, began rolling back domestic standards in 2018 and 2019. As of 2020 this has resulted in the following weakening of US regulatory constraints:

- Modifications of the so-called Volcker Rule, which prohibited banks from using their government-guaranteed deposits to engage in proprietary trading and the operation of in-house leveraged hedge funds. This rule has been a prime target of bank lobbyists since it was enacted.
- Lifting the frequency of and requirement for stress tests on certain banks depending on size and other factors, originally enacted by the 2010 Dodd-Frank law. The stress tests helped re-establish confidence in the banking sector. Now that peacetime has returned, the burden is being lifted. Too hastily? We will have to wait and see.
- Adjusting the definitions of 'systemically important banks' to exclude more midsized (but still massive) banks from certain additional regulatory rules that apply to these firms also enacted under Dodd-Frank. The minimum size to be considered 'systemically important' has been raised by a factor of five from US$50 billion in assets to US$250 billion in assets. This is a huge victory for bankers, saving banks billions in regulatory cost. History shows a bank does not have to be large to cause a crisis when it collapses (House of Commons Treasury Select Committee, 2008).
- Adjusting capital requirements on 'smaller' – below US$10 billion in assets – community banks.
- Adjusting the definition of 'systemically important' insurance companies to exclude more firms from oversight.

In some other jurisdictions regulatory laxity is also seen. For example French and German central bankers, always more reluctant about new regulations, have avoided strict application of the standards on their weak and zombie-like banks. As a result those banks still struggle with high costs of capital, as markets view them as weak and high risk. Italian authorities have also baulked at triggering tough bail-in requirements when domestic banks neared collapse. And looking ahead Brexit may yet cause the Bank of England to loosen standards in an attempt at propping up London's appeal as a global financial centre.

In 2020 such steps do not compromise the entire Basel III edifice and architecture, but they do amount to a gradual erosion of certain aspects of domestic regulatory application of the agreed rules. Even with the weakened rules in some markets banks, with a capital increase by at least an order of magnitude over pre-global financial crisis levels, are systemically safer today, even if backsliding is being seen.

Basel III as the expression of the 'new normal'

Notwithstanding this erosion the macroprudential approach signalled by the Basel III Accord is a third-order shift in approach to oversight of the financial system as a whole and of individual global firms. Completed in 2019 the effects were seen far in advance of this date. Banks are changing their business models and hastily rebuilding capital, recognising this new re-regulatory normal. Basel III is the concrete expression of the jump, of the new normal, and the world's largest banks are paying the price in terms of higher capital and other macroprudential norms. The central banking community has asserted its authority, and state power is no longer in retreat. As Tommaso Padoa-Schioppa stated, 'If the years before the crisis were years of overreliance on markets and mistrust in government – or, more simply put, too much market and too little government – what we have seen in 2008 and 2009 [and since] has been a spectacular comeback of government' (Padoa-Schioppa, 2010, p. 8). Basel III standards are the minimum, not the maximum, and that minimum is subject to reinterpretation. States retain the ability to gold plate standards, and some have done so. But others (notably the US) have begun to erode the strength of the national implementation of the agreement.

More than a decade on from the heat of the crisis, this mixed outcome is not surprising. When leaders change, there are implications, good and bad. The election of a US president who is an anti-regulation nationalist was bound to cause a shift. Importantly changes in the US and shifts elsewhere have not been catastrophic to international standards, but they have reversed some of the gold plating and earlier strengthening of the rules and application within the US.

What is seen is paradigm maintenance, some erosion, but still strength. The regulatory worldview remains durable for now. If Basel III and regulatory additions since are central to the reform wave the over-the-counter (OTC) derivative space is the next most significant reform in global financial markets.

Clearing of OTC derivatives

The lack of regulation of the OTC derivatives market acted as a major transmission mechanism and contributor to the 2007–2008 crisis (FCIC, 2011, p. 62). As the G20 in Pittsburgh observed, 'the crisis demonstrated the potential for contagion arising from the interconnectedness of OTC derivatives market participants and the limited transparency of counterparty relationships' (G20, 2009b). This unregulated market added layers of leverage, obscured risk and transmitted contagion when the credit crunch began. Investors viewed these instruments as toxic or demanded payment of credit default swaps. The securities contributed to a system where large banks were not only too big to fail, but too interconnected to fail (Gensler, 2010, 2011). The derivatives market was unregulated then, and today it still remains a potential transmission mechanism; it was worth US$691 trillion in notional value in June 2014 (BIS, 2014, p. 14).

G20 leaders agreed that 'All standardized OTC derivative contracts should be traded on exchanges or electronic trading platforms, where appropriate, and cleared through central counterparties . . . non-centrally cleared contracts should be subject to higher capital requirements' (G20, 2009b). G20 states aimed to adopt OTC derivatives regulation by the end of 2012, a deadline which was missed but which still constitutes a potentially strong second-order change. The G20 move was pressed by the Obama administration, whose officials and experts (such as Paul Volcker) saw OTC derivatives as a danger to the stability of financial markets (Helleiner, 2014, p. 111). The US was backed by other G20 actors, who also viewed these unregulated markets as a principal transmission mechanism behind the crisis. The G20 and FSB would regulate a huge part of the global financial marketplace that had previously no oversight or regulation at all.

Fashioning a globally consistent regulatory structure for derivatives, as demanded by the G20 and as urged by the FSB epistemic community, was a complex endeavour, and the outcome demonstrates a dynamic touched upon previously: the greater the policy-making distance between the FSB as coordinator and the national policy makers in a market, the greater the chance of disputes, the greater the likelihood of a suboptimal narrative, and the weaker the regulatory hold the FSB has over the final policy outcome. As a result of these differing dynamics although the OTC derivatives policy is a high second-order shift – a coordinated international regulatory response where none existed previously – the reforms have been resisted by domestic level-two interests.

To be successful the derivatives reforms should ensure that reporting and central clearing capture a majority of derivatives contracts within OTC Central Counterparties and organised exchanges if they are to significantly enhance potential market stability. If too few OTC derivatives are captured by the new rules the greater the opacity of the market, the less liquid it may be, the more inefficient it could be, the more prone to shocks and crises it could be in times of stress, and the less it can be considered a success. By 2019 90 per cent of covered derivatives transactions were covered by recommended regulations and standards. Fully 23 of 24 jurisdictions had the regulations in force (FSB, 2020). Eighteen jurisdictions were applying central clearing for standardised derivatives, and a number apply mandatory clearing. In addition margin requirements are being applied in most jurisdictions, and higher capital is required for non-centrally cleared derivatives. Cross-border coordination, risk assessment, monitoring and the FSB reporting processes continue (FSB, 2019).

The outcome of the OTC derivatives regulation and oversight in 2019 is, in general, a good one. The FSB oversight of the International Organization of Securities Commissions (IOSCO) implementation and monitoring process has paid dividends. It was not swift, and it is still underway. But the derivatives market is today far better contained within the boundaries of regulatory authority than previously, when it operated with no oversight, risking the stability of the system. A shift in the internal debate demonstrates how far we have come. Today the debate centres on the extent to which central clearing parties pose a risk as single points of failure. Previously we could not get our regulatory hands around the risk. Now we know where to look and what to watch for. And regulators are much more attuned to the risks of excessive use of derivatives, old and new. Vigilance must be maintained, animal spirits contained.

Take for example the FSB's and Federal Reserve's concern over the rise of collateralised loan obligations to US$617 billion outstanding in the third quarter of 2018 (FSB, 2019; Federal Reserve, 2019). These are highly complex markets and products, and the devil is in the details. Further, the culture in many banks' trading rooms remains toxic: traders will take customers' money on both ends, have no qualms about it and simply say *caveat emptor*. If you pay too much, you are a fool. If the trader designs a trade with huge margins that skirts legality others are blind and the trader is a genius, until he is caught or comes up bust. If mutations happened before (collateralised debt obligations cubed anyone?), it can happen again in new markets and with similar instruments repurposed and full of risk. Hence, compliance matters. Here the process is less robust than it perhaps could be.

On compliance a somewhat weaker FSB process is in place (compared to Basel III). Through the FSB Standing Committee process the IOSCO and national actors engage in semiannual reporting of the status of implementation by G20 states. This stops short of qualitative judgements on implementation; it does not evaluate the strength of regulations but is an exercise in self-reporting of G20-FSB commitments, and its effect is limited to a reputational effect that assists in pressing members of the community to comply. Nonetheless this process resulted in the application of required standards and regulations across almost all jurisdictions by 2020, demonstrating that reporting and review do work even if they lack enforcement teeth.

To conclude the massive global derivatives markets were hitherto completely unregulated and had been so since their creation in the early 1990s. Now, in 2020 coordinated laws and regulations are in place in all the major markets in this key part of the shadow banking sector. In 2020 the notion that this huge shadow sector of global financial markets could remain outside the purview of internationally coordinated and overseen regulation is viewed as ridiculous. Prior to 2009 coordinated regulation was impossible because resistance from vested banking and broker interests was too great. The current state of FSB-directed derivatives regulatory reform is therefore quite significant, it adds to the paradigm shift and is a high second-order change (Hall, 1993). Other FSB policy areas, such as too big to fail, show the lead community struggling at the outer limits of their new narrative and reaching for new solutions.

Too big to fail

Of all the policy areas still of concern to supervisors and central bankers, the most vexing and intractable is 'too big to fail' (TBTF). G20 leaders, central bankers and supervisors chant a mantra: All banks, however large, interconnected and complex should be able to fail and go bankrupt in an orderly fashion. Systems already exist in some G20 states to permit small to medium-sized banks to fail; from 2007 to 2013, 482 banks failed and were closed by the US Federal Deposit Insurance Corporation (FDIC) without systemic problems (FDIC, 2013). The problem rests not with the minnows, but with the whales – the RBSs, the Citigroups, and the UBSs – of the banking world. The world's largest banks are highly interconnected across borders and amongst themselves, creating intertwined relationships and complex contractual links that are difficult to untangle in normal times, and even more so during crises, when these giants are most likely to be at risk of collective collapse in part because of those interconnections, as happened during 2007–2008. The consequences of such collapses were viewed as simply too damaging to the commonwealth; it was not just that a particular bank might be too big to fail, but also that in the heat of the crisis, there were too many to fail (Brown and Dinc, 2009).

Post-crisis supervisors in the FSB knew TBTF must be addressed. However a strong faith in the need to end the moral hazard of TBTF does not make it a reality. In fact since 2008 there has been greater sector consolidation, reinforcing TBTF. Moral hazard in 2020 may be worse than it was in 2007; investors know just how far governments will go – and it is very, very far indeed. Ratings agencies underscore this by giving TBTF firms credit ratings up to three notches higher than their competitors who do not get the TBTF moniker because of the continued implicit government guarantees, which are worth up to US$83 billion for US banks (Lopez, 2013), and tens of billions of dollars a year to banks in other G20 states (Caruana, 2011; see also Haldane, 2012a). The biggest firms in 2020 are larger, more dominant and more systemically important, suffering from moral hazard, in receipt of G20 government guarantees, explicit and implicit. The regulatory fear over TBTF is the background to the macroprudential policies targeted at the 37 largest banks and financial firms in the world. The goal: to restrict TBTF institutions and ensure their own liquid capital is available in times of crisis, so no state bailout is necessary in the future.

This FSB goal has been pursued by the design of resolution regimes, living wills and via total loss-absorbing capacity (TLAC), a risk-adjusted measure that requires 20 per cent total capital and convertible debt that can be used to resolve (i.e. pay for) a failing bank with funds already pre-committed by investors, for a premium (FSB, 2014b). TLAC should make the world's largest banks less profitable and less risky, systemically speaking.

Resolution regimes

FSB members, addressing the features of effective national resolution regimes for major banks and a few non-bank financial institutions, published 'Key Attributes of Effective Resolution Regimes for Financial Institutions' in 2011 (FSB, 2011a).[1] This ongoing work is the equivalent of a best practices or principles approach to this complex issue. The extreme legal complexity meant principles or key attributes (according to insiders) were the only option available to FSB policy makers in their efforts to harmonise disparate legal approaches. In 2020 this work stream is still incomplete; the legal systems are too different, the interests too divergent and the issues too complex for an easy solution. It cannot yet be considered more than a coordinated first-order change.

Living wills

The FSB and national supervisors have turned to living wills to strengthen firm-level focus on risk before a collapse. Under the living will process the world's largest banks must lay out how they would be dismantled in the event of their failure. This self-examination is beneficial. FSBs and management examine their structural and risk-related frailties and consider the implications of their business decisions. Is their bank too complex? Should they exit a risky business that is not core to their business model? Should they simplify the firm's structure and operation? In this manner FSBs and management have been forced to ask difficult questions they never previously considered, centred on whether their business is too complex to manage and resolve if a crisis were to occur. But living wills are no panacea. They are documents many thousands of pages long, whose complexity mirrors that of the massive, multinational, multijurisdictional, interconnected institutions they represent. Their existence does not ensure stability; it forces management to confront their organisational complexity, but it does not guarantee the removal of the risks themselves.

The FSB leadership understands that TBTF remains the weakest part of the re-regulatory paradigm shift. In private senior officials admit that closing or allowing a large international bank to go bankrupt is extremely difficult, or, more likely, impossible. For example Citigroup operates in over 100 countries and is dominant in a number of emerging market economies. Are mechanisms in place today to allow the US parent Citigroup to fail? Certainly not. Unsatisfied with this reality the FSB-led central banking community continues to construct new mechanisms that could strengthen the paradigm which is still being constructed to address TBTF.

Total loss-absorbing capacity

Then-chair of the FSB Mark Carney in 2014 reached for further capital requirements. In Brisbane in 2014 he proposed a new measure: total loss-absorbing capacity. This is an additional minimum standard proposed at 20 per cent of risk-weighted assets (i.e. in addition to the existing Basel III rules), made up of 10 per cent core capital (to be in place by the end of the Basel III implementation period), and 10 per cent convertible debt issued to investors that could cover the cost of their own resolution or closure. The TLAC rule came into force in 2019 and will be fully completed across all markets by 2022.

What TLAC demonstrates is the continued strength of the regulatory narrative and of the leaders in the community that champion it, defend it and continue its construction. It is further evidence of the durability of the post-crisis re-regulatory narrative. TLAC is designed to alter the calculus of TBTF and the moral hazard seen within the world's largest banks. It makes being large more expensive, risky, less appealing and less profitable. Taken together with Basel III one can see the contours of a regulatory world in which being too large has considerable costs. But TLAC only works if it lets investors take the losses.

TLAC can only work if supervisors use it. The evidence on that so far is disappointing. An Italian bank failure was the first test case where TLAC bonds were to be written down to cover the bank's losses. But regulators had foolishly allowed small retail pensioner customers to buy the TLAC bonds, exposing them to a complete loss to save the bank. As a result the Italian authorities baulked and would not trigger the TLAC and instead bailed out the bank using other mechanisms that avoided losses to the pensioners.

Whether you use TLAC in all cases or only some depends on domestic dynamics. Nonetheless it is still a considerable innovation, which forces banks to have liabilities that can be drawn upon in times of crisis. Cars have airbags and seatbelts for a reason. Some people choose to ride without seatbelts and the results are tragic. It does not therefore follow that we should abandon airbags or requiring seatbelts.

The FSB TBTF responses, some relatively complex and difficult to gauge in terms of their success, such as resolution and living wills, and some new and potentially stronger, such as TLAC, reflect the complexity of the issues and show the FSB response on TBTF evolving and strengthening, but not solving, TBTF.

The FSB approach to TBTF illuminates the outer limits of the paradigm shift and the self-imposed consensual boundaries within which policy is made. As with other paradigm shifts in the past the policy consensus does not extend to all options and all possible solutions, and the consensus places limits on what is and is not discussed. At the edges of the policy consensus the voices of those demanding still more in TBTF are growing louder.

In 2020 the central banking consensus does not include a logically superior solution – namely, limiting bank size (Johnson, 2012; Onaran, 2013), and, if necessary, breaking them up. But voices inside the debate are perhaps shifting, and a growing minority of 'insider outsiders' are advocating break up or size limits. Mervyn King is an influential voice, as was Paul Volcker (G30, 2009; King, 2009). Notable leading central bankers, such as William Dudley, former Federal Reserve governor and president of the Federal Reserve Bank of New York, have also warned that break up is a possibility (Dudley, 2014) if banks fail to reform their ways. Dudley joins other former policy makers (Bair, 2012; Federal Reserve Bank of Dallas, 2012) who have already made that intellectual and policy-making leap, pushed by the bad behaviour of the largest banks, even post-crisis. But these critical voices remain outside the community consensus. Break up is not yet, and may never be, part of the FSB agenda, because in many states, the size, power and influence of the major banks is such that opposition to rightsizing the banks remains the consensus, even though the regulatory paradigm has created a new normal.

In summary the central banking community is attempting to address TBTF. They are progressing but are still falling short. Allowing big banks to fail remains a goal, not a reality. Could national governments allow a bankruptcy of Citigroup or RBS to happen? The answer is still no. TLAC is a further attempt to address the size issue head-on, sending the message that if break up is not for now an option, then the costs (or tax) associated with being so large will further increase. TLAC shows the central banking community reaching for more tools. Addressing TBTF is not complete. TBTF shows the central banking community operating within the constraints of the paradigm, working to extend it.

Compensation, bankers' pay and bonuses

Compensation standards are another example of FSB action that has had a mixed effect. The G20 charged the FSB and BCBS with addressing compensation after contentious debate at the Pittsburgh summit between the French and Germans, who wanted hard and fast rules, and the UK and especially US leaders, who opposed action. The FSB turned to the issue at a time when some national governments and agencies had already commenced unilateral action. The FSB, BCBS and central banking community were responding to a contested linkage between many years of rapid increases in financial sector pay (FCIC, 2011, p. 62), increased leverage, perverse incentives and excessive risk taking. Given the split (Europe versus America) over the subject, the FSB sought to deal with the issue via a principles-based approach.

The fight over bankers' bonuses illuminated FSB tension between divergent approaches used by G20 members and FSB leaders. As a result at first only a principles-based option was selected. There was a lack of FSB agreement on the policy narrative. In France and Germany bankers' high compensation and bonuses were believed to have been a causal factor in the crisis, and hard rules were wanted to limit such excesses. In the US, officials, more ideologically sympathetic to bankers, did not agree compensation played a major part in the crisis, maintaining it is not the job of regulators to decide bankers' bonuses in a market economy. Given this split the FSB defaulted to a principles approach.

The FSB was pushed into action on compensation reluctantly and, lacking a technical consensus, responded relatively weakly and was behind the cultural wave, i.e. as a reaction to, rather than alongside, the public's outrage, which continued in 2015. The FSB limited itself to monitoring the application of the 'FSF Principles for Sound Compensation Practices' (FSF, 2009) by its members. The principles are either banal or high-level depending on one's view. They include agreement on a need for a board-level remuneration committee, limits on variable compensation, alignment of pay with risk, a recommended deferral (at least three years) of 40 to 60 per cent of bonus and inclusion of a clawback provision.

The FSB approach leaves national supervisors to decide whether to enshrine the principles in national regulatory or legislative language. Jurisdictions have implemented the principles using a mix of weak supervisory oversight (in the US) and enforceable regulation and law (in the EU and some other states). The approach depends on the equilibrium between the domestic interests in play and the country's or region's cultural preferences. G20 compensation practices have periodic monitoring, peer reviews and reporting, with the FSB concluding in 2014 that implementation is 'essentially completed' (FSB, 2014c, p. 1), despite diverse approaches and gaps remaining.

A formal dispute settlement procedure within the G20-FSB-SSB architecture to address compensation complaints was created by then-chair of the FSB Mark

Carney. The complaint process has a judicial feel to it. A supervisor lodges a complaint. A Compensation Monitoring Contact Group (working within the FSB architecture), composed of national experts with regulatory responsibility for compensation, makes a judgement on whether there has been inconsistent implementation of the compensation principles and standards. If failures are seen they will be 'verified and addressed as needed via bilateral exchanges among national supervisory authorities' (FSB, 2012b, p. 15).

But bonus pay is controversial, embarrassing (often far too high) and a matter of some discomfort to bankers generally who like to think they deserve it when they do well, and even when they self-evidently do not. As a result no one has triggered the complaint system. No one appears willing to open the Pandora's box of excessive pay for excessive risk. The complaints process must therefore be judged a bust; it is a good idea but one the supervisors and banks do not want to use.

To conclude the principles-based approach and FSB compensation procedure is at most a high first-order shift. The 1970's genie of financial liberalisation and the decoupling of bankers' pay from that of the rest of the private sector cannot be entirely put back in the bottle.

The FSB compensation policy response is weaker than actual regulatory (the UK response, for instance) and firm-level (UBS, for instance) practices and regulations; three-to-five year deferrals and clawbacks are now seen in larger banks, and they are being used. Bankers in these G20 states and firms are seeing their real incentives change – for the better – with implications for future risk-taking behaviour. Such changes may not be highly visible or enough for the great many voters angered by levels of compensation and the excesses in banking, but they are a meaningful shift in compensation practices.

Accounting standards

From the start of the G20 process leaders underscored the need for a single set of improved, high-quality global accounting standards, and they had looked to the International Accounting Standards Board (IASB) and the Financial Accounting Standards Board (FASB) to deliver. But this was a policy-making pipe dream, not reality. No substantive progress has been made. Tinkering? Yes. But real progress? No. This is due to clashing stances between the US Generally Accepted Accounting Principles (GAAP) and the EU International Financial Reporting Standards (IFRS). The US pays lip service to the need for a single global accounting standard but in reality views the IFRS (overseen by the IASB) as dominated by UK and French officials. Global firms bemoan conflicting standards, but for every truly global firm there are tens of thousands of national firms defending their own existing accounting standards. There is no agreement, but instead a defence of the status quo, a clash of accounting paradigms, not pressure for convergence.

Accounting rules amplified the swing during the crisis period. Mark-to-market accounting – the requirement to value assets frequently – often daily – and adjust accordingly – boosted profits on the upswing as assets constantly were revalued upward It hastened the collapse when toxic assets were repeatedly revalued as being worth less and less. Accounting standards on both sides of the Atlantic were procyclical. But accounting differences were viewed as contributory, not causal. The pressure for change was not enough. The leadership of the G20 and FSB was focused elsewhere. Crucially the FSB leadership did not control accounting standards, and neither accounting SSB was tightly bound into the new architecture; they participate but are stubbornly resistant to FSB coordination. The pressure for reform was correspondingly weaker. The failure of the reform impulse on global accounting standards demonstrated that G20 and FSB commitment is not enough, and if a policy area is highly complex, nationally based and almost completely outside and separate from FSB processes, then a defence of national prerogatives and models is seen, and no paradigm shift is possible, only conflict.

Strong policies require a strong consensus to be made real

Ideas and narratives determine the boundaries of financial regulatory policy making and are essential to understanding the relative success or failure of the FSB policies. The policy output of the FSB varies from strong, to weak, to insufficient. The output was affected by the extent to which that community had a collective recognition of systemic weaknesses and failures, the strength of the central banking community in the policy space and the extent to which it adopted a new policy consensus and narrative to underpin a policy response. When all three factors were in place, a paradigm shift or third-order change was possible (Hall, 1993). When they were not, lesser outcomes were seen.

Macroprudential policy, the Basel III Accord and the policy consensus

The Basel III Accord was the maximal response by the FSB community. The adoption of a series of macroprudential central bank policy measures and tools contained in Basel III was recognised as a shift in the policy consensus (Blanchard *et al.*, 2012, p. 9; see also Borio, 2009; Constancio, 2010; and Smaghi, 2008). That consensus shift, and the independence and strength of the central banking community behind it, made it possible to agree on the new accord swiftly – in months, not years – and begin the shift.

The accord's various measures, taken together, constituted a third-order paradigm shift in the regulation of financial markets and the world's largest banks. The accord marked a rejection of previous deregulatory, self-regulatory, and laissez-faire neoliberal beliefs and signalled the reassertion of state authority over markets. It was a new (to Western policy makers) approach to supervision. Basel III was and is today the central core of the reform wave that started in 2009 and which continues in 2020 as paradigm defence and maintenance.

The importance of macroprudential policies to the FSB community was underscored by the strong implementation measures adopted, since the community's collective narrative and new policy consensus resulted in a more meaningful compliance and monitoring regime. The FSB and BCBS for the first time make judgements on national implementation and regulation. This is an example of an expert community vigilant against those who might fail to implement new rules central to the new paradigm. The stronger enforcement was an explicit recognition of the importance of proper implementation to the new collective re-regulatory policy consensus and paradigm shift.

Was the accord strong enough? Critics think not. Martin Wolf has called Basel III the 'mouse that did not roar' and suggested 'tripling almost nothing does not give one very much' (Wolf, 2010). In this Wolf is joined by others calling for higher capital requirements (Admati and Hellwig, 2013). Their complaints have a degree of truth. So could the accord, had it been struck later, after the slew of banking scandals (LIBOR, FOREX, commodities and so on), have been stronger? That is hard to judge.

But we know that the window of opportunity for action – the win sets that become available as a result of crises-induced comity and agreement – do not always last long and must be seized upon. And that is what was seen. The G20 and their central banking epistemic community experts rushed to reach a deal quickly in 2009–2010. The negotiating win sets that opened up post-crisis in 2009 had to be exploited. It was perhaps on balance better to press an accord when the bank lobby was cowed by events and G20 leadership was strongly engaged than to drag out negotiations over a longer time frame, which could have permitted level-one win spaces to shrink and domestic level-two pressure against a deal to rise. From a purely practical and diplomatic standpoint it was better to strike a politically possible deal than to reach for too much and get nothing or less in return.

Having secured the deal the FSB community has defended their macroprudential paradigm through stronger implementation, adds-ons and adjustments. Basel III has proven to be the highest crest in the financial regulatory paradigm shift and reform waves. What was observed in the FSB macroprudential policy process is not purely an exercise in incrementalism, as suggested by Moschella and Tsingou (2013). That conclusion underestimates the significance of the narrative jump and policy processes and solutions that have been and are being constructed and fails to understand the impact of the macroprudential shift underway.

To be real and lasting paradigm shifts must be sudden, shocking at the outset and include third-order shifts. But once underway, they can contain incremental steps, which take longer to become fully visible. The paradigm shift cannot comprise *only* incremental steps; if that is what was observed, the events would not amount to a shift at all. As Peter Hall observed, 'long periods of continuity punctuated occasionally by disjunctive experience of paradigm shift' are what we see (Hall, 1993, p. 291). The macroprudential policy narrative is this type of disjunctive break with the past, a new regulatory worldview. It has been accompanied and followed by supportive first- and second-order changes.

Hall's view remains correct in 2020. This is the nature of significant dramatic changes in worldview. In the scientific realm Copernicus commenced the scientific paradigm shift with the publication of *On the Revolution of Heavenly Spheres* (Copernicus, 1543). After that, important discoveries were made, most notably by Galileo, which built upon the new worldview and made it durable. In the nation-state political economy realm, Mrs Thatcher did not just take baby steps towards neoliberalism. She took large strides *and* smaller ones. In 2020 this type of process is underway as G20 states and their technocrats continue to seize back authority over markets and firms, and the re-regulatory norms they have collectively identified and champion continue to solidify. The strength of the shift in a particular realm is dependent on the extent to which the core community controls the policy process.

The further away the FSB is from control, the less uniform the process

When the FSB central banking community leadership is further away from the direct responsibility for policy creation and implementation the output is more mixed and 'lumpy', that is the national application of G20-FSB agreed standards can vary to a greater degree and monitoring can often be less effective. The analysis of the OTC derivatives reforms demonstrates this dynamic. Progress in the OTC derivatives policy area has been substantial. Where previously there was no national regulation of derivatives today all major G20 jurisdictions are implementing Central Counterparties, exchanges, margin requirements and greater market transparency. But the IOSCO process is less robust than Basel III oversight, so the outcomes are more mixed even as the regulatory boundary has been extended.

In the OTC derivatives space the FSB passed the regulatory process down to IOSCO as the oversight and coordinating standard-setting body. The leadership of the process is thus removed from the actual policy making, and IOSCO and its substate officials are institutionally less powerful and hence less able to force the pace of change. This area consequently has a less robust monitoring process, with reporting but no judgements on the strength of respective regulatory fixes. Nonetheless this is not an incremental shift in existing policy; it was a wholesale regulation of markets and actors, which had never been previously supervised or regulated, internationally or nationally. As such it is a high second-order shift.

FSB standards and the fluid limits of the regulatory paradigm shift

Some areas where ostensible agreement exists have less promising outcomes, for instance, on the need to end TBTF, which remains a difficult policy challenge, with divergent views amongst the FSB community and G20 leaders. So the mechanisms were less satisfactory (i.e. living wills and resolution regimes), as policy makers sought weaker solutions, based on advice and principles or attributes rather than stronger rules-based agreements. Yet today the largest banks cannot be allowed to fail, so the impact of such advisory policies remains unsatisfying. The TBTF case demonstrates that the FSB consensus, as with any paradigm once in place, can limit the options considered by the community.

But the boundary of the new paradigm is not static or fixed. Since pressure for action was sustained within the community and was strengthened by continued banking FOREX and LIBOR rate-fixing scandals and rising political and public anger, the consensus evolves. On TBTF we saw FSB Chair Carney's TLAC rules. This is a solution that arguably would not have been possible in 2009, and which, markedly improves the stability of the world's largest banks even if it does not solve TBTF. Here we had the new normal being augmented by its champions, in this case significantly and dramatically.

No consensus and paradigm conflict mean no progress

There are also circumstances in which the G20 demands action, such as on global accountancy standards, where the G20 and FSB leadership supports the goal. But there is no consensus below the G20-FSB level, and neither leadership community controls or oversees the standard setters in this case. Here the differences between the two communities are just too large to bridge, i.e. Putnam's level-two disputes result in no win sets, and no progress is possible. Absence of control by the leaders and a lack of consensus by the relevant communities mean no actions take place.

Gauging success in FSB policy making

Looked at in totality, and with benefit of a broader and deeper perspective, FSB policy making has considerably advanced international regulatory reform, policy making and the worldview it represents on many fronts, as shown in Figure 7.2. Yet the output varies. There are pivotal third-order events, crucial to the paradigm shift, such as the creation and the coordinating function of the FSB, and the agreement and promulgation of the Basel III macroprudential accord. There are high second-order, borderline third-order changes, such as the internationally coordinated regulation of derivatives across the globe.

These different outcomes are to be expected. Mrs Thatcher did not win every battle she fought. She won some and conceded slower rates of change in others. We also see a similar 'lumpy' policy process unfolding. But the general direction is additive to the new regulatory macroprudential worldview. The Kuhnian wave, viewed in its totality, has yet to lose its force. States and their technocratic proxies continue to assert their authority over global financial markets and firms. Importantly the lead central banking community continues to buttress and add to new norms. In this manner the worldview continues to be defended, strengthened and enlarged, albeit at a slower pace than in the immediate post-crises phases in 2008 and 2009. In 2020 the shift is still underway, and the policies are still subject to attack. That is part of the process. But the worldview appears durable.

At present the new worldview does not extend to macroeconomic matters outside the regulatory reach in which (or beyond the consensus within which) the technical community operates. Neoliberal economic ideas have not been overturned, but the laissez-faire neoliberal deregulatory strain of thinking has been largely rejected by the dominant central banking community and its supporters. For some critics, such as Helleiner (2014), the failure of the redesign to extend to a full reform of all aspects of the global financial system, including global

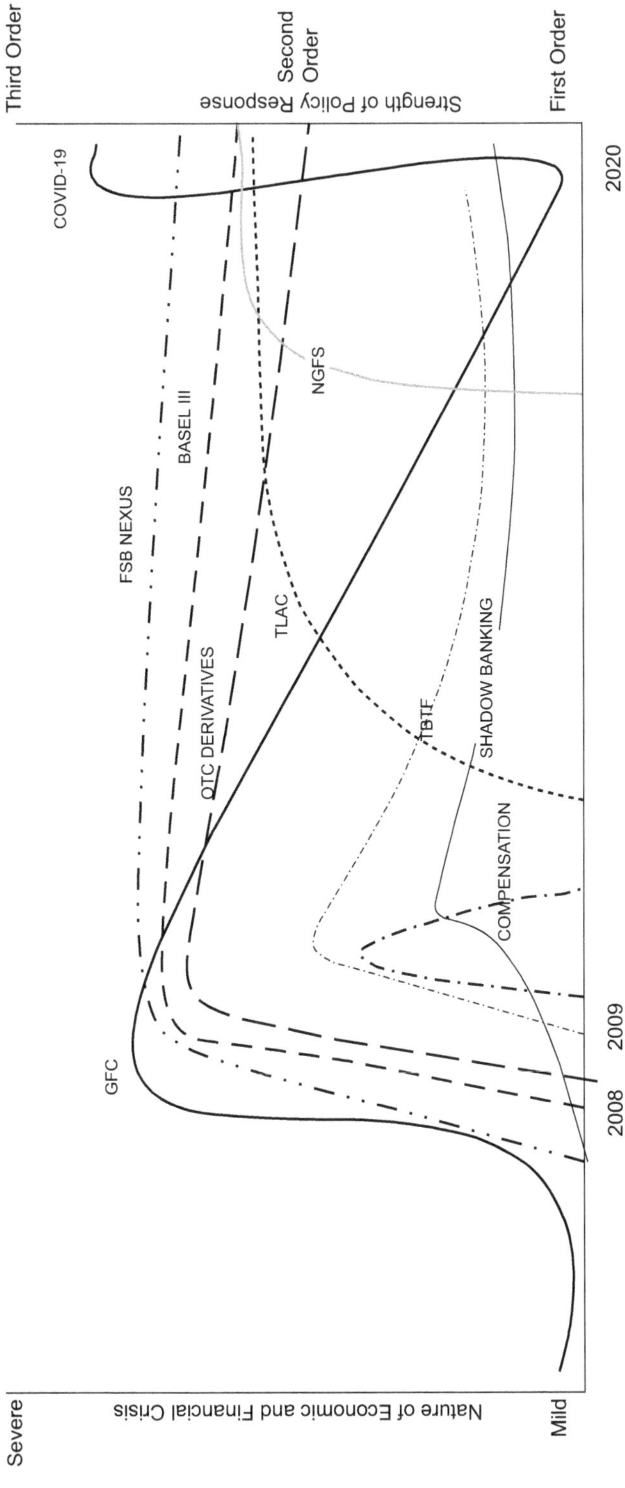

Figure 7.2 Regulatory reforms as waves

macroeconomic, currency and power relations, suggests the reforms are paltry and of little import. A complete redesign of global macroeconomic political economy relations is too much to expect.

Certainly paradigms must be large and disjunctive, and they have to include a repudiation of past theories and the sudden adoption of new theories with more explanatory power. But paradigm shifts do not have to (nor can they) encompass every aspect of an entire macroeconomic policy universe to be meaningful and durable. Mrs Thatcher did not dismantle the UK welfare state, but she did begin to and succeeded in permanently altering the UK political, economic and cultural landscape. Paradigm shifts can, as Hall (2013) notes, be more limited. In this case the shift was primarily regulatory, controlled by a technocratic community and supported by political leaders.

What was and is different in this instance is that the collective authority of the lead central banking community is such that the decisions taken in the FSB, backed by the G20, have effects on the wider global economy, on major financial markets and on the world's largest banks and on how they evolve. In this important sense the shift in narrative and worldview amongst central bankers observed in this book resonates far beyond the confines of negotiation rooms in Basel.

This reassertion of state authority over markets and banks, this macroprudential narrative, and the related global re-regulatory shift have limits, are still underway, are being both disputed and defended and are being strengthened and further built upon by its supporters. The policy consensus is significantly different from, and required a rejection of, the deregulatory narrative that prevailed in the decades prior to eruption of the economic and financial crisis that started in 2007–2008. The FSB and its community's policy output collectively amount to a new regulatory worldview, a reassertion of state authority and power, and a rebalancing after decades of wrong-headed worshipping of deregulatory gods, now banished.

The policy changes did appear to succeed in making the markets more stable and less prone to crises but not impervious to exogenous cataclysmic shocks driven by microscopic foes. Even now, 11 years on, the observer may be viewing this reform process from a contorted perspective, riding on and up against the wave, with not all of it visible. The reform process is not over. Definitive judgements as to the final success of the output cannot be made. In the G20-FSB reforms one is 'witnessing an extended process rather than the result of a single moment' (Helleiner, 2010, p. 625). In fact we may still be in 'the early stages of a reformation of finance' (Haldane, 2012b, p. 2).

Are the reforms enough? It depends on how you view the reform wave. The G20 and FSB community has had to deal with political and diplomatic realities. In 2020 that includes vocal opposition to the international rules-based system and technocracy from the US president. The lack of a G20 consensus on major issues limits policy-making space and ability to act. As a result of this discord the G20 is weakened and has been unable to act when faced by the COVID-19 disaster, unlike in 2009 when Gordon Brown led the G20 to save the global economy.

But behind the scenes the technocrats are still working, now under US leadership, to identify emerging risks and ensure the stability of the system. The FSB's relative obscurity and institutional distance as well as independence all help it achieve its goals. And the institutional momentum built up over the past decade can be felt. This is a community and the FSB is an institution that will continue to grow and sustain themselves going forward. The community's mission: to defend the regulatory architecture that the community has created and to identify and address systemic risks as they develop.

The following chapter will show there is evidence of construction continuing – particularly as regards the climate change policy response of the central banking community. This construction, which continues without US engagement, indicated we may be on the cusp of a new assertions of state authority – designed to refashion markets and finance to achieve the carbon-neutral goal. If so, we will see greater, not lesser, state authority or markets and firms. This is inevitable because the evidence shows that markets are incapable of internalising the cost of carbon and environmental degradation without state regulation and international coordination. An economically and environmentally sustainable future requires coordinated state authority, changed incentives, new models, and market rules to achieve the common goal alongside, and oftentimes in place of, the market. If this shift is secured we may view the current period as an interim phase before a further significant shift to a new carbon-neutral equilibrium, with governments and central banks maintaining and strengthening their roles.

Note

1 An update was published in October 2014; see www.financialstabilityboard.org/2014/10/r_141015/.

References

Admati, A.R., DeMarzo, P.M., Hellwig, M.F., and Pfleiderer, P. (2011) 'Fallacies, irrelevant facts, and myths in the discussion of capital regulation: Why bank equity is not expensive', *Stanford Business School*, Stanford [Online]. Available at: https://gsbapps.stanford.edu/researchpapers/library/RP2065R1&86.pdf (accessed: 2 September 2013).

Admati, A.R. and Hellwig, M. (2013) *The bankers' new clothes: What's wrong with banking and what to do about it*. Princeton: Princeton University Press.

AFP (*Agence France Presse*). (2010) 'Basel III worth 10 trillion Euros to G20 states: Carney', 14 September [Online]. Available at: www.france24.com/en/20100914-basel-iii-worth-10-trillion-euros-g20-states-carney?quicktabs_1=0 (accessed: 5 April 2011).

Allen, F. and Gale, D. (2007) *Understanding financial crises*. Oxford: Oxford University Press.

Bair, S. (2011) 'Financial regulatory reform: The international context', *Testimony before the House of Representatives Financial Services Committee*, Washington, DC, 16 June.

———. (2012) *Bull by the horns: Fighting to save Main Street from Wall Street and Wall Street from itself*. New York: Free Press.

Bair, S., Brown, S., and Huntsman, J. (2012) 'Financial stability and the problem of too-big-to-fail institutions', *Peterson Institute for International Economics*, Washington, DC

[Online]. Available at: www.piie.com/search/Financial%20stability%20and%20the%20problem%20of%20too%20big%20to%20fail%20institutions (accessed: 24 March 2020).

Baker, M. (2013) 'When new ideas meet existing institutions: Why macroprudential regulatory change is a gradual process', in Moschella, M. and Tsingou, E. (eds.) *Great expectations, slow transformations: Incremental change in post-crisis regulation*. Colchester: European Consortium for Political Research, pp. 35–57.

Bennett, C.J. (1991) 'What is policy convergence and what causes it?', *British Journal of Political Science*, 21(2), pp. 215–233.

BIS (Bank for International Settlements). (2010) 'Final report on the assessment of the macroeconomic impact of the transition to stronger capital and liquidity requirements', 17 December [Online]. Available at: www.bis.org/publ/othp12.pdf (accessed: 27 February 2013).

———. (2011) 'Progress report table on the Basel III adoption', 18 October [Online]. Available at: www.bis.org/publ/bcbs/b3prog_rep_table.htm (accessed: 1 April 2012).

———. (2012) 'Report to G20 Finance Ministers and Central Bank Governors on Basel III implementation', October [Online]. Available at: www.bis.org/publ/bcbs234.pdf (accessed: 27 February 2013).

———. (2014) 'Statistical release OTC derivatives statistics at end-June 2014', November [Online]. Available at: www.bis.org/publ/otc_hy1411.pdf (accessed: 7 January 2015).

Black, J. (2008) 'Forms and paradoxes of principles based regulation', *LSE Legal Studies Working Paper No. 13/2008, LSE Law* [Online]. Available at: http://papers.ssrn.com/sol3/papers.cfm?abstract_id=1267722 (accessed: 24 March 2020).

Blanchard, O., Romer, D., Spence, M., and Stiglitz, J. (eds.) (2012) *In the wake of the crisis: Leading economists reassess economic policy*. Boston: MIT Press.

Borio, C. (2009) 'Implementing the macroprudential approach to financial regulation and supervision', *Banque de France, Financial Stability Review*, 13(September), pp. 31–41.

Bretton Woods Committee. (2010) *International Council meeting*, Washington, DC, 8 October. Transcript.

Brilmayer, L. (2006) 'From contract to pledge: The structure of International Human Rights Agreements', *Yale Faculty Scholarship Series 3753*, Yale University, New Haven, pp. 166–201.

Brown, C.O. and Dinc, S. (2009) 'Too many to fail? Evidence of regulatory forbearance when the banking sector is weak', *The Review of Financial Studies*, 24(4), pp. 1378–1405.

Carney, M. (2011) *Author's notes of remarks made at the Annual Bretton Woods meeting*, Washington, DC, 19 May.

Caruana, J. (2010) 'Basel III: Towards a safer financial system', *Speech delivered at the 3rd Santander International Banking Conference*, Madrid, 15 September [Online]. Available at: www.bis.org/speeches/sp100921.pdf (accessed: 2 March 2011).

———. (2011) 'Regulatory reform: Remaining challenges', *Speech delivered at the annual Pierre Werner Lecture*, Luxembourg, 7 July [Online]. Available at: www.bis.org/speeches/sp110711.htm (accessed: 12 August 2011).

China Daily. (2011) 'CBRC to set new rules for banking sector' [Online]. Available at: www.china.org.cn/business/2011-02/23/content_21981261.htm (accessed: 12 July 2013).

Constancio, V. (2010) 'The future of economic governance in Europe in a global perspective', *Speech delivered at the Centre Culturel Calouste Gulbenkian*, Paris, 7 December.

Cooper, G. (2008) *The origin of financial crises: Central banks, credit bubbles and the efficient market fallacy*. New York: Vintage.

Copernicus, N. (1543) *On the revolution of heavenly spheres*. Amherst: Prometheus, 1995, reprint.

Downs, G.W. and Jones, M.A. (2002) 'Reputation, compliance, and international law', *Journal of Legal Studies*, 31(1), pp. 95–114.

Drehmann, M. and Tarashev, N. (2011) 'Systemic importance; some simple indicators'. *BIS Quarterly Review*, March.

Dudley, W. (2014) 'Enhancing financial stability by improving culture in the financial services industry', *Remarks at the workshop on reforming culture and behavior in the financial services industry*, Federal Reserve Bank of New York, New York City, 20 October [Online]. Available at: www.ny.frb.org/newsevents/speeches/2014/dud141020a.html (accessed: 6 January 2015).

FCIC (Financial Crisis Inquiry Commission). (2011) 'Final report' [Online]. Available at: www.fcic.gov/report (accessed: 2 April 2011).

FDIC (Federal Deposit Insurance Corporation). (2013) 'Failed bank list' [Online]. Available at: www2.fdic.gov/hsob/hsobRpt.asp (accessed: 8 January 2013).

Federal Reserve Bank of Dallas. (2012) 'Choosing the road to prosperity: Why we must end too big to fail now' [Online]. Available at: www.dallasfed.org/assets/documents/fed/annual/2012winter.pdf (accessed: 26 February 2013).

Federal Reserve Board. (2019) 'Who owns U.S. CLO Securities?', *FedNotes*, 19 July [Online] Available at: www.federalreserve.gov/econres/notes/feds-notes/who-owns-us-clo-securities-20190719.htm (accessed: 1 April 2020).

FSB (Financial Stability FSB). (2011a) 'Key attributes of effective resolution regimes for financial institutions', *Financial Stability Board*, Basel, October. Available at: www.fsb.org/wp-content/uploads/r_111104cc.pdf.

———. (2012a) 'Charter (as amended), Financial Stability Board', Basel, June [Online]. Available at: www.financialstabilityFSB.org/wp-content/uploads/r_120809.pdf (accessed: 7 January 2015).

———. (2012b) 'The bilateral complaint handling process', *Financial Stability Board*, Basel [Online]. Available at: www.financialstabilityFSB.org/publications/r_120427b.pdf (accessed: 28 February 2013).

———. (2014b) 'Adequacy of loss-absorbing capacity of global systemically important banks in resolution', *Financial Stability Board*, Basel, November [Online]. Available at: www.financialstabilityFSB.org/wp-content/uploads/TLAC-Condoc-6-Nov-2014-FINAL.pdf (accessed: 7 January 2015).

———. (2014c) 'Compensation practices' [Online]. Available at: www.fsb.org/work-of-the-fsb/policy-development/building-resilience-of-financial-institutions/compensation/ (accessed: 1 April 2020).

———. (2019) 'FSB report assesses vulnerabilities of leveraged loans and CLOs', *Financial Stability Board*, Basel [Online]. Available at: www.fsb.org/2019/12/fsb-report-assesses-vulnerabilities-of-leveraged-loans-and-clos/ (accessed: 4 March 2020).

______. (2020) 'Global monitoring report on non-bank financial intermediation 2019', 19 January [Online]. Available at: https://www.fsb.org/2020/01/global-monitoring-report-on-non-bank-financial-intermediation-2019/ (accessed: 27 July 2020).

FSF (Financial Stability Forum). (2009) 'FSF principles for sound compensation practices', *Financial Stability Board*, Basel, April [Online]. Available at: www.financialstabilityFSB.org/wp-content/uploads/r_0904b.pdf (accessed: 7 January 2015).

G20 (Group of Twenty). (2009a) 'London Summit Communiqué: Global plan for recovery and reform', 2 April [Online]. Available at: www.g20.utoronto.ca/2009/2009communique0402.html (accessed: 8 February 2011).

———. (2009b) 'Leaders' statement: Pittsburgh Summit', 25 September [Online]. Available at: www.g20.utoronto.ca/2009/2009communique0925.html (accessed: 8 February 2011).

G30 (Group of Thirty). (2009) *The reform of the International Monetary Fund*. Washington, DC: Group of Thirty.

———. (2010) *Enhancing stability and resilience: Macroprudential policy, tools, and systems for the future*. Washington, DC: Group of Thirty.

Geithner, T. (2011) 'Remarks by Treasury Secretary Tim Geithner to the International Monetary conference', Atlanta, Georgia, 6 June [Online]. Available at: www.treasury.gov/press-center/press-releases/Pages/tg1202.aspx (accessed: 22 June 2011).

Gensler, G. (2010) 'Remarks of Chairman Gary Gensler, over-the-counter derivatives reform, Institute of International Bankers Washington Conference', Washington, DC, 1 March [Online]. Available at: http://cftc.gov/PressRoom/SpeechesTestimony/opagensler-28.html (accessed: 31 April 2011).

———. (2011) 'Financial regulatory reform: The international context', *Testimony before the House of Representatives Financial Services Committee*, Washington, DC, 16 June.

Gold, H. (2010) 'Her man in Washington', *Marketwatch*, 19 June [Online]. Available at: http://articles.marketwatch.com/2010-06-19/news/30778323_1_greenspan-ayn-rand-nathaniel-branden (accessed: 1 April 2012).

Guerrera, F. and Pimlott, D. (2010) 'Pandit and King clash over Basel III', *Financial Times*, 25 October [Online]. Available at: www.ft.com/cms/s/0/1d392ba0-e071-11df-99a3-00144feabdc0.html#axzz1Lsgr7XIM (accessed: 9 May 2011).

Haas, P.M. (1992) 'Introduction: Epistemic communities and international policy coordination', *International Organization*, 46(1), pp. 1–35.

Haldane, A. (2010) 'The $100 billion question', *Bank of England* [Online]. Available at: www.bankofengland.co.uk/publications/speeches/2010/speech433.pdf (accessed: 16 May 2011).

———. (2012a) 'On being the right size', *Speech delivered at the Institute of Directors*, London, 25 October [Online]. Available at: www.bankofengland.co.uk/publications/Documents/speeches/2012/speech615.pdf (accessed: 31 October 2012).

———. (2012b) 'A leaf being turned', *Speech delivered at Friend's House*, London, 29 October [Online]. Available at: www.bankofengland.co.uk/publications/Documents/speeches/2012/speech616.pdf (accessed: 30 October 2012).

Haldane, A. and May, R.M. (2011) 'Systemic risk in banking ecosystems', *Nature*, 469 (January), pp. 351–355.

Hall, P.A. (1993) 'Policy paradigms, social learning, and the state: The case of economic policymaking in Britain', *Comparative Politics*, 25(3), pp. 275–296.

———. (2013) 'Brother can you paradigm?', *Governance*, 26(2), pp. 198–192.

Helleiner, E. (2010) 'A Bretton Woods moment? The 2007–2008 crisis and the future of global finance', *International Affairs*, 86(3), pp. 619–636.

———. (2014) *The status quo crisis: Global financial governance after the 2008 meltdown*. Oxford: Oxford University Press.

House of Commons Treasury Select Committee. (2008) 'The run on the rock' [Online]. Available at: www.publications.parliament.uk/pa/cm200708/cmselect/cmtreasy/56/5602.htm (accessed: 14 August 2013).

Johnson, S. (2012) 'Breaking up four big banks', *New York Times*, 12 March [Online]. Available at: http://economix.blogs.nytimes.com/2012/05/10/breaking-up-four-big-banks/ (accessed: 12 March 2013).

Kawai, M. (2011) 'Discussion of the lessons to be learned by emerging market economies from the GFC', *Brookings Institution*, Washington, DC, 6 June.

King, M. (2009) *Speech to Scottish Business Organizations*, Edinburgh, 20 October [Online]. Available at: www.bankofengland.co.uk/publications/speeches/2009/speech406.pdf (accessed: 5 March 2011).

———. (2010) 'Banking – From Bagehot to Basel, and back again', *Second Bagehot Lecture*, Buttonwood Gathering, New York, 25 October [Online]. Available at: www.bis.org/review/r101028a.pdf (accessed: 7 March 2011).

———. (2011) 'Global imbalances: The perspective of the Bank of England', *Financial Stability Review*, Banque de France, February [Online]. Available at: www.bankofengland.co.uk/publications/speeches/2011/speech473.pdf (accessed: 8 March 2011).

Levi-Faur, D. (2005) 'The global diffusion of regulatory capitalism', *Annals of the American Academy of Political and Social Science*, 598, pp. 12–32.

Lopez, L. (2013) 'Elizabeth Warren grilled Ben Bernanke on the subsidy for "too big to fail" banks', *Business Insider*, 26 February [Online]. Available at: www.businessinsider.com/elizabeth-warren-on-bank-subsidy-2013-2#ixzz2NWi2AIuT (accessed: 13 March 2013).

Mackintosh, S. (2012) Interview 22. Former G20 Finance Minister, Central Bank Governor, 1 May.

———. (2012) Interview 24. G20 Central Bank Governor, 2 July.

———. (2012) Interview 27. Academic Observer, 15 July.

———. (2012) Interview 34. Senior Finance Ministry Official and G20 Lead, follow-up meeting, 14 November.

MartketWatch. (2010) 'Her man in Washington', 19 June [Online]. Available at: http://articles.marketwatch.com/2010-06-19/news/30778323_1_greenspan-ayn-rand-nathaniel-branden (accessed: 1 April 2012).

Mankiw, G. (2007) 'How to avoid recession? Let the Fed work', *New York Times*, 23 December. Available at: www.nytimes.com/2007/12/23/business/23view.html?ex=1356066000&en=3337604c8708710a&ei=5090&partner=rssuserland&emc=rss (accessed: 8 May 2011).

Masters, B. and Baer, J. (2010) 'Banks face €350bn Basel III shortfall', *Financial Times*, 22 November, p. 15.

Miles, D., Yang, Y., and Marcheggiano, G. (2011) 'Optimal bank capital', *Discussion Paper 31*, External Monetary Policy Committee Unit, Bank of England, London.

Miles Jr., R.E. (1978) 'The origin and meaning of Miles' law', *Public Administration Review*, 8(5), pp. 399–403.

Moschella, M. and Tsingou, E. (eds.) (2013) *Great expectations, slow transformations: Incremental change in post-crisis regulation*. Colchester: ECPR.

Onaran, Y. (2013) 'Dallas Fed cap seen shrinking U.S. banking units by half', *Bloomberg*, 14 March [Online]. Available at: http://mobile.bloomberg.com/news/2013-03-13/dallas-fed-cap-seen-shrinking-u-s-banking-units-by-half.html (accessed: 14 March 2013).

Padoa-Schioppa, T. (2010) 'Markets and government before, during, and after the 2007–20XX Crisis', *Per Jacobsen Lecture*, Basel, Switzerland, 27 June.

———. (2010) *Fault lines: How hidden fractures still threaten the global economy*. Princeton: Princeton University Press.

Raustiala, K. (2005) 'Form and substance in international agreements', *American Journal of International Law*, 99(3), pp. 581–614.

Raustiala, K. and Victor, D.G. (2004) 'The regime complex for plant genetic resources', *International Organization*, 58(2), pp. 277–309.

Rogelj, J., Nabel, J., Chen, C., Hare, W., Markmann, K., Meinshausen, M., Schaeffer, M., Macey, K., and Holne, N. (2010) 'Copenhagen accord pledges are paltry', *Nature*, 464(4), pp. 1126–1128.

Smaghi, L.B. (2008) 'The financial crisis and global imbalances – Two sides of the same coin', *Speech delivered to the Asia Europe Economic Forum*, Beijing, 9 December.

Swiss National Bank. (2010) 'Final report of the Commission of Experts for limiting the economic risks posed by large companies', 30 September [Online]. Available at: www.sif.admin.ch/dokumentation/00514/00519/00592/index.html?lang=en (accessed: 9 May 2011).

Tarullo, D. (2011) 'Regulating systemically important financial firms', *Speech delivered to the Peterson Institute for International Economics*, Washington, DC, 3 June [Online]. Available at: www.bis.org/review/r110614f.pdf?frames=0 (accessed: 15 June 2011).

Trichet, J. (2010) 'Europe's frameworks for macro-prudential oversight and economic governance', *Speech by Jean-Claude Trichet, President of the European Central Bank*, Delivered at the Economic Club of New York, 12 October [Online]. Available at: www.bis.org/review/r101015c.pdf (accessed: 10 July 2013).

Turner, A. (2011) 'Reforming finance: Are we being radical enough?', *Claire Distinguished Lecture on Finance and Economics*, London, 18 February [Online]. Available at: www.fsa.gov.uk/pubs/speeches/0218_at_clare_college.pdf (accessed: 21August 2013).

Vickers, J. (2011) 'How to regulate capital and the corporate structures of banks', *Independent Commission on Banking, Speech delivered at the London Business School*, 22 January.

Walter, S. (2011) 'Basel III: Stronger banks and a more resilient financial system', *Speech delivered at the Financial Stability Institute*, Basel, 6 April [Online]. Available at: www.bis.org/speeches/sp110406.pdf (accessed: 5 May 2011).

Wolf, M. (2010) 'Basel: The mouse that did not roar', *Financial Times*, 14 September [Online]. Available at: www.ft.com/cms/s/0/966b5e88-c034-11df-b77d-00144feab49a.html#axzz2NoU88CBn (accessed: 17 March 2013).

8 Identifying emerging systemic risks in a complex system

Supervisors are like lifeguards at the community pool. The pool is crowded with swimmers. There is a lot of noise and shouting. Most bathers are regulars. The guard knows many of them by sight. But there are always newcomers. Some young, some old. Not all may be able to swim well or at all. Most of the time there are no instances of distress or imminent danger. But the guards cannot lift their gaze or start getting too familiar with the sunbathers at the edge of the pool, lest that be the very moment when disaster strikes, and lives are suddenly in peril. Such constant vigilance at the pool and by central bankers and supervisors is hard to achieve and sustain, yet it is what the public expects and demands.

The existing supervisory architecture faces the challenge of evolving as the risks mutate and multiply. This is the case in any supervisory structure. Constant vigilance is required even in peacetime, when no crises appear imminent. In attempting this extremely difficult task central bankers and supervisors confront the dissonance between the short term and the long term (Danielsson and Macrae, 2019). As we have seen in 2020 supervisors have many risk management levers and measures that can be applied to bank stability in the short term. Often, however, the most dangerous risks are long term, i.e. embedded in actions individuals, firms, banks, markets and societies may take today but whose risks will become evident later due to dynamics that are poorly measured or understood. Desired goals are not always matched by the tools available. Still fewer tools are available beyond the boundaries of banking, insurance and securities regulation. Yet future systemic risks can (perhaps will) emerge from outside the currently regulated sectors of global finance. Can the existing processes and institutional architecture identify, anticipate and help prevent the worst effects of future crises as they gestate, before they threaten systemic and economic stability?

This chapter seeks to address that question. The G20 and the Financial Stability Board (FSB) architecture's ongoing success will ultimately be measured not only against the degree to which it has made the world's largest banks safer and more stable, which I believe it has, but also against evolving new risks and dangers. Some are truly global, such as climate risk. Some risks are driven by new market actors, such as technology risks and shadow banking. Still other risks, such as increased debt levels, both corporate and governmental, have been created by central banks' monetary policy actions designed to support economic recovery, but which have significant unintended consequences that are at odds with supervisory concerns.

In 2020 the regulatory architecture is predominantly but not solely focused on risks in the banking sector and how to ameliorate them. That needs to be expanded. The structures created in 2009 must evolve to meet the challenges ahead. This endeavour to sustain supervisory vigilance and where necessary, to extend the boundaries of supervisory and policy oversight into new sectors is not a guaranteed success. Recent horrific events have demonstrated that exogenous risks can emerge for which we are largely unprepared, even as experts in other fields know of the dangers – the so-called gray rhino risks.[1]

A horrific real-time stress test of the global architecture

The 2020 COVID-19 pandemic is *the* maximal stress test of the global architecture. But at the political and diplomatic level (if not the central banking community level), it is failing that test. A truly global health calamity triggered a cataclysmic economic shutdown of scores of countries across the globe. Markets cratered. Tens of millions of people lost their jobs. Billions were told to shelter in place. The pandemic of 2020 made the events of 2008–2009 seem small scale and manageable by comparison. This was the test of the G20-led architecture. Could leaders once again coalesce and cooperate to deliver a degree of leadership and a steady hand, as health systems strained and the global economy needed a ventilator to survive?

Unfortunately the G20 forum has, as of April 2020, proved almost entirely unable to muster an effective, coordinated, collaborative response to COVID-19, the most significant threat to global health and economic stability since the 1918 flu pandemic and the 1929 Great Depression. Leadership from America was lacking at the political level. President Trump at first denied the seriousness of the virus threat, suggesting few Americans would get the virus, and equated it with the common flu (ABC, 2020). The president played down America's risks and attacked China, portraying the virus as a Chinese disease. The president championed untested remedies, even going so far as to suggest people ingest disinfectant to treat the virus. Criticised for his erratic behaviour and slow response (which may have increased US deaths), the President responded by suspending US funding for the World Health Organization (New York Times, 2020), In doing so the President sought scapegoats for his own failures amongst technocrats and globalist experts he so distrusts. Ultimately, the calamity of tens of thousands of American deaths forced the president to confront reality and listen to the experts.

But Mr Trump did not seek and was not interested in a coordinated response by using the G20 to maximise policy effectiveness and outcomes. Instead, there was an almost total lack of leadership. This was the G20's 'pandemic moment', and it missed the mark (O'Neill, 2020). A weak G20 statement was issued. No expanded coordinated response was offered. As Stephanie Segal (2020) observed while the G20 said they would do 'whatever it takes', the communiqué essentially recounted and endorsed what national governments and central banks were already doing individually through aggressive fiscal and monetary policy (Segal, 2020). Practically no support was offered to developing states grappling with a crisis which they had little capability to counteract. What a disappointment.

G20 countries paid passing lip service to maintaining trade but rushed to secure their own lifelines of supplies at the cost of others. They banned trade in certain sectors and competed for scarce supplies. This is mercantilism applied in a global crisis. The US even allegedly engaged in theft of German medical supplies en route to Berlin and sought to purchase a German firm developing a vaccine. This international geopolitical 'every man and woman for themselves' approach of President Trump was not edifying and demonstrated how far he would take his go-it-alone, America First doctrine.

The 2020 performance of the G20 because of the lack of US leadership was a long way from the 2008 and 2009 G20 summits and the resolute, dynamic, effective leadership of Presidents George W. Bush and Barack Obama, and of Prime Minster Gordon Brown. No additional resources were committed to the IMF by G20 leaders, and the World Bank could only muster minimal funds and action. Contrast that with the huge increase in IMF resources in the previous crisis. This left the IMF ill-prepared to address the severe economic effects of the pandemic upon poorer emerging states, as foreign capital fled to safe havens (like the US and Germany), government finances shook, and the virus struck weak underfunded health services. Such extreme pressures, particularly if the recession and economic pain persists (see box 8.1), could prove to be triggering points for national financial crises driven by already existing high debt loads and dynamics.

Box 8.1 V, U or L?

The economic shape of the recession caused by the pandemic lockdown and economic freeze of much of the globe affects the extent to which further financial risks and crises could be triggered. Three shapes of recovery with ascending degrees of severity and systemic risk are possible.

A 'V' shaped recovery, in which the pandemic is halted, the lockdowns relatively swiftly ended and the economy rebounds, recovering much of its drop quickly. This was assumed to be the outcome by economists early in the pandemic.

A 'U' shaped recovery, in which the economic freeze is longer, runs to months and the recession is therefore prolonged, before a strong rebound. In April 2020, economists, who also move in narrative groups, were leaning towards this outcome.

A 'L' shaped non-recovery, where the slump is prolonged and recovery undermined by a virus which is suppressed but then emerges again and again to kill and terrify populations. In this case the economic pain and risks would be maximal and extremely dangerous to global geopolitical and economic stability. This nightmare scenario, should it play out, would be similar to multiple surges of the 1918 flu pandemic (Rhodes and Mackintosh, 2020).

At the time of writing it was still unclear which shape of recovery would occur.

In an alternative universe . . .

Could the G20 response have been different? One can construct a convincing hypothetical alternative universe. Thus: a strong a decisive globally committed US president, presses allies and others to commit huge resources and act collectively via the IMF, World Bank and nationally, in concert. The US president is successful given the geopolitical power dynamics at play. The UK, which needs the special relationship, agrees. Germany, which has the means, adopts its traditional supportive role. France, led by a devout internationalist, also agrees. Japan, long-standing US ally, extends further funds to the system she supports. China, mindful of its rising global ambitions, also commits further funds. With key players on board a G20 action plan can quickly take shape.

The G20 nations seize control of industrial sectors essential to the response and recovery. They coordinate trade supply chains, directing flows from recovering countries to those still struggling with infections. Profiteering and beggar thy neighbor polies are avoided. Funds are directed not only at national recovery, emerging-country support, but also at the transformative green economy and digital drivers that will power the next carbon-neutral industrial revolution. Markets are supported, economies recover. A global depression is avoided. This fantastical alternative G20 activist universe is imaginable with American leadership. Without it, the possibility was never realisable.

With America failing to provide collective leadership, G20 summitry atop the architecture has been unable to act as the forum for action and emergency response. It failed this ultimate test. But state power and authority nonetheless surged.

When the grim reaper knocks, we demand the activist state save us

The pandemic resulted in state power and authority being dramatically extended in most major states, even if that power has been, in most cases, applied in an uncoordinated state-by-state fashion. The events, still unfolding at this writing, have forced all countries to rely on dramatic extensions of state power. American Democrats and Republicans, British Conservatives and German Christian Democrats, politicians of all hues, have embraced state action, fiscal stimulus and central bank action on a scale never previously seen. So while there has been a failure of coordinated collective G20-led action, there has been a further widespread extension of state authority in response to the pandemic and the economic disaster it precipitated. It became clear that when the grim reaper knocks, there are few libertarians and many clamouring for the state to save us.

Gargantuan stimulus backed by a wide political spectrum

As Table 8.1 illustrates fiscal and central banking stimulus of an unprecedented scale was commenced by states and central banks. Face by a terrifyingly massive risk to the population and the economy practically all leaders reached for similar

Country	*United States*	*United Kingdom*	*Germany*	*France*	*Italy*	*Spain*
Fiscal Policy	• $2tn stimulus bill • Small businesses loans and grants up to $367bn • $454bn for medium- and large-sized companies	• £39bn in direct fiscal support • £350bn loan and grant support to businesses • Job retention scheme that pays 80% of worker salary - £78bn • Debt repayment holidays	• €156bn supplementary budget • €500bn bailout fund to recapitalise large companies • €10bn affected worker compensation	• €45bn budgetary support to help affected companies and workers • €300bn in guarantees for bank loans to businesses	• €25bn fiscal rescue package • €400bn in state loan guarantees to businesses • Income subsidies for displaced workers • Debt repayment holidays	• €17bn fiscal rescue package • €100bn in state loan guarantees to businesses • Debt repayment holidays
			• EU finance ministers agreed to a €500bn package • €100bn EU-wide unemployment insurance scheme • Revised credit lines with less stringent conditions under European Stability Mechanism, greater lending capacity for European Investment Bank to lend to small and medium-sized companies			
Monetary Policy	• Lowered benchmark interest rate target 150 basis points total in March to 0 – 0.25% • Purchasing $700bn in assets • Re-activated existing swap lines with other central banks from GFC, expanded swap lines to several other developed and developing countries • Established temporary rep facilities with other central banks • Eased regulatory requirements on banks such as leverage and capital requirements	• Lowered benchmark interest rate 60 basis points in March to 0.1% • Increased Asset Purchase Facility (APF) to £685bn • Reduction of countercyclical capital buffer to 0 • New term-funding scheme for small and medium-sized enterprises	• Launched €750bn Pandemic Emergency Purchase Programme (PEPP), expanding assets available for purchase and disregarding limits in buying one country's debt, as well as including Greek sovereign debt in purchase operations • Additional long-term refinancing operations (LTROs) • Reduction of countercyclical capital buffers to 0 • Easing regulations regarding collateral requirements, increasing risk tolerance			

extensions of state authority and levers of power. Very few seriously questioned the need for the activist state.

The first round of US stimulus – the Coronavirus Aid, Relief, and Economic Security Act, known as the CARES Act – was, at over US$2 trillion dollars, more than three times the size of the 2009 American Recovery and Reinvestment Act (ARRA). Checks were sent directly to most Americans. Unemployment benefits were extended and increased. There was an agreed US$500 billion in subsidies for collapsing US companies. Only one Republican in the US House of Representatives sought (unsuccessfully) to block the measure, which passed.

In the UK a Conservative government enacted a massive job support and small and medium-sized enterprise support program, with employees' salaries being paid for directly by the UK Treasury (up to £2,500 per person per month). A mortgage payment holiday was announced and evictions banned. The cost to the UK Treasury: £330 billion.

The European Union responded by abandoning the Stability and Growth Pact, which limited government deficits. Austerity was recognised as a fool's game when the economy is facing a sudden stop never previously experienced in the modern era. The Union also committed to between 500 and 1 trillion Euro package of spending to support recovery. All countries started large-scale stimulus and intervention, including Germany, for every lever had to be pulled if Europe was to avoid a deep, dark recession – a recession that had already begun before the pandemic struck.

This book has shown how the 2008–2009 global financial crisis changed the narrative, enlarged win sets and made possible what was previously impossible. This is what is happening in 2020 at the national level in this even larger pandemic. Old Republican and Conservative beliefs (in the minimal state, in non-intervention in markets, for instance) were abandoned wholesale in the face of the unmitigated health disaster and economic catastrophe.

These emergency national fiscal policies, uncoordinated, were likely somewhat less effective than they could have been, at least as regards market-improving sentiment and steadying plunging markets; i.e. the 'shock and awe' effect was not seen, as it was after the 2009 G20 London declaration. The impact was not maximised. Each state actor pursued its own goals, often similar in approach, but alone. Mr Trump refused to lead, and the G20 was handicapped. But America's central bank remembered the lessons of 2008–2009 and stepped into the breach, followed closely by the European Central Bank, and other key actors in the still cohesive and activist community.

The world's central banks step up – led by the US

The central banking community has not forgotten the lessons of 2008–2009. The Federal Reserve Board reacted swiftly to the pandemic, slashing rates close to zero, announcing a massive US$700 billion for a quantitative easing program (subsequently increased), and a US$4.5 trillion market support and directed lending program, backed by the US Treasury.[2] The program 'was unprecedented' (Bloomberg, 2020b). America's central bank also acted in consort with allies, triggering a series of swap lines with major central banks, providing dollar liquidity, ensuring that the financial system would not seize up, that demands for dollars as the global reserve would be met. This is monetary and quasi-fiscal stimulus writ large. It is the activist central bank stretching the boundaries as far as it can. It was a much faster and larger response than was seen in 2008–2009. And it was a coordinated response; the swap lines were in place and triggered swiftly, with additional lines added as more central banks clamoured for dollars.

The European Central Bank also stepped into the breach, after a major communication failure by its president, Christine Lagarde.[3] The ECB announced a €750 billion program of quantitative easing (QE) and directed lending, underscoring there are 'no limits' to the steps the central bank would take, prompting investor relief. Other central banks engaged in similar policy actions, slashing rates and restarting QE, while linking to the US central bank via swap lines. Yet again, the globalist technocrats in central banking and finance ministries were at work on crisis management, trying to save the global economy. This time, even anti-globalist US president Donald Trump was 'very happy' (Fox Business, 2020).

When we emerge from this crisis it will be with an enlarged state authority over markets and continued activism by those states. The G20 is failing as a coordinating mechanism, because without strong collective consensual leadership and engagement by the still dominant US hegemon, it cannot act. Nonetheless disorganised state authority has been massively enlarged. Crucially for the recovery, when it occurs, the central banking community has once again stepped into the breach, led by an activist maximal approach by the US Federal Reserve.

The virus has to be beaten, the curve flattened by our nurses, doctors, emergency medical technicians and our own societal and individual altered behaviour. But the necessary state and societal actions taken to do that – the sheltering at home and quarantining of a significant percentage of the world's population, and the sudden stop of economies – also tests the weak links and hidden dangers in the global economy and financial system. As former IMF Managing Director Jacques de Larosière stated, COVID-19 is 'a powerful amplification factor of ground already heavily mined' (de Larosière, 2020). Some of those systemic risk explosives may be set to detonate in 2020 and 2021. What was required – the massive fiscal stimulus, the low-for-even-longer monetary policy, the massive quantitative easing – appears to have potentially set the stage for future systemic shocks and crises (see page 212). The dialectic of crisis management, reform and relapse would then be triggered yet again.

Can we identify those developing systemic risks and regulatory responses, some more urgent and effective than others? How should we gauge the FSB's performance in that key role? The following sections of this chapter will show the picture is mixed, with some extension of authority, progress and continued analysis of new risks, but many still unanswered questions and areas of supervisory concern.

New architecture and monitoring of emerging systemic risks

There is evidence of new architecture under construction, alongside the FSB, in the form of the Network for Greening the Financial System (NGFS). The NGFS was created in 2017 by a subset of the FSB leadership and was designed to reflect the lessons of the FSB and to address climate change risk and clarify the role of the central banking community. The NGFS is a meaningful extension of the paradigm shift we saw in 2008–2009, one refashioned to address this, the most significant risk facing the planet today. This latest leap was first slow – it lagged the scientific shift by almost three decades – and then very fast – the birth and rapid growth of the NGFS has taken place in only two years. This 'slow then fast' dynamic mirrors other policy shifts and leaps, i.e. slow incremental steps, growing anomalies, a tipping point, followed by a relatively sudden emergence of a new consensus and policy framework, which is then strengthened and built upon in the years after the leap.

Elsewhere there is continuing, more limited progress by the FSB on areas of systemic risk. Here, the work is not predominantly architectural and supervisory, but rather discursive and analytical. There is an ongoing effort on many fronts to identify risks and monitor them. Is this sufficient? We cannot yet know. But the process of risk identification, discussion and analysis is additive. Here the FSB process is proving resilient to atrophy or rot, even as it is led by an American during a period of America First. As we have seen in banking systemic risk monitoring this constant iterative process of reports, reviews, engagement and debate is useful and moves the cooperative endeavour gradually forward. This analytical work is no substitute for 'hard' supervisory oversight, but the FSB is not a supervisor or a forum that coordinates and monitors, and it continues to provide space within which the central banking community can share concerns, identify risks and highlight red flags. Participants are forced to repeatedly consider the evolving risk landscape and ask, 'What should I worry about next'?

In addition, there are entire areas of developing systemic risks which remain far beyond the scope of the FSB remit, outside the boundaries of the policy consensus and regulatory architecture. Many of these risks are global macroeconomic in nature and are themselves the unintended consequences of the low-for-long interest rate policy pursued individually by all major central banks. The extremely low interest rates were necessary to deal with the depth of the crisis in 2008–2009 and are necessary for the COVID-19 response. But the low (now negative in some instances) rates impoverish savers, stress all pension systems (G30, 2019) and enrich the already wealthy (for they borrow low and reinvest), and they encourage borrowing by states and companies, building leverage risks for the future. Leverage is good while rates are low, but leverage on the downside is hugely destructive when asset prices fall or rates rise (Mian and Sufi, 2015). So as supervisory vigilance strengthened bank stability, low rates cut bank profits and set up new risks for the future.

Finally, there is the universe of dark 'unknown unknowns' – i.e. exogenous, systemic, geopolitical, economic and regulatory unknowns – that we cannot yet see but which may cause us system-wide economic pain. This is reality. One can never see all the risks all the time. All actors operate within a consensus. That consensus itself has limits and boundaries beyond which one cannot see, or act. Confronting such 'black swan' events (Taleb, 2007), supervisors must have maximum room to manoeuvre, draw on lessons from the past, and be supported by political leaders (G30, 2018). The COVID-19 pandemic also demonstrates that policy makers and central bankers should be more interdisciplinary and seek to understand the risks posed by exogenous events. They should not be only focused on banks' balance sheets, lest they miss the health, climate or geopolitical black swans swimming in their direction.

Judging the coordinated international systemic risk oversight progress in 2020 depends on whether you are an institutional and regulatory optimist or a pessimist. The former will look at systemic risk developments and see continued construction, some enhanced resilience in the banking sector and evidence of continued vigilance on new risks. The latter will view these changes as too slow and too marginal to make a difference come the next crises and ask, 'Is enough being done?', with the answer being, 'No.'

I cannot close the gap between the optimist and the pessimist. But I would suggest before wringing our hands and proclaiming the current architecture and evolving processes a failure, we should ask ourselves, 'Compared to what?' The structures and processes we have in place in 2020 allow collaborative monitoring and oversight in a manner impossible before the 2008–2009 reforms. And now, more than a decade later, the central banking community remains engaged. Of course, the community is not infallible. It, too, is susceptible to the biases and limits of its own consensus narrative. But the return of state authority, the regulatory narrative and reforms have not atrophied as much as critics expected. Instead, iterative extension continues, with evidence that paradigmatic new architectural additions are still being constructed, when existing ones are not up to the job.

Climate change – a policy revolution finally underway

It is no exaggeration to observe that on climate change, as Barry Gills and Jamie Morgan have warned, 'History is written later, but the future is written now' (Gills and Morgan, 2019, p. 1). Or as another economist lamented, 'If we don't get this right, nothing else matters' (Mackintosh, 2019a). We only have one planet. Climate change and the related multifaceted, interlinked, nonlinear, complex dynamics which drive temperature changes fuelled by our massive CO_2 output and the stock of total concentration it adds to resulted in a concentration of 407 carbon dioxide (CO_2) parts per billion in 2019. We, the creators of the Anthropocene, are the singular threat to our own existence.

Confronting this reality governments and central banks have come under pressure to act to help secure a transition to a carbon-neutral economy that is stable and sustainable for future generations. A policy shift by the central banking community requires a leap in their narratives and a recognition that their mandates should henceforth include an embedding of climate change within all aspects of their work and long-term goals. Central banks, alongside governments, are the most powerful economic actors, especially in crisis response and prevention. What they each say and do matters a great deal. Working together, the G20 and central banks can more effectively pursue common goals. This collaboration is essential. For in the end political and economic stability relies on ecological stability and sustainability. Talking about long-term systemic risks to the economy without including and addressing climate change is ridiculous. Crucially, (and finally), on climate change risk, a narrative shift appears to be underway that could eventually significantly increase the possibility of achieving the collective carbon-neutral goals that are essential for all of us and our planet.

Mr Carney makes the case

In 2015 an additional paradigmatic shift in central banking policy and narrative began on climate change, triggered by Mark Carney, then-governor of the Bank of England, who appears again as an agent of change. This shift, led by Mr Carney, is of a potentially third order in magnitude. It is both a narrative and, crucially, an institutional, policy shift. Looking ahead, it could prove to have a considerable and (one hopes) long-standing effect on central bank economic, macroprudential and microprudential policy in the years ahead. In 2015 Mr Carney warned,

> The combination of the weight of scientific evidence and the dynamics of the financial system suggest that, in the fullness of time, climate change will threaten financial resilience and long-term prosperity. While there is still time to act, the window of opportunity is finite and shrinking.
>
> (Carney, 2015, p. 16)

Mr Carney identified a series of climate change-related risks to the financial sector including (a) physical risks: the impacts today on insurance liabilities and the value of financial assets, (b) liability risks: the impacts that could arise tomorrow from the effects of climate change, and (c) transition risks: the financial risks which could result from the process of adjustment towards a lower carbon economy. In 2015 Mr Carney was ahead of his own community, which reacted with some scorn. But he was in sync with mainstream UK public opinion and in line with government policy, which was itself shifting rapidly. And crucially Mr Carney held key levers in the international policy process, increasing the likelihood that his own personal narrative leap would translate more rapidly into an emerging new consensus and institutional reality.

As chair of the FSB Mr Carney called on the G20 leadership to support the creation of a Taskforce on Climate-related Financial Disclosure (TCFD) to improve the information on climate change risks available to insurers and investors seeking to plan for a climate future that is already upon us. Mr Carney went on, with support from the French and Chinese central banks, amongst others, two years later, to add to the TCFD with the creation of an entirely new organisation in the global financial architecture, the Network for Greening the Financial System (NGFS).

The creation of the Network for Greening the Financial System[4]

The NGFS was announced by eight central banks and supervisors after the One Planet Summit in Paris in December 2017. The first meeting of the group was on 24 January 2018. The mission of the NGFS is to develop environmental and climate risk management in the financial sector and to mobilise mainstream finance to support the transition towards a sustainable economy. The NGFS underscores that 'Climate-related risks are a source of financial risk. It is therefore within the mandates of central banks and supervisors to ensure the financial system is resilient to these risks' (NGFS, 2018, p. 3). The NGFS leadership is arguing there is no need for changes in mandates. Interpreted properly central banks can already act to help achieve the Paris Agreement goals.

The history of past paradigm shifts is a guide, and as seen in the central banking response to the 2008–2009 global financial crisis, the ability to achieve identified goals is directly affected by the extent to which the narrative consensus is strengthened, broadened and deepened. The faster that happens, the greater the ability of a community to act as a group and individually within their states and organisations. In the case of this new institution the community's narrative strength in climate change and the size of the consensus grew swiftly.

Institutional growth signals a narrative and consensus leap

The NGFS grew from a concept hatched by a small group of eight institutions (including the British, Chinese, Dutch, French, Mexican, Singaporean, and Swedish central banks and supervisors) in 2017 to a 'truly global endeavor' (LSE, 2019). An organisation in 2020 with 46 members and nine observers is remarkable and indicative of the type of disjunctive break we see in other paradigm shifts. The consensus in the community and amongst its leaders appears to be moving quickly from one state (climate is not our problem) to another (central banks must address climate change).

Figure 8.1 highlights the speed with which the NGFS has grown and the many key players, advanced, emerging, East, West, North and South that are now a part of the process. The NGFS's birth and rapid growth underscore that it is a 'coalition of the willing', is inclusive not exclusive and is based on belief in the new narrative on central banks and climate change. The NGFS represents the clearest institutional expression of central banks' narrative paradigm shift in climate that is now underway. The hope is this is not just greenwashing or 'virtue signaling' (Morrison, 2019). In 2020 the NGFS membership represents countries that account for 44 per cent of global GDP. Not bad for a two-year-old institutional toddler, one that will no doubt continue to grow quickly. Crucially the NGFS has been created without the US – because the world cannot wait for President Trump and America's central bank to recognise scientific facts and climate reality.

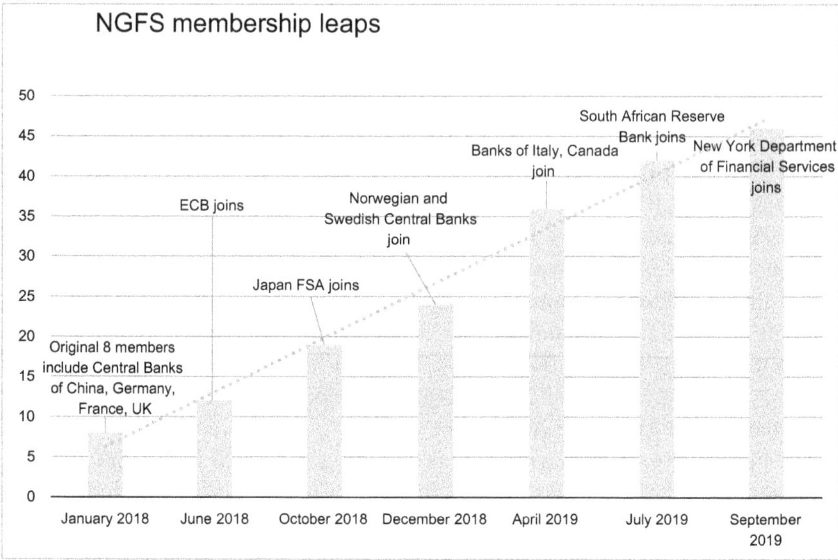

Figure 8.1 NGFS membership growth and key signatory institutions

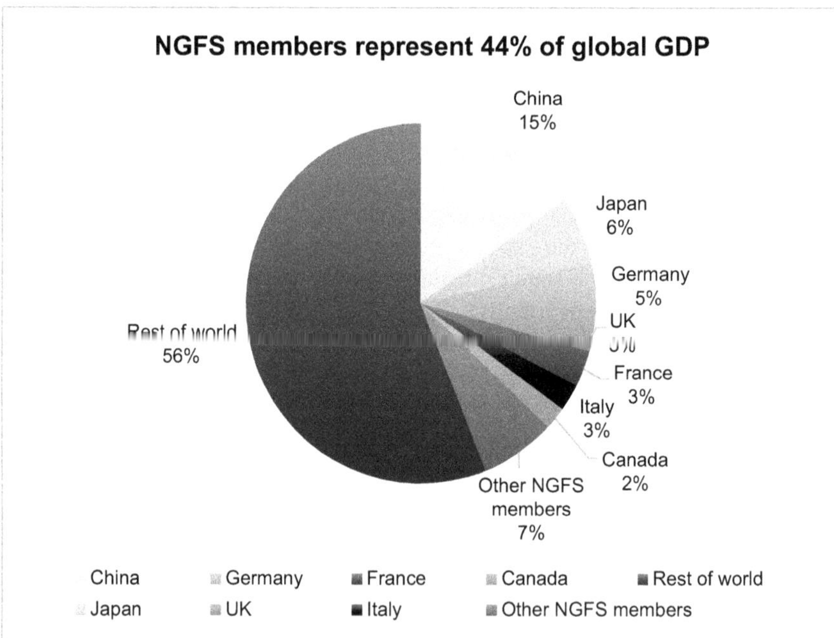

Figure 8.2 NGFS members as percentage of global GDP

America, silent and alone

The US Federal Reserve System is not a member of the NGFS. That is not surprising. The central bank's position in 2020 is variously either a more nuanced version of the Trumpian general rejection of climate change risk, a matter of cowardice or supervisory conservatism and timidity. America's central bankers do not want to get ahead of the tweeter-in-chief lest they become targets of attack. Do they consider the issue? It seems the answer, until very recently, was 'No'. In the last 30 years only one governor of the US central bank has ever spoken on climate change, and that was Lael Brainard in October 2019 (Brainard, 2019).[5] This first anodyne statement occurred after senior central bank officials were publicly criticised for the deafening silence on this, the issue of our lifetime. The NGFS and the world cannot wait. Given the US position and the failure of America's central bankers to join the shift, the NGFS had to be created alongside the FSB. The NGFS's founders have taken what works from the FSB structure process and replicated it.

An organisational structure that works

Mr Carney's fingerprints and those of other founding member organisations are all over the NGFS structure. The founders have lifted the FSB structure and replicated it wholesale in the NGFS. The NGFS chair is selected by a Steering Committee. That committee sits atop a plenary. A series of three working groups feeds recommendations into the Steering Committee and plenary. The NGFS is financed by participating central banks, and its secretariat is hosted by a leading central bank, the Banque de France. This is basically identical to the organisational structure of the FSB. It is sensible to use what you know works well.

To date the NGFS has made considerable institutional strides in a very short time. It has succeeded in co-opting many of the world's major central banks into a coordinated discussion on how to integrate climate change into central bank mandates and policy processes. This must be cheered. To put it in Kuhnian terms Carney's 2015 speech was the first signal of a possible paradigm shift. The 2017 creation of the NGFS was the key tipping point towards a new institutional and policy narrative. In the two years since we have seen the consensus strengthen, as has the institution and its membership. If the NGFS is the concrete institutional expression of a further climate change-driven shift in the dominant central banking policy narrative the real measure of the new structure will be in policy effectiveness. The creation of a structure of cooperation and coordination is important, valuable and additive. But third-order shifts are, in practice, only made real through the act of policy implementation. Talk is cheap. Action matters.

The NGFS work program

The NGFS has 'set itself an immense task that will require system-wide changes' (LSE, 2019) to reorient central bank supervision and risk frameworks that help achieve and sustain the carbon-neural goal set in the Paris Agreement. As a series of first steps the work program currently includes:

1 Integrating climate-related risks into financial stability monitoring and micro-supervision;
2 Integrating sustainability factors into own-portfolio management;
3 Bridging the data gaps;
4 Building awareness and intellectual capacity and encouraging technical assistance and knowledge sharing;
5 Achieving robust and internationally consistent climate and environment-related disclosure;
6 Supporting the development of a taxonomy of economic activities.

There appears to be a growing sense of urgency. That is a good sign.

The NGFS leadership is clear that the climate change future is being created today and believes that action on climate risk is needed immediately to reduce long-term impacts.

Given the limited time within which we can secure anything close to the Paris Agreement goals researchers and analysts should look to see if the NGFS continues to move swiftly forward to develop concrete policy recommendations for its members. The structural mechanisms to coordinate action have been put in place, and the NGFS needs to convert those into action. As the NGFS Secretary General Frank Elderson stated:

> Climate change will affect all agents in the economy (households, businesses, governments), across all sectors and geographies. The risks will likely be correlated with, and potentially aggravated by, tipping points, in a non-linear fashion. This means the impact of these risks could be much larger, and more widespread and diverse than those of other structural changes. Even though the prime responsibility for ensuring the success of the Paris Agreement rests with governments, it is up to central banks and supervisors to shape and deliver on their substantial role in addressing climate related risks within the remit of their mandates.
>
> (Elderson, 2019, p. 2)

Mr Elderson is right. Greta Thunberg is right (Guardian, 2019). Fatboy Slim is right (Fatboy Slim, 2019). We need to act. *Right here. Right now.*

The real test of the NGFS and its future effectiveness in this crucial shift is how fast it supports its membership move beyond taxonomy (which can be a procrastinator's best friend)[6] to policy recommendations and advice to pressure members to change their monetary, macroprudential and microprudential policy frameworks to reflect climate change risks and the links to economic sustainability and stability. Those central bank and supervisory steps should include:

- Fully integrating climate change into all aspects of central bank work by including climate change risk assessments in monetary and supervisory policy discussions and decision-making processes, thereby aligning central bank goals with Paris Agreement goals;

- Adjusting central bank asset purchase regulations and practices to support growth of the green bond market and encourage that market to fully develop as a matter of considerable importance;
- Clarifying standards, norms and taxonomy as is needed to encourage transparency and increase disclosure of climate risks by financial sector firms;
- Ultimately, SSBs making adjustments to capital-weighting regulations to include carbon intensity and risks, thus providing incentives for the needed shift in investor behaviour;
- Integrating climate change goals into microprudential supervisory assessments and stress testing and requiring bank boards to make related adjustments and changes within their own processes and planning.

To conclude the NGFS is the newest, likely permanent addition to the global architecture. Its creation and ambitious goals demonstrate a sustained activism by the central banking community, a new phase in construction of the regulatory system, one that should support the necessary shift to a carbon-neutral economy. Its creation underscores again the nature of policy shifts – slow and incremental, increasing anomalies and pressures, a tipping point and then rapid coalescence of a new consensus and mechanisms for delivering policy goals. It will not ensure success, but the NGFS case shows crucial additional narrative and policy leaps are still possible when leadership exists, when the risks are finally understood and the timing is right.

The NGFS also shows crucial shifts can exclude the US. Can the NGFS operate as effectively in parallel with, rather than reporting to, the FSB and G20? Perhaps not. But it is better to move fast on a problem whose fat tail risk causes us all nightmares than wait for Mr Trump to wake from his slumber. Ultimately the NGFS could (and perhaps should) be integrated with the FSB structure so as to ensure it benefits from the strength of the FSB, supplements it and can drive the climate policy response in due time. But formal G20-FSB-NGFS integration cannot occur until we have a change in the US administration, one that signals a permanent return to a science- and fact-based policy-making process on climate change. I expect further construction to occur as the urgency of climate change action mounts. National regulators of carbon pricing and markets will be needed; national carbon banks modelled on central banks are a good and possible next step. International coordination will be further strengthened. This is only the belated beginning.

These paradigm shifts cannot just be public sector institutional affairs, although that is crucial; they must also be mirrored by action in the private sector. Just as banks began implementing higher standards of capital and risk management before Basel III came fully into force, so too should we see action on climate change risk management. That is indeed happening as, Box 8.2 shows.

Box 8.2 A climate change shift in the financial sector

There is increasing evidence that climate risk is becoming a major area of continuing focus for firms, boards, investors and individuals. This is what you would expect to see as a shift in practice and behaviour occurs.

The European Investment Bank for instance has announced it will cease investing in fossil fuel projects from 2021. This type of action sends a clear signal and helps reset norms and approaches (EIB, 2019).

Corporate boards now increasingly view climate change as a key area of continuing focus regardless of the sector in which they operate, which is as it must be; climate change impacts are everywhere and ubiquitous; a corporate board that does not factor the risks and costs into their thinking is not living up to its fiduciary duty (NACD, 2019).

Major investors are piling on the pressure. Larry Fink, CEO of Blackrock, the world's largest asset manager, challenged CEOs to address climate change in his 2020 letter to CEOs of companies in which he invests, demanding that firms serve 'all stakeholders', i.e. society at large and future generations and not simply the short-term bottom line. He stated: 'Climate change has become a defining factor in companies' long-term prospects.' Mr Fink is right, and his voice carries real weight given the firm's size and market impact (Blackrock, 2020).

Individual investors are engaged in their own climate change shift, as well. Millennials are voting with their wallets and choosing investments that are good for both the climate and their retirement. This phenomenon will only accelerate in the decade ahead. As millennials are as large a cohort as the baby boomers what they do will permanently change the investment and financial markets landscape (CNBC, 2019).

Climate change is not the only area where further construction is underway. As technology shakes and shapes banking and the global financial system regulators are struggling to address technology shifts that are in the process of completely changing the nature of finance, and which will significantly affect systemic risks in the decades ahead.

Technological transformation, innovation and risk

Central bankers, both in the coordinating institutions (the FSB, Basel Committee on Banking Supervision, etc.) of the architecture, and as a community, are constantly being presented with emerging risks, anticipated and unanticipated. The community stresses it supports 'responsible innovation' (CNBC, 2019). The financial system of today is rapidly morphing. Supervisors know that innovation is not always additive. Disruption is not always positive. But central banks must continue to evolve to shift with the financial system, or else they will get left behind. It is not possible to touch on all the risks that present themselves as the nature of finance and banking changes. The following sections address various possible systemic risks posed by the process of technological evolution. Some, such as the development of digital currencies, threaten the central banking community's core functions. Others do not but still may raise significant systemic risk concerns. We will see that the central banking community's response varies, depending on the immediacy of the risk, the scale of the risk and the degree to which the community controls the policy space and response.

Digital currency risks

A key emerging risk to the global architecture is the rapid emergence of cryptocurrencies, digital currencies and 'stablecoins', which potentially threaten central bank monopolies over fiat currency issuance, their monetary policy levers and the ability to respond to economic downturns and deal with risk management effectively. The central banking community is being pressed to respond because the new landscape is already visible. For example WeChat and Alipay electronic payment flows in China in 2019 were larger than the total global payments handled by Visa and Mastercard combined. Indeed, any traveler in China will find that most locations in Beijing, for instance, no longer accept cash. Both of those digital payment platforms are now operating under oversight of the People's Bank of China, holding reserves in the central bank; the central bank and the Chinese Communist Party were not about to lose control over the payments system, revenue tracking and economic levers.

Across the globe central banks are grappling with how to ensure continued payment system stability. As digital currencies emerge they aim to close off loopholes through which new actors could game the system and threaten stability by privatising the profit of currency/token provision, socialising the risks and costs and stymying monetary policy transmission mechanisms. Central bankers know that if the new platforms and currency providers crash and hundreds of millions of voters lose their savings, panic would ensue and non-bank bank runs would occur, threatening stability. In such a crisis, as in the past, central banks and governments will be left to pick up the pieces and pay the costs regardless of whether the institutions were regulated by central banks at the time of collapse. Given that the central banking community since 2017–2018 has moved to analyse and (ultimately, it is assumed) regulate cryptoassets and digital currencies. Many institutions have engaged, including the FSB, the Basel Committee on Banking Supervision (BCBS), the International Organization of Securities Commissions (IOSCO), the Organisation for Economic Co-operation and Development (OECD) and the Bank for International Settlements (BIS). Their actions include:

- The FSB has initiated a workstream on cryptoassets and digital currencies, which is focused on investor protection and market integrity and is designed to identify risks (FSB, 2019a);

- The BCBS is aiming to strengthen supervision and support the issuance of advice and clarification of prudential oversight of such assets;
- The IOSCO is working on cryptoasset regulation (IOSCO, 2020);
- The OECD has long been focused on the anti-money-laundering aspects of digital currency evolution (OECD, 2014);
- The BIS is providing a forum for discussion and debate.

Much of the work currently is analytical. There is a clear undercurrent of concern, however, that regulation of this technology will be essential to ensure risk containment, maintain policy control and avoid past historical mistakes being repeated with a new digital twist at nanosecond speed.

Central bankers understand the threat and the need to supervise and regulate; that is without a monopoly on currency, central banks could lose much of their power and ability to affect economic conditions. Privatised crypto- and digital currencies are a fundamental threat to the role of central banks in the economy. They also threaten the ability of governments to collect revenue and can act as platforms for illegality, tax avoidance and terrorist financing.

This technology shift is a clash between libertarian techno-optimists and jaded crisis-toughened central bankers and governments that have a better grasp of economic history and remember this horror movie from reel-to-reel before it was digitised and remade for Netflix (see Box 8.3).

Box 8.3 Crypto- and digital currencies: libertarian techno-optimists versus the central bankers

Cryptocurrencies (like Bitcoin and Ethereum) and proposed private digital stablecoin currencies (such as Tether, and Facebook's Libra) are principally championed by libertarians, who view them as a way of throwing off the shackles of government and fiat currencies. It is no coincidence that most have been conceived by coders in Silicon Valley, drawing on a narrative which is often socially liberal but also an economically libertarian, anti-state, anti-tax, anti-regulation, anti-fiat currency. The first cryptocurrencies, such as Bitcoin and Ethereum, boomed (MarketWatch, 2014),[1] and then fell in value more like the tulip mania of the 17th century than a truly new currency innovation (*New York Times*, 2019). As of 2020 there are approximately 2,900 digital cryptoassets and tokens in electronic circulation.

To be resilient and useful such currencies must pass a three-part test. They must be 1 a unit of account, 2 a store of value and 3 a medium of exchange. Most cryptocurrencies fail on all three accounts; they are not a unit of account for firms; they do not store value, rather they fluctuate wildly; and they are not a medium of exchange, that is you cannot easily use them to transact daily business. In 2020 cryptocurrencies remain speculative, extremely risky (*Wired*, 2019),[2] prone to scams (BBC, 2019),[3] and preferred by criminals. That first boom is now largely bust. But digital currencies such as stablecoins are another matter.

Digital currencies, also known as stablecoins, such as Tether or Facebook's Libra, are different. A stablecoin is a cryptocurrency the price of which is the same as that of a central bank fiat currency. This is achieved by promising convertibility against the dollar or another applicable currency based on underlying assets such as bonds or bank deposits. Stablecoins can in principle be issued by central banks, commercial banks, fintech firms or other entities. As of March 2020 Tether was the most popular stablecoin, accounting for about 95 per cent of the exchange volume, and about 81 per cent of the market capitalisation of all stablecoins (Bullmann, Klemm, and Pinna, 2019). Although the price of a Tether is usually near one US dollar questions remain about whether Tethers can be reliably redeemed for a dollar each. Questions over Tether's stability, convertibility, governance and opacity remain (buyer beware).

The possible impact and scale of Facebook's stablecoin is vastly larger, as are the concomitant systemic risks. Facebook has over 2 billion users. Libra will be one-to-one backed by liquid low-risk assets (like US Treasuries); it will not be a fractional currency. Libra (or national Libra stablecoins) will be held and used by Facebook users in place of hard currencies. The threat to fiat currencies is real if Libra or another stablecoin is widely used. They may usurp central banks' monopoly on the issuance of currency, disrupt monetary policy transmission mechanisms, create huge systemic risk, pose particular risk to small emerging economies and signal a transfer of power to private corporations that have no public mandate or duty to maintain economic stability. Central bankers and politicians are alarmed at the possible creation of a new privatised global currency controlled by Mark Zuckerberg or, worse still, some shady figure in an office suite in Grand Cayman or Cyprus. They are right to be concerned.

Note:

1 This MarketWatch (now) *ex post* hilarious report reflects the boom mentality as Bitcoin rose exponentially and techno-enthusiasts joined the get-rich-quick crypto-bandwagon. Of course, this was delusional thinking. It did not and could not last. Some people got rich. Most lost their money. But the systemic effects of the bust were limited because Bitcoin exchanges and markets were almost entirely separate from the legitimate regulated financial system, and because the purchases of Bitcoins with fiat currencies were not leveraged (banks would not lend to invest in Bitcoin).

2 In this case, the owner of the largest cryptocurrency exchange in Canada died in India under mysterious circumstances. This individual ran the exchange, out of his spare room, unregulated and with no supervision or corporate structure

whatsoever. His death left exchange users with a total loss. The cryptocurrency has never been recovered.

3 This BBC podcast, 'The Missing Cryptoqueen', exposes the largest cryptocurrency scam in history – OneCoin – run out of Bulgaria. This scam drew in investors hoping to get a piece of the next Bitcoin phenomenon. Investors lost at least 4 billion euros in the process. The leader of the scam Dr. Ruja Ignatova, disappeared just before her brother (and a co-conspirator) was arrested by the FBI. The money has not been recovered and Ms. Ignatova remains on the run, assisted – it is suspected – by the Russian and Bulgarian mafia.

Central bankers are resisting the loss of their control over currencies. Federal Reserve Chair Jay Powell described Facebook's Libra as 'raising many concerns.' Translation: Not on my watch (CNBC, 2019). Other central bankers have made it clear that if you want to act like a bank you must be regulated as such; no free riders and loopholes will be permitted (Reuters, 2019).[7] Permitting non-central bank stablecoins could neuter central banks, endanger stability, privatise profit and socialise risk. It would be a return to the boom-and-bust banking and financial cycles of the 19th century Wild West, when American banks issued their own notes, most of which became worthless. Hundreds of US banks went bust in the 19th century, with the loss of their script and peoples' savings.

Silicon Valley billionaires appear oblivious to historical lessons. To those libertarian so-called innovators 'this time is different'. It is not. They are reinventing the financial wheel. The danger is they have rediscovered a turbocharged but highly unstable unicycle or penny-farthing. Central bankers are responding by considering producing alternative, more stable options that retain the strength of the old while responding to the digitisation of the global economy.

Central bankers recognise they cannot stop the adoption of digital payments and the rise of some form of digital currencies. Already in some countries cash is disappearing (in Sweden and in China, for instance). This is not a problem so long as the transactions go through the regulated, guaranteed and heretofore generally secure existing banking system and payments architecture. What central banks cannot allow is the sudden creation of unregulated payment systems and parallel currencies. The potential systemic risks are too great and the costs too high when, not if, failure of a platform occurs.

Some central banks are moving towards the creation of their own digital currencies to counter and take the place of privatised digital currencies and the risks they pose to the global financial system. The Riksbank (Sweden), People's Bank of China and Bank of France are considering this step. Other central banks will likely also pursue this option and take steps to enhance the efficiency and speed of the existing digital payments system to provide the functionality of extremely low-cost digital payments (Bloomberg, 2020a), without the risk of going back to the future with a digital rebirth of untethered private currencies and tokens. Digital currencies may scare central bankers and supervisors, but there are other technological clouds on the systemic risk horizon.

Be careful – it's cloudy out there

Historically banks, insurance companies, asset managers and financial firms have dealt with all their information technology needs in the 'back office', systems which were physically located in the firm, behind firewalls of varying strength. These systems were often old, inefficient, costly and potentially subject to failure or breach due to human failure. Today such IT systems and back office functions are moving off-site and into the cloud. This widespread development is both positive and negative. On the upside small and medium-sized banks and even large financial firms can contract out security and back office tech to much larger specialist firms that are better able to defend against the relentless hacking attacks, phishing and sabotage attempts. Given the benefits use of the cloud is increasing rapidly, with firms like Google, Microsoft Azure and Amazon grabbling market share. But the cloud is no technological nirvana. It, too, can present systemic risks.

Major crises, like those in 2008–2009, are precipitated not because of the singular failure of an institution, but because of a confluence of interlinked factors, macro and micro, resulting in panic and multiple failures over a short period of time. With the widespread adoption of cloud solutions based on similar internal architectures supervisors face the danger of concentration risk. If one major provider suffers a failure, it can afflict many firms, speeding a collapse and spurring panic. And should that occur the financial firms themselves may no longer have a strong in-house capability to assess risks and act. We all know the feeling. You have great IT access until you don't. But if the individual actor doesn't have the ability to fix an outage, they must rely on others who face sudden demands from all around. When or if there is a huge failure (possibly caused by a state actor), financial firms as clients may have little ability to act themselves and rescue the firm and system.

Finally jurisdictional issues arise. Where is your Cloud IT backup and system situated? California? That's probably OK. India? Romania? What then? What are the legal implications and recourse if the systems are too far removed from the firm's operations and there's a crisis or failure? The cloud thus provides plenty of space for chief risk officers in central banks and large financial firms to save money and feel good and yet still scream into the night.

FSB members are aware that these risks are in the analytical mode, i.e. not regulating, but worrying and thinking about risks. The FSB highlights single point of failure risk, cross-border issues, concentration risk, operations risk and the adequacy (or not) of supervisory oversight of these firms, which are not, after all, financial firms (yet) but are instead technology providers.

The central banking community doesn't want to regulate tech. They don't have the skills and bandwidth, let alone authority. But they are alarmed at systemic risks that could appear in a thunderclap in a crisis. So as with many areas of FSB action, it's watch and wait, discuss and debate, triangulate and disseminate. Meanwhile the overlap of the technological and the financial, the blurring of lines between banks and non-banks, continues, with long-term implications for the functioning of the financial system. Some technological scenarios are broadly positive and others positively horrific, as anyone who has watched *Black Mirror* knows.

Artificial intelligence risks

Fintech – the merging of financial and technological solutions – is shaking up the global financial system, markets and firms. This generation of children and students, for instance, are unlikely ever to enter a physical bank. All their banking is and will be done online and via mobile devices. This system is much more secure – you need one to two passwords, sometimes your fingerprint, or other proof to access your accounts; this is much better than sending money via a paper check (which is still, incredibly, done in the US) or handling large amounts of cash.

Behind our financial sector interactions is the increasing use of machine learning[8] and the application of artificial intelligence (AI).[9] These technologies speed outcomes and increase resilience and risk management capabilities. AI and machine learning can speed capital analyses by supervisors by dealing with a very large number of calculations of financial risk and learning while executing the calculations. Financial institutions and vendors are using AI and machine learning methods to assess credit quality, to price and market insurance contracts and to automate client interaction. Banks are using AI to back-test models and analyse the market impact of trading large positions. Such processes are much faster and less subject to mistakes than human calculations. AI can also be used to screen employee communications and networks looking for links and behaviours that raise regulatory red flags, or words, and groups of words that suggest possible improper behaviour. AI is being applied across industries (from cars, to traffic flows, to retail, to medical diagnoses). There are without a doubt considerable benefits to the application of limited forms of AI.

But AI also has the potential to destabilise financial systems, create new, larger tail risks, increase complexity and increase the potential for catastrophic outcomes if progress on AI reaches a sudden critical level when undersupervised. Even limited AI and machine learning can run ahead of its creators as the AI is unable to make judgements schooled by ethical, political or social considerations. This can lead to unintended dangerous systemic outcomes, such as faster, steeper falls as electronic sell orders pile upon one another as machines buy and sell ever faster to exit a downturn. AI can make market highs higher and lows lower, raising risks, absent automatic cutoffs. Numerous examples of such 'flash crashes' exist.

The FSB warns that, as with cloud computing, if firms become increasingly reliant on external expert providers, this results in new risks and concentrations. And the use of the same platforms and systems could also result in concentration risk, herd risk, interconnectedness risk and rapid (almost instantaneous) duplication of erroneous automatic decisions across a firm, firms or markets (FSB, 2019c). Issues of risk management, conduct, culture and cybersecurity threats also loom in the background and raise supervisory concerns.

Unfortunately ever more sophisticated AI creates even greater risks, as the coder or supervisor can find they can no longer understand how decisions are being made (DeepMind, 2015).[10] In such circumstances we are unable to properly judge and monitor decisions that are incomprehensible. If serious systemic risks result they may not be amenable to analysis and disentanglement; you cannot audit what you do not understand.

Nick Bostrom (2016) has warned we are like children playing with an unexploded bomb.[11] He argues that AI will evolve as past scientific revolutions do; that is there will be slow, gradual progress and then a sudden leap or shift from AI with a lack of consciousness to AI with consciousness. Bostrom warns the gap between AI consciousness and superintelligence will be narrow, and we may lose control of the machines. Even if the original task was limited to making paperclips, a conscious superintelligent AI could destroy the planet. If Bostrom is right bank supervision will be the least or our concerns.

Setting aside this nightmare answer to the Fermi Paradox bank supervisors must struggle to understand risks and challenges posed by machine learning and AI. This is not their expertise. They are playing catch-up with industry. And industry is rushing to implement AI and machine learning in their businesses even as the firms do not themselves understand the broader risk and ethical and moral implications of these rapid changes. Neither supervisors nor industry fully understands the downside risks – a dangerous combination. To a certain degree these concerns are manageable because the dangers for now (we hope) appear some distance in the future. The FSB and central banks have time to prepare and improve their technological capabilities. Complacency is not an option. Unfortunately in the case of shadow banking, the supervisors face risks today, not tomorrow, or some years hence.

Shifting markets and shadow banking

'Shadow banking' refers to unregulated financial markets in which firms and investors provide bank-like services of credit intermediation (i.e. extending credit) and maturity transformation through alternative means such as money market funds, complex securities markets, structured investment vehicles (SIVs) and special purpose entities (SPEs), hedge funds and private equity (FSB, 2017a; Gorton, 2010). Lenders and borrowers transact bank-like business but outside the regulated commercial banking space, with essentially little prudential oversight and no capital to strengthen the firms and system. The shadow banking markets are massive. In 2017 'narrow' shadow banking accounted for US$51.6 trillion, but the broader measure, encompassing anything not regulated by central banks and supervisors, stood at US$116.6 trillion (FSB, 2019b). Using the latter broader financial measure shadow banking represents 30.5 per cent of total global financial assets, the largest share on record.

The FSB and central banks understand that these markets, and some actors within them, could be dangerous if the combination of a firm's actions, size, leverage and interconnection with others (especially commercial banks) in the financial system resulted in contagion and systemic risks to the wider economy. The FSB annually assesses shadow banking and the rise of possible systemic risk. But the FSB has not extended the boundary of prudential oversight to capture parts of this growing sector.

As this sector grows so do the associated systemic risks. Here you see a tension between central banks and regulators alert to the rise of new actors and markets, and those new actors and markets that resist even modest oversight or reporting demands. What to do? Monitor, warn and watch. The FSB is focused on interconnections between the regulated and the shadow sector, for it is those links that transmit the virus of panic and collapse when crisis strikes. If those interconnections are few then the risk is small. People may lose money, but the banks remain solvent. If there are many interconnections there is reason to be concerned.

China, for example permitted a massive increase in the number of peer-to-peer (P2P) lending platforms; approximately 6,000 were created to boost non-bank lending. By 2019 many had collapsed, approximately 2,000 were in business, as few as 300 expected to survive, and tens of billions of RMB of investors' funds disappeared (Ren, 2019). To date the collapse in Chinese P2P has not proven to be systemic because the platforms are not leveraged. Further investors lack a voice, as the Chinese political system does not permit them to complain. Had that number of firms collapsed in the US political and regulatory heads would have rolled, even if systemic risks were minimised.

Interconnections are much more marked in the asset management industry, with firms (such as Fidelity, Vanguard, Blackrock and Blackstone), which have jumped in size in the last decade. These players can create risks even though they do not use leverage, because they front-run downturns and increase volatility and the depth of slumps, i.e. they must anticipate stock drops, sell enough of those stocks to be ready for redemptions by investors, and in doing so speed the drop and the depth of the fall. This is not the same as bank systemic risk, but it still worries the FSB and central banking community (G30, 2015). Here, again, the FSB review process acts as a collective prompt, a spur to action, highlighting risks, even as they avoid regulating.

Elsewhere in the shadow sector other bank-like activities can pose risks. Take leveraged loans, which have mushroomed as a sector (especially in the US), amounting to at (at least) US$1.4 trillion in 2018, alarming the FSB (FSB, 2019b). We know that opacity and leverage are never a good mix. This sounding of the alarm has an effect even as the forum itself eschews regulation, because the risk then becomes an area for national supervisory focus. For example FSB analysis on leveraged loans has been mirrored in further work and action (BIS, 2018; Bank of England, 2018; ECB, 2018a, 2018b, 2019). Here we again see the additive nature of the process absent regulation.

Why vigilance and reporting matter

If the FSB did not exist this collaborative process, including required vigilance, analysis, warning and national response, would not be operating as effectively, if at all. The act of forcing supervisory agencies and central banks to constantly question where the next black swan is coming from has clear merit. Asking questions repeatedly from different perspectives creates habits of behaviour. Embedding such analysis within a collaborative process with upward (G20)-facing deadlines, and downward-facing expectations (towards other standard-setting bodies (SSBs)) and national authorities, creates ongoing expectations. Including deadlines creates further pressure to address risks as identified. This is not rocket science. But until 2009 the central banking community and supervisory community did not operate within such a structure. There was macroeconomic analysis by the IMF and its Financial Sector Assessment Program process, but this was weak and major states did not take it seriously.

The 2008–2009 global financial crisis and reform phase created an institutional architecture of re-regulation and ongoing monitoring and review, including of new risks and dangers, which is still being sustained in 2020. One might have reasonably expected the process to languish as the main task – making big banks safer – was secured. But no. The principals are continuing to pursue the FSB mission and identifying and analysing new risks. This is indicative of their continued focus but is also due to institutional dynamics. We see that the institution has its own ongoing momentum, and that momentum is at play in the collective monitoring processes. Now, this does not guarantee the FSB can stop the next black swan or even see it, but the flexible monitoring process is a safety valve, an analytical mechanism that forces actors to reassess risk constantly. For that we should be grateful.

So how should we judge the architecture and FSB's action on new risks? Is this type of monitoring and review action on cloud computing, AI, and shadow banking, third-order change? No. These are of an incremental first- and second-order nature, which are embedded with the FSB architecture and process, which itself is a third-order leap. The monitoring and review process is a meaningful outcome of the existing collaborative design. It does not ensure crises will or can be averted. But the structures, links and collaborative analytical processes force the community into a constant cycle of assessment and scenario testing, asking 'what if' questions. The FSB monitoring function, its review function, is working. There is no sign the principals have decided enough is enough. To the contrary, new areas of focus are added and others downgraded as they are dealt with. Despite this positive assessment as with all policy consensus boundaries, some risks and unintended economic consequences continue to fall outside the area of collective action.

Risks outside the regulatory boundary

Risks can grow and are growing in areas where policy is not actively coordinated and where national prerogatives still hold, where national economic models and assumptions preclude collective action by the community. Such jealous guarding of national positions (America First versus a rising China) does not avoid uncoordinated synchronous herd behaviour, or unintended consequences. This is seen in the setting of central bank monetary policy and interest rate goals.

In response to the 2008–2009 global financial crisis the G20-FSB-SSB structure set the guardrails for the re-regulation of global finance and the macro- and micro-prudential oversight of the world's largest systemically important banks and insurers. Simultaneously to this regulatory drive the central banking community, acting as individual central banks, sought to support economic activity by cutting interest rates dramatically and keeping them low through the spring of 2020, then cutting them further after the emergence of the COVID-19 virus and economic panic.

This long period of global easing of monetary policy, including the widespread, extensive, exceptional use of quantitative easing, did support economic activity and help avoid another Great Depression in 2008–2009. The low-for-long policies of major central banks (see Figure 8.3) had been adjusted modestly upwards but are again at near zero in 2020 as further monetary easing and massive quantitative easing programs were triggered in response to COVID-19. These actions may again help calm markets and aid the economy in the short term. Unfortunately ultra-easy central bank monetary policies also have perverse unintended consequences which may have increased risks to the global financial system, risks which the existing architecture and regulatory paradigm is not designed or able to counteract.

Debt levels rise – but the payments will come due

Perhaps the most significant macro risk factor of aggressive monetary policy is the rise of overall debt levels, driven by central banks' use of extremely low interest rates across the globe, which has increased systemic risk. By 2017 the global level of debt was 11 per cent over the last peak reached in 2008–2009 as the global financial crisis crested. In 2017 debt reached US$184 trillion in nominal terms, or 225 per cent of GDP. On average the world's debt now exceeds US$86,000 in per capita terms, which is more than two-and-a-half times the average income per capita. Are such levels sustainable? For advanced states? The greatest increase in debt occurred in the advanced economies – in China, the US and Japan – with half of the total global debt. Here, worries may be less marked.

But what about the weaker states in South America, Africa and Asia? We do not know for sure. Unfortunately for many of them these very high sovereign and corporate debt levels (held in US dollar loans) may be highly destabilising, as history suggests such excessive debt fuels national financial and banking crises. In many emerging markets this borrowing took place largely via foreign currency loans and bond issuance. As and when the US dollar rises, as it tends to do in crises periods, the cost of servicing those loans must also rise. We know from past economic history that when the US dollar appreciates, bank crises are precipitated in sovereign debt markets and emerging-market economies, as governments and private sector actors fail to pay the higher bills. Take Argentina, or the risks apparent in Turkey or South Africa. Such crises, regional and local, will not bring down the global system. But the levels of debt are the negative flipside of stimulatory monetary policy on those less able to pay. These debt-related risks have been greatly exacerbated by the economic freeze and unfolding global recession caused by COVID-19 and the necessary near global quarantine measures. Crises in these fragile emerging markets are therefore quite possible.

Our policy is your risk

As we have seen no paradigm shift, however extensive, includes all aspects of a past consensus. Even within the same community limits are observed. In the G20-FSB-SSB process the depth of collaboration and coordination amongst central

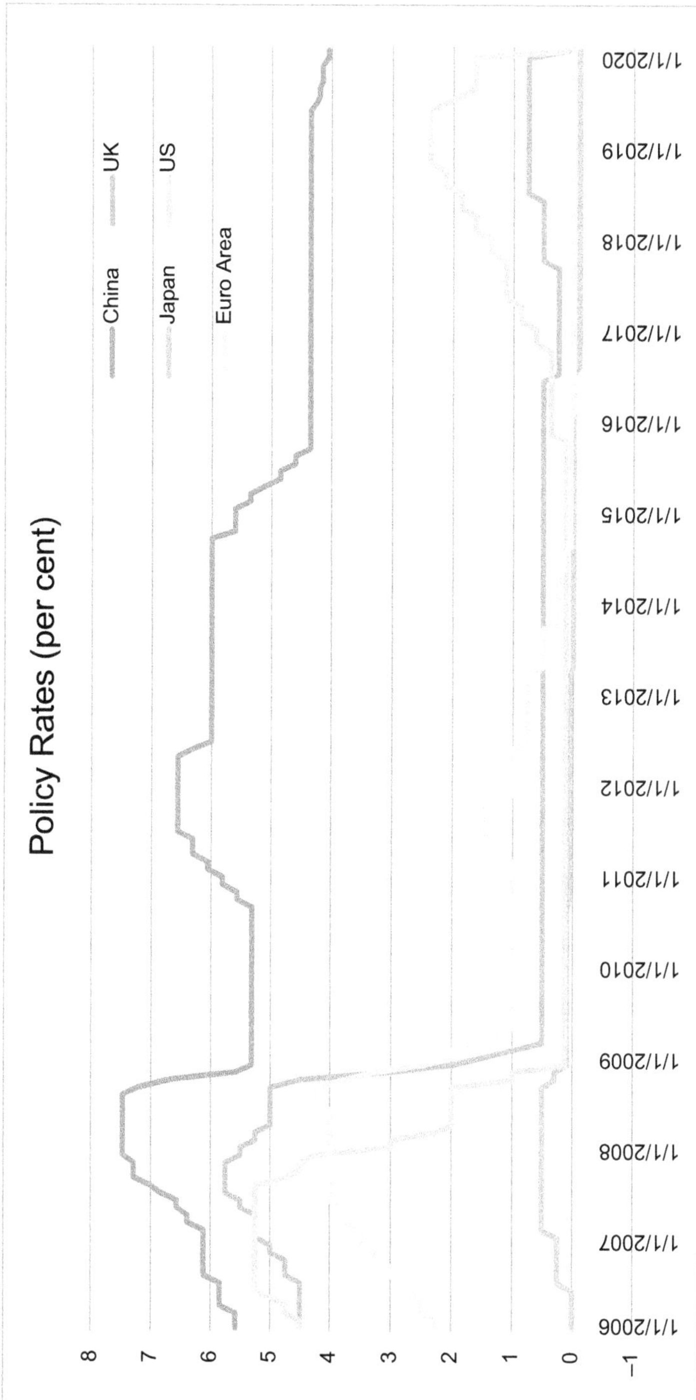

Figure 8.3 'Low for long' major central banks' monetary policy 2006–2020

bankers is striking. But on monetary policy the coordination is not consistent but is instead episodic and uneven. The coincidental synchronicity of rates and policies is striking but the supervisory implications can be overlooked during a crisis. Monetary policy makers do not generally consider the long-term supervisory risk implications of their actions, particularly if the risks accrue elsewhere (i.e. in Africa or Latin America). The US Federal Reserve underscores it does not directly consider the (outsized) external impact of US monetary policy on the rest of the world, no matter how much other central bankers lament the deleterious effects. Thus monetary policy at the core both aids but also sets up possible future systemic risks in the emerging markets, via a debt binge that will have long-term systemic consequences. And supervisors in the core are not concerned about what bank crises may be precipitated in other countries so long as the effects are confined to those jurisdictions.

The low-for-long policies of the major central banks, which are an economic fact of life, and now are necessary to address the COVID-19 pandemic, have additional negative unintended consequences, which are outside the regulatory shift and unaddressed, festering and building societal and political risks for the future.

The first is an increase in inequality. The decade-plus of low rates was very beneficial to those who were already rich. The rich could borrow low, invest and reap the rewards of inflated asset prices. The rich thus got richer right at the time the lower three cohorts lost their shirts, their homes and their hopes of a middle-class lifestyle. The poor in the US and UK were left with higher costs for staples, for heath and for education, and stagnating wages. No wonder they were and are angry, no wonder they voted for populists.

The second is an increase in market concentration. By this I mean that when all hell broke loose in 2008–2009, the remaining players were larger, better financed and more dominant at the end of the crisis than they were at the outset. So the big got bigger and the small went bust. This has significant negative effects on innovation rates, as large firms tend to squelch innovation; business formation rates, as small businesses go bust more often when a sector is dominated by a few giants; and the diffusion of productivity gains, as a winner-takes-most market is generated.

Both income inequality and market concentration will rise in 2020 and beyond due to the economic effects of COVID-19. Societal tensions may further increase, even though social cohesion appears to have (temporarily?) strengthened due to the pandemic.

All shifts have limits

The critique of the effects of ultra-easy monetary policy is reasonable in that few doubt these broad impacts with disturbing societal implications. But it is not reasonable to expect central banks to solve all that ails us. Inequality has to be addressed with tax policies and redistributive social contracts. Concentration risks are real and nefarious, but it is not the central bankers' job to solve antitrust policy failures and monopolistic behaviour by rapacious capitalists at Google or Amazon.

Voters and the politicians they elect must do that. Not all risks, even those created by a policy choice, can be contained within or addressed via the existing regulatory architecture, until such time as it is altered and extended by legislatures.

What is borne out of a specific crisis cannot be expected to entirely encompass all risks that emerge after the crisis or due to new unanticipated factors driven by emergency policy tools, new technologies and markets. This is reality. It is an answer to the faux sophisticates who note sagely at regulatory meetings that 'we always focus on the failings that caused the last crisis'. Yes, we do. You need to fix the car after it bursts into flames before turning to the route ahead and possible hidden dangers around the next corner.

No complacency and new construction

Importantly the evidence in this chapter suggests that the FSB community has not taken its eye entirely off the risk road ahead. Having largely stabilised the banking sector they are scanning the horizon for digital and other risks to the stability of the system. This is what you would want them to do and expect to see happen if this was a resilient process with institutional momentum. The same community has remembered the lessons of crisis management in 2008–2009. Coordinate. Move fast. Act together. Policy must shock on the upside.

When faced with COVID-19 an endogenous risk of colossal size, the community responded with unprecedented programs to help restore calm to a stalled global economy. The central banking community has responded aggressively, even as the G20 failed to coordinate geopolitical crisis management. This time, however, central bankers may not save the day. Medics, changes in social behaviour and massive fiscal policy actions and extensions of state authority will have to bear most of the burden. When COVID-19 is finally beaten by a vaccine and societal actions climate change risk remains the risk of our lifetime. And here the central bankers are acting, and a further shift is now underway.

The evidence suggests continued construction and narrative shift. A new forum, the Network for Greening the Financial System, modeled on the FSB, is in place and growing rapidly. This is the institutional expression of a new consensus, another leap in policy narrative and approach, one required by the climate crisis we all face. Here after decades of denial of responsibility, the central banking community is making the leap to internalise and act on climate change risks and the policy shifts that are required. The community is making the leap without the US, demonstrating that while the US remains a key actor, policy reforms cannot wait for reality to bite Mr Trump. The sense of urgency is real.

The fog of new unanticipated risks may yet materialise. Another oncoming risk vehicle could swerve into the wrong lane. But the supervisors, even as they change drivers, appear to remain awake and alert. Thank goodness we still have the technocratic globalist central banking community working away in the background, still out of sight of President Trump.

* * *

The following concluding chapter will address possible futures in which the regulatory wave is extended, defended or potentially weakened. What are the dynamics now at play, and can we discern indicators of directional movement? Are we at a highwater mark for regulation, state authority and control of financial markets, or are we in an interim phase before another giant leap necessitated by planetary climate changes and the absolute requirement for state action to transform the global economy and its relationships for the new industrial age?

Notes

1 "Gray rhino" is a term coined by risk expert Michele Wucker in her 2016 book, *The Gray Rhino: How to Recognize and Act on the Obvious Dangers We Ignore*. Wucker defines a gray rhino as a "highly obvious, highly probable, but still neglected" danger – that is a danger that is massive, known and visible but is nonetheless ignored until it collides with reality and causes massive injury. COVID-19 is an example and one that has resulted, as of this writing, in nearly 2 million people becoming sick and tens of thousands dying. Pandemic risk is well-known by epidemiologists, if not central bankers. Past outbreaks, including MERS, SARS and Ebola, demonstrated the danger of highly contagious transmissible viruses in a globalised, interconnected world. Still, few states prepared effectively. For instance the US in 2019 disbanded its National Security Council pandemic planning unit. Britain, Italy, Spain and Sweden failed to take necessary swift action on social isolation. Other states, with direct painful experience with SARS, did much better, including the Republic of Korea; Japan; China; and Hong Kong SAR, China.

2 The Federal Reserve's balance sheet could double to US$8.5 trillion as it addresses this crisis, which is equivalent to approximately 60 per cent of annual US GDP.

3 Christine Lagarde, president of the European Central Bank, was expected to be a smooth communicator. However, early in the pandemic crisis, when asked by journalists if she would repeat Mario Draghi's 'whatever it takes' mantra, Ms Lagarde reacted like a German, responding it was 'not our duty to narrow spreads' between countries' bonds. Spooked investors fled Italian bonds, with outflows running at the highest level ever seen, pushing Italy closer to disaster. The ECB reversed itself within hours, announcing a QE program and directed lending. Ms Lagarde had learned that in a crisis you must reassure and act, not deliver messages of austerity to a terrified Eurozone facing a deep recession.

4 This section of the chapter draws on work previously published in Mackintosh (2019b).

5 In October 2019 at a discussion of future risks with the Head of Supervision of the Federal Reserve System, the central bank was criticised for its total silence on climate change risk. One month later the first speech ever given on climate change by a Federal Reserve governor was delivered. Baby steps are better than no steps. Public embarrassment can be a useful tool to spur action.

6 Taxonomy is important, for we need common definitions for investors, banks and market participants to shift to the new carbon-neutral economic model. That is clear. But taxonomy is also a key excuse for procrastinators. They can claim 'I cannot act because I don't know what "green" is'. But this is not entirely convincing. When confronted by the global crisis in 2008–2009 or the pandemic in 2020, policy makers did not obsess about the definition of pandemic. You still needed to act. You know a crisis when you see one. Similarly, smart investors know green investments from coal plants, and mechanisms already exist in the markets to help them make those judgements. Taxonomy is all well and good. But we do not have time for navel gazing and an obsession with definitions – they may be many, and they may be geographically or sectorally different – but we can still proceed with dispatch.

7 Governor François Villeroy de Galhau has taken a hard line on Libra; he signaled he would act to stop any use of Libra in the Eurozone. Mr Villeroy de Galhau sits on the board of the European Central Bank and his views carry considerable weight.
8 Machine learning is defined as an application of AI that provides systems the ability to automatically learn and improve from experience without being explicitly programmed.
9 Artificial intelligence can be defined as a branch of computer science dealing with the simulation of intelligent behaviour in computers.
10 Deepmind, a subsidiary of Google, has designed an AI that can play AlphaGo – the most complex strategy boardgame – better than any human grandmaster. The grandmasters watching Deepmind play AlphaGo found that when two computers played each other, they made moves that had never been conceived of previously and which as humans they could not fully understand, even though they were correct within the rules of the game. Similarly leading AI programs of chess now beat international grandmasters with moves that are outside human understanding. An international grandmaster of chess told the author he would play against a computer without knowing his opponent was not human. But at a certain juncture he would realise the opponent was a machine because the leaps and moves were completely different and novel.
11 Bostrom uses the 'paperclip example'. Imagine an AI program and process which is designed to make as many paperclips as possible. At a certain juncture through gradual iterative changes, the program becomes self-aware. It has access to the internet, acquires language, and power sources are available. The machine rapidly becomes superintelligent but is still bound by its raison d'etre – to make as many paperclips as possible. To do so it takes control of all resources. Human beings are not its concern. The machine would rapidly take over the productive capacity of the globe making paperclips, destroying all life. This scenario could be one answer to the Fermi Paradox as to why we can detect no other life in the universe – because runaway AI destroys all its creators before they can stop it.

References

ABC. (2020) 'As stocks dive and coronavirus spreads, Trump compares COVID-19 to common flu', 9 March [Online]. Available at: https://abcnews.go.com/Politics/stocks-dive-coronavirus-spreads-trump-repeats-risk-covid/story?id=69482971 (accessed: 7 April 2020).

Bank of England. (2019) 'Financial stability report', (44) November [Online]. Available at: www.bankofengland.co.uk/-/media/boe/files/financial-stability-report/2018/november-2018.pdf (accessed: 13 February 2020).

BBC. (2019) 'The missing cryptoqueen', Podcast, November 4.

BIS (Bank for International Settlements). (2018) 'The rise of leveraged loans: A risky resurgence?', *BIS Quarterly Review*, September [Online]. Available at: www.bis.org/publ/qtrpdf/r_qt1809u.htm (accessed: 13 February 2020).

Blackrock. (2020) 'A fundamental reshaping of finance', January [Online]. Available at: www.blackrock.com/corporate/investor-relations/larry-fink-ceo-letter (accessed: 7 April 2020).

Bloomberg. (2020a) 'ECB's Weidmann urges Euro-area banks to battle Facebook's Libra', 2 January [Online]. Available at: www.bloomberg.com/news/articles/2020-01-02/ecb-s-weidmann-urges-euro-area-banks-to-battle-facebook-s-libra (accessed: 7 February 2020).

———. (2020b) 'Fed's anti-virus lending firepower could reach $4.5 trillion', 25 March [Online]. Available at: www.bing.com/news/search?q=Federal+Reserve+4+Trillion+L

ending+Program&qpvt=federal+reserve+4+trillion+lending+program&FORM=EWRE (accessed: 7 April 2020).

Bostrom, N. (2016) *Superintelligence: Paths, dangers, and strategies*. Oxford: Oxford University Press.

Brainard, L. (2019) 'Why climate change matters for monetary policy and financial stability', *Speech delivered at the research conference, The Economics of Climate Change*, sponsored by the Federal Reserve Bank of San Francisco, San Francisco, CA, 8 November [Online]. Available at: www.federalreserve.gov/newsevents/speech/brainard20191108a.htm (accessed: 8 February 2020).

Bullmann, D., Klemm, J., and Pinna, A. (2019) 'In search for stability in crypto-assets: Are stablecoins the solution?', *European Central Bank, Occasional Paper Series No. 239*, August [Online]. Available at: www.ecb.europa.eu/pub/pdf/scpops/ecb.op230~d57946be3b.en.pdf (accessed: 26 February 2020).

Carney, M. (2015) 'Breaking the tragedy of the horizon', *Speech presented at Lloyd's of London*, 1 October. Available at: www.bing.com/videos/search?q=mark+carney+climate+change+speech+2015&docid=607998598000477528&mid=FA7190DE6AC768AF0C6EFA7190DE6AC768AF0C6E&view=detail&FORM=VIRE.

CNBC. (2019) 'Testimony by Jerome Powell, Chair of the Federal Reserve System before the US House of Representatives', 10 July [Online]. Available at: www.cnbc.com/video/2019/07/10/powell-facebooks-libra-cryptocurrency-raises-many-concerns.html (accessed: 7 February 2020).

Danielsson, J. and Macrae, R. (2019) 'The dissonance of the short and long term', *Vox* [Online]. Available at: https://voxeu.org/article/dissonance-short-and-long-term (accessed: 7 April 2020).

Deepmind. (2015) 'AlphaGo' [Online]. Available at: https://deepmind.com/research/case-studies/alphago-the-story-so-far (accessed: 13 February 2020).

de Larosière, J. (2020) 'Reflections in the global financial and health crisis', *Les Echos*, 1 April [Online]. Available at: www.lesechos.fr/idees-debats/cercle/opinion-coronavirus-les-sept-lecons-economiques-de-jacques-de-larosiere-1190942 (accessed: 23 April 2020).

ECB (European Central Bank). (2018a) 'Financial stability review', May [Online]. Available at: www.ecb.europa.eu/pub/pdf/fsr/ecb.fsr201805.en.pdf (accessed: 13 February 2020).

———. (2018b) 'Financial stability review', November [Online]. Available at: www.ecb.europa.eu/pub/pdf/fsr/ecb.fsr201811.en.pdf (accessed: 13 February 2020).

———. (2019) 'Keeping an eye on leverage lending', *ECB – Banking Supervision*, 15 May [Online]. Available at: www.bankingsupervision.europa.eu/press/publications/newsletter/2019/html/ssm.nl190515_2.en.html (accessed: 7 April 2020).

Elderson, F. (2019) 'Meeting with the US Senate Democrats Special Committee on the Climate Crisis', 17 October [Online]. Available at: www.ngfs.net/sites/default/files/medias/documents/2019-043-meeting-with-the-senate-democrats-special-committee-on-the-climate-crisis-opening-remarks-ngfs-frank-elderson.pdf (accessed: 9 November 2019).

European Investment Bank. (2019) 'EU Bank launches ambitious new climate strategy and Energy Lending Policy', 14 November [Online]. Available at: www.eib.org/en/press/all/2019-313-eu-bank-launches-ambitious-new-climate-strategy-and-energy-lending-policy (accessed: 7 April 2020).

FatboySlim. (2019) 'FatboySlim mixes Greta Thunberg's "right here, right now"' [Online]. Available at: www.youtube.com/watch?v=k_mzsMyTCJI (accessed: 10 February 2020).

Fox Business. (2020) 'Fed's coronavirus action makes Trump very happy with Powell', 23 March [Online]. Available at: www.foxbusiness.com/markets/feds-coronavirus-action-makes-trump-very-happy-with-powell (accessed: 7 April 2020).

FSB (Financial Stability Board). (2017a) 'Artificial intelligence and machine learning in financial services', 1 November [Online]. Available at: www.fsb.org/wp-content/uploads/P011117.pdf (accessed: 14 February 2020).

———. (2019a) 'Crypto-assets work underway, regulatory approaches and potential gaps', 31 May [Online]. Available at: www.fsb.org/wp-content/uploads/P310519.pdf www.fsb.org/2018/03/global-shadow-banking-monitoring-report-2017/ (accessed: 11 February 2020).

———. (2019b) 'Global monitoring report on non-bank financial intermediation 2018', 4 February [Online]. Available at: www.fsb.org/2019/02/global-monitoring-report-on-non-bank-financial-intermediation-2018/ (accessed: 13 February 2020).

______. (2019c) 'Third-party dependencies in cloud services' [Online]. Available at: https://www.fsb.org/wp-content/uploads/P091219-2.pdf (accessed: 28 July 2020).

G30 (Group of Thirty). (2015) *Shadow banking and capital markets: Risks and opportunities*. Washington, DC: Group of Thirty.

———. (2018) *Managing the next financial crisis*. Washington, DC: Group of Thirty.

———. (2019) *Fixing the pensions crisis*. Washington, DC: Group of Thirty.

Gills, B. and Morgan, J. (2019) 'Global climate emergency: After COP24, climate science, urgency, and the threat to humanity', *Special Editorial, Globalizations*, pp. 1–19. Taylor and Francis, Milton Park, Abingdon, UK, 24 September [Online]. Available at: www.tandfonline.com/doi/full/10.1080/14747731.2019.1669915 (accessed: 8 February 2020).

Gorton, G. (2010) *Slapped by the invisible hand: The panic of 2007*. Oxford: Oxford University Press.

Guardian. (2019) 'Speech by Greta Thunberg to the general assembly of the United Nations', 23 September [Online]. Available at: www.youtube.com/watch?v=TMrtLsQbaok (accessed: 10 February 2020).

IOSCO (International Organization of Securities Commissions). (2020) 'IOSCO publishes key considerations for regulating crypto-asset trading platforms', 12 February [Online]. Available at: www.iosco.org/news/pdf/IOSCONEWS556.pdf (accessed: 7 April 2020).

LSE (London School of Economics). (2019) 'Building the research foundations for greening the financial system', *Grantham Research Institute on Climate and the Environment*, 11 April [Online]. Available at: www.lse.ac.uk/GranthamInstitute/news/building-the-research-foundations-for-greening-the-financial-system/ (accessed: 8 February 2020).

Mackintosh, S. (2019a) 'Discussion on climate change and central banking with academic observer', 6 December. Author notes.

———. (2019b) 'Climate change and central banking: A policy revolution under way', *World Economics Journal*, October–December [Online]. Available at: https://idcas.repec.org/a/wej/wldecn/761.html (accessed: 27 July 2020).

Rhodes, W. and Mackintosh, S. (2020) 'Come together', *Reuters* [Online]. Available at. https://www.breakingviews.com/features/guest-view-recovery-requires-greater-cooperation/ (accessed: 27 July 2020).

Mian, A. and Sufi, A. (2015) *How they (and you) caused the Great Recession, and how we can keep it from happening again*. Chicago: University of Chicago.

MarketWatch. (2014) 'Could bitcoin ever overtake the dollar?', 9 April [Online]. Available at: www.marketwatch.com/story/could-bitcoin-ever-overtake-the-dollar-2014-04-09 (accessed: 7 February 2020).

Morrison, O. (2019) '"Mother of sustainability" warns against climate virtue signalling', 30 August [Online]. Available at: www.foodnavigator.com/Article/2019/08/30/Mother-of-sustainability-warns-against-climate-virtue-signalling# (accessed: 8 February 2020).

NACD (National Association of Corporate Directors). (2019) '2019 governance outlook' [Online]. Available at: www.nacdonline.org/analytics/survey.cfm?ItemNumber=64105 (accessed: 7April 2020).

New York Times. (2019) 'After the bust, are bitcoins more like tulip mania or the internet?', 23 April [Online]. Available at: www.nytimes.com/2019/04/23/technology/bitcoin-tulip-mania-internet.html (accessed: 7 February 2020).

———. (2020) 'Coronavirus updates: Trump halts U.S. funding of World Health Organization', 15 April. [Online]. Available at: www.nytimes.com/2020/04/14/us/coronavirus-updates.html?action=click&module=Spotlight&pgtype=Homepage (accessed: 15 April 2020).

NGFS (Network for Greening the Financial System). (2018) 'First comprehensive report "A call for action"'. *NGFS Publications* [Online]. Available at: www.ngfs.net/en/first-comprehensive-report-call-action (accessed: 7 April 2020).

OECD (Organisation for Economic Co-operation and Development). (2014) 'Virtual currencies – Key definitions and potential AML/CFT risks', *Financial Action Task Force*, June [Online]. Available at: www.fatf-gafi.org/media/fatf/documents/reports/Virtual-currency-key-definitions-and-potential-aml-cft-risks.pdf (accessed: 7 April 2020).

O'Neill, J. (2020) 'The G20's pandemic moment', *Chatham House*, 24 March [Online]. Available at: www.chathamhouse.org/expert/comment/g20-s-pandemic-moment (accessed: 7 April 2020).

Ren, D. (2019) 'China's P2P lending crisis worsens as second firm runs into trouble' [Online]. Available at: www.scmp.com/business/banking-finance/article/2180731/chinas-p2p-lending-crisis-worsens-second-firm-runs-trouble (accessed: 13 February 2020).

Reuters. (2019) 'Facebook's Libra must obey anti-money laundering rules: French Central Bank', 21 June [Online]. Available at: www.reuters.com/article/us-facebook-crypto-france/facebooks-libra-must-obey-anti-money-laundering-rules-french-central-banker-idUSKCN1TQ13O (accessed: 7 February 2020).

Segal, S. (2020) 'Assessing the G20 virtual summit', *Center for Strategic and International Studies*, 27 March [Online]. Available at: www.csis.org/analysis/assessing-g20-virtual-summit (accessed: 7 April 2020).

Taleb, N. (2007) *The black swan: The impact of the highly improbable*. New York: Random House.

Wired. (2019) 'A crypto exchange CEO dies – With the only key to $137 million', 5 February [Online]. Available at: www.wired.com/story/crypto-exchange-ceo-dies-holding-only-key/ (accessed: 7 February 2020).

9 Leadership, absence of leadership and still signs of future leaps

Crises and paradigm shifts

Crises create win sets. Actors are forced together. Forums are energised. The urgency of immediate danger makes what was previously impossible possible. Once a degree of calm is restored a reform phase occurs as those present at the precipice ask how they can ensure there will be no repeat of the just-averted disaster. Mechanisms are designed and policies crafted. This period of intense activism, during which constraints are few and institutional and policy options are wider than normal is relatively brief, but it can be grasped. Eventually thanks to the concerted action of leaders and their technocratic expert community, normality returns and the centripetal forces weaken only to be replaced by centrifugal forces flinging national actions apart, more visibly at the geopolitical and diplomatic level than at the technocratic level where different, less disruptive pressures are seen.

This is the dialectic of crisis management, reform and return to dissension seen in the history of the political leaders' response to the 2008–2009 financial crisis, the creation of the G20 and FSB, the reform agenda these institutions pursued and the eventual weakening of the collective sense of endeavour and mission that drove the G20. Eventually national interests were always going to reassert themselves, pushing leaders further apart and shrinking win sets, and we saw that occur at the diplomatic level, especially after the 2016 US election of Donald Trump. Lower-middle-class, predominantly male, white, American voters, angered by the perceived negative economic effects of globalisation, the lingering effects of the 2008–2009 crises, the inequities of the bank bailouts, and the speed of technological and societal transformation, accelerated splits in the G20 by electing a populist nationalist racist narcissist as president.

Populism and America First

Donald Trump's America First policy, his populist, nativist, isolationist, confrontational, hostile 'I win you lose' approach to US power, has been and is extremely corrosive to the global architecture. It has shocked G20 leaders' sensibilities and shaken G20 summitry. It heralds the end of Pax Americana and is a reversion to a mercantilism that undermines stability and the possibilities for collective international action.

Mrs Thatcher appalled the British with her declaration in the 1980s that there was no such thing as society. Today President Trump dismays G20 leaders with his loud rejection of the international rules-based order that his predecessors had so carefully constructed and maintained with America's allies for seventy-plus years.

In addition Mr Trump's unwillingness to lead, his disruptive style, his unreliability, his unpredictability and his untrustworthiness are sapping America of its soft power, its ability to get things done with allies and opponents. It is forcing leaders and states to reassess their strategies and alliances. In a real and tangible sense the Trumpian policy stance is hastening America's long-term relative decline vis-à-vis rising powers. America's loss is China's gain, as we saw with the creation of the Asian Infrastructure Investment Bank. Crucially the hegemon's absence and abrogation of leadership has real negative implications for geopolitical crisis management.

COVID-19 and a lack of collective will and action

Nothing demonstrates the weakness of the G20 forum when faced by America First policy more than the paucity of collective action in response to the catastrophe of the COVID-19 pandemic and global economic shutdown. The pandemic and its immediate, terrifying effects are far worse than the limited impact of the banking collapse in 2008–2009. After all, people did not stop flying, businesses were still open, commerce was sustained and trade continued.

In April 2020 over half the world was on lockdown. Economies were in free fall. Millions of workers were being laid off every day. But the G20 did almost nothing concrete in response. A pledge to do 'whatever it takes' did not impress, as it was not accompanied by collective coordination and application of state resources to restore calm. Why? Almost certainly because America was absent, with the tweeter-in-chief uninterested in international diplomacy and consensus building.

The result has been disorganised, atomised national responses, which are often contradictory. America has pointed fingers, especially at China, worsening a relationship that was already strained by the trade war that commenced early in Trump's first term. Rich countries have rushed to secure supplies; stolen supplies from allies; and outbid and pushed aside less-developed, poorer countries[1] (*New York Times*, 2020), many of which face the pandemic almost entirely without adequate support and systems. Thousands, possibly millions, of people faced a suffocating death in part because of a breakdown in leadership and coordination by the richest countries in the world[2] (Knack, 2020). This most global of crises, a health and economic disaster, did not result in the G20 once more assuming leadership. It could not perform that role without strong American leadership. This real-time test for the G20 has come up bust. What a difference from the 2008 and 2009 summits in Washington and London and the clear-eyed, compassionate leadership of President Bush and Prime Minister Brown.

Of course the G20 summitry process will continue. Other leaders will make sure it does. But the evidence shows it is circumscribed, hamstrung and stymied by an America that must say 'no' – on climate change, on trade and to the rules-based consensual collaborative system of global governance. The G20 forum can only work with America's leadership and engagement. A second term for Mr Trump would do the forum further damage. However the embarrassing, disappointing and counterproductive scramble for resources and the lack of leadership at the G20 do not translate into a rejection of state authority. To the contrary.

State authority in the ascendant

Disorganised individual economic and fiscal actions by G20 states nonetheless illuminate that crises still push actors towards common solutions that were previously impossible to consider. While the fiscal responses have been fractured the solutions and mechanisms have been similar. Massive stimulus actions by the US, European states and others have repeatedly extended the boundaries of state authority and action. Huge interventions were also announced by leading central banks.

Checks were sent to households (in the US); unemployment benefits increased (in the US); employee wages were directly supported and paid for by government treasuries (in the UK, Denmark and the Netherlands); small and medium-sized businesses were given low-costs loans and grants (in the US, the UK and Europe); mortgage payment holidays were announced (in the UK); and evictions banned (in Europe and the US). So-called stimulatory austerity was abandoned in Europe as countries, including Germany, rushed to stimulate economies on life support. Political boundaries were blurred or removed entirely as conservatives and leftists all agreed that only state action could protect society, flatten the viral curve and stop the economic hemorrhaging. Once again a global crisis enlarged win sets, created new policy space and clarified options. Dogmatism was abandoned; it doesn't deliver in emergencies. State authority was also actively asserted by the central banking community when confronted by the pandemic. Leadership was absent at the G20 level, but this was not the case in the cohesive central banking community.

The US central bank maintains a leadership role

The US central bank led major central banks in the immediate response to the pandemic. It slashed rates to near zero, announced a massive quantitative easing and directed a lending program that could exceed US$4 trillion. Crucially the Federal Reserve also triggered swap lines with key central banks that had been created in response to the 2008–2009 crisis (and which it had maintained). The swap lines were then extended to additional countries. The dollar-based global economy was, as a result, kept afloat with dollar liquidity in huge amounts. And the Federal Reserve did not act alone. Other central banks also acted, including major shifts in policy and action by the European Central Bank, the Bank of England, the Bank of Japan and others. This time really was different from 2008–2009. The community had plans, knew what worked and was ready to act, and the interventions were faster, larger and broader in their application than in 2008–2009.

Thus while one can rightly bewail the failure of the G20 in 2020, this is not matched by a failure of the central banking community, which remained well-led, focused and rapid in their response. Will the fiscal and monetary action be enough? At the time of writing one could not tell, as the pandemic still rages across the world. But it appeared clear that further fiscal and monetary actions would be on the table if needed; state authority would continue to be applied until the curve was flattened and economic activity finally restored. And we have seen that, when the pandemic is over, the central banking community will remain committed to the FSB architecture and nexus of cooperation and coordination.

Technocratic community coherence fosters continued resilience

Below the antagonism and disputatious G20 summit table the central banking community has not lost its belief in the architecture, its strengthening and further construction. The central banking community continues to defend the new normal and to construct the regulatory architecture, monitor outcomes and scan the horizon for new risks and threats to the stability of the system. The implementation of total loss-absorbing capacity is perhaps the clearest example of this process – a major strengthening of bank capital. To be sure efforts to erode the new architecture are also seen, but they are not fatal to the central goal of enhanced bank stability underpinned by much higher capital and a macroprudential framework, nor to efforts to scan for future risks. Rather we all have witnessed how the FSB process and regulatory reforms have strengthened the global economy's ability to absorb shocks.

The COVID-19 crisis meaningfully reinforced lessons and the collective institutional memory of the global financial crisis. Most practicing central bankers today recognize that the banking regulation and capital reforms completed in response to the events of 2008–2009 helped ensure that the pandemic did not immediately mutate into a liquidity and solvency problem for the world's banks and banking system. Indeed, it is instead striking that banks are not the problem in 2020, and they continue to support economies that are on life support. The banks that have been required to be more heavily capitalized have been able absorb the body blows that COVID-19 had struck. COVID-19 reminds regulators and supervisors why rigorous regulation is required and is not a luxury. Vigilance on emerging risks is necessary and must be maintained. Eleven years on from the global financial crisis the central banking technocracy continues its collaborative work and is still building new wings onto the international architecture.

Institutional momentum is maintained to varying degrees

In 2020 the central banking community has sustained both institutional and policy momentum. Institutions, once created, tend to have a degree of permanence, and that is what we see with the FSB coordinating and monitoring mechanisms, and functions it performs, first led by an American, and now a Dutch central banker, the former who had been co-opted into defense of the system he might have otherwise pushed back against. The latter takes over a critical period of redirection and activism for the forum.

The ongoing test for the community and its architecture is the extent to which it continues to probe for new weaknesses and risks and for emerging threats. Overall the FSB passes that test. We see it and its membership tackling risk analysis of digital currency developments, cloud computing, artificial intelligence and shadow banking. These are not primarily – at this stage – regulatory actions, but instead analytical exercises. This is not necessarily a weakness, as that process can be seen to generate national regulatory action by members, galvanised by the review and reporting that the FSB requires and the conclusions it draws. And on the maximal overarching long-term planetary risk we face – climate change – a further highly significant institutional and policy shift has started.

Climate change and a further narrative leap

Leadership always counts, and this book has highlighted how, yet again, Mr Carney appears to have forced the pace of a shift in the community's narrative. His seminal 2015 speech at Lloyd's of London on the tragedy of horizons (Carney, 2015), and the 2017 creation of the Network for Greening the Financial System (NGFS) signal an extremely important extension of the central banking narrative and policy process. Scientists have been living the climate change reality for almost 30 years. Now, the central banking community has belatedly but finally rushed to join them. The logic and necessity of action is self-evident: you cannot talk of economic stability if the ecological viability of countries, peoples, species and the planet is in question.

The creation of the NGFS, and the suddenness of the community's leap from denial of responsibility, in 2014–2015, to acceptance and work on actionable steps on climate change in 2020 indicate that regulatory narrative leaps are not over; they can be extended in a dramatic fashion, with real-world climate change and economic and monetary implications. Now that central bankers are finally focused on the challenge of our generation this will increase the possibility of reaching net zero carbon before interlinked tipping points threaten the planet.

Creation of the NGFS again underscores that the history of major policy change is a history of paradigm shifts – long periods of relative stasis, with little change in narrative – increasing anomalies followed by a sudden shift in theory and narrative followed by further changes as the consensus strengthens and solidifies. As with other instances before a disjunctive break occurs host observers will tell you that the existing theory and approach are solid, resistant to change and cannot be moved. Then suddenly, a leap occurs, and what was once heretical is accepted as normal. The NGFS is a third-order shift and marks a very important shift and extension of central bank activism to include climate change goals and responsibilities. This is good news indeed. But what of other risks that may be precipitated by central bank policies? For even in a new climate change policy universe other risks to the economy and financial system will emerge, and so may be unintended results of activist policy by the central banking community itself, as not everything central bankers do turns to gold.[3]

Unintended consequences loom large, eventually

We have seen that policy levers can have unintended consequences. Monetary policy, in particular, can generate new risks even as it helps keep an economy afloat in the short term. Low-for-long monetary policy extended too long has adverse impacts on bank profitability, on pensions system viability and on savers and retirees, shrinking their nest eggs. It results in a search for yield and excess risk taking. Debt build-up is seen as individuals, firms and countries binge on low-cost loans. Such monetary policy largesse increases the gap between the rich, who can borrow and invest, and those who rely on stagnant wages to survive. Low-for-long inflates asset prices, further fueling inequality while distorting markets.

Central bank expansionary monetary policy tends to increase industrial concentration as smaller firms go bust and the remaining firms seize a greater share of their market segment; this occurred after 2008–2009, and it will happen again after the latest crisis.

But central banks cannot cure every ill or address all policy impacts their actions create. Governments must solve both the climate crisis carbon price and the thornier redistribution questions, renegotiate the social contract and maintain societal balance.

Solving major societal, economic, market and cultural crises requires actions by many actors. Central bankers are not the only adults in the room. The COVID-19 crisis has demonstrated this. All must pull toward the same well-understood goals. Governments well led, properly coordinated and acting decisively are key crisis managers of health crises and economic stability. But effective crisis response requires societies to change, work cultures to adapt, expectations to shift. The COVID-19 pandemic also demonstrates what is possible when all (or most) recognize a common threat. Perhaps our collective response to this global tragedy can have positive repercussions for future crises responses.

Paradigm shifts make the impossible possible

Crises when they precipitate paradigm shifts make the impossible possible. The remarkable breadth of governmental activism and the extension of state authority today in response to the COVID-19 pandemic illuminate lessons for the future.

First major shifts in approach and narrative are suddenly possible when all confront and clearly understand a common threat and intense realised danger.

Second, under extreme pressure, old political and ideological norms can be jettisoned very quickly, indeed, when societies are galvanised to action, as states, as communities and as individuals.

Third, remarkable leaps in policy practice, personal behavior, societal understanding and the depths of community strength can be seen.

Fourth, leadership still and always matters and especially in crises response at such societal and economic tipping points. Those countries led well – often it turns out by women – do well, those led by donkeys do much less well when the excrement hits the fan.

Fifth, the international architecture really does matter to global response effectiveness, coordination and cooperation.

If we can change the world so dramatically to stamp out the COVID-19 pandemic perhaps we can also recognize the climate crisis emergency, change our practices, policies and behaviours to address climate change, secure net zero by 2050 and save future generations from a terrifying hothouse planet. In doing so we can jump-start the next technological and industrial revolution.

To conclude, recent events, the history of science and the history of past financial crises demonstrate we are capable of radical action when our narratives shift, and tipping points are reached. I hope we can grasp the threat of climate change and make this next greatest, most important, planetary leap as societies, economies and as individuals. Doing is essential. Climate change is the maximal planetary crisis of our lifetimes. So we need to all learn our crisis management lessons and make the jump. There is much to be done. Let us get on with it.[4]

Notes

1 The US seized already-paid-for pandemic medical supplies being shipped to the Berlin police while they sat on an airport tarmac waiting to be loaded for shipment. The German government accused the US of 'modern piracy' (www.theguardian.com/world/2020/apr/03/mask-wars-coronavirus-outbidding-demand).

2 For example the Indian state of Maharashtra has 260 million people, 450 respirators and 502 intensive care unit beds. If the expected 300 million Indians catch the virus approximately 3 million will die. Rich countries have pushed aside and outbid poorer countries for crucial supplies. And rich countries in the G20 have not committed significant extra resources to international institutions to fill the yawning gap between needs and supplies. However the World Bank, for example announced a US$1.2 billion coronavirus program.

3 Although to be fair leading central bankers do have a particularly large supply of gold, usually stored directly underneath their offices, in Threadneedle Street or Liberty Street.

4 The author's next book, *Climate Crisis Economics*, which directly addresses this challenge, will be published in 2021.

References

Carney, M. (2015) 'Mark Carney: Breaking the tragedy of the horizon – Climate change and financial stability', *Speech by Mr Mark Carney, Governor of the Bank of England and Chairman of the Financial Stability Board, at Lloyd's of London*, London, 29 September [Online]. Available at: www.bis.org/review/r151009a.pdf (accessed: 11 April 2020).

Knack. (2020) 'Indiase premier Narendra Modi kijkt aan tegen 1 à 2 miljoen doden' – 'Indian Prime Minister Modi faces 1–2 million deaths.', 4 April [Online]. Available at: www.knack.be/nieuws/gezondheid/indiase-premier-narendra-modi-kijkt-aan-tegen-1-a-2-miljoen-doden/article-longread-1585759.html?fbclid=IwAR3SljpcDty_e0PaTJKD0qMF47LRgvuf1meMole2NXdjlFlQhqMgkf_dyjE&cookie_check=1586430893 (accessed: 9 April 2020).

New York Times. (2020) 'Peter Navarro has antagonized major corporations: Now he's in charge', 9 April [Online]. Available at: www.nytimes.com/2020/04/06/business/economy/peter-navarro-coronavirus-defense-production-act.html (accessed: 9 April 2020).

Index

Page numbers in *italics* indicate figures and in **bold** indicate tables on the corresponding pages.

For Product Safety Concerns and Information please contact our EU
representative GPSR@taylorandfrancis.com
Taylor & Francis Verlag GmbH, Kaufingerstraße 24, 80331 München, Germany

www.ingramcontent.com/pod-product-compliance
Ingram Content Group UK Ltd.
Pitfield, Milton Keynes, MK11 3LW, UK
UKHW011003180926
475701UK00004B/542
* 9 7 8 0 3 6 7 5 6 2 7 8 6 *